..., who continues to serve those who served.

...ne and Souvenir
...lles S Cole Jr
"Sam"

...iam R. Robbins

Russell W Gustafson
T/Sgt. Russell W. Gustafson
Flight Engineer/Top Turret

1st Lt. Donald J. Gott
Pilot - K.I.A.

...rt A. Dunlap
...tor - K.I.A.

2nd Lt. William E. Metzger, Jr.
Copilot
K.I.A.

2nd Lt. John A. Harland
Navigator

The Lady Jeannette

2nd Lt. Joseph F. Harms
Bombardier

Joseph F. Harms

The Last Flight Of
'The Lady Jeannette'

* * * *

A grave's mystery and place
Called through time and space
For its path to be traced - -
So this grave's man can be graced
With name, home and face.

* * * *

This book's charge to all must also be
COMMEMO
now and evermore.

COPYRIGHT © 1998 BY WILLIS S. COLE, JR.

All Rights Reserved. No part of this publication may be reproduced, stored in a retrieval system, or transmitted in any form or by any means, electronic, mechanical, photocopying, recording or otherwise, without the prior permission of the copyright holder.

ISBN 0-9662728-0-3

PRINTED IN THE UNITED STATES OF AMERICA
Snohomish Publishing Company, Inc., Snohomish, Washington, U.S.A.

The Last Flight Of
'The Lady Jeannette'

Willis S. Cole, Jr. "Sam"

Battery Corporal Willis S. Cole Military Museum

A NONPROFIT CORPORATION
13444 124th Ave. NE, Kirkland, Washington, 98034-5403   U.S.A.
E-mail: ww1@ww1.org -- http://www.ww1.org

Acknowledgments

I have been helped by many people during my research for this book. I have tried to include them where I could. However, without a doubt, I have missed giving credit to some who so deserved it. To them and to anyone within the book where I might have misspelled a name or missed an accent, I apologize. Special acknowledgment must go to my son, Willis S. Cole, III, and my daughter, Rebecca Lynn Cole Willsey, for their ongoing moral support during the years I have been working on this book.

A small number of people from 1944 to present helped make this book possible. Without them, I could not have linked all the events together. Beginning with the elders of Cartigny of 1944, Emile Berger a member of *Le Souvenir Français*, and several excellent French friends who deserve special recognition, Marcel Gauthier, Bernard and Claude Leguillier, Robert Lefevre, Richard Boniface and Pierre Segers.

Early in my life my parents, Luella Claire King Cole and Willis Samuel Cole, instilled a heavy burden upon me. One that continues to effect my life today, **The Burden of Wonderment**. This book is a result of that burden. A new challenge was placed before me and, as usual, I can not stop until all wonderment has been erased and replaced by knowledge.

This Book Is Dedicated
To The One Person
Who Made it Possible.

Carol Lorraine Reinbold Cole

Perhaps the one thing worse than the

"Burden of Wonderment"

is being married to one who has it.

Table Of Contents

PROLOGUE vii

Chapter One, The Beginning 1

Chapter Two, The Beginning Of The Search 19

Chapter Three, The Legends Of The Grave 33

Chapter Four, And then, I thought It would Be Easy! 41

Chapter Five, The Last Flight Of *The Lady Jeannette* 69

Chapter Six, The Americans - After The Crash 87

Chapter Seven, The French - After The Crash 103

Chapter Eight, 'On The Home Front,'
          After The Crash 9 November, 1944 - 4 April, 1949 111

Chapter Nine, Remembrance - 1994 157

Chapter Ten, Remembrance 97 181

Chapter Eleven, The Men Of *The Lady Jeannette*
          And The 452nd Bombardment Group (H) 219

Chapter Twelve, Related Crashes and Evaders 245

Chapter Thirteen,
          So You Always Wanted To Go To France, But You Needed A Good Reason! ... 263

Epilogue 277

Authorities And Sources 278

Index 281

Maps:
    Map 1: 452nd Bombardment Group (H) Mission 162 Briefing Map viii
    Map 2: Péronne area - showing crash sites and grave 218
    Map 3: Large area map showing travel area written about in this book . 218
    Map 4: Last flight path of both the B-17 and B-26 and memorial location . 262

PROLOGUE

A comprehensive study of the research into the identity of a grave in France containing the remains of an Unknown American Aviator of World War Two.

The events I have written about actually happened. A bomber, '*The Lady Jeannette*,' did crash on November 9, 1944. The pilot and co-pilot were both awarded the **Congressional Medal of Honor** for their attempt to save the life of the wounded radio operator. Unknown to them, a fourth man was also riding to his destiny with the wounded bomber. Four men died in the crash of '*The Lady Jeannette*' that day, the pilot, the co-pilot, the radio operator and the tail gunner.

To my knowledge, the only known documented case of American soldiers, of World War Two, recovering American War Dead and hiding most of the remains they recovered. Each of the four dead men have an Official War Grave, they also have a combined 5th War Grave. At the time this book was completed, the United States of America still does not recognize the existence of the 5th grave, even though the French government has recognized the grave for over 50 years.

As I researched the book over a period of six years, I found the events so entangled that in the end, I decided to write the book in an autobiographical form. The book begins with the events that lead to my being asked to identity the American aviator in a grave marked "UNKNOWN" and ends, not with everything I promised the men in the grave, but with the end of my research into what happened aboard the bomber and on the ground in France and the beginning of our effort to introduce before the Senate of the United States of America a request that the United States of America recognize by Act Of Congress the World War Two Isolated **Congressional Medals of Honor** 5th Grave at Cartigny, France.

Other events and bombers which entered into the research and tied together over the years are also included as they came to light.

I have told the story, just as it happened to me and as I determined it happened to the men and women I have written about. I have not only told the story of the service men involved, but also the story of the wives and families they left behind on '**the home front**.' The story does not stop with the death of some of the men or when the war ended, it follows all the men and their families from the birth of the men to their destiny today.

Willis S. Cole, Jr. "Sam"
Executive Director/Curator
Battery Corporal Willis S. Cole Military Museum

Member:  *Le Souvenir Français*    **COMMEMO-RANGERS**

 Les Amis De Vauquois    Western Front Association

 Great War Society    The American Legion (Life)   452nd Bomb Group Assoc. (Life)

 Veterans Of Foreign Wars (Life)    Ninth Air Force Association (Life)

 Graves Registration-Mortuary Affairs Assoc.

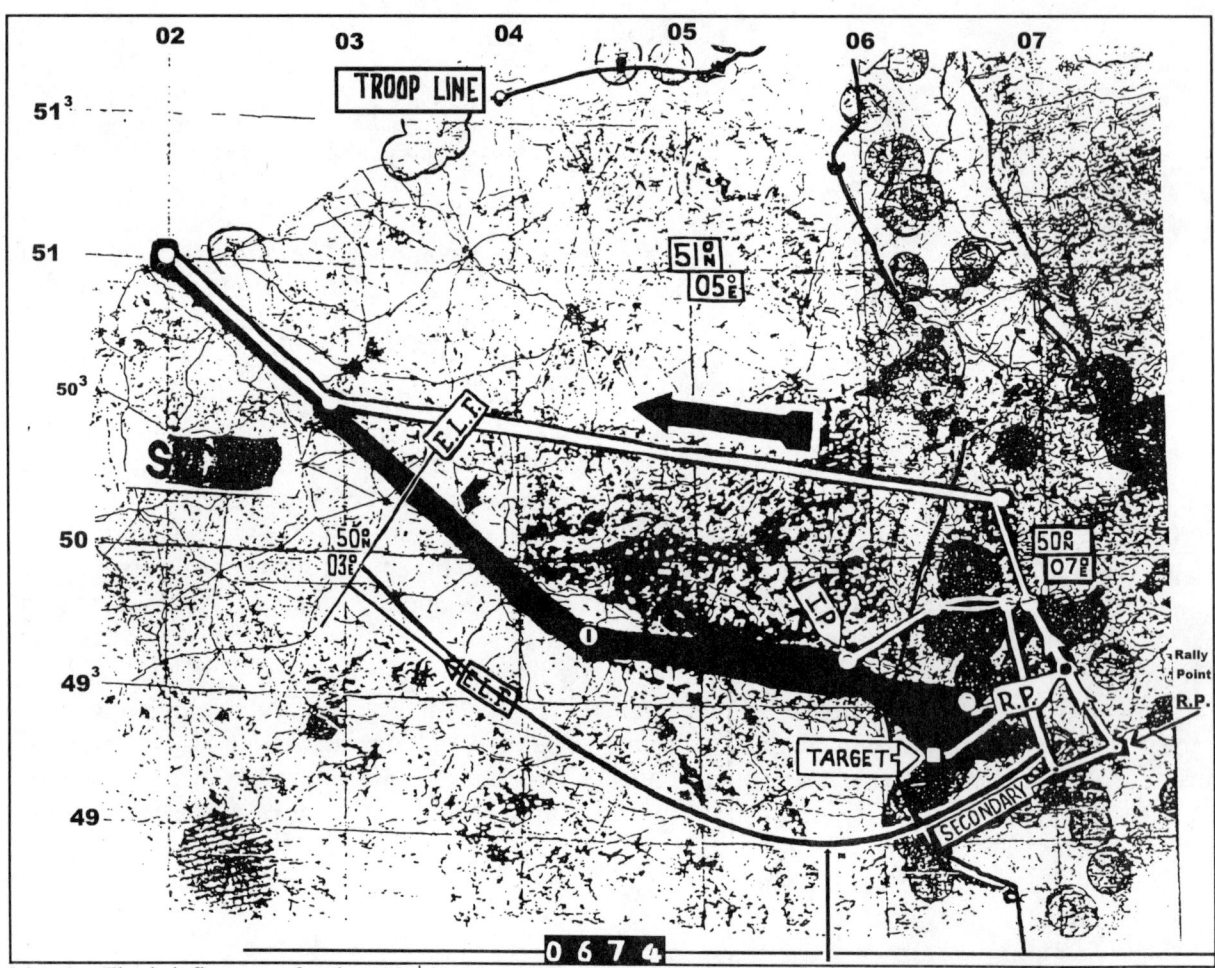

Map 1: The briefing map for the 452nd Bombardment Group (H) for the 162nd mission of 9 November, 1944. The primary target being the Metz-Thionville area. The 452nd diverted to the secondary target, the railroad marshaling yards at Saarbrucken, Germany. The circular route marked ending just below the 50 degree north, 03 degrees east is the point where '*The Lady Jeannette*' crashed. The marked route is the Author's estimated route of the bomber from the time it was hit by flak until it crashed. The E.L.F. (Emergency Landing Field) was about 5 miles southwest of the crash point. The crash point is in-line with the southwest-northeast runway that existed at that time, indicating the bomber crashed as the pilots attempted to turn the bomber to line up with the runway. The round circles along the Troop Line are flak concentrations and the mission flight paths are routed around them as much as possible. I.P. = Initial Point R.P. = Rally Point

Note: The author had cleaned the microfilm printout and improved the markings to make them more visible for the purpose of this book. See page 674 group history microfilm for as-is viewing.

Chapter One

The Beginning

"I picked up a man's face," was Bernard Leguillier's answer to my question. I'm sure, that I had a most astonished look on my face when I replied, "What do you mean you picked up a man's face?"

Bernard, whom I had met an hour before, had just answered the question I ask many French people of the right age when I first meet them, "Quick, without thinking about it, what is your first memory of World War Two?"

My wife Carol, Bernard and I were sitting in the home office of Bernard Leguillier at Flamicourt, France, a village connecting to the southern edge of Péronne. Péronne is located in the valley of the Somme River, about 70 miles north of Paris. We had been introduced to Bernard by Marcel Gauthier, whom we had met the year before on our first visit to Péronne and the World War One lines located around it.

My name is Willis Samuel Cole, Jr. and my son's name is Willis S. Cole III. We are named after my father, Willis S. Cole.

When I was very young, I received the nickname Sammy, which I use to this day, shortened to Sam. That way, two named Willis did not come when one was called. When my son came along, his first name Willis became his call. To this day, if some one calls for Willis, I still look to see whom they are calling. It was when I was in the seventh grade in New Concord, Ohio, that I found out my name was not just Sammy Cole.

That first day of school, the teacher called the roll and when she asked for Willis Cole, I looked around the room to see the boy with the same name as my father. Then she looked at me rather sternly and said, "Sammy, aren't you going to answer?" I replied, "Why?"

With much laughter from the other students, she explained that Sammy was not my real name, that Willis was. When I got home, I asked my mom and she agreed with the teacher that I did have a hidden name, my legal one, Willis Samuel Cole, Junior. I had been named after my father.

My father, who died when I was nine,

Corporal Willis S. Cole, (Sr.), 295th Military Police Company, 6th Division, Regular Army.

was a World War One Veteran who served with the Sixth Division in France and with the 3rd Army in Germany. He was in the 295th Military Police Company and he was a motorcycle dispatch rider for the division headquarters. The division was called '**The Sightseeing Sixth**' because they marched all over the United States' area of action in the Meuse-Argonne and Verdun area of France during and after the war. They were always in reserve and never participated in the fighting.

The memorials to the people of Malmédy killed by the American B-26 bombers that bombed the town twice by mistake. T/Sgt. W. Henderson, 606th G. R. helped recover the dead in December, 1944.

I have always been very interested in the United States' military history. I went through a Civil War phase, a World War Two phase and fixated on World War One after a quick four day visit to the World War One lines in 1977. The trip was made on a large rented motorcycle and it was planned to be my only trip along the World War One lines.

I was in Dusseldorf, Germany, at the D.R.U.P.A. printing equipment show and took five days off to rent a motorcycle and head into Luxemburg, Belgium and France for a quick tour of the lines. The lines were only 400 miles long and that would be an easy 100 miles a day on a big motorcycle.

I traveled though several famous World War Two cities and towns that first day. The trip flashed through Aachen, the first German city taken by American troops in World War Two. Then through Malmédy, and Baugnez, or the Five Points crossroads, the location of the massacre of the men of Battery B, 285th Field Artillery Observation Battalion. I learned something that day that led to my speciality type of military research, '**site**

The men who served in the Malmédy during liberation and the Battle of the Bulge. One company is missing, the 606th Graves Registration Company to which T/Sgt. Wilmer Henderson was assigned.

specific.' As I visited the memorial[1] to the men who were killed there on December 17th, 1944, by Kampfgruppe Peiper, I realized that the pictures I remembered and the place I was standing did not match.

It seemed to me that the actual place was on the other side and somewhat further down the road. Later research[2] allowed me to show that exact spot to my wife, Carol, and son, Will, on a second visit and to be able to explain exactly what had happened there.

The field in which the men of Battery B, 285th Field Artillery Observation Battalion were murdered, at Baugnez on Dec. 17, 1944. T/Sgt. Henderson later helped pick up the 86 bodies.

The first night I stopped at another famous town, Bastogne. In fact, after checking into the first hotel, the Hôtel Lebrun, that had secured parking for my motorcycle, I walked into my room and there on the wall was a plaque that read: This room had been occupied by Brigadier General McAuliffe, the American Commander, who had became famous for his answer, "Nuts," when asked to surrender by the Germans when Bastogne was surrounded.

Battle Of The Bulge Memorial, Bastogne, next to an excellent World War Two museum.

I arrived at Verdun the next day and as I drove toward Verdun from the north, I approached a rim of hills. As I drove up the side of the hill, men were working on the roadside with a bulldozer and I had to stop. I watched and waited for the go flag, as the dozer cut into the hill and the bulldozer blade brought a group of rusty German helmets to the surface. As the flagger waved me on, I saw the dozer run right over the helmets and mash them. I was half sick to my stomach. It was obvious that such finds were of no importance to this road crew.

At the top of the hill was a crossroads with a sign pointing toward Fort Tavannes, Fort Vaux, the Museum, the French National Memorial Ossuary and Fort Douaumont. Heck, it was early afternoon and I had lots of time. I would go see a fort or two.

Soon, I was wandering through a woods along a path leading to Fort Tavannes. At the entrance to the path was a sign saying, Danger - De Mort. Meaning do not enter, one could get killed. At least that was the way I interpreted the sign with it's exploding bomb image. Well, it was a well worn path and I didn't see any large new holes indicating someone might have recently been blown up.

About three blocks back along the path, I came to a masonry fort with great big blocks of stone lying all over the place. It had obviously been well shelled. I did know, that Fort Tavannes had not been captured during World War One. After walking around the fort for a while, I was soon on my way to Fort Vaux.

I pulled into the vehicle park and saw nothing, except a line of school buses and a grassy slope. I parked between two of the buses and when I turned the engine off, I could hear the loud voices of children on the top of the slope. I looked around for the fort, but saw nothing. So, I started up the path to the top of the slope.

There were lots of kids and some adults wandering around on the shell hole pocked hill. It was very rough with paths winding around the various high and low spots. I started exploring and soon I knew that I was on the fort for lying on the ground in front of me, were pieces of a huge steel gun cupola about 18 inches thick. It had to have been blown up and out of it's proper position in the fort. It was split right down the middle and the edges looked just like the jagged edge of a cracked egg shell.

I walked around the top of the fort for 20 or 30 minutes and decided that it would be more interesting if I could have gotten inside. I went back to the motorcycle and started back to the main road. About a half mile up the road, I saw a new rough and muddy road that had just been cut by a bulldozer. Though there were De Mort signs all along the road, I figured if the bulldozer did not blow up as it cut the new road, why should I?

I parked the cycle and started walking down the new road. I had not gone over ten feet before I realized that I was walking on lots of fragments of shells and stuff. After a short walk, I saw what looked like a loop of rope hanging out of the newly cut bank. When I walked over to it, I realized that it was a belt stuck in the dirt. I pulled on it and it came out of the dirt easily and hanging on it was a mashed, rusty German Potato Masher Hand Grenade. The handle had rotted away and only the grenade was left. The belt was very interesting to me, because I knew that a German Grenadier went into combat with 14 grenades hanging from the belt. As the belt was still buckled together, the German it had been looped around had long ago rotted away, but his belt was there in my hand and so was his last grenade.

That mashed, broken grenade became the first World War One relic I kept. Not much further away, I picked up a twenty-five pound fragment of a large shell and decided that I had picked up enough. That fragment still props doors open here in the house.

Rusted, bent German potato masher grenade from Fort Vaux, Verdun, France, 1977. Next to it is another in good relic condition.

After driving down to the next crossroads, where there was a memorial with a large lion on it, I took the fork to Verdun to hunt for a room for the night. Later, I found that the memorial[3] marked the furthest point the Germans had advanced during the Battle of Verdun in 1916. I quickly found a hotel and went for a walk around Verdun. Not far from the hotel, I located the Tourist Bureau and collected every brochure they had about Verdun and the battles around it. At a bookstore, I found a couple of books about the Battle of Verdun that I did not have and I was long into the night reading about all the things to see and do in the Verdun area.

The next morning, I was up and at them early. Back up the hill to visit the places I missed the afternoon before. The first place I went, was back to Fort Vaux. For I had read about the fort and I found out the secret. There was a door into the fort. I had just not seen it tucked into the bank, as it was hidden by one of the busses.

This was just the beginning, there were several more forts to be seen, the Ossuary, the Trench of the Bayonets and much more. Plus, about 20 miles south was St. Mihiel, where the Americans made their first official attack, as an American army, September 12, 1918.

The Ossuary and cemetery above Verdun. Under this building, visible through small windows are the bones of tens of thousands of unknown dead.

When my time was up and I had to hurry back to Dusseldorf three days later, my last stop along the World War One lines was at the Meuse-Argonne American World War One Cemetery at Romagne-s/s-Montfaucon, located about 15 miles northwest of Verdun. I had to return to Dusseldorf and I had only covered 40 miles of my planned trip along the lines.

First, I stopped at the office to find the location of the graves of several men that I wanted to visit. When I signed the guest register, I found that I was the first registered guest in four days. It appeared that visiting the dead of a long ago war was not a current tourist destination at that time.

I had parked my motorcycle near the east wall of the cemetery to visit the grave of Lt. Frank Luke[4], **Congressional Medal Of Honor**[5]. As I dismounted, and looked out under the trees, in the far distance I could see

The reclining lion marks the furthest advance of the Germans during the 1916 Battle of Verdun.

Entrance to Meuse-Argonne American World War One Cemetery, located at the village of Romagne-sous-Montfaucon.

A view of the cemetery when completed in the mid-1920s.

From the headquarters of the Meuse-Argonne World War One Cemetery looking toward the chapel.

The field next to the cemetery was covered with red poppies. The first thing that popped into my mind was the beginning of Lieut.-Col. John McCrae's poem. A doctor, from Canada, he wrote the poem in 1915. It was first published in **Punch**, Dec. 8, 1915. Lt. Col. John McCrae died of pneumonia on Jan. 28, 1918.

'In Flanders Fields[6].'

*"In Flanders fields the poppies blow
Between the crosses row on row"*

Just before I left, while visiting the cemetery's chapel, I never felt more proud of being an American. Standing there above the row upon row of dead American soldiers of World War One, I knew that someday I would return to this cemetery and that tower in the distance.

Thirteen years later, I returned and we visited that tower in the distance. In 1990, Carol L. Cole my wife, Willis the III, and I took a quick tour of Germany, Belgium and France. We drove over 2,500 miles in those two weeks. Not only did we visit the Verdun area, we quickly visited most of the First World War Line, the Beaches of Normandy and we made a fast trip to London to visit the Imperial War Museum.

We found the tower I had seen in the

2nd Lt. Frank Luke, Jr., **Congressional Medal Of Honor**. Known as the balloon buster for shooting down German observation balloons.

a large tower. The map told me that it was an American memorial for World War One. As much as I wanted, I didn't have time to drive to it and I stored that visit in my mental wish-list file.

Aerial view of the American Montfaucon Memorial of World War One.

distance 13 years before, the Meuse-Argonne Memorial at Montfaucon,[7] the most imposing American monument in Europe. The tall monument commemorates the victory of the American First Army in the Meuse-Argonne during World War One.

As we drove along the roads in the Argonne, I felt the presence of another man who had driven these very roads, 72 years before, in search of the Sixth Division on his return from Army Headquarters. I told Carol and Willis III about the one story I remember my father telling someone, long ago.

He was searching for his unit's H.Q. on his motorcycle. He came to a place where another military policeman was directing traffic at a crossroads. Not knowing which way to turn, he stopped and got out his map. Soon the traffic slowed and the M.P. came over and asked, "Where you going buddy?" When my father pointed to his map and told him, "I have to find Avocourt and follow that road from there, but I have not found the village yet." The M.P. said in reply, "Buddy, you see that pile of bricks there and the one next to it? Well, Buddy, you are in the middle of Avocourt," and he pointed, "that's the road you take."

On the way to the cemetery during my visit in 1977, I had stopped at a crossroads not far from Avocourt and looked at a hill in the distance. It was cleaved open, like a giant knife had cut it from one end to the other. I knew right away what I was looking at. I was looking at a hill that had been mined and blown up. Mining[8] was used to dig under the

Willis S. Cole, III, at sign pointing to World War One French soldier's grave.

other fellow's defense lines, when the mine was complete, explosives would be placed in the end of the mine to blow up the enemy's lines above, so they could be taken in an attack.

Over 1,600 mines had been exploded during the war and usually they did not succeed, other than killing some of the other guys who were in the trenches above the explosion. The Allies never had much luck blowing up mines under the German lines. The Germans were experts at rushing new men to the blown up trenches and taking the big hole back from the attackers.

This trip, following a Michelin map Guide[9], we were able to get to the top of Butte de Vauquois and visit that blown up hill. We had to park quite a ways down the hill and walk to the top, but what we found was worth it. First, one could see a long way to the north and it was obvious whoever controlled this hill could control what they saw there. In the same way, one could see a long way to the south. The Germans, to the north, wanted it to protect themselves, while the French, to the south, wanted the same.

By the way, for a rule of thumb, you can tell the age of a French village by where it is located. If it located on the top of a hill, it is very old. A very long time ago, they built their villages on top of the hills so an enemy had to attack up the hill. Later, when the country became more occupied and better protected, they located the villages down in the valleys where the weather was modified and water was easier to obtain.

The memorial signs at the top told us the story. When the war began, in August, 1914, the Germans attacked from the north. When the French retreated, they flowed around the hill of Vauquois upon which sat the village of Vauquois, while the Germans[10] attacked up the hill to take the village. The Frenchmen in the village had fought the Germans, however the Germans managed to push the French out of the village and 200 meters down the other side, before fierce counter attacks by new French forces drove the Germans back to the village. They fought over that village for the next four years.

In due time, the Germans dug mines and the French dug mines and by the end of the war 16 large mines had blown the village away and blown the center of the hill up and over the sides. The Germans had been forced to surrender when the American 35th Division went around the hill during the first day of the Meuse-Argonne Battle, September 26, 1918.

Carol and I crossed over to the German side of the hill and walked part way into the woods. As we entered the woods, the first thing we had to do was to scramble down into a trench and up the other side. As we looked around we could see the trenches stretching out in both directions.

We crossed over several of them and came to a couple of concrete emplacements. From the way they pointed, I was certain we were in the German trenches. About three feet to the north of one of them, someone had dug a fresh hole. There in the hole was a set of fins on an iron pole about two inches thick. The hole went down around the fins and a bomb shaped top was showing. It was obvious that whoever dug the hole decided to stop when they realized that what they were digging up was a large aerial torpedo, a French mortar bomb.

We had so little time there in the Verdun area and we found more and more interesting places to visit. Willis suggested that we find the airport and see if we could hire an airplane for a tour over the major Verdun Battlefield area. From overhead we saw many places that we just couldn't visit. By the time the plane landed Carol and I were already planning on coming back to Verdun.

On our way down the back roads to our next stop, we were caught up in a column of tanks. Yes, tanks on the back roads of France. It seemed we had arrived during a military exercise and the military had first right to the roads. We followed along between two tanks for some distance. It was interesting to get close up views of the front and back of them in motion, especially when the guy behind us tracked us with the turret and cannon. The hole at our end of the barrel looked very large from that angle. For quite a while, we saw military vehicles of all types parked back in the woods and camouflaged in the open spaces.

When we arrived at Péronne to visit '**The Battle Of The Somme**' lines, Willis suggested, "We should hire a guide to insure we see what is most important during our short time there." With that in mind, we located the tourist office and asked the young lady there if she knew of someone we could hire.

She told us that her father, an English professor, would be the best one, but he was in England. However, she knew a student of his who might be available. Arrangements were made to meet Marcel Gauthier early the next morning at our hotel.

We spent that evening hunting for the place of death and the grave of an American, Alan Seeger.[11] He had joined the French Foreign Legion[12] and was assigned the Serial Number: 195522,[13] just after the start of the war on August 21st, 1914. Alan was killed on the Fourth of July, 1916, on the fourth day of '**The Battle Of The Somme**,' about six o'clock in the evening, at the southwest corner of Belloy-en-Santerre[14] located a few miles southwest of Péronne. Alan was among the over 800 men of the Legion killed during the two days the Legion was in combat at Belloy. The village square is named after him and his name is on the memorial at the edge of the square with others who died that day.

We had found his place of death, but could not find his grave in any of the several French military cemeteries close by. I have since read, that one of the men who buried Alan and his comrades had returned to Belloy-en-Santerre in November, 1916, and he could not locate the common grave in which Alan and so many more had been buried. The shell fire had totally torn the ground apart, the higher mound where they had buried them was totally erased and the remains torn apart, mixing them with the earth, lost forever.

That evening in the sunken road where the German machine guns had been located that had killed Alan and so many others, Carol and Willis listened as, I read his most famous poem. When I first read this poem a few years earlier, it became one of the forces driving me to my second trip to the World War One lines. I had found a map of France and as I read the book which contained the poem, I marked his travels and thought about duplicating them.

I HAVE A RENDEZVOUS WITH DEATH

I have a rendezvous with Death
At Some disputed barricade,
When Spring comes back with rustling shade
And apple-blossoms fill the air---
I have a rendezvous with Death
When Spring brings back blue day and fair.

It may be he will take my hand
And lead me into his dark land
And close my eyes and quench my breath---
It may be I shall pass him still.
I have a rendezvous with Death
On some scarred slope of battered hill
When Spring comes round again this year
And the first meadow-flowers appear.

God knows 'twere better to be deep
Pillowed in silk and scented down
Where Love throbs out in blissful sleep,
Pulse nigh to pulse, and breath to breath
Where hushed awakenings are dear . . .
But I've a rendezvous with Death
When Spring trips north again this year,
And I to my pledged word am true,
I shall not fail that rendezvous.

Alan Seeger
American
Poet
Volunteer, Legionnaire

HE HAD A RENDEZVOUS WITH DEATH

On a summers eve, close to the Somme,
Over a flat field he charged.
Side by side with comrades blue
To his pledged word he kept true
He had that rendezvous . . .

From sunken road surprise blew.
A Hun's missiles of death flew
Rat-a-tat, rat-a-tat
Across the field through chest high corn
His squad advanced in file and line.
Rat-a-tat, rat-a-tat, rat-a-tat.
He had found his rendezvous . . .

His flesh was torn, blood flew
His breath was quenched
Thus he fell, to take God's hand
To keep his rendezvous.

T'was not long till he was borne,
Along with eight hundred and more,
Lost on that combat's day,
Placed in common grave, in battles way.

The war roiled on blast on blast,
Year on year, the soldiers died,
Sixteen, Seventeen and Eighteen roared,
And the grave was lost among the crust
Of attack, attack, attack . . .

Quiet came where the soldiers rest,
To the fields where they lie.
Comrades came to see their place

And think of the fallen's face.
Except for Alan and his friends,
Where in unmarked earth they laid.
In common grave, where they were borne
Lost in war's earth so torn.

The farmers returned, the fields asunder
Their plows found soldiers graves.
Unlike other's who fell that day
Whose cemeteries bloom nearby
These broken bones were transposed
To lay now far from where they fell.
Near Lihons these thousands decompose
Many known placed side by side
Seven hundred and more,
'Unknown But To God'
Share a common grave.

Alan's shattered bones may moulder there
Mixed in among the seven hundred.
Marked 'unknown' in this grave.
He had kept his rendezvous.

If one day, by Lihons you stray
Stop and visit this common grave.
For in this grave, marked 'unknown' you see
May lie a man you know.
Alan Seeger, American, Poet
French Legionnaire, volunteer.

Willis S. Cole Jr. "Sam"

Yes, Alan had found his rendezvous at the edge of the only village, in France, where the French Foreign Legion fought the Germans during both World Wars[15]. When the Germans shelled and destroyed the church steeple during the Second World War, they also destroyed the bells that Alan's family had donated to the village in his Remembrance. The broken brass was hauled away to Germany. One small piece was kept by the village policeman and it now is in a museum in southern France.

Alan's family came to France several times, his mother's last visit, in the 1970's, is remembered by several people in the village. His poem, *I Have a Rendezvous With Death*, became quite famous during the war and you will often find reference to it in World War Two books. Alan is well know at the Mairie and they are proud of their memorials to him.

In 1917, Alan's family had his writings printed in two books, **_Poems_**, Alan Seeger, Charles Scribner's Sons, 1917, and **_Letters And Diary of Alan Seeger_**, Charles Scribner's Sons, 1917. Through them, you can follow Alan's travels to his Rendezvous and today you can visit all the places he mentions. I recommend the visit. The country side is very quiet now and it is in a beautiful part of France, especially Château Bellinglise.

The reflecting pond at Château Bellinglise.

BELLINGLISE

Deep in the sloping forest that surrounds
The head of a green valley I know,
Spread the fair gardens and ancestral grounds
Of Bellinglise, the beautiful château.
Through shady groves and fields of unmown grass,
It was my joy to come at dusk and see,
Filling a little pond's untroubled glass,
Its antique towers and mouldering masonry.
Oh, should I fall to-morrow, lay me here,
That o'er my tomb, with each reviving year,
Wood-flowers may blossom and the wood-doves croon;
And lovers by that unrecorded place,
Passing, may pause, And cling a little space,
Close-bosomed, at the rising of the moon.

Alan Seeger

Marcel Gauthier, whose English was quite passable for a young man of seventy-six years, and who had just started taking English courses a couple of years earlier, gave us an

Australian 1st Division Memorial - Pozières

Delville Wood South African Memorial

excellent tour the next day. We drove along through the lines and visited the most famous of the places to see. In the process, we passed many military cemeteries, interspersed with memorial after memorial. Truly a great battle had been fought here, as we drove to the most famous places, we passed so many others. Carol and I agreed, as we left that afternoon, what we had seen would bring us back to the valley of the Somme. During our travels, Marcel wanted to know if we had ever seen the Black Hills Monument to the American Presidents? When we told him we had seen it, he asked many questions. He told us he had always wanted to visit it, but when he was finally able to do so, Helene's, his wife, health would not permit international travel. We asked for his address and promised to send him any pictures we happen to run across. This original contact with Marcel is truly the beginning of this book.

Upon returning to the United States we started to plan for our next trip to France.

Later that summer of 1990, I visited my family back in New Concord, Ohio, for a family reunion. While there, I was out late, about midnight one Saturday night, with my nephew, Rick Cole and his wife Robin. They insisted that we go close out their favorite new night spot, *The Outback*, in Zanesville. A half block after we left the main road, we started to turn a corner when suddenly I shouted, "Stop, stop, STOP RIGHT NOW!" There, sitting in the weak light of the street lamp above, was a fantastic cannon. I bailed out of the van before it had come to a complete stop, the whole time listening to Rick saying, "No, not yet, '*The Outback*' is the across the street."

It was big, one of the bigger cannons I had ever seen. And there it was, sitting on the back lot of a rental store. In the dark, under the weak street light, it didn't look very safe to me as the wheels were rusted through in places.

Robin and Rick came walking up, after parking at the club to see what weird Uncle Sam was up to now. After explaining to them that I always brake for cannons, I told them I had never seen one like this. Rick supplied a lighter and from its flickering flame I could make out the word KRUPP and 1917. I knew then, I was standing in front of a German World War One relic, and I also knew at that time, it had to be a rare one.

This was the beginning of the second step to this book, except the full story of our restoration of "**How the Howitzer**" could be the subject of a book on its own.

Through Rick, I was able to find who paid the taxes on the lot and sent him a letter about the cannon. To show how small the

Péronne city hall and square.

world is and how intertwined it is, about three weeks later, I received a telephone call from my brother, Dick Cole. He asked, "Did you write someone about a cannon in Zanesville?" When I answered, "Yes," he went on to tell me that he had worked with the owner's wife for twenty years and never knew they owned that cannon.

I later found out that my sister's children knew the owner's wife, she was a leader of the marching team they had belonged to. Rea, my sister, and Dick Huff, had also known Warren White and Barbara White for many years without knowing they owned that cannon.

Saved from the junkyard in 1972 by Warren, the cannon had sat on the store back lot for 18 years, always with the hope he could restore it. Now, the rental store had been sold and he had to move the cannon. My offer was the lowest he received, however I promised to conserve it's condition and restore it.

Two months later, Carol and I were in Zanesville and with my brother, Dick, and my cousin, Bud Wortman, we prepared the 16,000 pound monster for shipment back to Seattle.

It took 3,000 hours of restoration, and that cannon, a KRUPP 210mm Lange Mörser,[16] is the pride of our World War One Museum collection today. But what good is a cannon, if you don't have a shell for it? Another very good reason to go to France again, to see if we could locate a shell.

Wait a second, why don't we write Marcel and have him ask his friends if they could find us a shell before we go over. So off to France went a letter asking a big favor of Marcel, included, of course, were some pictures of Mount Rushmore.

A solid block of metal and rust?

Within two weeks, we received a letter back from Marcel telling us that he had located a shell for us. A friend from his Air Club was going to be able to get us one from a friend who was a Bomb Remover. Now that was a real good reason to go to France.

In the middle of May, 1991, we arrived at Charles DeGaulle Airport, Paris. We got our reserved rental car, drove to the end of the airport road and turned right, heading to the north away from Paris and on our way to Péronne. Our first stop after the Assevillers Exit for Péronne was at Belloy-en-Santerre where we again thought of Alan Seeger and the Legion.

Soon we were in Péronne at the town square. A beautiful spot where one can sit at the outside tables of the cafés and watch the people walk by. We had Marcel's telephone number and were to call him to come meet us.

I found a telephone and placed the call. Marcel answered and asked me the name of the café. I looked up at the sign and it said Jupiler, so I passed it on. A long time went by and no Marcel, it's not that big of a town so something must be wrong. I got up and walked up and down the square. Soon, something did become very obvious to me. Almost every café in town was named Jupiler.

Just like in the U.S.A. the beer companies furnish signs, but the difference here was that the name of the café was in small type in a corner. I had just told Carol of my findings when I saw a car coming across the parking lot in the middle of the square driven by a very dapper gent. Yes, Marcel had found us at last.

He told us about the shell that Richard Boniface had gotten, from Christian Kowal, the Bomb Remover. It was big and heavy and it would take two or more to load it, so he had not brought it into town. He thought it would be best if we met his English Professor that evening, as his interpreting skills were much better and Marcel had made arrangements for him to go to Richard's home with us the next day to pick up the shell.

That evening Marcel introduced us to Bernard Leguillier, Régine his wife, and Valerie his daughter, whom we recognized as the girl we had talked to at the Tourist Bureau the year before. They invited us to stay for a visit and later, when Carol and I were sitting in Bernard's home office I asked him about his first memory of World War Two.

"Yes, I picked up a man's face, it was the face of an American aviator," Bernard restated. The third link to the beginning of this book.

"One day in November, 1944," he continued, "my brother, Claude, and I were eating lunch at our home in Driencourt, a few kilometers from here. Off in the distance we heard the sound of a B-17 bomber. By that time in the war, we had spent many hours listening to all the airplanes and we could tell German from American and what type each airplane was."

"We used to lay out in the courtyard of our home compound and watch the sky fill with American planes. German soldiers were living in our house and they always hid under the different sheds and hollered at us to get out of sight. They were worried that the Americans might strafe our house."

Bernard continued, "The bomber came closer and closer and we could tell by it's sound that it was in trouble. Suddenly, we heard a loud explosion in the distance and a

It took a 100 ton hydraulic jack and special high test chain to finally break the barrel loose and slide it out.

few seconds later a much louder one. We ran outside and up the road to where we could look south toward Tincourt-Boucly. There we could see a column of smoke over the ridge near the village. We ran back to the house to ask mother to let us go to the crash, but she made us finish our lunch first."

"We walked straight across the valley and up over the ridge, through the woods," he said, "Everyone was used to walking everywhere. We had no gas and bicycle tires were hard to come by. When we topped the ridge we could see a very large hole near a small woods, close to the crossroads north of Tincourt-Boucly. We could see lots of people there and we hurried down to the crash site. From the distance, we could see the hole was in the shape of a airplane."

"When we got to the crash, it was a big hole, about 5 meters deep and 30 meters wide. When we arrived, the Americans were there with an ambulance. We talked to some of our friends and they described what they had seen before the crash".

"The bomber had come from the east, flying about 400 meters in the air. It's right engine was gone and there were flames flowing clear back past the tail. The outside left engine was stopped and the inside one next to the pilot, was smoking. As it passed over the large field just to the north of the village, one man bailed out. Even from that distance, they could tell he had something wrong with his right leg. His parachute opened and as he slowly dropped to the ground, some men from the village started running toward him."

"A few seconds after his parachute opened the bomber started to bank to the south. It rolled over on its back and started to dive toward the earth beyond the woods. Almost immediately it exploded once, some parts broke loose, and it continued it's dive straight down. When it hit the earth, it exploded again very loudly."

"My friends had no sooner finished telling me what happened when the Americans asked all of us to line up in a long straight line from the hole and to walk in a big circle. We were to pick up anything that looked important, such as clothing and pieces of people. One big door had broken loose during the first explosion and fluttered to earth. The Americans had us put the human pieces we found on the door."

"During that walk around the crash hole, I picked up the man's face. It was the flesh starting at the edge of the upper lip, up around the eye and across just above the eyebrows and back down around the other eye, down to the lip again. It was the shape of a mask such as a woman might wear to a masquerade ball. The eye brows, eyelids, and nose were there. No eyes, just the eye holes, it was just the skin of the face. I put that face of an American flyer on the door."

Bernard finished his story, "When we were done, the door had a pile of human remains almost a meter high, there was as much as 300 or 400 pounds of remains. Soon, the Americans, with the help of some Frenchmen, put the door in the ambulance and drove off toward the American Airbase at Estrée-en-Chaussée. After it left, we picked

The cannon trail is upside down and we are ready to begin rebuilding after months of disassembly.

up a large yellow container, about the only thing of any size that came through the explosions and we went back home."

Bernard and I talked about the crash of the B-17 a bit more and he promised to show me where the bomber crashed sometime. He told me, he had also walked through the hull of a B-26 that had crashed in the woods near where the B-17 crashed. It was interesting, but as I told Bernard, I was mostly into World War One and air warfare was not the most interesting to me. However, since I would know the exact place the bomber crashed, someday I might try finding out something. Right now, I was mostly interested in getting my cannon shell and exploring the Somme Battle Lines.

The next day, we drove out to Richard Boniface's home and found that it was quite different from any I had visited. On the way out, Bernard told us that Richard had been a National Motocross Champion back in the late seventies and he was now the operator of a dozing and excavation company. He also loves to work with explosives and he implodes large buildings and chimneys. His home is attached to the workshop of his business, like the French house/barn of old. However, Bernard warned us that Richard is a very private person and that we should not be upset if Richard did not pay much attention to us. He had to know someone very well before they became a friend.

When we arrived and looked though the large sliding door, we saw the KRUPP 210 mm shell we had come to get, sitting in the middle of the workshop floor. Richard was not there, but his wife, Michelle, and their two sons, Peter and Romain were. We were in the final process of rolling that 246 pound monster out the shop door, when a four wheel drive utility came shooting up. We've found that whenever you go some place with Richard, expect to travel at full warp speed and limited braking.

By now, I knew they all belonged to the Aero Club and after Richard helped us load the shell he decided to show his friends what he does with explosives. We followed him into a small room, that I later found to be right under his bedroom, and he pulled out some small squares of explosive, fuse cord and detonators. In the process, he showed us a box of World War One Mills Bombs (hand grenades) that he had recovered from a newly discovered dugout. They looked brand new and were fully operational.

The author, Bernard Leguillier and Marcel Gauthier inspecting the KRUPP 210 mm shell donated by Christian Kowal and Richard Boniface.

All this time, I had my video camera turned on. I can carry it and aim it without looking through it, so I can watch the action myself. We went out into his large equipment yard to where a couple of disabled trucks were sitting. Richard led us over to one and we watched as he attached a two gram block of dynamite against one of the frame's cross supports. He lit the fuse and we followed him fairly slowly over near the other truck. Soon, there was a loud crack and smoke flowed out from under the truck. We walked back and Richard showed us the broken and bent cross frame. He explained, in French of course, how the two gram block special explosive he was now mounting to the other end of the frame was much stronger.

During these demonstrations, I would occasionally ask Bernard to translate a question to Richard. I noticed that Richard would usually have an answer ready before Bernard even got started and I realized Richard understood technical English. I have found out, over the years, that mechanical and electrical terms are standard in lots of languages.

This time, when Richard was finished and lit the fuse, he walked quite a bit quicker and insisted that we get behind the other truck's wheels and when he ducked, he motioned for us to duck also. It was a much stronger and louder explosion followed by a whirring sound, at the end of which was the sound of metal on gravel. When we looked around the truck, we saw that cross piece lying where we had stood for the first explosion. The grin on Richard's face spread from ear to ear.

He asked us to go back into the shop and he was going to show us a very large explosion using several sticks of dynamite. He had it stored under a shelf in that same room. We all followed him into the room and I zoomed the video camera tight into the box as he started to pick up the first stick of dynamite. What I saw, startled me and I quickly told Carol, who was standing behind me, "Back out, Carol, back out fast, the dynamite is sweating."

As we quickly retreated out the door, Richard gently placed the stick back in its box and asked me directly, "What does sweating mean?" I told him, that sweating meant the dynamite was old and very unstable and the nitroglycerin was separating and leaking out. All it would take to make it explode was for one of those drops to strike something and not too hard. The only safe way to get rid of it was to burn it. He agreed, and from that moment on we have been fast friends and Richard became the fourth, and very vital, link to this book.

For the next two weeks, we spent a lot of time with the Bonifaces getting to know this French family. Richard began helping his father use explosives when he was only seven years old and he has an outlook on life that is quite different than anyone I had ever met until then. Often, when discussing his work and the dangers he rubs his fingers together, as we rub them together to indicate money, shrugs his shoulders, looks up and says, "poof!"

Richard and I were speeding down the roads one day and he slid, yes slid, to a stop at the front door of a large business. He flung open the door and bounded around the front of his 'Cat-Cat' (or four by four, as we would say) and waved for me to follow.

Inside, he entered into an animated conversation with a man behind a very cluttered desk. I was soon introduced to Bernard, the culvert factory owner and soon thereafter his brother, Pierre Segers, a trucking company owner. Richard has known the Segers family for most of his life and when you are a good friend of one Frenchman, you are given every chance at becoming the friend of his friends. Pierre would later provide a vital data link in my research, become a great friend and help in **Remembrance-Souvenir**.

Richard would also become the second most important person in helping this book to be written. For in mid-November, 1991, I got a telephone call from Richard. He wanted me to come over to France during the Christmas season to uncover and remove a German 77 mm cannon he had found for me. His firm had a contract to remove a large woods to create larger fields when one of his men pulled up a tube with the long teeth dragging the earth behind his bulldozer. When they took a close look at it, they realized it was a cannon and what should they do with it, but cover it up and ask Sam to come over and get it.

A cannon, what could I do, but go! I made arrangements to stay with Richard from

Richard Boniface with interesting junk from his shop yard.

Christmas Day to New Year's Day, when he would take me to the airport. I immediately called Bernard and made arrangements to stay with him for a week until Christmas Day.

I arrived at Charles De Gaulle Airport and was met by Bernard and his brother Claude. I had a most excellent stay at Bernard's and we often went out to the family home at Driencourt where Claude lived, with his wife Françoise, and his sons, Hérve and Alain. Claude had managed to get a metal detector and we spent quite a bit of time in the family fields and woods hunting for relics of World War One.

By this time, I had found that when I spent a little time with a French person, we could soon communicate quite well. I don't speak French, but most of them had some school English and between the French words I understood and the English words they knew, we would get along, especially when they talked about military items. In the same sense, I can read French military books well

Large gears, large springs, but beginning to come together.

enough to understand most of what is written.

During this time, I was invited rabbit hunting with Bernard's and Claude's hunting association. They have an old bus in the orchard near the farm house and the men use it as their meeting place. Several come long distances, one from Paris. They meet almost every winter weekend and often during the summer, some of them go out to place feed and water for the birds, rabbits and other game animals they hunt.

I didn't carry a gun, but I walked through the fields and woods with Bernard and Claude. At one time, we met some fellows from another association and several fellows from Bernard's group also came up. There in the field they had a heated discussion of where the trenches had been, the gun positions and where relics, such as machine guns and such had been found. At one point Bernard turned to tell me what they were saying and I told him, I already knew, and repeated what I thought I had heard. He agreed that I could understand much of what was being said. I did learn right then that I can't seem to say one word in French that they understand. One word was, d'accord, which means OK; no matter how many times I repeated it, they did not understand me. Finally, I gave up trying and just listened.

Soon, Christmas Eve Day was upon us and according to French custom, we were going to a late feast at Bernard's son's home. Gérard and his wife Catherine, and Baptiste the grandson, were to host both sides of their families and some friends, like me.

Bernard had received an invitation from a man in Bernes, asking him to bring me along, to see his private military collection. We decided we had enough time that afternoon to go see it. On the way, as we came over the top of the hill on the road from Driencourt to Tincourt-Boucly, Bernard pointed out a low spot in a field where he told me the B-17 bomber had crashed. Close to it was a bank with some bushes growing on it and he told me the bomber had crashed near the edge of a small wood that had been there. The place where he, "...**had picked up a man's face**."

Mr. Robert Lefevre's private collection.

Robert Lefevre greeted us at his door and we were shown his collection. His family has been collecting military relics since the War of 1870 with Germany. He has one of the best uniform displays I have seen. Not in number, but in how complete they are, down to the underwear. I told him, "I knew how they must have got them. The lonely soldier was walking down a village street when the woman of the family stopped him, saying, "Hi, big boy." When he woke up the next morning, lying nude in the street with a knot of the back of his head, he really wondered what happened."

As we were leaving, it was starting to get late and we had our evening planned, Robert asked Bernard to translate a request to me. Robert was a member of the **Le Souvenir Français**, a volunteer organization first formed in 1872 to maintain France's military memorials and tombs. He asked, that we stop by the cemetery of the village of Cartigny and visit the grave of an Unknown American Aviator, of World War Two, that he had been tending for some time.

It would not be far off our route back to Péronne and perhaps, I, as an American, could find out the identity of the man in the grave. The 50th Anniversary of France's Liberation was coming in three years and he thought it would be very nice if the man in the grave could be identified and memorialized by the French people during the upcoming 50th Anniversary, in 1994.

At once, I told Bernard that I just didn't believe such a grave could exist. A member of our Museum Board, Will Henderson, had been in Graves Registration during World War Two. He had landed on Omaha Beach at 11:30 a.m. on June 6th, 1944.

A Sergeant in a platoon of the 606th Graves Registration Company, he was one of the first G. R. personnel in France. His Platoon had later picked up the remains of the men killed at Malmédy. Together, we had thoroughly researched Graves Registration[17] service in Europe, during and after the war.

To quote directly from the QMC Historical Studies, pages 107 and 108, "Here again army took action with a view to speeding up search and recovery operations in rear of the battle line. In contrast to the conventional method of "area sweeping," when lulls in combat permitted the diversion of attached graves registration personnel from evacuation and burial activities, the new one may be described as a secondary phase of battlefield evacuation.

Organized by the Army Graves

It moves, up and down, for the first time in over 75 years.

Registration Officer for this specific purpose, collecting teams were deployed to recover bodies which had been overlooked during the primary phase." At this time, the search was restricted to areas where unburied bodies had been reported, however they would not have left a buried American soldier where they found him.

I knew that Graves Registration had made several sweeps through France from just after the Liberation on through 1951. During each sweep, they went to every city, town and village and asked the mayor, police and church leaders if they knew of any missed graves of American military men existing in their area of control. It was my belief, if such a grave had existed, especially one in a cemetery, they would have found it and removed the remains to one of the temporary American military cemeteries.

I also knew there were several Isolated War Graves of American Soldiers, from both wars, in village cemeteries spread around France. The graves, located in remote village cemeteries, are marked with an American military tombstone. Each of these officially recognized war graves are visited and maintained twice a year by employees of the American Battle Monuments Commission.

I really had to doubt if the grave Robert was telling us about, could actually be the grave of an American soldier. However, Bernard and I, agreed to stop by the cemetery and see the grave Robert described. We had some time to spare and it would only take a few minutes, even if it would be dark soon.

In no more than ten minutes we were at the gate of the Cartigny cemetery and we entered in search of the grave.

There it was, right in front of us, a grave where no such grave should exist. The first grave on the left, just past the shrubs beyond the storage area. It was a grave, just as Robert had described it, surrounded by a concrete berm, with a red, crushed stone covering and a large rose bush at its foot.

At it's head was a French Military Concrete Cross with a *Le Souvenir Français* roundel at its top and mounted on that Cross was a plaque stating:

* *

* *

Aviator AMERICAN UNKNOWN
DIED FOR FRANCE-IN 1943

I made several promises to the man in that grave that Christmas Eve of 1991. I would make every effort to identify him and to inform his family that he has a grave in France. I would see that the grave was properly marked and that our nation would officially recognize his grave in this small village in France. And, I promised that his fellow countrymen would know about his grave.

Chapter Two

The Beginning Of The Search

I left the cemetery that Christmas Eve with a deeply rooted resolution to identify the remains in the grave, knowing I had no information to aid me in such a search. As Bernard and I drove back to his home, we had our first discussion about the grave and how we might go about finding the identity of the man who had lain in the grave marked INCONNU (UNKNOWN) for so long.

It was obvious to me, that the real secret to the grave had to be in Cartigny. Someone there had to have buried the remains and surely someone would remember under what circumstances the grave had come to be in their cemetery.

Bernard's family had been selling their crops to the village grain elevator (owned by the Mayor) for a long time and they knew many of the people in the village. We agreed that Bernard and his brother, Claude, would ask some of the people they knew in the village what they might know about the grave. Bernard promised to begin right after Christmas and before I left for home.

That Christmas Eve at the home of Bernard's son, Gérard and his wife Catherine, is one of my great memories of my many trips to France. They live about 20 km south of Péronne in the small village of Punchy, across from the farm of Catherine's parents.

The village of Punchy was right in the middle of the World War One battle lines for sometime and farming the area right after the war must have been quite interesting, what with all the unexploded bombs, shells and bullets lying around. They come to the surface still.

Attending this special evening were the extended family and several friends. A boon, as each new person I meet widens my network of friends across France.

As many of us might know, the French do not sit down to early dinners. Most do not begin to eat before 8:00 p.m and many even later. The Christmas special is Foie de Gras, or overfed goose liver pate which I found to be an acquired taste. This is but one of the special French foods that each family presents.

I continue, to this day, to forget about the many different courses such a dinner might have and I usually eat too much of the first courses and have little room for the following ones. Several of the courses come with a different wine to complement the taste of the food and there I sit with an allergy to wine and food has never been very important in my life, as it is for most people. I have been told by a Japanese friend that I have what they call, "A cat's tongue." Meaning that I don't care for spicy food at all, and I don't care to experiment with my meals, just give me basic meat and potatoes and I am happy.

The Leguillier and Lercher family Christmas with guests, Christmas Eve, 1991.

I remember well, my first experience with a French dinner and wine. I was a young man in the United States Air Force serving 13 months at a remote radar site in Morocco. I had met a French girl, Evelyn Lombardo and her family, at the beach on an R. & R. run and they had invited me to visit their home in the city of Meknes. I put in for a pass and dressed in my civilian suit and headed down to the road to hitchhike my way to Meknes.

There are times in life when one can be lucky, the first car coming down the road stopped and picked me up. I managed to convey that I was going to Meknes and showed him the address of my new friend's family. The fellow's face broke into a wide smile as he told me that he parked his car in the garage of that building. Now this conversation was between two people who did not speak the other's language, but we understood each other.

I arrived at Evelyn's front door, a day early. I had expected to get to Meknes in the evening and go to their house the next morning. The door was opened by a woman, whom I found out later was her grandmother. She knew I was coming and she insisted I enter and make myself at home. Soon I was eating French bread, spread thickly with butter and drinking tea.

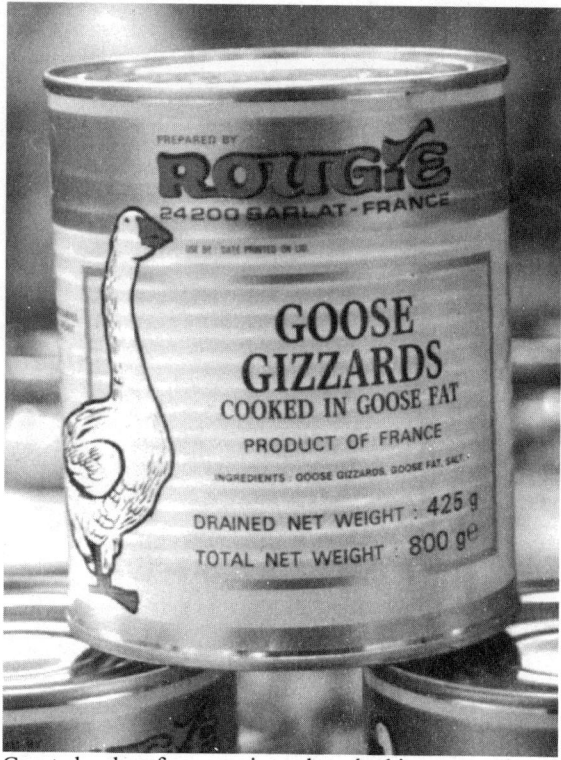
Great chunks of goose gizzard cooked in great gobs of goose grease!

The front door opened and Evelyn's younger brother came in. He could speak some English and we discussed my trip. Before long, Evelyn arrived from college and she showed me the book she had told me about at the beach. She had been awarded an English book by the King of Morocco for her good grades and on the flyleaf of that book was the statement: "Do not practice your English with an American, they do not speak English!"

As the family arrived, it was agreed that I should stay for dinner. When I told them that I had to find a room, Evelyn told me not to worry, her father had already made arrangements for me.

The dinner started and we ended up with eleven courses and seven different types of wine. Each bottle was a new one and as the guest, I got to smell the cork and have the first drink from the new bottle. Well, to shorten the story, I'll just say, "Her 11 year old brother drank me under the table." And I'm very thankful my first impression did not remain their final impression of me. They blamed my quick reaction to my day's travel, and the next day I was able to tell them that it was the first time I had ever drank wine and at home we never had alcohol at all. On my later visits, I was only required to sip a bit of each wine and I never repeated the first experience, except I got a severe headache each time. At that time, I was only seventeen and a half years old with lots to learn about myself and life.

My biggest inconvenience in France, besides not speaking the language, is that allergy to wines. It takes just a sip or two for me to quickly have a hard time breathing, followed very soon by a splitting headache.

I guess, I do speak a few words of French. Two of the main ones are allergique and mal de téte (headache) and by now, I know the hand and arm movements to go with the words. It can be hard sometimes, but I can usually get by without having to sip the fermented juice. However, after some words of astonishment by those in attendance, all of whom, including the children, are drinking wine, I am quickly offered something of a different type so I can join in with the toasts. My problem is becoming common knowledge and there is usually diet cola and bourbon when I show up to visit, scotch works in an emergency. Just to be safe, I usually carry Pepsi Max, as Diet Pepsi is called 'over there,' in my car boot, or trunk. I finally met a Frenchman, Bernard Delsert, a man with an equal passion for World War One who, we discovered, also shares the same wine allergy. Now, I don't feel like the only one on the ark with the problem. Bernard Delsert, like Christian Kowal works for the Bomb Disposal, North France.

Gérard Leguillier is a textile factory technician and Catherine is a school teacher. Their son Baptiste, being the only grandson at the time of this visit, was quite the center of attention by all.

That evening and early into Christmas morning, I had a wonderful opportunity to observe and be part of a true 'French Family' feast and Christmas observation. As with most families, the grandparents presented fabulous presents to their grandchildren. Baptiste received a large battery operated, rideable plastic jeep. The children are allowed to stay up late on Christmas Eve and the families were busy chasing the jeep as it explored the obstacles of the house, at a scale French highway speed, fast.

Bernard's son and his wife, owned a typical village home across the street from Catherine's parent's Ferme de LERCHER, in Punchy. Their farm ground is split by the motor highway from Paris to the north. A fairly long portion of the highway was built over the old World War One Lines. Causing a lot of problems during its construction as lost dugouts would collapse and they found hundreds of tons of unexploded shells that had to be cleared away.

The new T.G.V. high speed train line had been built just to the west of the motor highway. After it had started its normal schedule, they found they had to put a speed limit on the trains because hidden dugouts were starting to collapse under the tracks. Even now, one can see concrete pumper trucks parked near the rail line, as they pump concrete into newly found dugouts before they cause the train to leave the track.

Many of my relic collecting friends called the construction of these two projects 'the golden age of World War One collecting'. It was important that you made friends with the ground moving personnel, so they would call you when they broke into a dugout or made a new find.

Today, whenever the ground is moved in the Somme Battle areas, more relics come to the surface. During a trip in March, 1997, I found a new stack of explosives that had been removed from an area about 50 meters by 100 meters where they were building a new farm building in Ginchy, just south of Delville Wood.

I counted over 50 shells in the stack, there were shrapnel, fragment and stokes mortar shells. Any one of which might detonate.

On Christmas morning, just before we left for my visit with the Bonifaces, Bernard and I reviewed my growing collection of World War One relics in his basement. The KRUPP 210 mm shell Carol and I had obtained during the summer was there, along with new items of interest collected along the way. These were going to have to wait for our next visit during the late spring of 1992, when we were going to fashion a crate and pack them all for transportation by ship to the United States and Seattle. Today, it is all considered scrap metal (when demilitarized, or made safe) and a large volume can be shipped to the United States at a reasonable cost. Of course, our valuation of reasonable cost for this scrap metal is quite different than others, for each piece has a story to tell us.

As Bernard drove me out to the Bonifaces, we again discussed the 'Grave at Cartigny' and the best way to research its identity. Bernard again promised to talk to some of the villagers and see if he could discover anything of interest before I left for home.

I was welcomed at a house in full Christmas spirit, which like his driving, meant

Richard had lots to do and we moved fast all week. That Christmas Day was very cool and foggy, Richard and I drove over to the field with a metal detector to locate and start digging out the cannon they had found and reburied just for me. We soon found the spot in the newly torn up field, that used to be a woods, where Richard thought the cannon should be. We searched and we searched and we could not locate that cannon. Finally, even Richard agreed that it was just not there any longer.

However, the search had not been a failure for me, for we had found many old bottles that the cannon crews had thrown out in front of their cannon positions and we found several 77 mm cannon cartridge cases which had been blown up. One, I kept for my collection, as it still had the primer intact, meaning it had exploded by some other means. We also found bits and pieces of a cannon ammunition caisson which was used to carry the cartridges for the cannon. In one large clump we found a bunch of fuse coverings. These indicated that we were at the exact spot where the cannon crew set the time fuses for the shells they were firing.

Over a year later, I was visiting the World War One Museum under the Basilica "Notre-Dame de Brebieres," in Albert, when I heard the curator telling how he had discovered a blown up German cannon near Mesnil. Immediately, I knew who had **stolen my cannon**. He had actually rediscovered it, after Richard's crew had discovered it and then hidden it again for me to rediscover on my forthcoming trip. You can visit my second German cannon there.

All was not lost you see, I learned a lot that day. We found the original position of the cannon battery and a bit later, we located where the battery had moved, just over the top of the ridge and away from the sight of the gun that had blown up one of their group.

I found, that one way to locate a cannon position is to look for glass bottles in an arc and then look behind them, an arm's throw away, for the actual cannon position. They probably threw them out there, because people do not walk in front of firing cannons.

Later, I came across an entry in a book about the French coming over the top of the ridge near Combles and seeing a German cannon position in the far distance firing at them. The French brought up one of their famous 75 mm cannons and on its first shot, it hit the position and there was quite an explosion. I believe, we were at the same German battery position upon which they fired and two of the bottles from that position, still with the dirt of the Somme on them, are sitting here on my desk.

Fuse cap covers, blown up cartridge case and bottles from the German 77 mm battery position found by Richard Boniface in November, 1991.

They could have contained wine, but more probably they had contained carbonated water. Much of the water in the battlefield area was polluted and most soldiers would not drink what was found in shell holes and such, unless they were really desperate. However, the Germans often had facilities to carbonate and bottle drinking water near the front. Of course, they would reuse any bottle they could to fill with carbonated water to send to the men in the front lines.

I realized that day, France is quickly losing its remaining World War One physical history as each year, several more miles of lines are plowed and restored to fields.

That night, I was a guest at the family Christmas dinner. One evening while visiting one of Richard's employee's home for dinner, I ended up dancing with all the wives and girl friends and giving away a sweater. I'm still not quite sure how that sweater ended up a permanent gift, but I still get a big smile when I see that fellow.

The first work day after Christmas, all of Richard's employees showed up early and we were off to cut down the trees along a stretch of road north of Bapaume. I am not one to watch others work and after I had taken the pictures I wanted, I was soon pulling limbs to the fire and helping move the logs to the storage spot. We built a big fire that day and burned the tops of quite a few trees.

I had already learned from Bernard, how dangerous that was. There can be a shell located not too far down and the heat from the fire can cause it to explode. However, I also knew that Richard did not seem worried and if he wasn't, then I wasn't...too much. Since that day, I have read and heard about several people being killed and injured under similar circumstances.

The trees growing along the roads of France are not the property of the Highway Department, they belong to the Forestry Department and they control when the trees are cut, trimmed and such. They are treated like a crop and from trip to trip we will find the big beautiful trees along a road gone and new seedlings in place. The tree lined roads go back to the early days when in the summer the shade of the trees made life easier for the horses pulling the loads. In winter, when the leaves are gone, the sun helps melt the ice and snow on the roads, as well as warming the horse at work.

Richard's home has one of the largest working fireplaces I have seen. He needs such work to secure the large tree trunks he burns. I told him, we could measure my visit by number of tree trunks used, for a large one takes all day to burn.

When visiting along the war lines, one will often see shells lying alongside a tree or near a marker along the road. It is OK to look at them and take pictures, but don't go picking them up and playing with them. That advice is for your safety, they can and do explode. Not often, but often enough to keep you informed. You may find, the hard way, that they can kill you.

One day, we went to the village of Lesbœufs where Richard bulldozed an old cattle field into a flatter farm field. He had brought his metal detector and told me to keep myself busy hunting for buried relics while he worked. So there I was, about thirty feet in front of his bulldozer waiting for that detector to signal its find.

I wasn't there very long when my imagination and more sane mind asked me, "What are you doing here?" Looking around, I realized, that if Richard hit and exploded a shell, he was somewhat safe because of the large and thick bulldozer blade. But there I was, in front of the blade which would focus any explosion exactly where I was standing. For the rest of the job, I following closely behind the bulldozer.

One of the reasons the farmer had Richard at work was a series of depressions surrounded by low banks. I realized, that I was looking at an artillery position and from its location it had to be a German one.

The end of a 77 mm German Artillery Battery position. Notice metal detector in foreground.

Shortly after I returned from that trip, I read in one of my books about an English unit's attack against the north end of Lesbœufs and how they were under direct fire from a cannon battery located near the sunken road at the north end of the village. And I knew, I too had become a participant in the destruction of history at that battery position, as the last physical evidence of the position was pushed and smoothed over.

I was somewhat sorry that I hadn't found any good relics at the position, except for the rifle cartridges one finds everywhere in the Somme, both fired and unfired, and an empty shrapnel shell or two. I know now, that such a place would have been picked clean by other relic collectors long ago as it was next to the road. I drive past that spot, almost every time I go to the Somme now and I think of what I saw and what was, and not of what I see now, a field of sugar beets or wheat.

Writing of wheat, you will often find the mention of corn in British and French writings. When they write of corn, they are writing about wheat, as they use the word maize for corn, as we know it. In Alan's Seeger's Poem, **_I Have A Rendezvous With Death_**, when he writes of *chest-high-corn*, he was writing of chest high wheat. The French use a breed of wheat that has much higher stalks than most farmers in the United States.

An interesting story Bernard once told me, was about the French people at the end of World War Two. An American telegraphed the French Relief Agency and asked what food stuffs the United States could send to help alleviate the food shortages. The French person telegraphed back, "Send us corn, shiploads of corn." Well, they got shiploads of corn products and Bernard remembers his mother learning to make new foods of corn (maize) content, instead of the usual corn (wheat) content they were so used to. They had received corn meal, corn flour and lots of whole corn (maize) for people to eat and not a kernel of the corn (wheat) they thought they had requested .

Shooting and Poofing in France
Shooting

I also went rabbit hunting with Richard, several brothers and some friends. Now that was an experience to remember until one dies. I had heard of hunting rabbits with ferrets, but I had never done it. On the morning of the hunt, Richard's brother, Sylvan, arrived with a cute little ferret in a straw-filled lunch box hanging from his waist. As we prepared to go, the first indication that this might be a bit different was that each of the twelve men present loaded a minimum of two boxes of shotgun shells into their hunting jackets. The second, was when Richard handed me a shotgun and told me to pick up some shells.

When I told him, "I shouldn't carry a shotgun as I was just visiting and not licensed." He laughed his very deep and rumbling laugh and told me, "Not to worry, because we were going to hunt on his property and the game warden was a very good friend." During my visit to France in 1994, I had dinner with Richard and his family at his good friend's, the game warden's, home.

When Richard Boniface tells you to do something, I have found the best thing is to do it. That way he will invite you along on the next adventure. So I picked up the shotgun and put six shells into my pocket, as I wasn't expecting to bring home the meat that day.

I have found that Richard has many friends and that he is a hero in the Somme locality. Richard and a brother were national Motocross champions in the late 1970's and early 1980's. Richard's brother is still a crew chief of a national Yamaha Motocross team. In France, they take Motocross big time, there are tracks everywhere and they remember their champions.

Off we went 'a hunting,' thirteen in all with a ferret and ten or so dogs. Now they hunt differently than Bernard's group, as they use the ferret. I also found they hunt differently than anybody I have ever seen in my life, or in the movies, for what followed would not be believed if one saw it in a movie.

Part of Richard's property is filled with the excess soil and rock from the digging of the Canal du Nord which is located just north of his home. This pile of chalk and flintstones is about 40 feet high, one half-mile long and a quarter of a mile across.

Rabbits in France are diggers and they have Swiss-cheesed the ground in the woods with warrens. As the hunters approach they dive into a hole and unless you have a ferret or you surprise them out in the open, they are gone.

As we approached the first large warren, about seventy-five feet across, Sylvan climbed half way up the very steep bank and stopped next to an obviously used hole. The rest of the hunters arranged themselves in a circle around the rabbit warren holes. Some are on top of the spoil mound, others at the base and the rest along the sloped hillside. I was standing about halfway up the slope with one foot about 12 inches above the other, the bottom foot was in the entrance of a rabbit hole which looked unused, as it was covered with light twigs and spider webs.

Then, I did a double take, as I looked around, I realized in amazement, that all these hunters are facing in as they jack shells into their guns and get ready to shoot. "0h'well," I say to myself, and I went ahead and loaded three shells myself. At the same time, the dogs were running in and out of the circle, climbing up and down the hill and generally letting us know they were very happy at being out hunting.

When Sylvan feels we are all ready he hollers, "Depart", which sounded like 'de-par-tay,' and releases the ferret into the entrance of the hole. The ferret sniffed the air around himself and the hole opening and he started into the hole. Sylvan bent over listening at the hole and as he listened he could hear the noise of the ferret scurrying through the hole and soon he could hear a rabbit moving.

From the many different holes he could judge which way they were moving and he started pointing toward me and hollering "Attention, Attention, Attention." No sooner had the last "Attention" left his mouth when a rabbit came bursting out of that unused bottom hole and over my foot. The rabbit took off down the hill, with ten dogs starting right after him.

BlaBlaBlaBlam,BlaBlaBlam, the shots ran together as many of the hunters shot at that rabbit, which was about five feet down the hill from me by that time. None hit him, and thankfully none hit me. But, the rabbit swerved up the hill and started right back toward me, dogs in hot pursuit.

I was laughing so hard from that rabbit running over my foot and all those people shooting at each other and me, that all I could do was stand and observe. The rabbit was running as hard as he could with the dogs jumping all over themselves trying to get to the rabbit, I couldn't even lift my gun. And, to this day I can't figure out how the rabbit, the dogs and the people all missed being hit by some of that lead.

Before the rabbit got too close to me, the guns roared again and again and again as that rabbit looked like a ball in a pin ball machine. Here, there, back here, over there he ran with dogs nipping at him and people shooting at him. Just when it looked like he had it, that rabbit burst between two of the hunters at the bottom of the slope and with dogs hot at his heels he took off into the winter wheat in the field at the foot of the slope. He was helped along by several more shots, but he lived to be hunted another day as they called the dogs back.

Now this would be funny enough, if it had happened just once, but as soon as the rabbit took off they all laughed and talked about how close they had come. Sylvan let the ferret go again and again he roared "Depart." This time, even I could hear the noise of the ferret and the rabbit running thru the tunnels. There in the center of this wonderful bunch of shotgun shooters stood big Sylvan pointing and saying, "Attention" and as that rabbit burst from a hole beyond him the guns roared again. Now this is one of those parts of my story that has to seem like fiction, for that rabbit darted this way and that way and the dogs followed as the guns roared again and again. And again, only this time at the top of the slope, the rabbit burst through the circle to freedom. So far, a minimum of two boxes of shells had to be gone and we didn't have a rabbit.

Well, now the laugh is on me, as Sylvan insists I come and stand by him when he sends the ferret into the hole. Richard led the laughter, as he told them what I saying about their hunting practice. It was interesting to see that ferret sniff and head into the hole for the third time. This time as Sylvan hollered, "Depart," I was looking at the grinning circle of gun nuts surrounding us.

Soon the ferret started moving faster and we could hear the rabbit heading nearer and nearer. Sylvan hollered, "Attention" and pointed at a hole between our feet. He smiled a great big smile and he placed his shotgun barrel about six inches above the entrance to that hole where it sounded like the rabbit was headed. Sure as heck, that rabbit came out of that hole scrambling like the devil, and as soon as he could react Sylvan pulled the trigger. Blam went his shotgun and off went the rabbit, but he left something. There blown into and around the hole in the ground, the shot had made was a scattered poof ball of rabbit tail. This time, when the ferret reached the head of the hole the rabbit had come out of, he looked a bit worried as he smelled the bits of hair and gun powder.

As Sylvan picked the ferret up, the battle was going on around us and this time the mighty hunters overcame and as the rabbit bounded up toward the top of the slope, he suddenly flopped over and expired as the dogs fought over which one was to have the pleasure of gumming the carcass a bit.

When the dog's owner got him to release the rabbit he gave it to Sylvan, who tore off a small piece of meat and gave it to the ferret as his reward. Not too much, he explained, or the ferret would go to sleep, just enough to keep him interested.

After running the ferret a couple of more times and with him coming back to the head of the hole when he didn't smell another rabbit, we moved along the spoil pile to the next rabbit warren. Once Sylvan talked to Richard, who told me that Sylvan wanted me to watch out for the ghosts of dead World War One Germans, as the ferret occasionally drives one out and they don't like being shot at. While moving, I climbed to the top of the spoil bank and walked along with Richard as he teased me and told the others what I was saying about this new experience.

At the next warren, they got the first rabbit with the use of no more than a dozen or two shells. The second bounced back and forth and came tearing up the bank and through two of the hunters, on the bank side to our left. The dogs, led by Richard's dog were hot on his tail as they disappeared into some brush. Richard's dog bounced out of the brush onto the level top before the rabbit came tearing out just beyond him. Richard's gun flew up and he fired, with the shot passing under his dog's belly and hitting the ground just behind the rabbit. No prize doll for Richard, but I did see what the expression on a surprised dog's face looks like.

Richard had purchased the piled up dirt pile to use as a Motocross training area and it is laid out in various runs with very steep hills and valleys. The flat area we were on was only about 12 feet wide and then it sloped down and up again across the way. The rabbit beat the dogs over the hill and down he ran, everyone hollered at their dogs and they stopped chasing and started coming back. We stood there and watched the rabbit run down the slope, across the track at the bottom and start climbing the hill on the other side at full speed.

Meanwhile the hunters who could see, were telling the ones over the bank about Richard's dog's close hair cut via his missed shot and Richard was telling me, "The dog had to learn not to be where he was going to shoot!" Me, I still had my eye on that rabbit and as he came to the top of the ridge, about eighty feet away, I lifted my shotgun and as he hurtled into the air at the top, I shot.

You could hear the intake of breath, as the hunters on the hill watched that rabbit tumble over in mid-flight that far away. It turns out, they don't shoot at any long distance as they are not used to it. I grew up hunting rabbits with no dogs and no ferret and when they broke out and started running most shots were at distances the French would not think of pulling the trigger.

I instantly became the great hunter with just one shot. We continued our hunt and we quit only when the shells were gone. In the end, we had seven rabbits and I had gotten three of them with my fantastic long distance shooting with just four shells. The other four took an average of one hundred and fifty twelve gauge shotgun shells each.

Everyone trooped back to Richard's house where the champagne was served and the stories continued to grow and grow.

Now honest, the above is true and this book is not fictional though portions of it reads like it must be. Of course, Sam had to have whisky, cokeka. I kept waiting to go back down and clean the rabbits, however I was to be introduced to something I had read, but really not believed. At Richard's, one does not clean freshly shot game right away, it must lay there for a few days until it is 'Gamey' before one cleans and cooks it. Believe it, all the odor doesn't go away when it is cooked either, but it was good rabbit when we had it for dinner the night before I left, as long as you didn't pay much attention to your nose.

Richard is a storehouse of locations to find dud shells and he is often called when people find shells they aren't sure of. Each run into the Somme countryside with Richard has the possibility of leading to treasure.

One day we stopped by my favorite café at Pozières. More Australians were killed within one mile of Pozières, during the Battle of the Somme, than anywhere else during the Great War.

Much later, Carol and I would find out one reason why this village always seemed to pull us there during our trips. Here, the Canadians also fought one of their most famous battles, when the first tanks entered into combat on September 15, 1916.

The café, Madame Brihier's of Pozières, was purchased in the spring of 1997 by Dominic Zenardi, who has renamed it **'Tommy's Café.'**

At one time he owned a café at Longueval[18] and then he was Curator of the museum at Albert, remember the fellow who *found* my cannon. He already has one cannon out front, we saw it when we were there in May, 1997. I expect that he will repeat the trench displays that were the big draw when he had his café at Longueval. It will be an excellent place to stop for lunch and a view of his large collection of relics.

Madame Brihier's husband lost his right hand above the wrist when he was working in a house doing plastering work. His partner reached up through a hole in the ceiling and pulled out an American World War Two aircraft rocket that had flown through the roof and stuck in a rafter during a strafing attack. When he threw it to Mr. Brihier, it went off just as he caught it. Another very good reason to be very careful of anything you might find 'over there.'

Richard and I were there for a reason, when Bernard and I had visited the week before, Mr. Brihier took us outside to see what had been found when the main road in front of the café had been torn up to rebuild it after Carol and I visited the café in the past June.

The road construction crew had found three Australian skeletons, lots of bent rifles, shells, some tank parts and about half of a five gallon can full of unexploded Mills Bombs, or

Mills Bomb, the spring loaded handle is held in place by a cotter pin. When the handle is released, the time delay fuse starts.

hand grenades. They had been found in two bunches, probably where a bomb carrier was killed or where one left, or lost a bag of bombs. The Mills Bombs looked brand new, except that they might have been rolled in muddy water.

Mr. Brihier took one of the Mills Bombs, placed it in the crook of his right arm and checked the cotter pin, that holds the handle in place, to see if it was rusted through. If the handle flies off, the grenade is armed and will explode in a few seconds. Not a good thought at the time.

He then turned the grenade over and unscrewed the bottom. He showed us how to cut the slow burn fuse in the bottom and pull out the detonator so it could not explode, but he did not cut the fuse. After screwing the bottom back on, he rechecked the cotter pin and handle and grasping the bomb in his left hand, he threw it onto the concrete with quite some force.

I can't tell you the expression on my face at that moment, but I can tell you that Bernard's eyes opened very wide and his mouth flew open.

Being around Richard, you have to think fast, and as Mr. Brihier wasn't moving, I didn't move, but I did think about it. With much laughter, he bent down and picked up the Mills Bomb and stuck it into my pant's pocket. Bernard interpreted, as he said, "Here, take this as a souvenir of this visit."

A week later, I was back with Richard so he could see the new stuff and check on the shells that had been found to see if they were still explosive. Richard had shown me how to lick my finger, to wet it, and to stick it into a dud shell and taste what was there. If it had an acid taste the explosive was still able to explode. Several of the shells had their fuses missing and even though they had been in the ground all those years, they were still deadly as the insides tasted like acid to me. I thought, they still had active explosive in them and they could explode. When Richard tested them, he agreed.

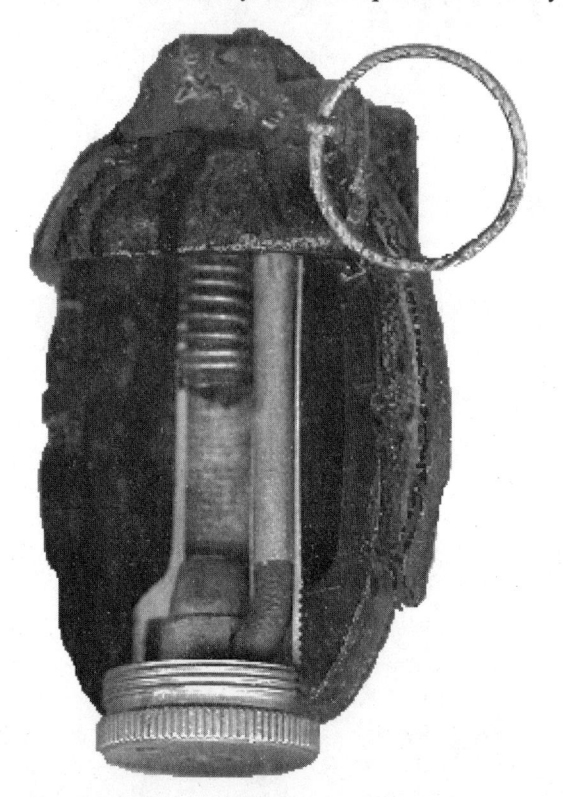

Mills Bomb Cut-A-Way. The mills bomb has a cast iron body that has grooves cast into the side, so that the body of the grenade breaks into chunks when the time delay fuse detonates. These cut-a-way relics are for sale and make a great paper weight.

Left to right: Richard Boniface, Josiane Brihier and Mr. Brihier. He lost his hand to an old W.W.II American aircraft rocket explosion. December, 1991.

We loaded the shells into the back of Richard's four-by-four, or 'Cat-Cat,' and later unloaded them onto the pile outside his home. And to think, to this day, I still can't get Richard to stick his finger into an automobile battery and lick it. If it has a sharp, bitter acid taste the battery is good. A weak or dead battery does not have that taste. A shell, he will, a battery, he won't!

On one of those days, we headed out to Bancourt to find a shell that Richard had uncovered during one of his excavations for the Segers brothers. It was another short shell used in the KRUPP 210 mm cannon we have. It had been fired, but for some reason it had not exploded.

In the 'Cat-Cat' were Richard his two sons, a brother and me. When we arrived, we found the big shell and several smaller ones, all duds, with the fuses installed. Some had been fired and some had not and they could all be active. Soon we were heading down the road toward home. As we drove past a field with the fences still alongside it, I laughed to myself and Richard asked me what I thought was funny? I told him that I had been thinking about what would happen if the shells suddenly exploded. All they would find, perhaps, is some twisted metal from the 'cat-cat' and some strings of our guts on the fence. Also, that it was the first time I had ever ridden with him at such a slow speed.

Now that was a mistake, for at once he stepped on the gas and we proceeded across the back roads of France at his more usual speeds, this with around 500 pounds of dud shells in the back, shells that contained some tens of pounds of high explosive. Since you are reading this, we must have made it.

Christian and Richard among Christian's tool and relics of the trade. If you want to know anything about cartridges, ask Christian.

One day, Richard took me to meet Christian Kowal, the bomb remover, who provided the KRUPP 210 mm shell during our last visit. Of interest, is Christian's collection of educational tools. Most are the first one of that particular type of explosive he has had to defuse. He often uses them to educate new employees how to safely defuse various types of explosives.

Richard is always happy to 'poof' things and one afternoon we placed a few of the smaller shells, from his pile, in the four-by-four, along with an eight inch British one. We bounced around the spoil pile to a place where he tests his explosives and we proceeded to blow up World War One shells. He would tape a small block of TNT to a shell, add a primer and fuse and he would light the fuse as we ran to hide behind the 'Cat-Cat.'

The resounding boom was quite satisfying and the whirl of the fragments brought to mind descriptions from the many books I have read. Soon, we were down to the big one, the one that would make the really big noise.

Up the hill from us, a farmer was winter plowing his field. He was over the ridge, but there was a gap where he crossed from one ridge to the other. Richard had been timing his crossings so that we would set the shells off when he was behind a ridge. It seemed a long distance to me, but I always listen and observe Richard's actions.

Soon, he was happy and we placed the eight inch shell against the bank and placed the last of the blocks of TNT against it, three or four of them. Soon, the fuse was lit and this time Richard did not look over the hood of the four by four, he crouched behind it and told me to get part way under it. The fuse was burning and the shell was going to explode.

Just then, the farmer's tractor came into sight, crossing the gap between the ridges. For some reason he had cut his turn around and arrived early. Richard looked at me and did his 'Poof' sign and crouched down further.

The **WHAM** and **BOOM** of that explosion echoed off the surrounding hills just as the farmer disappeared behind the ridge. The air was full of whirling noises as the fragments flew and as we watched, we saw one very large piece fly up into the air and head right for that gap. It seemed to move in slow motion as it whirled through the air, leaving behind a distinct sound. Slowly, slowly it seemed to fly and then it plunged to earth. Right in the center of that gap and very close to where the farmer had just made his passage.

The people around Richard's home have to be used to large explosions coming from the direction of his property. I expect, the farmer never realized that we had chased him with that fragment. I expect, he just said the usual swear words about having such a noisy neighbor and plowed on.

Poofing

"What is 'Poofing," is a fair question. As you have read, Richard is most happiest when he is blowing something up. When he discusses an explosion he will hunch his shoulders and raise both hands up in front of him while turning the palms upward and saying, "Poof!"

When Carol and I had visited Richard in the spring of 1992, he had shown us a very large amount of explosive that he had temporarily stored in the building for the next day's job, a building that is both his shop and his home.

When I asked him, "Just how big of a hole it would make," he replied, "It would make a hole about 40 meters wide and 10 meters deep when it went 'Poof.'" I looked around and told him, I thought the building we were in must be about 20 meters wide by 40 meters long and did he mean, he and his family would be blown up if it happened to explode while they were home. Without a second thought, he looked me right in the eye, with a big smile and said, "Oui, Poof,' while giving his "Poof" sign. I knew then, that Richard and his family all accept his dangerous way of life and live life, 'day by day.'

All too soon, it was New Year's Eve and I was to leave early the next morning. It had been a working day and several of Richard's brothers and workers were there celebrating the end of the year and payday. By now, I knew most of them quite well and we had gotten to know each other's style of humor.

Suddenly, we were all heading down the stairs, as they were going to give Sam a big send off show of 'Poofs.' First, out came the army surplus magnesium aerial flare with it's firing tube, so we could see it go off among the low clouds.

The flare tube was placed out in the middle of an open spot and the fuse string was pulled. Everyone ducked behind a car and waited expectantly. No flash, no fire and no flare, it just sat there mocking them and I wasn't much help with my remarks.

Well, that called for a conference while they figured out how to next impress me. Out came a container of essence, (gasoline), two small squares of 'the special stuff' and some fuse. The fuses were cut under the supervision of all, one a bit shorter than the other, as the first 'special poof' had to break the gasoline container and vaporize the fuel so the second one would cause it to flash when it exploded. Back to the open spot, next to the flare, with the second, 'let's impress Sam shot.' Now, not only will we get to see the gasoline flash, it will be augmented by the flare.

The fuses were lit and we retired behind the bulldozer to observe the dramatic results. Soon there came a small flash and the muted sound of an explosion, however the second shot failed and we now had an area covered with gasoline and its fumes, a missing square of 'special poof,' the dud flare and even more remarks from me.

This called for another conference and plans to figure out how to take advantage of all this for a really, really big send off for Sam. Well, let's see, we need a hot enough flash to set all the gasoline off, we need a big enough shot to tear the flare apart and to set the flare off. It also has to be big enough to insure that the missing 'special poof' block of explosive also would ignite, wherever it was.

Sylvan's face opened with that big smile of his and he said he would be right back and out the door he went. Soon, he was back with two small hand tanks of propane from the service truck. "Simple," he said, "just wrap two sticks of Nitro Express dynamite onto the two propane tanks and when they go, the flashing propane would surely do the job." So, I watched Richard crimp the electrical primer onto the electrical firing line, splice the fuse into the sticks of dynamite and tape the bomb together. By now, it was agreed it was none to safe to have a burning fuse with the low lying gasoline fumes, so the electrical firing system had been gotten out to remotely detonate the bomb.

This time, when we went out to the open spot, everyone did not troop right up to the previous explosives. When I saw most of them slowing up, I slowed even more and while we stood far back, I was the furthest back. We watched as Richard gingerly walked into the middle of the open spot and placed the new device on the ground next to the flare tube.

By now, it was pitch dark and the misty evening had turned into a light rainy night. Boy, it was dark and though I would not have traded places with Richard, I would have walked out with him, if he had asked. But, I took his failure to ask to heart, and knowing Richard as I do, I let the rest of them stand between that open spot and me.

Soon Richard came back, trailing the wire from the spool behind him. With great showmanship he hooked the wire to the plunger box and prepared to fire the 'poof.' This time, there was no one peeking around the bulldozer to see that very special 'poof,' when Richard pushed the plunger down. Whomp, went a very muffled explosion. 'Poof' was just about the word I would have used, until I learned the French meaning of the word. It was a very small explosion with a very small flash of light and an extremely disappointing amount of noise.

It was a sorry group that walked back to the shop with me that night, for by now there were gasoline fumes in the air, unfired; a magnesium flare, unfired; a small block of 'very special poof,' unfired and missing; one or more small tanks of propane, unfired; one stick of Nitro Express that didn't fire and one laughing American talking about the French "Poof" experts.

Well, they all agreed that the open spot was just too dangerous to go near in the dark and when it was light, Richard would have to gather up the goodies and give them a special New Year treat. One that Sam would not see.

I sure missed that big 'poof, as Richard had taken me to the airport early that New Year's Day and I was on the plane heading west when he finally got the big display. Perhaps, an incoming airplane wondered what the flash of light was. Still, the real memory is of the night it wouldn't go 'poof' for all the tea in China, or all the champagne in Reims.

As we drove to the airport that morning, I didn't have a cannon to send home and I didn't see the big flash, but I had gotten the most rabbits and my luggage was full of fuses, grenades and other goodies, all fixed so they were not dangerous, of course. They do check those things before they let you on the plane and there had better be no questions about them.

Most of all, I had a new passion. A passion to identify the Unknown American Aviator, who died in 1943, for the Liberty of France. One who lies in a grave at Cartigny, France, in a grave marked:

**AVIATEUR AMERICAIN
INCONNU
MORT POUR LA FRANCE - EN 1943**

My quest had started, for on that last day Bernard called and told me about the first of the **'Legends' of the Grave.**

SOUVENIR FRANÇAIS
AVIATEUR AMERICAIN
INCONNU
MORT POUR LA FRANCE

Chapter Three

The Legends Of The Grave

Bernard had called me the evening before Richard took me to the airport and I must admit I was a bit excited, for I really thought that he might have found a good lead to the identity of the remains in the grave of the Unknown American. However, as he repeated to me the story he had been told, I began to realize that the story didn't provide any real information that would help in my new quest.

Bernard told me that the person he had talked to about the grave, "Didn't know too much about it, except that he had heard the remains in the grave were found by a farmer on a fall day, during World War Two." He had been told, that the farmer walked out of his home one fall morning and when he looked toward his farm pond in the distance, he saw birds diving down to the surface and back up. As it was the wrong time of year for the birds to be feeding on insects in the pond, this did not seem right and the farmer walked to the pond to see what the birds were feeding on.

When he arrived at the pond, he saw the birds diving at something floating in the water and after finding a limb he pulled the floating object to the side. As he pulled, he realized that he had hooked onto what was left of a human floating in the pond, so he left the remains there and went to contact the village authorities.

The authorities came to the pond and looked over the situation and helped remove the remains. There was enough clothing on the remains to identity them as being an Unites States Army Air Force airman, but there was no other identification.

As the remains were American, it was decided that the authorities would go to the American Somme Military Cemetery at Bony, which is located about ten miles from Cartigny, to see if they would take the remains. It is the cemetery that contains the American dead who lost their lives in the Somme area of France, during World War One.

When they arrived, there were no Americans there. The Supervisor had left at the beginning of the war and he had not come back yet, however there was a Frenchman still working at the cemetery. The men from Cartigny asked him if the cemetery would take the remains they had found? The French worker told them it was no problem and for them to bring the remains to the cemetery where, "...they would put the remains in a grave for the unknown."

As people quite familiar with French Military Cemeteries, they knew that the usual grave for the INCONNU (Unknown) is an Ossuary, or a pit in which a large number of unknown remains are placed and covered. On top there will be a marker declaring that so many unknown remains are buried in the common grave and there may even be some names listed, stating they are known to be in the grave.

Somme American World War One Cemetery, Bony, France

The Cartigny delegation discussed it among themselves and they decided, that this American airman had died fighting for the Liberty of France and he deserved a grave of his own, not a burial in an Ossuary pit. So, they went home and buried the remains in the Cartigny village cemetery, next to the four French soldiers who had been killed in the area during the French Army's retreat before the Germans in 1940.

The story seemed somewhat plausible to me, except how did the United States Army Air Force flyer arrive in a pond? Did he come from a plane that crashed nearby, or one that had crashed some distance away. Perhaps, he fell from a airplane that was damaged as it flew over Cartigny? To me, the explanation of the grave that Bernard had been told, created more questions than it answered.

Bernard said he would continue to ask about the grave's origin and we discussed the next time Carol and I would be in France.

Just before saying goodbye, we also discussed the need to ship our collected relics home, as the pile was growing and he was going to need the room in his basement when his wine shipment arrived next summer.

Bernard heads a co-op of friends who buy their wine together to get the best deal and each June a large truck pulls up and Bernard unloads several pallets of wine into his basement. The first time I saw the truck unloading the wine, I wondered if it was all Bernard's, you know those Frenchmen.

I spent that New Year's Day flight back to Seattle, thinking of the events of my visit and uppermost in my mind was the grave and the strange story I had heard. The more I thought about it, the more I thought the only thing that made real sense was the tale of the visit to the American Cemetery. Carol and I had visited hundreds of military cemeteries in France, there are over 200 British military cemeteries in the Somme (80) Department and many French and German cemeteries. It is fairly rare to find a grave marked INCONNU in a French Military Cemetery. Finding an Ossuary with many INCONNU is quite normal. It just didn't sound like something someone might make up.

The only other help was the statement that it was fall when the farmer saw the birds at his pond. Since the grave was marked MORT POUR LA FRANCE - EN 1943, it would allow me to date the grave to sometime in the fall of 1943.

I arrived back home and Carol and I discussed what kind of books we should be locating at the local libraries to begin researching the grave's identity. We needed to look up any information we could find on missions during the fall of 1943 that might have flown over the Péronne area of France, with the hope that something would catch our eye that might help.

From earlier reading and Bernard's conversations, I knew there had been large flights of bombers and fighters over that area to targets further away. However, local bomber and fighter sweeps didn't begin until the ones to disrupt traffic for "D-Day, 1944" and as the Germans were driven back away from northern France.

Although World War Two aviation was not an area of research to me, I had read many books about it. Especially when I was in school and the military, if a book was available, I read it. The two years I spent at remote sites in Morocco and Korea, added a lot of such books to my reading history.

Carol and I spent many enjoyable afternoons and evenings at libraries looking through military history books and reading about the Army Air Force in Europe. We found lots of information about bombers over Europe. There were hundreds of missions going in the right direction, but without any real date to research there wasn't any way to search for lost individuals.

It didn't seem very long before we were on our way back to France for another visit. With luck, Bernard, Claude, Carol and I could meet some of the people of Cartigny and get a good lead.

When we arrived in Péronne in late May, 1992, one of the first people we met was Bernard and we reviewed the information he had been sending us via the fax machine. He and Claude had talked to several more people and all they had heard, were several versions of the story Bernard had first told me.

Each person had told them almost the same story, with each version having several points in common. The time of year, the birds, the pond, the American Cemetery and the grave at Cartigny were in all the stories.

However, some versions began to differ when the person described the remains recovered. Bernard and Claude had been told by one, that he had heard there were the remains of two airmen in the grave. And one said that the grave contained the remains of several airmen and that the remains had been in very small pieces.

Sam and Bernard discuss the 'Legends of the Grave' at Cartigny.

As we discussed the several stories they had been told, we realized that none of the stories provided the basic information needed to solve the mystery of the grave at Cartigny, a solid who, what, why, where and when.

The story of the small remains of several Airmen, really puzzled us. For how could they have pulled small pieces of remains from a pond? They should have sunk or been eaten by the fish.

It could be possible that they had found parts of two airmen, perhaps a navigator and bombardier who had fallen out of a damaged bomber together. But the pieces of several people just didn't seem possible. I had seen pictures of B–17 bombers that had returned to England with the front of the bomber gone, along with the men within it.

Two stories stated, that a large weight of remains had been recovered and put in the grave, in fact, several hundred pounds. That would support the two person story, but it sounded like to much weight for just two people.

In some ways, the more we found out, the less we knew.

All we had **for certain, we thought**, was a time in the fall of 1943.

We became busy in our usual activities of such a visit, researching points of interest of World War One. One day, we cleaned the grave and repainted the cross. We often walked in the woods with French friends and metal detected for relics of soldiers past.

Grave keeping, cleaning and repainting the cross of the grave of the Unknown American Airman, Cartigny, France, May, 1992.

During this visit, we were also told the story of an American bomber that had crashed somewhere in the vicinity of Péronne. The crew had gotten out and had been hidden by the French in a hunting cabin in a woods.

After some time had passed the Germans overheard someone talking about the American crew in a bar. Later that night they went to the man's home and took him away, he never came back. That same night, the Germans surrounded the woods and captured the crew.

Quickly, my mind jumped to the thought that just possibly, one of the crew had managed to escape the German circle and had fallen into the pond and drowned while running away in the night.

The only problem was the person who told the story could not provide any dates, not even an approximate date of the crash and we could find no one else to support the story. And that theory would not account for the new stories of the remains being more than one American airman, nor the small pieces.

We did have one major job to begin to collect our relics from all our storage places at different friend's homes and pack them. Layer by layer the crate was filled and each layer was photographed so we could show customs, at home, what was in the crate.

One person's scrap metal is another's treasure. Note 210mm shell in corner.

For a few days, we drove south along the lines to visit Reims and the Verdun area again. I was lucky one afternoon when we arrived at the Butte de Vauquois for another tour of the blown up hill and long gone village. When we pulled into the parking lot, we found the men and women of an organization called the **'Les Amis De Vauquois et de sa région.'**

All volunteers, they were clearing out tunnels on the German side of the hill and they would give a tour of the tunnels they had already cleared for a donation to their organization. Since I had on my heavy boots and work clothes, I quickly made the donation and was soon carrying my video camera towards the German tunnels, following my guide, Vincent Bentz, who could speak English fairly well.

On the way, we crossed through the mine holes from the French side to the German trenches and walked past the concrete bunkers where Carol and I had seen the aerial mine (bomb) a few years earlier, however it was no longer there. Vincent, took the time to show me a carving made by a German soldier on the stone side of the trench leading to the tunnels.

Looking out of the craters of Vauquois toward the French memorial.

Soon, we were passing down through a small hole into the tunnels. It was inspiring, for the Germans had spent the entire war improving their position by digging five kilometers of tunnels. They had dug out large barrack rooms, offices, dinning rooms, a hospital and workshops, all connected by the network of tunnels. The tunnels had been lighted during the war by the use of large electrical generating systems.

As I walked through the tunnels with Vincent, I began to count the small light bulbs hanging along the tunnel walls. They were providing a somewhat dim light that made travel through the tunnels a bit bumpy. I

Looking east out of the crater of Vauquois toward Avocourt in the distance.

suddenly remembered the very small portable generator humming back down the trail on the way to the tunnel and the wire lying along side the path. It was not much of a generator and there were a lot of lights. I was glad to have my spare flashlight and hoped that I would not need it. We had come a long way into the tunnels and it was just as long to get out if that small generator suddenly quit.

We walked along the tunnels for over an hour and Vincent told me how they had been lined with wood paneling. In the barracks rooms, I saw the metal screening left from the beds used by the German soldiers. All the wood was gone, but there was lots of evidence of the German occupation. A woman's shoe had been found and the usual rumors were present. The mess hall area was obvious next to the kitchen and through a fallen area, I was shown the hospital.

At one doorway, Vincent told me of the skeleton of a French soldier they had found when they cleared the stairs going up to the trench above. During a French attack, the soldier had made it to the German trench and down the stairs, when the earth behind him fell in and crushed him against the closed door. He was trapped there for seventy-five years until he was discovered by his fellow Frenchmen.

The Germans had developed a tunnel system where they could just climb up a set of stairs and they would be in their front line to counter any French attacks. The French spent the entire war on the other side of the hill in holes in the ground as their leaders did not want them to become comfortable and cease having the will to fight.

As I wrote in Chapter One, the Germans had attacked up the hill toward the village at the top called Vauquois. The French army had retreated around the hill and counter attacked the village. They had fought on top of the hill for four years and here I was, walking through the tunnels the Germans had labored so hard constructing, over 70 years later.

Before I left that day, I had submitted my membership application to the French organization, *Le Amis de Vauquois*, and have duly paid my dues each year. They continue to clear more and more tunnels and conserve these important relics of World War One.

The are so many memorials and places to visit all along the First World War lines in this area. One, Cote 304, or hill 304, near Verdun, meaning the hilltop is 304 meters above sea level, is just another hill in the region until you drive up to the top and find the beautiful memorial located there. Ten thousand and more Frenchmen disappeared in the mud on this hill during the Battle of 1916, when the Germans attacked here trying to flank the French defenses at Verdun.

French memorial on Cote 304, or hill that is 304 meters high. The far left flank of the Battle of Verdun, 1916.

One can drive the little back roads here and find something to look at, just about anywhere. I walked back into a small woods one day and found a large, long distance, 210 mm shell for our cannon lying on the ground. It had been fired and the fuse was in place in the base. Not wanting to disappear in the sudden making of a large new hole, I reluctancy left it there and walked off, dreaming of the day I could find a demilitarized one.

In no time at all, our visit was over and we flew home, anxious to get our relics shipped so we could have them and also sad that we had found nothing to help identify the man in the grave.

During the next year, after our crate of scrap metal arrived back home, we showed them to anyone interested in our collection of goodies. From our short 210 mm shell for our

KRUPP 210 mm Lange Mörser, with its time fuse to the many cartridges and shells from World War One. Each item had a story to tell about where we found it and what happened during World War One at the place it was found.

Two years quickly passed. We made another trip to France, visiting more and more of the World War One lines. Each time, we made several visits to the grave at Cartigny. We raked the gravel, painted the cross, pruned the rose and we continued to promise the man buried there, that we would find out who he was.

There are many memorials and places of military history along the World War One lines. However, you don't have to limit your visits to just that period. As most couples will, Carol and I do not always agree on what to visit next. So, we also visit places that might be of more interest to her. And, she has her shopping visits while I spend my time reading or visiting another war place.

World War One American Oise-Aisne Military Cemetery.

The Somme valley is beautiful with many interesting places not connected to either war to visit. The Cathedral in Amiens is known throughout the world. One will often pass beautiful châteaux, castles, and fortified towns in France. France is a country of museums. Most are not war orientated.

We always stop at the newly named Tommy's Café at Pozières and of course we visit John Middleton Brodin's grave, Carol's Australian cousin, at the British Pozières Cemetery.

Carol and I had always been drawn to the British Pozières Military Cemetery. Whenever we passed it we stopped and walked around reading the names on the crosses and on the Wall Of The Unknowns, men who have no known grave.

Just after Christmas, 1992, I received a letter from Carol's family's newly discovered Australian relatives. The family of an uncle a few times removed who had been thought to have been lost at sea. It turned out, that he was the only survivor of a ship that sank in the South Seas and he ended up in Australia where he raised a family.

I had written to them about a son of Eric Brodin that had been killed during World War One that they had told Carol's mother, Anita Smith Reinbold Luiten, about. Their letter stated that he had been killed in 1916 at Gallipoli. I wrote back and told them, if he had been killed in 1916 it could not have been at Gallipoli as the Australians were gone by 1916.

I also wrote to the Australian army records center and requested John Middleton Brodin's service records.

What we received back greatly surprised us. John had been killed on the 25th of July, 1916, at Pozières, and you can guess what cemetery he was buried in. Yes, we had been drawn to that cemetery, many would say by John Middleton Brodin. On our next trip we found his grave and though we had walked up many of the aisles in the cemetery, we had not walked up his particular one before.

Carol is the only family member to have ever visited John's grave.

One place not to miss is Delville Wood and Janet and Tom Fairgrieve, the caretakers at Delville Wood. Delville Wood is a Memorial to the South African Forces that fought in both wars and there is a most interesting museum on the grounds.

Janet serves coffee and tea at the visitor's center and she also sells war relics. Each visit to Janet and Tom's at the start of a vacation is great and we are always sad to see Janet at the end, as that is the sign it is time to go home. Always one of our last visits during each trip, we go back to Delville Wood to see Janet's "for sale collection." She quickly relieves me of of any French francs (money) I might have left and I have a few more goodies to explain when they x-ray my luggage at the airport.

At home, most of our free time continued to be taken up in the restoration of the German KRUPP 210 mm cannon. I wrote letter after letter to assorted government organizations in different countries hunting for other KRUPP 210 mm cannons and for manuals and information about them.

We have found there are about twenty of them left in the world. Most in Australia and the United States. We never have located a manual or drawings. I have visited many of the KRUPP 210 mm cannons and hope someday to have been able to visit each and every one of them.

Most of them are in poor condition and we are worried that they will end up in a scrap yard somewhere if they are not maintained better. First, the wheels rust through and soon the people get worried about their safety. It is just a matter of time, before the ones that are left outside, without proper conservation, disappear. There are so few, and most of the ones located in large museums will survive until some future museum director decides that World War One things belong to a period of time so far removed in time that they don't need them any more and they too will go.

In March, 1994, I visited and stayed with old friends, Gail and Charles Kettlewell, in Manassas, Virginia, so I could spend some time at the National Archives in search of information on KRUPP cannons. I thought I might be able to find how and when our cannon arrived here in the United States. However, the National Archives could not direct me to any stored information on the return of war trophies in 1925 and 1926. It appears the American Legion helped with the distribution and final records were not kept, or if they have been, I haven't been able to find them.

The question has been and still is, what happened to this 16,000 pound cannon from World War One to the summer of 1961, when it appeared at the Army Reserve Compound at Newark, Ohio? If anyone out there knows where it came from, please contact me.

When the written archives could not help, I went on to the next goal of the trip. I had planned on looking through the Army Air Force photographs of World War Two, hoping to find a picture of the bomber's crash site. When I had called before I left, to check to see where the motion picture film of World War One was at and where the Army Air Force photographs were kept, I was told they would all be moved to the new College Park Archives building by the time I got there.

A major goal of the trip was to look for still and motion pictures of the cannon firing. I had seen such pictures on television, so I knew they existed. However, I had never seen a complete series from loading through firing. As my luck usually goes, the move to the new archives building at College Park had been delayed and I could only look through a small portion of what would be available in the near future. It would take another two trips and three years before I actually got to look for what I wanted.

During the spring, Bernard sent a fax telling me that he had learned who had restored the grave some 20 years before. A fellow named Emile Berger, who had died in 1988. His grave was located near the grave of the unknown airman.

It is nice to have friends such as Bernard Leguillier. Early in 1994, Bernard and I were talking about my next visit to France, when he offered to find a place where I could stay for a long period of time, **for free**.

After talking it over with Carol, we decided that I could go to France for two months beginning in early May, 1994. I quickly called Bernard back to tell him that I was going to take him up on his offer. A few days later, he called back and told me he had found an empty house in his home village of Driencourt where I could stay.

Almost before I could get ready, it was time to leave for France and a long stay in the Somme. I was full of plans, time to blow something up with Richard, find some real fine goodies that have been buried for years, and to discover the secret of the grave.

KRUPP 210 MM LANGE MÖRSER, SN: 1748
MANUFACTURED: ESSEN, GERMANY, 1917

Willis S. Cole, Jr.   "Sam"   Carol L. Cole
' The Corporal'   'The Popsie'

William and Nicolas Cilliez, it helps to play soldier when dad is a collector.   Photo: Jean-Pierre Cilliez

Chapter Four

And then, I thought It would Be Easy!

Almost before I could think about it, I was on my way to France on May 3, 1994. Ever-faithful Bernard and Claude picked me up at the airport, early on the morning of May 4th, and we headed to Péronne and my temporary home at Driencourt.

On the way, we discussed the latest they had heard about the grave. So far, no one from the village had told Bernard or Claude anything that was not in another of the stories they had heard earlier. Either, no one knew how the grave actually got there or they had not talked to the right person. Claude told me he had set up a visit the next weekend, with a man in Tincourt-Boucly who had seen the bomber crash.

The Family Berger-Lardier tomb. It is just a short walk from the Unknown grave that Emile saved from being lost.

That day I made all my first day visits, with the first visit being to the Cartigny cemetery to visit the grave and let him know that I was still trying, though I wasn't having much luck. Then I walked up the nearby aisle and found the tomb of Emile and Leona Berger-Lardier and thanked Emile for his efforts on behalf of our fallen American Airman.

Then, I was off to visit many of my friends to let them know I was there and available for adventure. One stop was at John Middleton Brodin's grave, another was to Jean-Pierre Cilliez's home to start to plan for some metal detecting trips into the fields around Bapaume.

No sooner had I paid my first visit to Richard Boniface, than he asked me if I wanted to go for a ride with him and off we went. Soon we were at Pierre Segers to wish him a happy birthday, or Anniversaire as a birthday is called in France. Suddenly, we were across the street, at the family home, for a family dinner in celebration of Pierre's special day.

We had been talking a bit when Pierre asked me if I was, "Going to Normandie to the Débarquement en Normandie?" I had to ask him just what he meant and he explained that he meant, the Normandy, 6th of June, 'D-Day Anniversary.' I told him that I had been reading about it a lot in the States, but you had to have a pass to go to anything there and as I couldn't get a pass, I was not planning on going. He quickly told me about a group he belonged to, the **COMMEMO-RANGERS** and said they were going to the 'D-Day Anniversary.'

They were a group consisting mostly of French people, with some from Belgium, who restored American World War Two vehicles. I had seen the 6x6 truck that Pierre had and the 4x4 that his friend Claude Coquel had at Pierre's company's truck repair shop earlier that day.

Pierre said that it was very simple, I could join the **COMMEMO-RANGERS** and go as a Frenchman, if I couldn't go as an American. Well, it was late enough in France to catch Carol just before she left for work, so

I called her and explained Pierre's idea and I asked if she would mind if she had to spend part of her vacation in France by herself so I could go to Normandy? I could tell it hurt a bit, but she said I had better jump at such an opportunity. I told her about the need to have a World War Two type uniform and to contact some uniform sellers we knew to see if they could supply one for her to bring over to me.

The next night, I was with the rest of the group at a meeting in Péronne as we planned our trip. I had become an official member of the **COMMEMO-RANGERS** and they gave me several unit shoulder patches to sew on my uniform when Carol got to France with it.

The month of May passed quickly as I spent my days doing what I love best in the Somme, searching out new spots along the World War One lines. One Sunday, the Leguilliers, Bernard and Claude, and Jean-Pierre Cilliez and I went metal detecting in a field where the battle line of the British was located at the end of the Battle of the Somme in mid-November, 1916.

Jean-Pierre turned out to be one heck of a metal detector operator. His finds quickly surpassed ours in quantity and quality. Working our way out of the large field we were in, Jean-Pierre suddenly shouted. He had found something quite large. In no time at all, we were digging a very big hole in the field. I had also located it while testing my new metal detector, but I thought such a large object had to be a false reading. I learned to trust the metal detector and Jean-Pierre.

By the way, we metal detect in fields that are in fallow and we do not intrude on planted fields at all. Plus, we always ask the farmer's permission first.

The longer we dug, the more I paid attention to the hole we were digging. I soon had to tell everyone that we had better hope that an airplane did not fly over. They would call the police and tell them that someone is hiding a body in a field, for our hole did look a lot like a grave.

In due time, we started to uncover a very odd looking, large metal object. It was about four feet long and a foot and one half

A real treasure! Probably from a tank from the 2nd ever tank attack of September 29, 1916.

wide and it had two rows of knobs running the length of it. Just as we got to where we could turn it over, we realized what we were looking at. We had found a large section of track from a World War One British Tank.

It wasn't long before Jean-Pierre had driven his car into the field and we were man-handling the track into his small station wagon. As we left the field with our new find, the bottom of the car was dragging along the ground. Today, you can see that track on display at our museum. Later, I found that it was probably from one of the first 50 British tanks. Some of them were in the second-ever tank attack on September 29th, 1916, near Flers. The first attack[19] took place along the line from Pozières to Delville Wood and one tank drove down the streets of the village of Flers followed by British soldiers.

Jean-Pierre Cilliez, master detector. Digging out buried stokes motor shells from final 1916 battle line on the Somme. Too dangerous to transport, we dug the hole deeper and reburied them armpit deep.

As a **COMMEMO-RANGER**, I volunteered to paint the portable toilet/wash station/shower that Pierre and Claude Coquel had built. They were very kind and gave me free rein on the color scheme. Our large red white and blue portable outhouse with its big white General's Star on the olive drab outhouse door drew quite a bit of attention as it later made its way to Normandy and back.

Pierre introduced me to a friend of his, Michael Vieillard, whom I call a Flossy. Mike was born in Australia of parents from Bapaume. To me, a Flossy is a French Aussie. His family had moved back to France where Mike is employed in computer work.

Mike had had a heart transplant about a year earlier limiting what he was allowed to do. But he was getting to where he could do a lot more.

Mike speaks fluent English and French and he became my interpreter and partner during our visit to the Normandy beaches.

I took him on a tour of the 1916 Battle area one nice day. Mike had been in France for many years, however he knew very little of the World War One battle areas around Bapaume.

War Memorial for 36th Ulster Division that fought here, July 1, 1916.

At the Ulster Memorial near Theipval a car was broken down in the parking lot. It was getting late in the day and the people didn't know what to do. They asked Mike if he knew where they could get some help.

I had my Leatherman Tool hanging from my belt, it is a combination tool that folds up and fits into a small belt case. I told Mike to let me check their battery first and as I worked on the battery with the amazing tool, Mike was telling them about us.

I found a lot of dirt on the battery cable connections and quickly cleaned and reattached them. Since we had no jumper cables, we pushed the car down the steep road and it soon started running well, problem solved.

Somewhere in France, people must still tell the story. It had to have seemed that we dropped in from Mars. A Yank with a magic tool and an Aussie with a heart transplant had saved their tourist day.

Carol arrived about a week before I had to leave for Normandy. She brought the uniform I needed with her, including a helmet which she wore aboard the airplane as her bags were stuffed. She told us that the flight attendant asked, "If she was afraid the flight might be rough?"

It was cold and dreary when I picked Carol up at the airport, it seemed that the weather was going to be a repeat of the bad weather of 50 years ago during the Invasion.

We left the airport and drove along the back roads to the Château de Pierrefonds (Oise), a beautiful castle about 40 miles from Paris.

I saw Walt Disney during a television interview one time and he was talking about his World War One service in France. He was stationed near Soissons behind the lines at a headquarters doing map work or something like that.

He had a side business selling war souvenirs. He used to stand by the road when the troops that had been up front marched back. By the time they got to where he was they were getting tired and those souvenirs that seemed so nice when they started out were getting rather heavy.

Walt would buy them from the tired marchers and then prepare them for sale. He had learned that a pristine German or French helmet didn't bring nearly as much money as one that showed war damage. So, Walt would take the helmets he bought into the woods and

43

shoot a few holes in them.

Back at headquarters he would sell his war damaged souvenirs for top price. Of course, some of the people he sold to were the very same soldiers he had bought them from a few days earlier. They were rested up and been paid, and now they had to find a different souvenir to send home to the little brother and sister.

Château de Pierrefonds (Oise)
Built in 1857 for Napoléon III.

One can't look at this Château from many different angles before one becomes certain that Walt Disney walked the same walk. For this castle has to be the one that he modeled his castles after.

Early on Sunday morning, Carol and I took off across France for a one day visit to the Verdun area where we attended the Memorial Day Ceremonies at the American Meuse-Argonne Cemetery. I was dressed in my World War One uniform and since we had reserved seats at the services we were right among it all.

After the memorial services, I enjoyed having my picture taken with many of the people who came. They wanted a souvenir showing them with a real Yank.

Each year, at the closest Sunday before Memorial Day, unless it is a French holiday, the American Military cemeteries hold their Memorial services. If it is a French holiday, the service is held two Sundays before Memorial Day. Troops assigned to Europe come in buses and perform the honors. When the services are finished, the troops and most of the guests line up and march down into the village.

Afterward, we visited the grave of Alfred E. Leach who was with the 6th Arty, 1st Division. I believe, there is a movie scene showing the shell explosion that wounded him near Fléville. He died later the same day of the effects of the wound. Then we joined the U.S. Military people in the town. The town makes them feel at home with food and drinks and we all had a good time.

Plot C; Row 28; Grave 22
American Meuse-Argonne Cemetery

ALFRED W. LEACH
PVT. 1 CL. 6 FIELD ART. 1 DIV.
WASHINGTON OCT. 7, 1918

On the way back, we stopped at the Sommepy Monument on the top of Blanc Mont ridge. It is surrounded with the remains of German trenches and defenses and commemorates the service of the 70,000 American troops that served in this area of France, and who captured the ridge in 1918.

We took the back roads all the way back to Driencourt and enjoyed a good look at the real country. Almost all the way, we traveled through the World War One area and we stopped at every memorial we came to.

The distances in France are really short, compared to what we are used to driving here in Washington State. We don't think much of driving over to visit Carol's family farm on a weekend, which is a 275 mile trip one way.

Almost all of our French friends find it hard to believe when we make such a trip. However, reality strikes home when you purchase gas. It is quite easy to put $ 40.00 worth of gas in a small car. If possible, it is best to rent a diesel engine car, as diesel is much cheaper. The essence as gas is called 'over there,' costs over a dollar per liter which is around $ 4.00 per gallon.

The next morning, Claude Leguillier walked over to the home where Carol and I were staying and we hiked over to the hillside to the west of the village. From the sunken holes on the hillside we could tell it had been a cannon outfit's position during the Great War. And, it had to be a German position because it was on the wrong side of the valley to be an British one.

One of the bomb dumps that Richard Boniface knew about. Visited by the author and the Leguillier brothers, Bernard on the left and Claude on the right. The Bomb Disposal people are finding it harder and harder to find places to store the 'iron harvest' that surfaces each year. Now, they are blowing up the found shells and bombs in place, if possible. Claude, now deceased, was one of my great guides to new places and people in France. He found my proof of Americans being in his home village of Driencourt.

The cows in the field were very interested in the metal detector's humming. They would come right up to us and put their nose near the buzzing noise.

We found bits and pieces of stuff, including some metal dugout roofing. We determined that two of the low spots in the field were the covered-over entrances to dugouts that were probably the command dugouts for the cannon battery.

At one of the gun positions we found a German 150 mm powder cartridge, so now we know what size the cannons had been. We also found hundreds of unfired rifle cartridges. You find them all over the place. Mostly German and English as the French weren't as spread out in this area of France. I am certain you would find French and German rifle cartridges if you searched in an area where they both were. You find so many, you wonder how they had any left to shoot at each other.

Claude and Bernard had always told me, that no American troops had been around Driencourt in World War One. However, one

Willis Samuel Cole, Jr.. "Sam"
Carol Lorraine Reinbold Cole
Romagne-sous-Montfaucon
Memorial Day Services, 1994

night back home in the U. S., I had found an entry in one of my research books[20] saying that the American headquarters had been located in the Bois de Buirre from the 22nd of September to October 12th, 1918. I faxed the information to Bernard and he told Claude, who went metal detecting in the Bois de Buirre several times before we arrived in France. That afternoon, Claude took us to the woods and we found a few American items, such as a spoon and empty first aid kit, proving the Yanks had been there.

In the fall of 1994, Claude sent me a dog tag he had found in their family woods. It had belonged to a Sgt. Edward McCarty of Company D, 108th Infantry of the 27th Division. I was able to look up the unit's information and send Claude a fax telling him the McCarty's unit[21] had been in Driencourt from October 2 to October 4, 1918. They were finally convinced that the Yanks had been right there, in their own home town.

Since our time together was very short, Carol and I took off the next day for the Belgium Military Museum, in Brussels, where we had located another KRUPP 210 mm cannon. Their cannon is in the best condition of any we have seen, as it has been stored in a heated building since the mid-twenties.

The barrel is not mounted in the cannon. It is located on a barrel carrying wagon which was used to reduce the road weight of the cannon and to carry spare barrels back and forth to the factory. It looks like the Germans released the barrel mount locks and raised the mount a bit with the crank. That very effectively disabled the cannon, because the barrel could not be slid in from the barrel wagon.

I was allowed to climb all over the museum's cannon to look for serial numbers and such. I do that with all of the ones I have visited trying to find a reasoning to the serial numbers. So far, every serial number trend I think I have found, has failed on the next cannon I visit.

We continued on north and arrived at Nijmegen, located on the Waal River, in the Netherlands that night. We spent one night there and we recommend visiting this town to anyone who goes to Europe. Overall, It had the most reasonable prices we have found in our travels in Europe.

We spent several hours walking around and visiting the town. You can sit at a sidewalk café on the river front and watch the huge river barges slowly moving up the river and rushing down.

The next morning we visited the American Airborne museum at Groesbeek. An interesting place, especially when you understand that the gliders landed right around there.

Afterwards we took a very small car ferry across a canal to visit Overloon and the Oorlosgmuseum. The village woods was the scene of a hard battle during the battle for the 'bridge to far.' The people used the war relics that were left to start this museum. They have added many vehicles and airplanes along with a new Holocaust museum. Carol was at once very interested and very sickened when she saw a piece of tanned human skin with the concentration camp serial number on it.

The museum is located directly south of Nijmegen just off of the A73-E31 road and it is a must see museum. Plan to take a few hours there and food and drink are available.

That evening we pulled into Pierre Segers to get my final instructions for the trip to Normandy. Pierre and Claude Coquel were busy loading supplies into various vehicles. They said goodbye to Carol and we headed back to Driencourt, tomorrow morning I was leaving with the **COMMEMO-RANGERS** convoy for the beaches and villages of Normandy and the 'D-Day 50th Anniversary.'

We left from Péronne, after a late start, and I rode in the back of an open-sided jeep. It had turned cold and was raining. Carol later told me that all she could see of me as we left, were my glasses and eyes.

From all over Europe, and some from the United States, the restored World War Two vehicles started to converge. At every stop and as we went through every village we heard the clapping and cheers of people, many who could remember convoys of these vehicles full of their American Liberators fifty years earlier.

COMMEMO-RANGER Convoy on way to Normandy Landing Anniversary
50th ANNIVERSAIRE DU DÉBARQUEMENT
6 June 1944 -- 6 June 1994

The trip took much longer than they thought it would, the old vehicles did not travel as fast as planned and when one jeep blew its engine, Pierre and Claude came to its rescue. They had prefabricated an emergency hitch attachment in Pierre's shop that bolted to the front of the various vehicles and attached at the back of Pierre's 6x6. Soon the jeep was hooked to the back of the 6x6 and we were back on the road.

Late that evening, we arrived at our temporary home, a barn at the bottom of the hill near Ste-Mere du Mont, just below St Martin-de-Varreville, Le Vallee. The Ferme de LELOUEY was located just at the edge of the beach lowland leading to Utah Beach. Fifty years before, the Germans had been present at this farm when the Americans came calling. The farm reminded me of my grandparent's farm during my youth, as the people still used a hand cream separator and cooled their cream in a pool of water. Normandy is known for its wonderful butter, made from the cream from such farms.

That night, I found that I just couldn't sleep in one long barn room with so many people. Since being in the service a long time ago, I have become a light sleeper, each noise caught my attention and if I did get to sleep, I was soon awake again. Late in the night, I picked up my sleeping bag and marched out through the mud to Pierre's 6x6 and settled in on the stacked supplies in the back. I was soon sound asleep, until the break of dawn.

Suddenly, I was jolted awake by quacking, very loud quacking. Crawling to the end of the truck bed, I leaned out in the light mist and found the source. The farm's ducks, that spent their night in the farm compound across the road, were on their way to the pond just behind the truck.

My friends the duck family at the LELOUEY family farm on the Utah Beach shelf at St. Martin-de-Varreville, le Vallee.

It appeared that the mother duck had gotten ahead of her ducklings and she stopped under the truck while she called to them with encouragement, as they worked their way through the mud and high grass. For the rest of my stay, just at daybreak, I was awakened each morning by momma duck and her ducklings quacking away. I could swear that she knew just when I fell into my deepest sleep to make her appearance.

COMMEMO-RANGERS take over one small part of Omaha Beach. 6 June 1944 - 6 June 1994

It was soon one of the jokes of the group, that whenever they saw me dozing suddenly the air was full of quacks. The farm family, Eugene and Gisele Lelouey, their daughter Catherine and grand-daughter Charlotte and their son, Michel and his girlfriend from San Francisco, Cathy Osmont all joined in, enjoying Sam's relationship with those farm ducks. So much so, that upon my return to the U.S., I received a gift of two stuffed ducklings from them. They grace my living room shelf to this day. I can't look at them without thinking of that family, the farm and especially the **COMMEMO-RANGERS**.

When you have that many people so anxious to show off their determined labor of love on their American trucks, jeeps and ambulances you don't sleep in. We were out early each day, running in convoy through all the villages that are famous from 'D Day.'

When we got to Omaha Beach, the road to the Beach was blocked and guarded, but that never kept a good **COMMEMO-RANGER** down. Many of them were retired policemen and public servants. No one would really give them a hard time, so up the road beside the beach we went, until we found a place where a good old fashioned American Army vehicle could quickly climb across the unguarded, high road block made out of sand. Within minutes, the beach was marked by our tire tracks as the convoy moved along Omaha Beach.

I have never seen such a look of pleasure on Pierre Segers face, as when he was running his 6x6 up and down Omaha Beach that day. There were television networks from all over the world covering the event and some were on the bluff above the beach that day and when you saw those restored vehicles driving along the beaches, it could have been us.

We invaded Utah Beach the same way that evening and Mike and I went to the bar while the rest showed off their trucks. Soon, we were approached by a Portuguese television crew for an interview. We didn't manage to have a French or U.S. television interview, but we did get on TV in Portugal.

On June 5th, the group decided to attend the parachute drop by the 82nd Airborne Division and some of the original men from 'D-Day.' Pierre had made arrangements to purchase two souvenir bottled wines for the **COMMEMO-RANGERS**. His truck was piled high with cases of them, one a Bordeaux and the other a Muscadet. Each bottle had a 'D-Day' scene screened in color on it, in place of a label. One showed a beach scene, with paratroops falling and four flags, American, French, Canadian and British. The other featured Corporal John Steele, of the 82nd Airborne Division, hanging from the church steeple at Ste-Mere Eglise.

Pierre and Jacques Notebaert, our fearless leaders, led the convoy around Ste-Mere Eglise and onto the four lane highway. We soon came to an exit where the convoy pulled off and they talked to the police guards. Bottles of wine had passed hands at each road block and this one was no different. The guards accepted our gift and pointed up the road leading away from the exit, but our leaders knew a better way. We quickly pulled back onto the highway and drove about a mile further to park along the side of the four lane highway.

Everyone else parking around us, walked back toward that exit but not the **COMMEMO-RANGERS**. We all unloaded and followed our leaders down the bank and into the field next to the road. The best I could understand, is that we were going to sneak into the drop area as this was the way to get the best view. We were going to be right where they dropped.

There was a large herd of beautiful horses running around the field as we made our way across it, avoiding horse deposits as we went. The horses, with their manes streaming in the wind, would run past us on one side and turn and run past us again on the other side. They were as interested in all these strange people sneaking through their field as we were in them.

The **RANGERS** walking through the fields had a Flossy, with another's heart and an 84-year-old member, both gamely trying to keep up with the group as we crept along. We were brave, we were not afraid, for we were the **COMMEMO-RANGERS**. We hid when the helicopter roared overhead at low altitude, for we were sneaking in.

After a while, we came to hedge rows with small creeks full of water running through them. The weeds were broken down and helping hands were offered to help cross the muddy banked streams. There was no German fire, but I got a very up close and personal view (as well as a wet foot) of the hedgerows and streams that the Americans had fought through 50 years before.

After what seemed to be a long walk through the fields and hedgerows, we came to a small road running across the fields. The road was full of people, all walking in the same direction. I stopped and waited for the Flossy and the elder who were lagging behind and soon we joined the walking crowd.

After walking quite some distance, part of it down a larger road, we began to come closer to a gate leading into the fields where everyone was to watch the parachute drops. We were not in front, we were a long way toward the back of the crowd. There were thousands of people there and they were walking through the gate, there was no charge, just walk in, **it was free**.

The rest of the **RANGERS** had gone through the gate and joined the crowded mass of people by the time we got there. Mike and I did not like such large crowds, so we stayed on the road outside the gate.

82nd Airborne Division storms Normandy again, 50 years later.

Soon there was a roar from behind us and here came the drop aircraft. As they went over us, the returning parachutists from World War Two bailed out just above us. We had a great view after all. As they landed, along came the rest of the 82nd Airborne dropping out from the large aircraft streaming through the air over us. One of the many memories

Brigitte Coquel has cleared one ditch/hedge row and heading for much larger hedge row.

that I will carry to my death, will be that great sneak across the fields of France to arrive at the gate behind everyone else, when we could have been in front. We were the only people in the world to sneak into that special, free event.

When it was over, the **RANGERS** slowly gathered together and instead of walking back through the fields, hedgerows, creeks and mud, we walked down the larger road with the departing crowd. Surprise, surprise, after a short walk down that road, just past where we had joined it on the way in, we came to the highway exit where we had given the guards the wine. They had offered us the shortest way and they were going to let us take the trucks to the landing site, instead of walking like everyone else. We would have been much better off, if we just followed their directions. But, that's what great memories are made of. If it had been easy, it would not be such a strong memory.

After we arrived at the trucks, we had to wait a long time for everyone to show up. When they did, off we went back to our farm compound. One of the members of the **COMMEMO-RANGERS** was a four-star chef by trade and he loved cooking. He would stay at the camp site all day and cook for the evening meals. The group ate very well during its stay at Normandy.

The **COMMEMO-RANGERS** chow down.

The problem, Mike and I found, was that once the meal and wine started no one wanted to leave, they spent each evening having a great time eating, drinking and talking World War Two vehicles. But for us, it was the night before the actual 'D-Day Anniversary,' and we wanted to go to Ste-Mere-Eglise for the dance that night. Luckily, two other members were as uninterested in such talk as we were, when great events were taking place just over the hill.

Jocya Charlet was a young nurse on leave, riding in her father's neat jeep, which she could also drive. The other was Claude's son, Olivier Coquel. He had come home from Tahiti, where he now lives, to attend the 'D-Day Anniversary' events with his mom and dad. Jocya and Olivier also wanted to see the lights that night, so Jocya borrowed her father's jeep and off we went.

Mike Vieillard and the author survey the scene in Ste-Mere-Eglise.

Ste-Mere-Eglise was ablaze with lights and as crowded as could be-there were people everywhere. Mike and I walked around to all the different bars and met many Americans who had been there 50 years before. Up there in a spotlight, hanging from the steeple of the church, was a mannequin dressed as an 82nd Airborne Paratrooper. It represented Corporal

Corporal John Steele - 101st Airborne Div.
6 June 1944 -- 6 June 1945

John Steele, who had landed there when the 82nd Airborne Division dropped in, just 50 years before. Red Buttons played his part in the movie, '**The Longest Day.**' We were told, that Corporal Steele had died in the late sixties, but he had visited the village several times and that he had been there during the filming of the movie.

I love to dance and later, we could hear the sound of music by the church. Mike and I wandered up and found a band playing and lots of young French people from the area, dancing. This was the biggest thing to happen in their lifetime and they weren't about to miss out on the fun.

Soon I was dancing away and having a good time. It started to rain lightly and it was not long before the only people left out there dancing were the young French and one old Doughboy in his World War One uniform.

I was having a grand time.

All of a sudden the band stopped playing in mid-song and I wondered what was going on. The announcer talked a bit and pointed up to the representation of Corporal Steele. The band starting playing the Star Spangled Banner and everyone clapped and cheered. It was 23:15, or 11:15 p.m., on 5 June, 1994, 50 years to the minute that the 82nd Airborne Division began to drop into the village of Ste-Mere-Eglise. I was pleased that I was the only American, as far as I know, dancing there in the rain with the French on that Anniversary night.

We danced and danced and finally the rain got heavy enough that even I was starting to feel damp, so I took off to find Mike at the Bar across the street. I found him and lots of interesting people. We talked to soldiers of the 82nd Airborne and their General, who had made the parachute drop that afternoon, and invited them to visit the **COMMEMO-RANGERS** campsite. Among the crowd was another from a famous American company, Peter Coors of Coors Beer fame.

It was late when we finally had our rendezvous with Jocya and Olivier and headed back to the camp. When we arrived, I expected to find everyone awake and *COMMEMOing* the Invasion, for it had already started by this time 50 years ago. The 82nd had landed around Ste-Mere-Eglise and the 101st Airborne Division had landed around Ste-Maire du Mont by now and here all the **COMMEMO-RANGERS** were all asleep. By golly, we had come to Normandy to commemorate 'D- Day' and we were the *COMMEMO*-**RANGERS**.

Well, I can say quite honestly, that it is hard to wake up a bunch of French people who have had a long dinner, with lots of special wine. They were quite grumpy for some reason and not wanting to wake up. So it was time to honk truck horns and turn on the siren on the ambulance. Wake up, wake up, they are here. The reason we came is now upon us, it is officially the 50th Anniversary of 'D Day,' the first Americans had landed 50 years ago.

Soon, the **COMMEMO-RANGERS**

were stumbling from the trucks, tents and where ever they slept. What's all the noise? Oh it's that damn Yank!

After a few drinks to celebrate the start of the Invasion, I was soon alone in the mess tent with Pierre Segers and Jacques Notebaert, talking about how I was actually feeling very down, because I had made no progress on the identification of the grave at Cartigny, and now the 50th Anniversary was here. It was beginning to look as if I couldn't keep my promise to the man in the grave.

I knew that Jacques was a retired policeman and that Pierre had pull, so what better to do, than place a challenge before the **COMMEMO-RANGERS**. **_COMMEMO_** was part of their name and we needed to **_COMMEMO_** the grave located at Cartigny. I challenged them to go to the village when they returned, ask the hard questions and find out the real truth of the grave. I knew, the truth had to be in that village and so far no one would tell it to me. If they were really **COMMEMO-Rangers**, then show me some real **COMMEMOing** and not so much _Rangering_!

As had the rest, I had registered my name in the **COMMEMO-RANGERS _GOLD Book_**, a souvenir book. I had written:

* * * *

A grave's mystery and place
Called through time and space
For its path to be traced--
So this grave's man can be graced
With name, home and face.

* * * *

This book's charge to all must be **_COMMEMO_** now and ever more.

* * * *

Before long, it was getting to be morning and I found that the group was going to the services at Utah Beach, as that is where the French landed, and not to Omaha Beach. Me, I wanted to go to Omaha Beach, quite some distance away, for that is where Will Henderson landed. So, I started out to walk and hitchhike to Omaha Beach. It turned out that the roads were blocked and I had one heck of a time getting there. When I did arrive, I was told that President Clinton had arrived a few minutes earlier and they would not let me in.

Standing at the gate of the Normandy American Cemetery and Memorial[22] was another person who had been refused entry. He seemed confused and I started talking to him. It turned out that he was English and he had been an assistant to the Beach Master at Sword Beach on 'D-Day.' He had not gotten his pass to Sword Beach in time and he was not able to go there either because of high-up government officials attending. He had been staying in Caen and he had been told by a group of American 1st Division people, staying in the same hotel, to come on their bus and he could attend the American Ceremonies with them. However, President Clinton had arrived and the Secret Service would not let them take him in. They were guests of honor, so they got in, we didn't. We found each other standing outside that gate and he was as disappointed as I, but not as mad.

As I talked to him, I realized that he was a bit more than sad. He had been traveling on a prepared, strict time schedule and he was getting very confused. It became obvious to me that he was suffering from age-related memory problems.

He told me that he had to get to Paris and catch a train to Nijmegen as he was to visit a friend there. He had his bag with him, but now he was going to miss his train and he didn't know what to do. I did. I had found some luck in hitchhiking in my World War One uniform and I told him I would take him to Paris if he wanted, Normandy could wait.

We were lucky and got a ride with an American who worked for the Paris Embassy. He was there, with a government car, to move important people around to different ceremonies. We were important enough to him, that he dropped us off right at the train station in Carentan. We were able to catch a train to Paris within the hour and arrived in Paris late in the afternoon. I shepherded my charge through the subways of Paris to the Gare de Nord where I was able to get him right on a train to Nijmegen. Myself, I had to spend the night in a small hotel near the station until I could catch a train to Amiens the next morning.

I had enjoyed Normandy, but I had not seen much, except from a truck or jeep. I was determined to return to Normandy to have a much slower trip along the places of interest and to stop at every memorial.

It was a few days before I saw a **COMMEMO-RANGER** again, until one afternoon, I saw a 6x6 roaring down the streets of Bapaume. I quickly turned around and followed it. As I got closer, I saw it was Pierre's 6x6. When it stopped, I stopped and we talked about Normandy and my challenge. He said that they were going to take it up.

I had made arrangements with Mike to visit his home in the Loire River Valley on my way back to Normandy. He lived near some of the famous châteaus and castles and he had promised to show them to me.

We left Bapaume and rushed along the highways of France, around Paris, on to Tours, and to his house. I swear, I have a few more gray hairs from following Mike, as he rushed and cut his way through the traffic of France. That afternoon we toured all the promised places and they were beautiful.

I met a man who crash landed a B-17 bomber in the east yard of this house. It stopped 300 feet short of the wall.

Late that evening, as we talked about my plans to return to Normandy the next day, he said, "Oh, by the way, I have something for you." He went and got a piece of paper and told me what it was and how he had gotten it.

Claude Coquel, Jacques Notebaert and Pierre Segers had gone to Cartigny the day after they had gotten back and talked to the Mayor about the grave. In the end, the Mayor had given them a certified copy of a statement that was in the Church Archives. It was written by the village Priest, CURÉ Étienne Serpette, on 23 November, 1944.

"Did I want him to interpret it for me," he asked. I could immediately tell, Mike was not as interested in the grave as I was. "Of course," was my quick answer. Mike looked over the statement and began his translation.

American Unknown
Cartigny Cemetery, Military Tombs
1939-1944.

It is not an American Soldier but only human remains that came from one or several American Soldiers.

These remains were brought by a U.S. Military Car and buried by the people who were in this car in a field along the road to Péronne, at a very small distance from Cartigny.

As the remains were not buried very deep in the ground, they were soon discovered and after an agreement between the French Police and the American Army was reached, the remains were taken to the cemetery in Cartigny on November 23, 1944. They were placed near the French Soldiers killed in 1944 and on the top stands a wooden cross, just like the French one, bearing the inscription:

U. S. Soldier
Unknown
23 November 1944

As Mike read on, I was almost busting with excitement, I now knew where the grave came from, now I could document a tie to the grave to the bomber crash at Tincourt. The place Bernard Leguillier had shown me where he had "**picked up a man's face.**"

A few days before all this took place (night between 9th and 10th November, 1944) a large American bomber (Fortress or Liberator) crashed near Tincourt: People were killed. It is thought that these remains belong to one or several of the people killed.

However, these human remains could be parts of human bodies that could have undergone operations in a campaign hospital and that the head nurse would have buried near Cartigny to hide them.

Américain Inconnu.

U.S. Soldier Unknown.

23 Nov. 44.

Cimetière de Cartigny.
Tombes militaires 1039-104

Il ne s'agit pas là d'un soldat américain mais de restes humains ayant appartenu à un ou plusieurs militaires américains.

Ces restes ont été apportés par une voiture sanitaire américaine et mis en terre par les occupants de cette voiture dans un champ en bordure de la route de Péronne à peu de distance de la sortie du village de Cartigny.

Enfouis peu profondément, ils ne tardèrent pas à être découverts et après entente avec les polices française et américaine averties du fait, ils furent transportés le 23 novembre 1944, dans le cimetière de Cartigny par les soins de la municipalité du village. Mis à côté des soldats français tués en 1940, ils sont surmontés d'une croix de bois, semblable à celle des français qui porte l'inscription "U.S. Soldier Unknown" - 23 novembre 44".

Quelques jours avant (nuit du 9 au 10 novembre 1944) un gros bombardier américain (Forteresse ou Liberator) est tombé près de Lincourt-Boucly : il y eut des morts. On pense que ces restes appartiennent à un ou plusieurs de ces morts. Il est possible cependant qu'ils soient des déchets (peut-on parler ainsi de restes humains) d'opérations faites dans un hôpital de campagne que les infirmiers pour les faire disparaître ont enfoui ainsi sommairement près de Cartigny.

COPIE - PHOTOCOPIE
Certifiée conforme à
l'Original Présenté.

CARTIGNY, le 6.06.1994
Le Maire.

The preceding interpretation was later provided to me by Alain Leguillier, Claude Leguillier's son, as Mike did not make a written copy of his translation.

The **COMMEMO-RANGERS** had kept true to their pledged word, they had provided the key to the secret of the grave.

Mike went on to tell me, that they had been told the story by the Mayor and Mayor said that the village Elders of the time, one had been his father, had made the decision to bury the remains in the village cemetery, after the offer to bury the remains in an unknown grave at the Somme American Cemetery, at Bony. He also told me, that there was no doubt in the villager's minds that the remains were from the bomber at Tincourt. They had what they thought were some very good reasons for not telling the Americans, who had just liberated them, about the remains. I will continue to respect those reasons. I knew a lot about that crash and now I had a set date. However, there were already problems flashing through my mind

Was there just one American in the grave or more than one? All the people who saw the bomber crash and who had helped pick up the remains had said several men had died, so there must be several men entombed there. Why did the priest say the night of 9th/10th November? B-17s only flew during the day, the British flew at night. Everyone knew the bomber at Tincourt was a Fortress, why did he write it might be a Liberator?

What did he mean by an agreement, that it was OK for them to rebury the remains? Every American regulation was against such a thing. Even if they did, why was the grave not disinterred during the Graves Registration unit's sweeps through France after the war. The hospitals in the area were not campaign hospitals, they were recovery hospitals, besides regulations said such surgical remains were not to be hidden but turned over to Graves Registration for burial at the site of consecrated military cemeteries. Why did the plaque now on the cross give a date of death in 1943, instead of the original 1944 as stated? All were questions that had to be answered, however, for the first time I had a real starting place.

I was on the telephone that night to Carol before I went to bed. We discussed the steps to take, first she should call Sally McDonald, of *The Seattle Times* and let her know what I had just learned. Also, she should go to the library and see what she could find for those dates.

Early the next morning I was off to Normandy and a shortened stay, as I was anxious to get back to Richard Boniface's office to pick up Carol's faxes and see what she had found.

Omaha Beach, Normandy, France.
T/Sgt. Wilmer Henderson helped establish this cemetery. He landed with the 29th Division. He landed on the beach not far from here at 11:30a.m. and carried machine gun ammunition up the hill until 4:00 p.m. when they were released to do G.R. work.

It is not all research and work.

At nine that evening, I was standing in the square at the Ste-Mere-Eglise Church where I had been dancing just one week before. There was a great difference though, I was the only person in sight. When I went to the bar where Mike and I had met so many people, there were just two other customers there and they soon left. The 'D-Day Anniversary' had come and gone and the village had gone back to sleep, to wake slightly each year on June 6th, before dropping back into the slumber of the ages, all was well in Ste-Mere-Eglise.

Each day, I called Carol to see if she had found anything for certain and each day she answered in the negative. She had found some books, but so far she had not found anything about the bomber.

After two days, and quick visits to all the Normandy sites and memorials I could, I felt I had to get back to Péronne so I could write some letters and fax them to people I thought might be able to help.

On the way back, I tried to drive along the path that Will Henderson had described to me as the route his platoon of the 606th Graves Registration had taken until the break out in late August of 1944. I made such good time, that I had time to stop by the American Monument at Cantigny and I pulled a bit off of the route to visit Alan Seeger's Belloy-en-Santerre before going on to the grave at Cartigny to tell the <u>men</u> that I was getting closer to fulfilling my promise.

I had previously planned to visit further along the World War One line toward Verdun and as soon as I got back, I prepared a fax to the National Commander of **The American Legion** and to Sally McDonald, telling them of the Priest's statement and the tie between the crash site and grave. The next morning, while leaving on my trip, I drove by Richards and used his fax machine to send them. I told Richard that I would be back in a few days and please keep any faxes that might come in.

Every two years, the French Army sponsors a military show at the Mourmelon Army Base, some miles south of Reims. I had heard about the show and I was going to visit it while on my drive along the path Alan Seeger had taken to his **Rendezvous With Death**.

I visited many places of World War One fame and Alan's path, as I drove along. One was the Bellinglise Château, where Alan had written his poem about being buried there.

From there, I visited the memorial in the Bois de Compiégne where the Germans signed the armistice for World War One and

The countryside is full of beautiful memorials. Many in disrepair as those who placed them are no longer here to care for them.

A memorial to the French Navel personnel that served in the front lines during World War One. On the Chemin des Dames.

Hitler forced the French to sign their surrender after the German invasion of France during World War Two.

Soon, I passed through Soissons and was visiting all the memorials along the road to the Chemin des Dames and Laon. As I drove along the Chemin des Dames, the road on the ridge, I thought of the years it took for the Allies to win it back. Just at the edge of the road, I found one of the German's largest World War Two cemeteries, located next to Fort de la Malmaison.

There are so many such places of

A very interesting and beautiful area to visit and it is really not very big. One can cover much history in just one day.

interest to list all of them, however I did visit the beautiful Château at Craonnelle where Alan Seeger's Corporal was killed and where he read books in the shell torn library. Of course, the Château has been totally rebuilt. There is an interesting memorial at Craonnelle to the men of Napoleon's army who were killed there many years earlier during another war.

At the edge of Craonnelle, I found the road leading to le Blanc-Sablon, a Château located down a fairly long dirt road. On each side of the road, one could see the surface was seamed throughout the woods with trenches running in all directions. Alan had spent time there and now the rebuilt Château will draw me back sometime. I hope to walk in those well preserved trenches someday.

Three days into my trip, I arrived at Reims on a Friday afternoon, in time to get a reasonable priced room on the road to Mourmelon. I spent the rest of the afternoon and evening visiting the wonderful military

1994 - French Infantry Soldier
A poliu, or hairy one.

museum at Fort de la Pompelle, the Champagne hillsides where the Champagne grapes are grown and Alan Seeger served for a long period and I went walking around Reims, including a visit to the famous Cathedral.

If you want to visit France and you like military history, make certain you select a year and time to allow you to visit the Military Review at Mourmelon. It is held in late June and lasts for two days over a weekend. Dressed in my World War One uniform, I was waved past the gate and allowed to wander all day long among this wonderful display of the French Army and the people with their passion for military history.

I walked over to the Big Red One Division site, based upon a compound in Vietnam in the 1960's, and found no one who could speak English. From there I walked over to the American 5th Calvary display and found that no one there spoke English either, however I did well enough with one person to find out that their leader could speak English and I made arrangements to return when he would be present.

My trip was very limited in time and I could only stay one day, but in that day I saw people in uniforms going back several hundred years and in uniforms that went back just a decade or so. The group representing the oldest military unit were roasting an ox over an open fire and when they went into sham battle at the display ground, the women followed along with baskets of wine and bread. It was great as they fired their very old, rope wrapped small cannon.

One had to watch out, to make certain the tanks had lots of room to move around. You could get run over by a tank of any war and age, or perhaps by a horse drawn wagon or cannon.

I can't wait to go back with Carol some year and have even more time to enjoy the displays. We may join them and have a small Doughboy and Nurse camp of our own.

I arrived back to find no new information from anyone. I called Carol and she told me about the talks she had with Sally McDonald. Talks, which to date, had produced no new information other than a 1,000 plane raid had been made to Metz/Thionville and Saarbrucken, during which forty planes had been lost.

The next day, I was off with Richard Boniface and his crew to blow up and fall a 172 foot tall factory chimney. It was no longer used and the top was starting to break

Janet Fairgrieve, Tom's fair bride. Janet runs the coffee shop and souvenir shop at the Delville Wood Memorial. It is usually my last stop before leaving for home as Janet always has excellent souvenirs. The shell she is holding is on our shelf today. The mask was made by Carol. Worn upon request.

up and the loose bricks were falling and endangering the people around the factory.

The foundation and smoke pit base of the chimney had walls about twelve feet thick and the manager thought it would be a great challenge for Richard. He asked Richard where he thought it would fall and Richard pointed out a clump of weeds in the distance.

Richard started by blowing out large chunks of the foundation to create holes on the side he wanted it to buckle. Richard and crew would drill a hole into the bricks and stuff it full of dynamite and set the explosion off with the electric detonating system. I was given the job of supplying the mud to stuff the holes with, the mud forced the explosion inward.

Tom Fairgrieve - Superintendent of the South African Delville Wood Memorial.
Splendid display, great fellow.

They do not wear hard hats and when we went into the chimney after each explosion I saw new bricks laying on the floor. It was obvious to me, that they were falling down inside the chimney from the top. Well, you can't chicken out or no more explosions in the future. I put my imagination away and supplied the mud.

After some hours, the only thing holding up the chimney on one side was a column of bricks in line with where Richard said the chimney would fall. He asked me, how I would set the explosions of the several charges we were about to install? I told him, I would set the outside ones to go off first to force out the bricks in front to prevent the falling chimney from pivoting as it fell. Then, I would set the rest to explode in a quick series from the outside in. He told me I was right, and we crimped on the timed detonators.

We were soon standing behind the trucks at a safe distance away and watching that chimney buckle and fall. I walked out to where the top struck the ground and Richard had missed those weeds. The chimney fell in-line with and 18 inches short of the weeds. Another fine day with my friends of France.

The 1st of July is a real big day on the Somme each year, as it is the Anniversary of the first day of the Battle of the Somme, when the English lost over 20,000 dead and suffered over 40,000 wounded in 1916. The crowds are actually increasing in size most years, as more and more English begin to search for their pasts.

I was up early, dressed in my American World War One uniform and by 7:15 a.m. I was at the Lochnager Mine Crater, just south of La Boisselle. Each year, there is a service there on July 1st, at 7:30 a.m., the hour the attack began in 1916.

I was very impressed by the Bag Pipe band that was there. After the services when I tried to talk to them, I found out that they were mostly French people who did not speak English. This band, which had become the French participant's passion, plays at many memorials and ceremonies each year. Later, I would get to know several members of the band and one, Freddo Loyer, would provide great service to my quest to fill my promises.

I talked to Janet and Tom Fairgrieve who were dressed up in their full Scottish dress. Tom very dapper in his Kilt and all. Janet was busy getting donations for the Poppies that help the memorial organizations keep operating.

After a stop at the Café at Pozières for a cooling beer, I drove over to the Memorial at Theipval for the ceremony that would be held there soon. At the edge of the crowd and out of the sun that very hot day, I found Janet again hawking her Poppies. We stood there in the shade and watched the Memorial Services together.

As the people were leaving, I was approached by an English man who asked, "What I was doing at an English memorial service? There weren't Americans in this area during the war, so I didn't belong there."

At times like that, it is nice to know the American history in the Somme. I quickly told him how the American 11th Engineers[23] had helped the British at Gouzeacourt in 1917, and helped the Australians stop the Germans at "Villers Bret" in March of 1918. Plus, I told him to look across the valley toward Serre. There, he could see where an American battalion, the 2nd of the 317th Infantry of the 80th American Division[24] had attacked with a New Zealand battalion in 1918. They had taken a position east of Serre that the British could not take for months in 1916. The ANZACs and the Yanks had taken in it one day. Later, the Americans had broken the Hindenburg Line at the St. Quentin Canal, to the east. We Americans had paid in blood for the right to be there at the memorial service.

Janet stepped in and reminded us that it was a memorial service, besides she told the fellow, "Sam is right."

Soon, I was approached by several people who wanted to have a picture taken with the Yank in the World War One uniform. I was very pleased to pose with a French World War One Veteran at the Theipval church as I left.

As I was getting in my car, which was parked in a field on the northeast corner of the village, my foot hit a large Mills Bomb fragment. After examining it, I asked the people who were getting in the car next to mine, if they might want it? Now, there was a happy British couple, they had a real souvenir of their trip to the Somme and their visit to the memorial services. Soon, the camera was snapping as they recorded the incident on film, here was a Yank giving them a real piece of their history.

An hour or so later, I was at Montauban-de-Picardie, where a new British memorial was to be dedicated to:

The Liverpool Pals, 17, 18, 19, 20th Battalions, The King's (Liverpool Regiments) - To the glorious memory of the Liverpool and Manchester Pals who as part of the 30th Division liberated this village - 1 July, 1916.

It was getting hotter and hotter and I soon developed a deeper feeling of sympathy for the soldiers who had to wear these uniforms with such tight necks and heavy cloth. At least mine was cotton, the British men dressed up in period uniforms had on wool outfits and full gear.

I was looking out over the crowd, when I saw my friend Bernard Leguillier. I made my way over to him and he told me, he was to act as the official interpreter during the ceremonies. We talked about the new memorial and he told me, that it had taken the people about five years to get all the permissions required to emplace the new memorial. That was a shock for me, for I wanted to have one in place in just four months at the crash site and grave.

There were two bands playing, a French one and the kilted pipe band. When the ceremonies began, the participants first laid memorial wreaths at the village memorial to their dead of the two wars and then they marched to the new memorial for its dedication.

After the ceremony, I stopped by the guest tent and had a beer with Tom Fairgrieve and further discussed the time taken to place a new memorial. He also thought, that it could take several years to get permission to place a new memorial. I talked to several other people I knew and left to drive over to the Delville Wood Memorial to have a cup of Janet's tea. Tom had told me she would be there.

By that time, it was just too hot for me to attend some of the other ceremonies that were going on later that day. So I went off to talk to Pierre Segers and found him busy at his business. It may have been a memorial day for the British, but it was just another work day for the French.

July 2nd did not bring any new information, however the day was topped by dinner with Richard, Michelle, Peter and Romain at the Le Stromboli, a pizza place in Bapaume owned by Richard's cousin. During our animated dinner conversations we talked about my dancing during my visit in 1991 and my giving a sweater away, at least Michelle promised me a dance the next time I could collect it.

During this visit, I had stopped by the Somme American Cemetery several times to talk to Joel Felz, the Superintendent. We had discussed the grave at Cartigny and the lack of burial record history available to visitors at our American Cemeteries, compared to the rather extensive ones the British have on their cemeteries. He could help me find a person who was buried in an American Military Cemeteries overseas, however once a remains had been returned to the U.S. his organization had no remaining record of that person. I have found the only record on most of the men returned to the United States for burial is a statement, "buried in private cemetery in (name of the State where buried)."

During my last visit, Joel had told me about the 4th of July ceremony at Cantigny. A village located about 20 miles southeast of Amiens. It was the village where the first Americans fought as a full Division. The First Division had attacked the village and drove the Germans out on May 28th, 1918.

There was an American Monument, in their village square, to the attack and each year the village held a memorial service on July 4th. Joel told me, that he would be there and that I would enjoy it. That seemed like a good place to visit on July 4th, as my trip wound down.

I called Bernard and told him about it,

but he had something he had to do and he could not go with me. We also talked about my plan to visit Alan Seeger's place of death, at Belloy-en-Santerre, about 6:00 p.m to remember him on the 78th Anniversary of his death. Bernard told me, he would try to meet me there.

I arrived at Cantigny already dressed in my uniform pants and shirt. As there was no one around yet, I drove around the village and out some of the local roads to familiarize myself with the village and to lay it out in my mind to fit the maps I had seen of the action there.

An American 1st Division memorial on the south outskirts of Cantigny, France.

Cantigny, France, 11:00 a.m., July 4, 1994. Pick your year and they will be here, even if no Americans are. The American Memorial to the 1st Division attack on 28 May, 1918.

When I returned to the village, some people were beginning to gather, so I completed dressing in my uniform and gear. Soon, I was walking up the street to the monument and at the same time, I saw Joel coming from the other direction. We talked about what was going to happened and he told me, that the care of the monument was one of his responsibilities. At the 11th hour of the day, July 4th, 1994, the services began. I soon realized that of the 200 or so people there that day, Joel and I were the only Americans. It became obvious to me, that even if no Americans turned up, these French people would still hold these Memorial Services in memory of what the Americans did for them during World War One.

If you can ever make it to France, I recommend that one stop you make is at Cantigny for their 11:00 a.m. services on July 4th. Make certain you identity yourself as an American and after the services at the American Monument, please march with the French out to their village cemetery where they hold services to honor the war dead of their village at their World War One/World War Two Memorial.

This is the only village in France, that I have seen that does not have its war memorial in the village. They have placed their Memorial in their village cemetery so as to not take away from the beautiful American monument.

At southwest edge of Belloy-en-Santerre, France. From this sunken road the machines guns fired into the field beyond. Alan Seeger died just out there, around 6: p.m. on July 4, 1916. The Legion attacked from their trenches, located just beyond the trees in the distance.

Here's to the Legion!

After the march to and from the cemetery was over, the Mayor, Mr. Joseph Lefever, invited everyone to his home compound in the village, where he has a small museum to the First Division. Of course, The champagne flowed. Everyone was introduced, including me, and I got to make a short speech.

I left there, feeling proud to be an American and feeling prouder of the French people of Cantigny, who after all these years still remember the United States Army and its actions on their behalf. It seems to me, that here at home in the United States, our people hurry to forget those who made the life they live possible. I know our schools are failing in teaching respect for our military past, the cause of our current success. While the French succeed in teaching their young how they obtained their liberty and to remember and honor those who have helped them maintain it.

Late that afternoon, just before 6:00 p.m., I approached the sunken road where the German machine guns were located that killed Alan Seeger 78 years earlier, as the Legion and he charged toward Belloy-en-Santerre.

I placed French and American flags on the bank among the red poppies blowing in

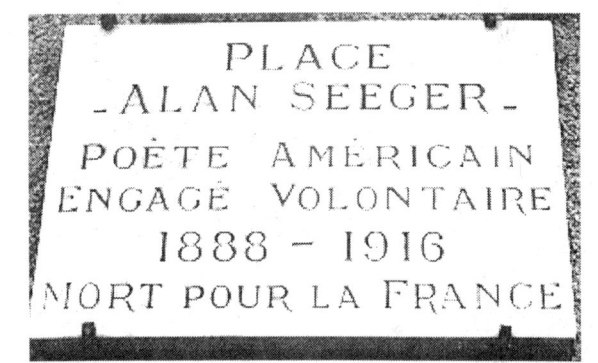

The village square of Belloy-en-Santerre is named after Alan Seeger.

the wind. As I stood there, having a drink in honor of the Legion and Alan, a car pulled up. Bernard had arrived for our private memorial to Alan Seeger.

I read two of Alan's poems, **Maktoob** and **I Have A Rendezvous With Death**, followed by my own poem, **He Had A Rendezvous With Death**. Bernard and I stood there that afternoon in **Remembrance-Souvenir** of Alan Seeger and his fellow dead of the Legion and we discussed how much the French appreciated those Americans of World War One.

We left there and drove to the Grave of the Unknown American Aviators at Cartigny and remembered them on this special

American day.

Early on the morning of the 7th of July, I stopped by the outdoor telephone booth at Nurlu to call United Airlines to verify my flight on the 10th. At least it was the 10th in my mind, as I had not looked at my tickets since I arrived.

When I got through, the very nice United Airlines operator told me, that I was due to be on an airplane in just three and one half hours. "**What**," said I? "**Yes**," said she! And, she went on to prove that I was due there today, the 7th, in just a very short time. My only response had to be that there was no way I could get there in time and that I had to make new reservations.

She came to my rescue and told me, "That I had called just in time, as I had beat the check in deadline and she could change my reservation for a fair extra charge." I thanked her and she started to find when I could return home.

I was on a cheap seat ticket (we recommend that low expense travelers like ourselves, leave before the 30th of May, as the high cost tickets start after that date) and she had to find an open seat at the same fare. She quickly came back and told me, there was a cancellation on the 11th and could I make it. I assured her that I could and she fixed me up with the new reservation.

That day, the information I had been waiting for so long began to cascade in via faxes from Carol. Each fax began to shorten the range of possible choices.

One contained information that Sally McDonald had faxed to Carol.[25] Sally had contacted the Air Force History Center and in return, she had received the basic information about a mission on 9 November, 1944. The 8th Air Force, in conjunction with the 9th Air Force, hit tactical targets in the Metz and Thionville area in support of Third Army forces. Other targets included the Marshaling Yards of Saarbrucken, Germany, bombed by over 300 heavy bombers. Over 40 heavy bombers and fighters were lost.

Another, forwarded to Carol by **The American Legion**, stated that only 4 bombers were lost on the mission of the 9th and one of the bombers had blown up in midair.

It seemed to me, that the bomber that blew up in mid-air had a much better than 25 percent chance of being our bomber. That evening, I told Carol to try another library and that we were getting close, what we needed was some real detail about the four lost bombers, especially the one that blew up.

Back and forth went the faxes and telephone calls, Carol making trip after trip to the library and finding nothing new. She found the basic mission information again and again. However, none of the books she located gave the required informational break down of the mission.

Early on the morning of the 10th of July, 1994, the day I thought I was to supposed to leave France, I arrived at the Bonifaces to see if Carol had any luck in finding more information about the missing bomber that blew up on the Saarbrucken mission, of 9 November, 1944.

When I arrived, Michelle first asked me if I wanted a cup of tea and then handed me the fax that had arrived from Carol during the night. Her message was simple and to the point, she had gone to the Bellevue library and found a book[26] which gave the basic information on the mission and she couldn't find anything new on the blown up bomber. However, the book also referenced a section containing all the **Congressional Medal Of Honor** award citations awarded to the 8th Air Force during World War Two. For my information, she included a copy of the two citations involved with the Saarbrucken mission about a bomber, '*Lady Janet*.'

As I began to read the the two **Congressional Medal Of Honor** citations, I could again feel great excitement welling within me.

GOTT, DONALD J. (AIR MISSION)
Rank and organization: First Lieutenant, U.S. Army Air Corps, 729th Bomber Squadron (H), 452nd Bombardment Group (H)
Place and date: Saarbrucken, Germany, 9 November, 1944
Entered service at: Arnett, Oklahoma
Born: 3 June, 1923

G.O. No.: 38, 16 May, 1945

Citation: On a bombing run upon the marshaling yards at Saarbrucken, a B-17 aircraft piloted by 1st Lt. Gott was seriously damaged by antiaircraft fire. Three of the aircraft's engines were damaged beyond control and on fire; dangerous flames from the No. 4 engine were leaping back as far as the tail assembly. Flares in the cockpit were ignited and a fire raged therein, which was further increased by free-flowing fluid from damaged hydraulic lines. The interphone system was rendered useless. In addition to these serious mechanical difficulties the engineer was wounded in the leg and the radio operator's arm was severed below the elbow. Suffering from intense pain, despite the application of a tourniquet, the radio operator fell unconscious. Faced with the imminent explosion of his aircraft, and death to his entire crew, mere seconds before bombs away on the target, 1st. Lt. Gott and his copilot conferred. Something had to be done immediately to save the life of the wounded radio operator. The lack of a static line and the thought that his unconscious body striking the ground in unknown territory would not bring immediate medical attention forced a quick decision. 1st Lt. Gott and his copilot decided to fly the flaming aircraft to friendly territory and then attempt to crash land. Bombs were released on target and the crippled aircraft proceeded alone to Allied-controlled territory. When that had been reached, 1st Lt. Gott had the copilot personally inform all crew members to bail out. The copilot chose to remain with 1st Lt. Gott in order to assist in landing the bomber. With only one normally functioning engine, and with the danger of explosion much greater, the aircraft banked into an open field, and when it was at an altitude of 100 feet it exploded, crashed, exploded again and then disintegrated. All 3 crew members were instantly killed, 1st Lt. Gott's loyalty to his crew, his determination to accomplish the task set forth to him, and his deed knowingly performing what may have been his last service to his country was an example of valor at is highest.

METZGER, WILLIAM E., Jr.

(Air Mission)

Rank and organization: Second Lieutenant, U.S. Army Air Corps, 729th Bomber Squadron (H), 452nd Bombardment Group (H)

Place and date: Saarbrucken, Germany, 9 November, 1944

Entered service at: Lima, Ohio

Born: 9 February, 1922, Lima, Ohio

G.O. No.: 38, 16 May, 1945

Citation: On a bombing upon the marshaling yards at Saarbrucken, Germany, on 9 November, 1944, a B-17 aircraft on which 2nd Lt. Metzger was serving as copilot was seriously damaged by antiaircraft fire. Three of the aircraft's engines were damaged beyond control and on fire; dangerous flames from the No. 4 engine were leaping back as far as the tail assembly. Flares in the cockpit were ignited and a fire roared therein which was further increased by free-flowing fluid from damaged hydraulic lines. The interphone system was rendered useless. In addition to these serious mechanical difficulties the engineer was wounded in the leg and the radio operator's arm was severed below the elbow. Suffering from intense pain, despite the application of a tourniquet, the radio operator fell unconscious. Faced with the imminent explosion of his aircraft and death to his entire crew, mere seconds before bombs away on the target, 2nd Lt. Metzger and his pilot conferred. Something had to be done immediately to save the life of the wounded radio operator. The lack of a static line and the thought that his unconscious body striking the ground in unknown territory would not bring immediate medical attention forced a quick decision. 2nd Lt. Metzger chose to remain with the pilot for the crash landing in order to assist him in this emergency. With only one normally functioning engine and with the danger of explosion much greater, the aircraft banked into an open field, and when it was at an altitude of 100 feet it exploded, crashed, exploded again, and then disintegrated. All 3 crew members were instantly killed. 2nd Lt. Metzger's loyalty to his crew, his determination to accomplish the task set forth to him, and his deed knowingly performing what may have been his last service to his country was an example of valor at its highest.

There was no doubt in my mind, that I was reading about an event that had been described to me in full detail by several Frenchmen, including Bernard, who had "...picked up a man's face.'

The citations and the stories were too close not to be the same airplane. They had to be the same bomber and with the priest's statement the same men in the grave.

Now, I knew the names of two of the men, 1st Lt. Donald J. Gott and 2nd Lt. William E. Metzger, Jr., both had been awarded the **Congressional Medal Of Honor**.

The first thing I did, was call Carol back in the U.S. and tell her the news about the break provided by the faxed copies of the **Congressional Medal Of Honor** she had sent. I was far more than twenty-five percent positive, I was now one hundred percent certain it had to be this bomber and these men.

I called Bernard and told him about the fax and the citations. I thought, that we could assume that the face that he had picked up belonged to the radio operator. He would have been above the bombs, so his face might have come out of the explosion, while the Pilots would have been beneath or directly in the explosions.

Next, I went out to the car and drove to the cemetery at Cartigny. There, I knelt down and read the citations to the men in the grave and promised Gott and Metzger and the still unknown radio operator, that I would get their grave recognized as soon as I could and that I would also contact their families and tell them about their loved ones buried in the Unknown Grave in France.

On 10th of July, 1994, 49 years, eight months and one day after they were killed in the crash of '*The Lady Janet*' at the village of **Tincourt-Boucly, France**, two of the three men in this grave heard their name spoken over their real grave for the first time. If I had left when I was supposed to have left, I would not have been in France to personally speak those names over the grave.

It was just one day before I had to go back to the United States and I had partially fulfilled the promise I had made to the remains in the grave that Christmas Eve so long ago. Except, I knew for certain now, that there were three men buried in the grave.

As I stood before the grave, I set forth more promises to fulfill to the men in the grave. I had to prove out my research, identify the radio operator, contact the families and tell them about the grave of their loved ones in France. I had to get the grave recognized for what it truly was, the grave of two men who had been awarded the **Congressional Medal Of Honor** and the man they had died trying to save.

I left the cemetery that afternoon, happy that I knew the names of two of the three men in the grave and sad that I had to leave the UNKNOWN plaque upon the cross.

I also knew the nickname given the bomber, '*The Lady Janet*.' I also thought, it should be easy to prove the crash site and grave were connected now. One would think, that two such medal awards would have been fully investigated and since the bomber crashed in friendly territory supporting documentation would provide the necessary evidence to prove the bomber that crashed at Tincourt-Boucly was '*The Lady Janet*.' Once I was able to obtain and read that documentation, I would know the name of the radio operator, the third man in the grave.

With this knowledge the people of the village would surely let me remove the plaque of the 'Unknown American Aviator' from the cross on the grave and exchange it with one with the men's names on it.

Well, the **COMMEMO-RANGERS** were the people to help me now, so I headed to Bancourt and Pierre Segers and my 2nd large crate of war relics, almost ready to ship home. It was time to ask Pierre's help again.

As Pierre helped me complete the task of closing up the crate of relics I filled him in on what I had found out about the men in the grave at Cartigny.

I had another challenge for the **COMMEMO-RANGERS**, they had provided the Priest's statement to me, that made the identification possible and now they could help provide the recognition the crash site and grave so deserved.

Pierre and I, discussed what they might do to help get the crash site and grave recognized during this 50th Anniversary of the Liberation of France in 1944 and the 50th Anniversary of the death of the men in the grave on November 9th.

I left Pierre, promising to keep him posted on what I found in the States and he promised to keep me posted on what they were doing in France. He also promised the full help of the **COMMEMO-RANGERS**.

Early the next morning, Bernard and Claude took me to the airport for my flight home. On the way, we discussed the grave and what might be done to be able to put the correct names on the marker. Bernard promised to talk to Mayors of both villages and see what they thought would be required to do so.

On the flight, I was looking at the '**D-Day**[27]' book I had asked Carol to bring over for me to carry to Normandy. All during my activities at the coast and later, I had people sign my book as a souvenir. The person in the seat next to me, asked me if I knew, "Who General Collins was?" I quickly answered, "Jolting Joe Collins, was the commander of Seventh Corps, the forces that took Cherbourg and later was in the drive through northern France into the Aachen area." She seemed a bit amazed that I knew that (my special thanks to Will Henderson who thought so much of General Collins, he made sure I knew of him). She then told me she was the grand-daughter of General Collins, Margarit Rubino.

The General's surviving family had been invited to Cherbourg, as guests, for the 50th Anniversary of the Liberation of Cherbourg. While there, they were the Guests of Honor when the city named a street after their grandfather. Soon, my souvenir book was making its way around the family on the flight and her autograph was added to its pages.

It turned out, that her husband had to leave France early for the U.S. and I was sitting in his canceled seat. The problem that had called him back to 'The Firm,' had opened a seat for me next to her. The living history of a famous general of World War Two.

My United Airlines flight left from Charles DeGaulle Airport, Paris and landed at Washington, D.C., where I had a two-hour lay over and I was able to call James Ryan Arthur of the Center for Air Force History in Washington. Sally McDonald had given Carol his number to pass on to me. We talked a while and he told me, he was on a summer vacation job from college, however he would help me as much as he could. He also told me who to contact at the Air Force Historical Research Center at Maxwell Air Force Base and he promised to see if he could pinpoint some more information, if so he would fax it to me at home.

Thus, I returned from France,
on 11 July, 1994.

Almost four years have passed since then and I am now committing to paper all that has happened to me and what I have found to be the truth of the Grave at Cartigny, from that Christmas Eve of 1991 to December of 1997.

I now know, what really happened during '**the last flight of 'The Lady Jeannette'** and in the over 53 years from early in the morning of 9 November, 1944, to now. Here, I believe, is the best place to insert the true story of the bomber's last hours.

The following, Chapter 5, has been read and approved **"as accurate"** by the three surviving crew members of '**the last flight of 'The Lady Jeannette'**.

*A grave's mystery and place
No longer called through
time and space*

Chapter Five

The Last Flight Of 'The Lady Jeannette'

Early in the cold and damp fall morning of 9 November, 1944, a Flight Engineer/Top Turret Gunner stood on the hardstand next to the forward escape hatch of a B-17 Bomber. He anxiously awaited the arrival of the overdue Bombardier. The rest of the crew had arrived over an hour ago and were all on board. Beside him, hanging from the hard mount on the wing was a 1,000 pound bomb.[28] There was another 1,000 pound bomb on the other side and eight 500 pound bombs in the bomb bay. All the checks had been done and it was almost time to 'start engines.' Soon, the bomber would have to begin its taxi to the runway.

The bomber he was standing under was a B-17G-35VE Bomber, Sn: 42-97904. It had been built at the Lockheed plant at Burbank, California, and delivered to the Army Air Force on 1 April, 1944. Just over two months later it was delivered to the 8th Air Force in England, on 'D-Day,' 6 June, 1944. It was a slick, silver-skinned bomber, with the group's large white identification letter L inside the black box painted high on its tail. Just under the box was the bomber's serial number, with the 4 left off the front, so it read 297904. A large R was just below that, the squadron's call letter for the bomber. A previous crew had named the bomber somewhere along the line, and its name, '*The Lady Jeannette,*' was written in red script across the nose.

Most of the regular crew would be on board for this flight, however there was a substitute copilot who was there to gain experience with a combat hardened crew. 2nd Lt. Gerald W. Collins, their crew's normal copilot, would be flying aboard another bomber giving that crew an experienced pilot to help them through their early missions.

As he waited, the flight engineer had a lot on his mind. It was his job as flight engineer/TTG, to work with the ground crew chief to insure the bomber was ready for the mission. If there was an in-flight equipment problem, the FE/TTG was supposed to know how to fix it. In flight he had no seat, he would stand behind the pilots the whole time and help provide instrument checks and fuel control, that is, unless he was in the Sperry top turret where his job as FE/top turret gunner, was to provide defensive cover fire against German fighters in the air space above and around the bomber.

This was this crew's first flight aboard '*The Lady Jeannette,*' as they had just been assigned the bomber after their last mission to Ludwigshaven.[29] It was to become the crew's permanent bomber, the one upon which they were to complete their tour of 35 missions.

On all their previous missions, the crew had flown in whatever bomber was available. As that flight engineer/top turret gunner[30] has told me, "It was kind of like working at a bus barn, on a bus that needed nine men to run it. We went to the office and they told us to take number ten one day and number three the next. It was a good sign that we were fast becoming an old crew when we were assigned a permanent bomber."

As he waited, he thought of home and the letters he and the rest of the crew had been writing, telling their families[31] that they were planning on being home at Christmastime. He would have to do just eight more missions, after this one, to reach the magic number and at the rate the Squadron was flying, they should easily reach that number by early December and he would be home for Christmas, 1944.

The crew were members of the 729th Bombardment Squadron (H), one of four bomber squadrons assigned to the 452nd Bombardment Group (H), the others being the 728th, the 730th and the 731st Bombardment Squadrons (H), the (H) meaning Heavy Bomber, such as the B-17 and B-24.

The 452nd Group, along with the 96th and 388th Groups made up the 45th Combat

Wing of the 3rd Air Division of the 8th Air Force, of the United States of America. The group was based on Station 142, at Deopham Green, England, not far from Norfolk.

Though the group contained four squadrons, it was common practice for only three squadrons to go on a mission, while the fourth squadron, in rotation, **Stood Down** for rest, repair and maintenance. It would take an average of 48 group missions for a crew to fly their required 35 missions if they flew every available mission. However, most crew men missed one or more missions due to sickness, training and other squadron duties.

If a crew member lost his position on a regular flying crew, he would fly future missions as a fill-in crew member and it might take weeks longer to complete his required number of missions.

The flying personnel of the squadron woke up at 2:00 a.m., that morning for the 162nd mission of the group. They grumbled as usual, got up, washed, shaved well, so the oxygen mask wouldn't itch as much, got dressed, and went to eat breakfast prior to reporting to the briefing room to be briefed for the day's mission.

In their briefing that morning, the 729th was told that the target of this mission of over one thousand planes was the Metz-Thionville region of France. The purpose was to provide softening up of targets that might hinder the planned advance of the Third Army, General George S. Patton's command. A secondary target was also designated, it was the railroad marshaling yards of Saarbrucken, Germany.

The navigator made copious and methodical[32] notes, listing altitudes, headings and the **E.L.F.**[33] (Emergency Landing Field) assigned for this mission. The mission's flight path, was charted on the large wall map and he had a flimsy (a light paper that was easily destroyed) upon which was the needed information for him to navigate the bomber to the target, even if the rest of the bombers were missing. His briefcase was stuffed with the maps of the area to be flown over, supporting documents and instruments.

The navigator took special note of the **E.L.F.** It was a recaptured French air base near Péronne, France, one that had been occupied by the German Luftwaffe until the end of August. Now referred to as Station **A-72**, it was the current base of the 397th Bombardment Group, a B-26 outfit, part of the 19th Tactical Air Command and an air transportation unit. It was located about 150 air miles west-northwest of the primary target and 190 air miles from the secondary target. If they got in trouble after crossing over into Europe, this was the place to land, if possible! The weather was reported as being about 8/10ths that day, meaning the clouds covered about eight tenths of the sky.

The pilot was introduced to the stand-in copilot, a new member of the squadron who had flown only two previous missions and as he looked for the navigator and bombardier to introduce them, he realized the crew's regular Bombardier, 2nd Lt. Earl L. Penick was not to be found. He reported this to the squadron operation's personnel and, with the rest of the crew, departed for the bomber located on its hardstand.

Upon arriving the crew did all their checks, installed the machine guns and ammunition, crawled into their flight suits and assumed their positions in the bomber. It would soon be time to start the engines and begin the mission as the wheels first rolled. Below the nose, the flight engineer/TTG shuffled his feet, talked to the ground crew chief and waited for the still missing bombardier.

Other bombers were starting their engines as a jeep pulled up to the bomber. The officer in the passenger seat got out and hurried over to the men. The officer told them he was the replacement bombardier for their crew's still missing bombardier. To complete the bombardier line on his flight manifest, the flight engineer/TTG asked the replacement bombardier for his name and serial number. While the officer swung up into the hatch, the flight engineer/TTG finished filling in the form on his clipboard. He removed a copy of the manifest for himself, which he stuffed into his uniform pocket. He gave the ground crew chief the manifest clipboard and swung up through the escape hatch and made his way up through the passage between the pilots to take his position behind them.

As soon as he was in position the pilot and copilot started the engines to warm them before they began their trip along the taxi way to the runway.

Within minutes, the wheels of '*The Lady Jeannette*' began to roll. For them, Mission 162 had begun and soon the bomber would depart Deopham Green.

As the bomber began its roll, the ground crew chief walked away, reviewing the flight manifest he was to turn over to flight operations. It listed each man's name, his serial number and previous missions. The crew of the departing bomber was:

27 Pilot: Gott, Donald J., 1st Lt.,
          Sn: O-763996
2 CoP: Metzger, William E., 2nd Lt.
          Sn: O-558834
19 Nav: Harland, John A., 2nd Lt.
          Sn: O-723355
1 Bomb: Harms, Joseph F., 2nd Lt
          Sn: O-2056698
25 RadOp: Dunlap, Robert A., T/Sgt.
          Sn: 39696406
26 B.T: Fross, James O., S/Sgt.
          Sn: 38462533
26 T.T: Gustafson, Russell W., T/Sgt.
          Sn: 12139299
22 T.G: Krimminger, Herman B., S/Sgt.
          Sn: 34890339
25 R.W: Robbins, William R., S/Sgt.
          Sn: 11051000

As the '*The Lady Jeannette*' began its mission roll, the crew worried about all the things that could go wrong in the next few hours, during take off and assembly. The take off and assembly could be considered the most dangerous time of any mission. The bomber was weighted down with a full bomb load, full ammunition, and full fuel load. The loss of one engine at a critical time could cause the bomber to crash in explosion and flame, with the loss of the entire crew.

Once the bomber had completed a successful take off, it still had to circle and climb to the correct altitude to rendezvous with the other bombers of the squadron and group. This late in the year, they were taking off in the dark and the air over East Anglia, England would be full of bombers and fighters as one thousand and more airplanes gathered into the formations required to best protect the bombers in combat. The East Anglia, Norfolk area was nick named 'Little America'[34] because of all the Americans stationed 'Over There.'

During the rest of this chapter about '**The Last Flight of '*The Lady Jeannette*'**, I will use 00:00 hours to indicate the 24:00 hour military time system, I will usually shorten the crew's names to the last name only. In places, I might switch between names and positions.

At 05:30 hours, Group Time, 9 November, 1944, the 729th lead squadron took off. One of those many bombers thundering safely off the runway, disturbing the early morning sleep of the English people, was the '*The Lady Jeannette*.' She had begun her last flight, with nine crewmen on board.

When the last bomber had taken off, the group had 35 bombers en route, plus four PFF aircraft.[35] The primary target was a German defense strong point line located twenty miles northeast of Metz and ten miles east of Thionville.

Referred to as the "A" Squadron in all the 162nd Mission reports, the 729th Squadron was the group's lead squadron in the group formation. The Hot Dog Unit's (as it was called by members of the other squadrons[36]) Lead Navigator,[37] 1st Lt. Stephen H. Rhea, reported that the leading squadron of the 45th Combat Wing had left the ground to begin forming over the Buncher Beacon[38], Number 20, located at their base, Deopham Green.

The Buncher Beacon was a low powered radio beacon used by the group to assemble the squadrons in flight formations. The bombers would fly a box pattern, using the signal from the beacon, as they climbed at a specified climb rate. As they assembled, they formed into their combat formations.

'*The Lady Jeannette*' climbed slowly, burdened by the 6,000 pound bomb load, 50 caliber machine gun ammunition and most of its full load of 2,800 gallons of 100 percent octane gasoline. Four thousand pounds of bombs were hanging inside the bomb bay on their shackles and two 1,000 pound bombs were hanging on the external hard mounts, one on either side between the fuselage and the inboard engine.

Two and one-half hours later, the group completed its formation and left the Deopham Green Buncher Beacon area for the First Wing Assembly Point at Mildenhall at 08:05 hours, at altitude of 18,000 feet.

During this period of time, the crew completed their tasks required before combat and the right waist gunner, Robbins, pulled the safety pins from the bombs. They were pulled before reaching high altitude, as they might freeze in the fuse if the crew waited too long to pull them. As was his usual practice, Robbins placed a couple of pins in his pocket as a souvenir of the mission.

Photo: S/Sgt. William R. Robbins
Little Friend: P51
Markings: CVX, Tail No: 2106702

As altitude was gained, the crew put on the ever uncomfortable oxygen masks and began breathing the oxygen from the large oxygen tanks placed throughout the bomber. In addition, they had portable oxygen bottles in case they had to leave their positions at high altitude.

At 08:36 hours they joined the other four Combat Wings, the 4th, the 13th, the 92nd and the 93rd, of the 3rd Air Division at the division assembly line to complete the divisional formation. Once achieved, they flew toward the coast and crossed the English coast at 08:54. Three hours and twenty-four minutes after take off. While over the English Channel, each gunner fired a short burst to insure the machine guns were in working order. As they continued to climb, the bombers gained a tail wind at the altitude of 20,500 feet, blowing from 330 degrees at 32 knots. The further they flew the more they became part of a stream of bombers and fighters heading for Europe.

The group crossed the Enemy coast[39] at an altitude of 20,500 feet, at 51-00 degrees north and 02-00 degrees east, which is just north of Calais, France. As they continued along the planned flight route the clouds covered eight tenths of the ground and as they got closer to the primary target the cloud cover was increasing.

The group reached the bombing altitude of 23,000 feet at 09:13 hours at 50:37 degrees north and 02:50 degrees east as it approached Lille, France. As the bombers continued along the flight path, at bombing altitude, they encountered winds from 303 degrees, blowing at 60 knots.

Photo: S/Sgt. William R. Robbins
I'm here buddy. P-47, Tail No.: 74645

When the group closed on the I.P., or Initial Point of the bomb run, of the primary target, they noticed the group ahead had turned off the bomb run and started for the secondary target. As the primary target was at this time, obviously covered with clouds, our group followed in turn.[40] The Secondary was to be bombed on the decision of the 45th "A" (729th) Leader.[41] The dust raised by the bombs dropped by the preceding groups and the increasing clouds obscured the primary target forcing the remaining groups to select the mission's secondary target, the railroad marshaling yards of Saarbrucken, Germany.

At 09:57 they reached the secondary target's I.P. The I.P. is a landmark easily visible from the air and one which could also be seen on a radar screen. The group turned south, toward the secondary target, which was about fifty miles south of the I.P.

The lead bombardier's report states that the bomb bay doors had been opened three times during this mission. First, over the Channel, again at 05 degrees east and again after leveling off after the turn at the I.P. en route to the secondary target.

To continue his report, "At I.P. it was seen that the run would have to be started PFF, or radar controlled. Strong drift was encountered but Mickey (a cover term for the H2X airborne radar) operator got it killed early. Mickey checks were coming in good and the dropping angle found by synchronizing short held good. A break developed in clouds and I picked up marshaling yards and began relining rate. Flak came up pretty accurate and did its best to interfere with run. I was knocked off sight (Norden Bomb Sight) by Flak and did not have a chance to pick up target again before bombs away."

But, what of '*The Lady Jeannette*' flying in the number four spot in the formation? It was flying behind the lead bombardier's bomber and as did the rest of the group, the bombardier opened the bomb bay doors once the bomber had leveled onto the bomb run after passing the I.P.

The crew were all in position, with flak jackets and helmets on. In the nose, the Bombardier, Harms, was watching the lead bomber so that he could toggle the bombs away when the first bombs left the lead bomber. The Navigator, Harland, was sitting at his table plotting the flight and assuring himself that the plot was correct.

In the cockpit, the pilot, Gott, was attempting to keep the bomber flying in its formation position and as smoothly as possible in the wake of the bombers ahead. The copilot, Metzger, was scanning the dials and helping control the bomber in its final bomb run. His hands were lightly on the controls in case the pilot was suddenly put out of action.

Sitting on the bicycle seat of his Sperry turret was the FE/top turret gunner, Gustafson. He was facing toward the front and scanning the sky for enemy fighters. After flying 26 combat missions, he knew that the major risk to the bomber was from flak from German anti-aircraft guns and not from German fighters.

As the front lines shrunk during the German's retreat, the Germans were able to concentrate their guns in the vicinities around probable targets. The Germans now had radar fire control for their AA batteries. These enabled the Germans to track the height and direction of flight and best aim their guns, so that the shell would reach the correct height and location before it exploded.

In the radio compartment behind the bomb bay compartment, the radio operator, Dunlap, was sitting at his station working his radios. Behind him, down in the ball turret, all scrunched up behind his guns was the ball turret gunner, Fross. He was looking forward, as he would count the bombs as they dropped from the bomb bay, so he could tell the pilot and bombardier they were all clear and the bomb bay doors could be closed.

Sgt. Harold E. Burrell at waist gun position. Original crew member, Lt. Metzger's crew.

Standing at the right waist machine gun was right waist gunner, Robbins. Not far away was his duffel bag, for Robbins[42] always took everything he had along with him. If he was going to bail out, he was going to have his stuff.

When this crew arrived at the 729th Squadron, as Army Air Force Crew 33-C (Crew AC-75, PV900CJ/16349CJ-4/4)[43], on August 17th, 1944, all the enlisted men were corporals, they were given an automatic promotion to Sergeant (Temp).[44] However before their first mission, one of the ten men on the crew, waist gunner, Sgt. Irving (N.M.I.) Hirsch,[45] was relieved from his crew assignment. He left the Squadron for a replacement depot, after the rest of the original crew had flown its first mission. From there he was later shipped to the 15th Air Force in Italy and served as a ball turret gunner aboard B-17s until the end of the war.

The Army Air Force was short of qualified gunners and since the enemy fighter threat was greatly reduced, the arriving crews were stripped of the 2nd waist gunner. Another reason, was the fact that the waist gunners aboard full ten man crews had shot other bombers if their side of the bomber was on the side of the formation. When German fighters flew through the formation, the gunner would shoot away and sometimes spray another bomber. Therefore, it was safer to have just one waist gun position armed, the one facing away from the formation.

As they approached the target, flak began to blossom around the formations.
Photograph: S/Sgt. William R. Robbins

Tucked away back behind the tail wheel and under the bomber's tail was the tail gunner, Krimminger. Just behind him, along the small crawl way to the front, was a small escape hatch that opened just under the right horizontal tail plane. As with all the men at the guns, he was scanning the sky for enemy fighters and watching the other bombers following behind.

Though none of the Gunners aboard *The Lady Jeannette* had ever shot their machine guns at an attacking German fighter, they were busy scanning the skies, just in case. After their first few missions, they had accepted the German fighter situation. They had a chance with them, they could shoot back at attacking fighters. However, the possibility of the flak ahead caused each of them to be uneasy. They had all seen bombers go down, bombers shot down by flak! Bombers, where few or no parachutes were seen to follow the bomber down. They could do nothing about flak but hope 'Lady Luck' was on their side.

As the bombers approached the bomb drop point, three flak bursts opened up and stained the air in front of the group. From the position of his bomber in the formation, Collins could see that they were right on in altitude and directly in front of the formations path. The squadron was just four minutes from bomb drop and they would soon be through it, he thought. No sooner had the thought crossed his mind, when another bracket of German anti-aircraft shells burst.

Aboard *The Lady Jeannette*, Gustafson's turret was facing forward when he heard and felt the flak burst strike the bomber which suddenly jerked and wobbled. She had been hit, and hit hard.

Gustafson looked quickly to his right and what he saw amazed him. He had seen several bombers return with an engine missing, however the engine had torn off the engine mount and the mount was still on the wing. *The Lady Jeannette's* number four engine was gone! It was gone clear back to the leading edge of the wing, mount, and all.

He quickly rotated his turret to his right, so he could take a good look and what he saw sent a cold chill up his spine. There was a stream of fire billowing out from beneath the wing and streaking back past the tail. Taking an extra good look, he realized that the missing engine's fuel line had to have been bent down below the wing's bottom surface by the explosion and the escaping fuel had caught on fire.

The fuel line fire was like a huge blow torch and Gustafson quickly realized that they had been very lucky. If that fuel line had bent upwards the fire would have melted the wing and set the fuel in the wing tanks on fire and the wing would have fallen off the bomber. The way it was bent, the fire was very visible, very scary, but manageable.

As flight engineer, he had to keep the pilots aware of the condition of the bomber and to help as needed. Fighters weren't a problem right now, they were in the flak concentration now and German fighters stayed away from that. The condition of the bomber was more important, he had to get to the pilot and tell him what he knew about the fire and its immediate threat to the bomber.

The bomber was bouncing up and down and starting to turn out of the formation as Gustafson started to rotate his turret to the rear, so he could step down out of it. Behind him, Gott and Metzger struggled with the controls to get the bomber under control.

Meanwhile in the formation, Collins was fighting his own control problems as his bomber was also jerking around from the concussion air waves formed by the flak explosions and as he watched, he saw '**The Lady Jeannette**' begin to leave the formation. Just then another bracket of shells burst, one of which burst right under '**The Lady Jeannette's**' left wing.

Gustafson had completed swinging his turret to the rear and he had started down and out of it. As his right foot touched the deck of the cockpit and took his weight, a fragment from the bursting shell broke through the side of the cockpit and flew through his right leg. It continued on into the hydraulic tank, located behind the copilot on the bulkhead wall, puncturing it and releasing the hydraulic fluid.

Gustafson fell down, to end up sitting, in agony, behind the pilot's seat, still conscious enough to think about his parachute that was stored behind the copilot, Metzger. When he reached for it so he could clip it onto his parachute harness, he realized that it was soaked with the hydraulic fluid from the punctured hydraulic tank.

Back in the rear of the bomber the first thing Robbins thought of, after being shaken by the first explosion and seeing a wall of flame out his gun position's window, was Fross in the ball turret. Robbins had to crank up the ball turret and help Fross out of it. The second thing was to drop the main rear hatch door so it would not impede bailing out. This done, he hurried to the ball turret position and began to turn the crank to get the ball turret and Fross up, so Fross could get out through the small ball turret access hatch.

Just then, the bomber shook from the second burst and bounced all over. Robbins held on to the ball turret mechanism and listened to the flak shell fragments flying through the bomber. They were crashing and crunching through the aluminum of the bomber and, as he was soon to realize, through the flesh of his fellow crew men. His mind flashed back for a second, back to the time a fragment of a fuse cap had broken into a bomber he was aboard, where it dropped into his open duffel bag, then he began cranking even harder.

In the radio compartment, just after the engine was blown off the wing, the radio operator Dunlap was alone and probably scared by the noises he was hearing, but he stayed at his position in order to transmit anything the pilot wanted.

When the second flak shell burst, some fragments entered the number one Engine, the outboard engine on the pilot's side of the bomber, and the engine died. Other fragments entered the number two engine and broke something that caused it to lose power and start smoking. Some ripped their way through the bomb bay destroying the bomb drop mechanism and tearing through electrical lines causing the intercom and other systems to quit working. The jolts of the flak bursts caused the bombs to jam in their shackles.

Another fragment tore its way through the side of the bomber, continuing upward at an angle through the radio compartment's front bulkhead, striking Dunlap in the left leg and tearing through his desk. As it burst through the desk, it struck Dunlap's right arm, which was stretched across the desk to his teletype key. The fragment's sharp edges cutting just above the wrist, nearly severed Dunlap's hand from his arm.

In the nose of the bomber some fragments flew past the navigator and the bombardier, cracking and hissing through the air. Holding on the best they could as the bomber seemed to stumble and catch herself, they looked first at each other to see if they were okay, then quickly looked back through the side windows. On the right side they saw the continuing flame from the missing number four engine and on the left they noticed that the number one engine had stopped rotating without being feathered and that the number two engine was smoking and struggling.

The engine was designed to conserve enough oil when it was hit to allow the pilots to turn the blades of the propeller so that the narrow edges faced forward, an action called feathering. However, it was obvious that the prop could not be feathered and that it was creating drag as the flowing air pressed against the three big paddle shaped propeller blades of the dead engine.

Still sitting on the cockpit deck, Gustafson took a good look at the his leg and realized that the fragment had torn out a great hole in the front of his lower right leg and broken the bone cleanly. His foot just flopped around when he moved his leg. The pain was serious and he reached over and opened the medical kit attached to the cockpit wall. He removed one of the morphine syringes and began the process of injecting it into his leg, just as he had been taught.

The pilots, Gott and Metzger struggled to get the bomber under control as they began to slowly lose altitude and move to the west away from the group's combat bomber formation. Throughout '*The Lady Jeannette*' each compartment had its own emergencies!

Collins, seeing his regular crew's bomber turning away from the group's formation, appearing to be under control, told his crew to watch for parachutes. As the bomber went out of sight, no parachutes had been seen. Collins told his navigator to record the location, A/C was last seen at 49-13 degrees north, 07-00 degrees east, Time: 10:04, Altitude: 23,000 Heading: 208.[46]

Within the next two minutes, another of the squadron's bombers, No. 833,[47] would close up the formation into space number four. There, it also was immediately struck by flak. One engine lost power and aircraft B-17, Serial #833 later crashed in Germany. The crew[48] was captured and carried as Missing In Action until after the war ended. The German flak may have been fairly light that day, but one unit's guns were right on heading and altitude. That afternoon, they painted two more stripes around their anti-aircraft gun barrels.

Aboard '*The Lady Jeannette*', each man found himself in great danger. Each one's mind handled it differently. For most, the actual time they remained aboard this flaming and smoking bomber compressed into a short period of time in their memories. Gustafson was hurting so much from his wound, that he felt and remembers each and every second the bomber would remain airborne to this day.

After inspecting his hydraulic fluid soaked parachute, Gustafson realized his parachute would probably not work when needed. He needed the spare parachute he knew was in the radio compartment. Gustafson tried to call Metzger over the intercom he was still hooked up to. Finding the intercom did not work, he reached up and tugged on Metzger's coat.

At about that same time Gott and Metzger realized that Gott was able to control the damaged bomber well enough by himself to keep it flying. It would be a risk as Gott could always lose it in a moment and the bomber would quickly start to spin in, trapping the crew inside due to the centrifugal force.

Gott and Metzger had tried their intercoms to get a crew check as soon as the second shell burst had hit the bomber and they had received no feed back from any crew position. With the intercom out, and Gustafson down, someone had to find out the bomber's condition. Metzger told Gott, he would go check the bomber and he got down out from his seat. Responding to Gustafson's tug, he bent over Gustafson who was now trying to open his heavy flight suit to be able to poke the morphine syringe into his upper leg.

The reader has to remember that the bomber was filled with the noises of the two

'The Lady Jeannette' B-17G-35VE Sn: 42-97904
Model showing damage as described by the survivors and witnesses.

working engines and whistling winds blowing in and out of the holes and the open doors and hatches of the bomber. Just to be heard, all communications in the bomber now had to made by hollering loudly.

As Gustafson asked Metzger to get him the spare parachute from the radio compartment, the flares contained in the flare bag on the bomb bay bulkhead behind the pilot suddenly burst into flame. The flares were for a Very Pistol, a pistol used to fire colored flares from the cockpit to inform the people on the ground if the bomber had damage or wounded men on board when they returned to their base after a mission. Either the flak or a damaged and over heated electrical line had started them on fire. Thinking quickly, Gustafson grabbed the burning flare bag and pitched it through the passage way between the pilot seats toward the front escape hatch. Harland had already pulled the emergency release and dropped the hatch. He grabbed the burning bag and threw it out the open hatch.

In the rear of the bomber, Robbins had gotten the ball turret cranked up and as he helped Fross out, he noticed that Fross had had his bell rung and that Fross was very dazed and confused. Not only from the two flak bursts, but also, we would find out many years later, from wounds in his head where small metal fragments had entered his ball turret and whizzed around and around, some striking him in the head. Fross had his leather flight helmet on as he got out of the turret and Robbins does not remember seeing any wounds at the time.

As Robbins was getting Fross out of the ball turret, Krimminger came crawling up from the rear. He too, seemed very dazed and he was obviously nervous.

Krimminger, the tail gunner, had been in the very back of the bomber when the first flak burst tore the engine off and suddenly he had seen flames blowing back past the tail on his left.

He had probably, quickly released his seat belt and started toward his escape hatch when the second flak burst caused the tail to whip and gyrate wildly throwing and banging him around in the small passageway. When he recovered enough to look around, he saw the flame off to his position's left (the bomber's right as he was facing to the rear) and he now saw the smoke pouring back from the damaged number two engine on his right.

At that moment, adding to his terror, he thought the bomber was going to crash immediately. He had to get out, now!

However, as Krimminger crawled forward to the escape hatches, he saw Robbins at the ball turret position and he proceeded past the two escape hatches into the main rear body of the bomber to join Robbins and Fross, who was emerging from the ball turret.

Realizing that they had not seen Dunlap, they opened the door into the radio compartment and found it covered in blood which was flowing from Dunlap's torn arm. Dunlap was fast becoming unconscious from the shock and loss of blood.

Robbins immediately grabbed the medical kit and began binding up Dunlap's wounds, with the dazed men helping as well as they could. As they worked on Dunlap, the fill in co-pilot, Metzger, came through the door from the bomb bay.

Metzger, after hearing Gustafson's request, had without hesitation unclipped his own parachute and gave it to Gustafson. It was much easier to walk along the bomb bay catwalk without a parachute than it was with one on. On his way through, he tried to kick the jammed bombs loose, until he realized it was hopeless. He continued on into the radio compartment. There he found the rear crew working on the wounded Dunlap. Together, they completed binding the wounds as Dunlap lapsed into full unconsciousness.

In the cockpit, Gott tried again to use the radios and contact Dunlap. He soon realized that they had no contact with the outside world, nor within the bomber itself. He continued to nurse '*The Lady Jeannette*' through the skies of Germany, drawing closer and closer to the front lines where they would pass over into friendly territory before they reached Verdun. Harland stood up in the passage way and they discussed the direction the bomber was heading and what was out in front of them.

Collecting the spare parachute for himself, Metzger told the crew in the rear about the Flight Engineer's broken leg and that he was trying to inject himself with morphine. Metzger also told them about the burning flares and the punctured hydraulic tank. He told them to stay calm and he would go back to the cockpit and tell Gott what he had found in the rear. They realized that Dunlap would not be able to use his parachute on his own and they didn't have a static line, which would let them drop Dunlap out and let his parachute be pulled opened by the static line hooked to the bomber.

As Metzger went back to the cockpit,

Across the skies of Germany and France, '**The Lady Jeannette**' struggled to reach the Emergency Landing Field at the A-27, Péronne Air Base. Model interpretation.

the three crewmen left Dunlap lying on the floor of the radio compartment and went to the rear of the bomber near the escape hatch and watched the fire stream back past the tail, as they waited for an order to bail out.

Metzger arrived back at the front with the spare parachute, and went past Gustafson, who was sitting on the cockpit floor. "Just about out of it," he later told me. "I was sitting there out of the loop and just hurting. I'm still not sure if I ever got the morphine in," he continued.

Metzger got back into his seat and he and Gott discussed their situation. Harland was probably standing there giving his input as to their location, when they would pass over enemy lines and where the E.L.F. was located. They were in a bomber with the number one engine not running and not feathered. The number two engine was smoking and delivering only partial power. The number three engine was the only one delivering full power and, of course, the number four engine was gone and the fire continued unabated below the right wing. Gustafson, sitting behind the pilots was out of it, not hearing much of what was going because of the noise in the cockpit and the pain in his leg was intense.

The non-working engine and its propeller were creating great drag on the left side of the bomber, pulled by the damaged engine. The right side, with its strong engine and ripped engine position completed the picture of a bomber that could barely stay in the air. The bomb bay doors were open and could not be closed. The 6,000 pounds of bombs were still on board, as they could not be dropped by the automatic controls or by any manual method.

The bomber had a lot of holes and open areas, but it was still flying. Gott and Metzger had to have felt the bomber would continue to fly as long as they could keep enough altitude and speed. Altitude and speed would be their savior and the loss of either would be their death.

Gott and Metzger must have learned from Harland that they had one hundred and ninety miles to fly from where the bomber was hit to the emergency landing field, near Péronne, France. They would have discussed the possibility of the crew bailing out over enemy territory. The crew might land safely and become captives, however, Metzger would have injected that Dunlap was unable to bail out and if he didn't get the fastest possible medical attention he would die. The land in the direction of the E.L.F. had lots of large flat fields, however with the bombs on board such a landing would be a great risk and the odds of Dunlap getting the medical aid he needed in time was nil, even if they landed safely in a field.

After discussing all the possibilities, Gott and Metzger had to have made the decision to try for the E.L.F. where Dunlap and Gustafson would have their best chance of getting the medical care they needed. Harland went back forward to check the course and tell Harms what was going on. Harms placed himself close to the escape hatch and stayed there. He was going to be close enough to get out quickly when told. While sitting near the escape hatch, Harms reviewed the proper way to parachute to safety. The major thing to remember, was to not pull on the 'D' Ring of the parachute too early, he had to wait for the bomber to pass before pulling on the 'D' Ring which pulled the rip cord from the parachute pack releasing the parachute packed inside. Once it was released from the pack, it would quickly be filled by his movement through the air. If a person bailing out opened their parachute too early, it could catch on a part of the bomber and be ripped or torn off the parachute harness. If that happened, one would fall to his death.

To save altitude loss, the pilots agreed that it would be necessary to throw out all the extra weight they could. Again, as Gott held the controls, Metzger went back to the back and told the men there that they were going for the E.L.F. and to throw out everything they could to lighten the plane and then to continue to stand by the escape hatch where they could bail out quickly in case the bomber started to crash. He checked Dunlap's condition again and went forward.

Back in the cockpit, Metzger got into his seat to help Gott control the wallowing bomber and guide it to safety. As they flew the bomber west, the crew threw out what it could, however the men in the back were not able to jettison the ball turret, so its weight continued to help pull the bomber down.

After about ten minutes, the pilots and navigator saw the beginning of the Moselle River valley, between Metz and Thionville, not far from their original primary target. Surely, they saw the smoke rising from the primary target area and Robbins and Harms both report flak bursts near the bomber when they got close to the front lines. They would soon be on the friendly side of the Front Lines and though some flak bursts spread across the sky, the bomber received no further damage.

The flak soon stopped and they could see the Verdun area, site of the titanic World War One struggle between the armies of France and Germany. They had passed over the front line and into friendly territory.

At some point, they passed into a low enough altitude that they did not need oxygen any longer and the men could take off their oxygen masks. The bomber continued to thunder west toward the E.L.F. As '***The Lady Jeannette***' struggled to the west, it became obvious to the pilots that they could not hold it in a straight line. It was staying airborne, though they were constantly losing altitude, but the damage was such that even though the number three engine was putting out full emergency power, the number two engine was pulling just enough more to keep the bomber in a slight turn to the right.

The bomber was barely able to stay in the air and to try to change and balance either engine's speed might cause the bomber to stall and fall out of the air. They just couldn't take the risk, for they were going in the right direction.

Harland, busy as he was, did take time to check his parachute and he found it had been damaged by flak which had torn its way into the parachute pack. He and Harms looked it over and decided that it probably would not work. Harland told the pilots and without any hesitation at all, Metzger removed the spare parachute he had gotten from the rear, the only one on the bomber, and handed it to Harland[49] who quickly removed his damaged parachute, threw it aside and clipped on the good one. It was the second parachute Metzger had given away that day, now he had none for himself and he was committed to staying with '***The Lady Jeannette*** to the end.

There was time to think now, they were probably in safe territory, the bomber was flying, not well, but flying. There is no living witness to the discussions Gott and Metzger must have had, Gustafson was there behind them, but he was on the floor and not listening, nor could he hear over all the other noise in the bomber.

These two professional army pilots had to have discussed the bomber's condition, the condition of the wounded, the condition of the rest of the crew and their own situation.

I believe Gott knew right after the first flak burst took off the far right engine, that he had little chance of getting out of the bomber alive. However, he was a determined young man and he did things by the book. Keep it flying and take care of your crew. Metzger now had no choice, for he had no parachute. There was another parachute, the one with the unconscious Dunlap, but no one would take a wounded crewman's parachute.

Gott was now doubly committed to staying with the bomber. I believe, Metzger probably volunteered to hold the controls to the last to let Gott get out, but I also know Gott would not have left. It was Gott's bomber and Gott's crew.

Metzger didn't have to give away a parachute, let alone two. But, he was committed to his ingrained belief[50] of what a man was and he had his own words to uphold. Just before his original crew left for England, they had a crew meeting and Metzger had told the crew, "I will never leave a bomber with a wounded crewman on board[51]."

As they nursed '*The Lady Jeannette*' across the cloudy skies of France, these two men must have closed a pact with each other. They would fly the bomber to the E.L.F. and slide it in, trusting it would not blow up and that Dunlap would get the medical attention he required. They would bail out all the crew that could, including Gustafson, just before their attempted landing at the emergency landing field. That way Gustafson would land close to the medical attention he needed. They, Gott and Metzger, would be sitting side by side all the way.

One can picture the bomber as it crossed Germany and eastern France on its way to the E.L.F., so far away. Every French kid could tell you what airplane was coming from the sound of it. They had been listening to them for five years now. Many could tell you which German vehicle was coming down the road without having to see it. When they heard a plane coming low and slow and the engines not sounding right, they rushed out to see what was wrong.

Looking to the east, they would see a great shiny American B-17 coming toward them. As it passed over head they would see fire streaking back past the tail on one side and smoke flowing back from the other. It was moving so slowly, they would wonder how it was able to stay up there. As it got lower, the people looking up could clearly see that one engine was missing and one was not turning at all. Each watched as it passed over, half expecting it to fall out of the sky at any moment.

Inside, Gott and Metzger stayed alert and followed Harland's directions to reach the A-72 Base. The men in the rear, after tossing out what they could and checking on Dunlap, gathered near the rear escape hatch and waited for further instructions from the front. Each prepared to bail out in a moment, if necessary, notice from the front or not.

Slowly, ever so slowly, they mushed across France, getting nearer and nearer to the E.L.F. The bomber was giving up altitude to gain the airspeed required to stay in air. An hour had passed since the first flak strike and they were flying over broad open fields already plowed in fallow or planted in winter wheat. Too far away from anywhere to help Dunlap out, even if they lucked out, they had to keep the bomber going, keep it going, keep it going.

Another half hour passed and they were starting to travel over rolling hills with large and small roads crisscrossing it and they were getting low, just a few thousand feet of air space left. They were beginning to see more villages and off to the left, a large town sat on a hill, one could easily see the large church. Harland told them they were abreast Laon and that St. Quentin was coming up just off to the side. The E.L.F. was 20 miles beyond.

They were close, ever so close. Throughout the bomber the crew was getting anxious and signs of fright were becoming even more obvious in the Tail Gunner. Krimminger was watching the ground getting closer and closer and the lower the bomber was, the less chance they had of making a successful parachute jump. All three men in the rear began to discuss the situation. No one

'The Lady Jeannette' as the people of Tincourt-Boucly saw the bomber just as T/Sgt. Gustafson bailed out.
Model Interpretation.

had come back for the past 45 minutes to tell them what was going on. It seemed to them, that they should have jumped when the number of villages increased and before they had lost so much height.

At about the same time, up in the cockpit, Gott and Metzger could look out to the west and see the runways of the emergency landing field. They had gotten so close, oh so close. It had taken every bit of Gott's skill to control the bomber over Saarbrucken and keep it flying and now it was obvious that they would not be able to line up with the east/west runway of the emergency landing field. They were going to pass to the north of the airport and there wasn't much they could do. The condition of the bomber would prevent them from an easy turn, they were going to have to risk changing engine speeds and banking to the left to align up with Station A-72's northeast/southwest runway.

``*The Lady Jeannette's*' last flight had a few minutes left, the end was near. It was time to get the men out, the pilots told the men in the front to get ready to bail out and Metzger got out of his seat to go to the rear again to tell the men back there to bail out. Dunlap was going to have to ride it out with him and Gott, and true to his word, he would be there in the bomber with Dunlap at the end. Gustafson gathered himself and began to decide how he would get through the passageway to the escape hatch in front.

In the back things were getting desperate, Krimminger was getting really nervous and wanting to bail out. He was checking and rechecking his parachute webbing and holding onto the 'D' ring.

Robbins, the only one who had not been concussed or dazed attempted to control Krimminger, and Fross was not much help. Fross just seemed to be somewhere else part of the time, his bell was still ringing, Robbins thought.

All of a sudden, Krimminger made up his mind and started for the escape hatch, his hand instinctively pulling on the 'D' ring as he went. Robbins and Fross grabbed for him, as his parachute was released and pulled from the parachute pack by the strong winds blowing through the bomber from the front and out the open escape hatch. There was nothing they could do as Krimminger's parachute blew through the hatch and flowed over the horizontal tail plane just behind the hatch door. Though they tried to hold him, Krimminger was pulled out of their arms and through the hatch. His weight took him down and held by the parachute lines he was whipped up under the tail plane to be held there by the flow of the air around the tail surface.

Krimminger had just been jerked from the bomber as Metzger came through the rear bomb bay hatch door. Through the open radio compartment door, he could see that there were only two men in the rear and that they were bailing out as he watched. He quickly turned around, went back to the cockpit and got into his seat, next to Gott. They would see this mission out to the end aboard '***The Lady Jeannette***.

When 2nd. Lt. Joseph Harms rolled over, he was looking up as the bomber passed. Model Interpretation.

In the back, S/Sgt. William R. Robbins, right waist gunner, bent over, looked at his fellow crewman Krimminger pinned under the tail and rolled forward and down from the hatch. Right behind him, S/Sgt. James O. Fross, ball turret gunner, stepped up to the hatch, took a good look at his friend Krimminger hanging there, hoped he was unconscious, as Dunlap was, and then he rolled out and down, passing just a few inches below Krimminger hanging there, then Fross pulled his parachute's rip cord.

As Metzger was getting into the seat, he hollered to Harland who had backed up a bit to give him room to get into his seat. Metzger told Harland what he had just seen in the back, one man was gone and he saw the other two men preparing to bail out when he looked at the rear escape hatch from the radio compartment. Then Metzger told Harland and Gustafson to get out as fast as they could.

2nd Lt. Joseph F. Harms, bombardier, was at the forward escape hatch and he was gone in a heartbeat. He stepped through the hatch and fell into the open air below. As he fell, he rolled over so the wind was at his back and he was looking up at the belly of '*The Lady Jeannette*' as it passed. Suddenly an awful sight passed in front of his eyes. As the bomber passed, he saw a parachute trailing and thought to himself, "My God, some poor guy opened his chute too early and it was torn off."

Right behind him, 2nd Lt. John A. Harland, stepped over to the hatch and dropped through, his hand grasping the 'D' ring of the parachute given to him by Metzger.

Gustafson grabbed his right pants leg and holding his leg he scooted along on his butt using his left hand and leg to get into the passage way. As he moved down through the passage he looked up, and became the last man to see Gott and Metzger alive, both looking intently ahead and moving the controls in tandem, committed together to follow through to the end.

As he got to the hatch he dropped his leg and flopping foot through the hatch, squirmed forward to get his rump on the edge of the hatch and then, T/Sgt. Russell W. Gustafson, flight engineer/top turret gunner slid through the hatch and down and away from '*The Lady Jeannette.*

Back along the flight path, Robbins popped his chute and dropped toward a woods. As he approached the tree tops he heard explosions. Fross dropped into an open field. Harms, having cleared the bomber, pulled his 'D' ring, was jerked as the chute opened and drifted toward an open field. Harland was slowly falling in his chute and nearing the ground when he heard an explo-

T/Sgt. Russell W. Gustafson bails out of '*The Lady Jeannette*' just seconds before it rolled over and dove to earth, exploding once in mid-air and again when it hit the ground at Tincourt-Boucly, France, 9 November, 1944. Model interpretation.

sion and seconds later another very loud explosion came over the rolling hill from the direction the bomber had disappeared, he prepared to hit the earth.

"My chute opened up into a beautiful white umbrella and to this day I don't remember actually pulling the ripcord," Russell Gustafson once told me. Looking down, he figured he had about 1,200 feet to fall. The air was cool and heavy so he was falling slowly, he should be able to land alright even with his broken leg.

The parachute turned in the light wind and it rotated Russell so that he was looking right at the end of the bomber flying away, moments later it rolled over and dived towards the earth.

Within a hundred feet, the fire from the ruptured fuel line was pulled back into the fuel line by the suction of the fuel pouring toward the front of the fuel tanks which were pointing straight down and the flame sparked an explosion of the tanks. A bomb bay door broke loose and started to flutter to earth as *'The Lady Jeannette'* continued to plunge straight down. Still at the controls, were 1st Lt. Donald J. Gott, pilot, and 2nd Lt. William E. Metzger, Jr., copilot. Side by side they had flown this mission and side by side they would end it. In the Radio Compartment, was T/Sgt. Robert A. Dunlap, radio operator. In the back, unknown to the pilots, hanging from the tail, but with them to the end, was S/Sgt. Herman B. Krimminger, tail gunner.

The bomber continued its dive and as it contacted the earth, just at the edge of a small woods. *'The Lady Jeannette'* ended its last flight as it was engulfed in a massive explosion as dirt, flame and smoke rose high into the air and a huge sound wave passed over the earth, as the 6,000 pounds of bombs on board detonated.

Technical Sergeant Russell W. Gustafson, flight engineer/top turret gunner, slowly drifted to earth.

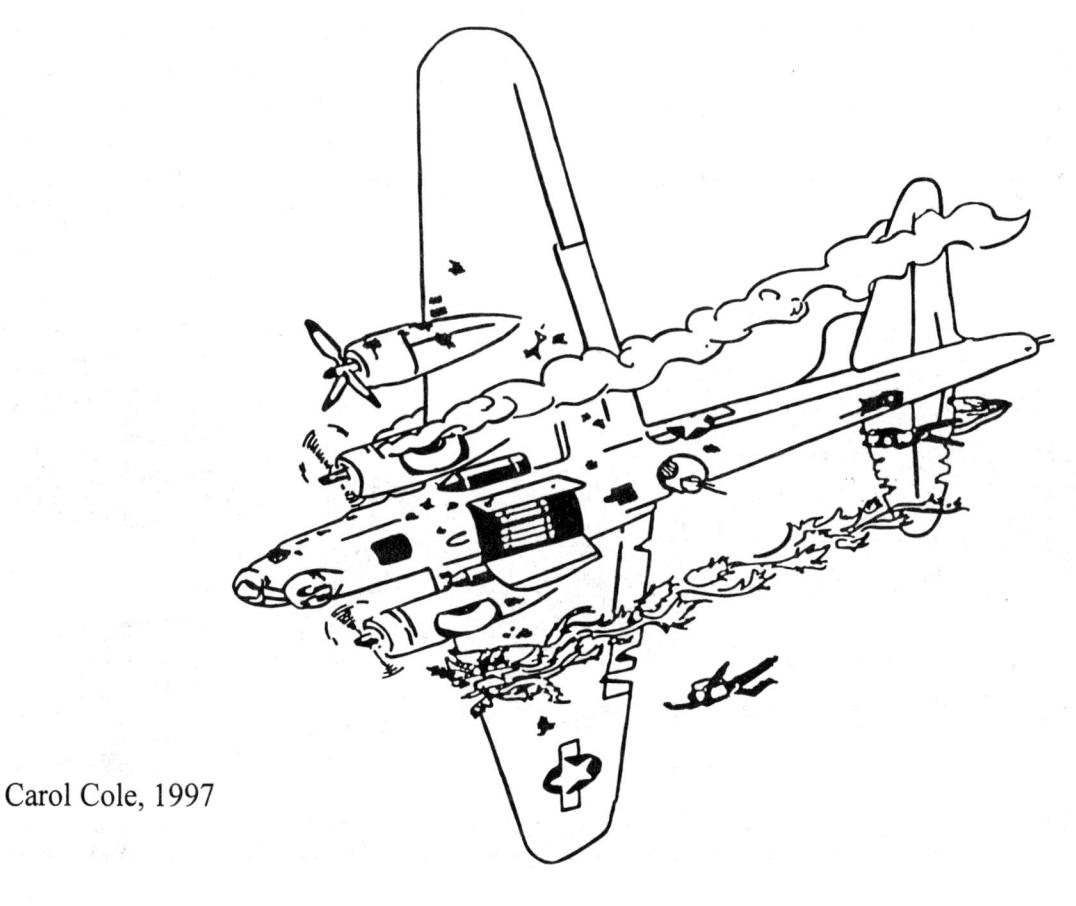

Carol Cole, 1997

Here ended, on November 9, 1944,
the physical existence of four men
and one B-17 bomber
The Lady Jeannette.

1st Lt. Donald J. Gott
2nd Lt. William E. Metzger, Jr.
T/Sgt. Robert A. Dunlap
S/Sgt. Herman B. Krimminger.

Chapter Six

The Americans - After The Crash

When the five parachuting survivors landed in France, time split into two streams, one American and one French, which were to meet again almost 50 years later.

The American events in this chapter will tell of the search for and the recovery of the official remains of the men killed in the crash of '*The Lady Jeannette*,' the survivors return to England, the background of the awards of the two **Congressional Medal Of Honors,** and the survivors return to the United States and civilian life.

For those who survived, both crewmen and families, life had to be lived and for each their stream of time meandered along between its banks of job, love, children and just plain living. Some to continue and some to end as the ebb of their lives broke against the sands of time. That is, until the 11th of June, 1994, when I first received the priest's statement and the two streams, American and French began to co-mingle again in this on-going story.

Chapter Seven, The French - After The Crash, will cover the events from the French view of their stream of time, until it joined with my life on Christmas Eve, 1991, when I first visited the grave and made my promise.

Chapter Eight, The Home Front, begins with the notification of their loved ones being Killed or Missing In Action, the award of the **Congressional Medal Of Honor** to the Gott and Metzger families, the return of three of the men's official remains to the United States for burial and the fourth's reburial at St. Avold, France.

....

Robbins fell through the trees of the small woods and though his parachute caught in the trees, he landed on the ground. He quickly checked himself all over and to his surprise found that he was unhurt and was still hanging onto the 'D' ring. He unbuckled his parachute and walked away, leaving it hanging in the trees as he started toward the edge of the woods. However, he kept that 'D' ring as a souvenir of the last flight of '*The Lady Jeannette.*'

As he approached the field at the edge of the trees he could hear an engine and as he walked into the open, he saw a jeep bouncing across the field. The driver stopped and asked him how he was. As he climbed into the jeep, Robbins told the driver that he was fine and the driver took off back across the field. Off in the distance, Robbins could see a column of smoke rising from where he was sure the bomber had crashed.

Soon, the driver drove out of the field and onto a road. But, instead of driving toward the column of smoke, he turned onto a road leading away from it. He explained to Robbins, that he was taking him to the nearby air base.

One of the many strange things I found, when researching this story, was the fact that the American soldiers who picked up the crewmen made no effort to collect the survivors together to account for all the crew. Except for the two men who were together for a ride to the hospital, the men each went their separate ways. Quite unlike the Germans, for it was normal for the Germans to keep captured crewmen in a local jail until all the crew could be gathered together or accounted for before sending them on their way to the prisoner of war camp.

At the airbase, Robbins was checked over at the medical station where they found nothing wrong. He doesn't remember being questioned about what had happened and his mind quickly related the parachute hanging over the tail, as a parachute passing under the tail and when he saw it, he jumped.

From the medics, he was taken to the operations building. There, he told them what base he was from in England, his squadron and group numbers. Within an hour, they got him a place on another plane which took him to Paris.

Once he was checked into the Transit

Barracks in Paris, he was given a pass to visit the city. Within a few hours of bailing out of *The Lady Jeannette*, he was walking around the streets of Paris. He was wearing his flying gear and it was still covered with the dried blood of his friend, T/Sgt. Dunlap. He walked a long time, that night in Paris, looking in the windows and seeing several things he would have liked to have bought for his wife, Shirley. However, he had no money that could be used in France. With a sigh, he remembered the emergency packet attached to that parachute harness hanging in the woods. For in it, along with the map and emergency rations were French francs. Hell, here he was, it had been an emergency and he forgotten it.

He spent a couple of days at the transit barracks before he was given transportation orders to permit him to fly back to England and rejoin the 729th Bombardment Squadron (H).

Fross landed with a jar and rolled over in the field as he came to a stop. His parachute was billowing so he got to his feet and, though still wobbly from the flak concussions, he ran it down as they had been taught and collapsed it. Unbuckling it, he gathered it up and began to walk to the large factory he saw in the distance.

When he arrived at the sugar beet refinery office door, the French people there called the police who contacted the military and an American army vehicle came and took Fross to the 109th Evacuation Hospital, a tent hospital, where he was treated and awarded the Purple Heart on November 10, 1944.

He spent three or four days at the hospital before they sent him back to England. He could speak some German and the hospital staff used him to help translate for some German prisoners being treated at the hospital and he helped with the care of the wounded American soldiers.

Harms landed well, collected his chute into his arms and set off toward the column of smoke that he could see over the hill. As he walked, he realized that his face was striped with several small wounds. He contributed them to the cords of his parachute whipping his face when it deployed.

I have not heard of him being seen at the crash site by any of the French, so I believe, another American driving a jeep saw him walking across the field toward the crash site and picked him up.

The driver took him to a large tent hospital located close by. As soon as he arrived, he was checked by a doctor and put to bed where they kept him sedated for a period of three days. When he awoke, he found that he had been awarded the Purple Heart and he was positive about the picture in his mind's eye. He had seen a parachute hanging from the bomber's tail, which was sticking up out of a hole in the ground.

He spent a few more days there under observation and, as he was able to move about he was asked to help the other wounded in various ways, such as pushing their wheelchairs. In due time, he was given travel orders and was taken to a small observation plane which flew him to England, where he was sent on to Deopham Green.

Harland swung to earth, rolled and got up. He quickly rolled up his parachute and started walking toward the column of smoke. As he walked toward the bomber, he saw an ambulance in the distance and headed for it.

Gustafson drifted to earth slowly and he was able to land taking up the shock with his good left leg as he crumpled to earth. However, he could not stand and he was lying on his back. His parachute drifted onto the earth and remained filled due to soft wind.

Billowing, it began to pull him across the large field in which he had landed. He started to try to roll over onto his chest, so he could try to collapse the chute when two Frenchmen and an American soldier ran up to him.

They grabbed him and brought him to a halt. Gustafson told the soldier to get his hunting knife from its sheath and cut the shroud lines to stop the chute from pulling him along. As they collected the parachute an American ambulance drove over the field to them.

When it got to them, the men in the ambulance lifted Gustafson onto a stretcher and began to load him into the ambulance.

Gustafson still complains that the soldier who helped him didn't give him back his prized hunting knife when he was loaded into the ambulance. However, they did load his parachute in.

As they were preparing to lift him though the door, Lt. Harland walked up. When Gustafson's stretcher was settled into its mounts, Harland got into the ambulance with him. Just before the driver closed the door to drive off, Gustafson asked him if he wanted the flight list manifest copy that he had in his pocket, so they would know just who was on board the bomber and could tell who died and who survived. The driver showed no interest as he closed the door and soon they were off.

In just a short time, they were at a large tent hospital where Harland got out and they lifted Gustafson's stretcher down. The doctor, who had come out to meet the ambulance, told the stretcher bearers to take Gustafson right into the operating room. Harland told him, "good luck," and that was the last time Gustafson ever saw Harland, who was soon back in England.

Within 15 minutes from the time he bailed out of the sick bomber, Gustafson was on an operating table and they were giving him an anesthetic. The two pilots had fulfilled their internal promise to him, they had gotten him close to the medical help he needed.

Gustafson awoke the next morning to find his leg in a cast and a doctor there to hand him his Purple Heart. That day everyone asked if they could have a piece of his parachute, as silk was scarce, and all he ended up with was a piece about the size of a handkerchief. Within two days, he was placed in an ambulance and taken to Paris.

There he was placed into the evacuation stream and loaded upon an ambulance train which took two days to reach Cherbourg. Upon arrival, he was taken aboard a hospital ship which took him back to England.

The large hole made by the explosion of the 6,000 pounds of bombs that were still on board '*The Lady Jeanette*' quickly became the point of interest, as the ambulance left carrying the American with the broken leg. Soon, there were several American soldiers, an American ambulance and a growing crowd of French people that began to collect as they came walking to the crash site from nearby villages.

The Americans waited for some time before entering the hole to allow it to cool off and to insure that everything was done exploding. However, there wasn't much to check in the hole, except for torn and twisted metal, the largest parts to be seen were some oxygen tanks that had been blown out of the hole and the large bomb bay door that had fluttered down when the fuel tanks exploded in the air.

The Americans began searching around the crash site hole and they began to pick up the larger pieces of human remains. It soon became obvious to them, that remains were scattered all around the bomber and for some distance out. If they were to complete their gruesome task today, they would need the help of the French.

They asked all the French to gather together and requested their help in recovering the remains of the dead American flyers and any personal possessions that might be found, such as identity tags, watches and items of uniform or equipment.

They explained their plan, they wanted everyone to line up in a long line, shoulder to shoulder. Once the line was complete, they would circle the crash site like the hand of a clock. Each person looking closely at the ground for remains as they moved forward.

Soon, people were hurrying to place recovered remains on the bomb bay door and back again to assume their place in line. Slowly, the line moved around the hole. The outside people had a very large area to cover, but the people closer in had to make many more trips to the bomb bay door.

Most brought small pieces to place upon the door, however as the line proceeded in its sweep, some large pieces began to be found in one quadrant. Including larger bone pieces and scraps of clothing.

Finally, the circle had been completed and the hole re-searched for remains. The door was stacked high with about two to two and a half feet of human remains, estimated by the French who helped to weigh several hundred pounds. It was heavy and some Frenchmen helped the Americans as they struggled to load the door into the ambulance. When the bomb bay door and its collection of human remains were in the ambulance, the Americans got in and started the engine.

The ambulance drove across the field from the crash site and began its journey back to its base. In the ambulance quite a conversation must have been going on. I don't know who was in the ambulance, it may have been enlisted/drafted men only, or an officer may have been present, but I believe, I have a good idea of how the conversation went.

In the back of the ambulance, there was a bomb bay door with a large pile of human remains that were mainly small to very small pieces. However, they had found some fairly large pieces. There was the crushed skull, mandible and maxilla, the shoulder found in the tee shirt with the laundry mark, as well as the pelvis found in the shorts with the same mark. There were several large joints, including another shoulder joint and knee, elbow and ankle parts. The rest was made up of small pieces of flesh and bone.

There were also the personal effects that had been found. Seven identification tags (Dog Tags) had been found and between them, they accounted for four men whose shattered remains were on the bomb bay door in the rear. Two were officers, named Gott and Metzger and two were rankers, named Dunlap and Krimminger. A broken and damaged wrist identity bracelet, with the name, William E. Metzger, Jr., engraved on it had been found, along with various ripped and torn apart uniform and flight suit pieces. The I.D. bracelet was covered with soot and dented. A wallet had also been found with personal effects of a T/Sgt. Robert A. Dunlap inside. It was probably protected by being in a pocket of Dunlap's heavy flying suit.

What happened next poses the greatest unknown still remaining in my research. I can only imagine what happened inside the minds of the men involved. There could be several reasons that might have made sense at the time. Especially, with what they had in the back of the ambulance.

I really believe, if they had been exposed to death at the front lines, as a friend of mine, T/Sgt. Will Henderson, of the 606th Graves Registration Company had been, they would have acted quite differently and this book would never had been written. But, the fact is, they didn't and I am sitting here writing this true story. I hope that someday, I will locate these men and be able to tell them about the French side of the story. For those men have been carrying a deeply hidden, dark secret within themselves since that 9th of November, 1944. They need to know about the grave at Cartigny, perhaps it would help erase their guilt. The families have sincerely forgiven them.

The door with its large pile of mixed human remains in the rear posed a great problem to them, for regulations called for such remains to be buried in a common grave. But, <u>no soldier</u> wanted his parents to know that he had died in such a manner as to require burial in a common grave with one or more other soldiers, so mangled and mixed together as to be inseparable.

I can see the soldiers in the ambulance asking each other, "Are you going to separate the remains in back?" "Hell, no," you do it! "I'm not going to touch it," the retort. This continued for a few minutes as the ambulance proceeded further from the crash site.

Suddenly, the ambulance pulled to the side of the road at a place that was out of sight of any homes in the villages spotted around the country side. The men got out, looked in all directions to see if they were observed. When they figured they were not being observed, they took a shovel from the ambulance and began to dig a hole in the field at the side of the road. They worked for sometime to get a hole large enough to accomplish what they had set out to do.

When they were finished digging, they opened the back of the ambulance and removed the greatest portion of the recovered human remains that had been collected at the crash site of the B-17 bomber and transferred it into the hole. In order to provide each man with official remains for an individual grave, they kept the largest pieces of the recovered remains and placed the rest in the hole beside the lonely French road.

When they had completed their self-assigned task and covered the remains with dirt, they drove away from this new grave in the countryside of France. They left the shallow unmarked grave, trusting it would remain hidden forever. The hidden grave of four American airmen of the 8th Army Air Force.

Upon arriving back at their base, they divided the remainder of the larger recovered remains into four somewhat equal portions and prepared each portion to be forwarded for burial. Included with each man's now Official Individual Remains, were his recovered dog tags (two stainless steel identity tags worn around the neck). One of Gott's identity tags was kept by the 19th TAC Graves Registration Officer for some strange reason. Both were supposed to be forwarded with the individuals remains. The movies always show soldiers cutting or pulling the dead's dog tags off. That should never be the case, as it left a basically unknown remains. I often wonder, could that dog tag be in the grave in France?

Included with the four sets of remains when they were forwarded for burial, were the two items of personal property recovered at the crash site, Metzger's damaged identity bracelet and Dunlap's wallet.

I am still searching for that Graves Registration Officer and hope to find an answer to that question. It also seems strange that the only unrecovered I.D. tag was one belonging to Krimminger as he was the one furthest from the explosion. I wonder if it graces some French metal detector's souvenir shelf as a relic of the bomber? His remains came out in the largest pieces, his skull was found, his left shoulder was found, his pelvis was found and we know his face was found.

I would like to remind the reader at this point, that I am writing this story with the approval of the four men's surviving families! They all know the details in full and wish that the story be told as close to the truth as I can, for this is a true history about a real event that happened during World War Two. An event, that the people and government of the United States Of America needs to accept as an accomplished fact of a war long gone.

As of the time of this writing, the United States has not officially given these men's Fifth Grave, in France, the honor it deserves through official recognition. During the second week of November, 1997, I received notification that my request on behalf of the men and their families had been forwarded to the Senate Committee on Armed Services for action. Perhaps, in the near future, we will get the Act of Congress required to recognize the grave.

When the bomber, diving straight down, started to contact the ground, the nose began to crumple in and the forward motion of the body of the aircraft continued driving it into the earth. From the moment the nose first hit the ground to the true end of the bomber took little more time than it did for you to read this paragraph.

My **_Bomb Disposal, North France_**, friends have the job of removing the shells and bombs of both wars, as they come to the surface or are dug up during construction projects. Each year, they continue to collect nearly 100 tons of unexploded World War One ordinance and occasional World War Two material. Just as we arrived in France, in May, 1997, a dump of unexploded German World War Two shells was found in a covered over ditch next to a railroad station. A train transporting them had been bombed during the war and the shells had been lost in the covered over ditch.

Christian enjoys his job greatly and he knows a lot about the American bomb fuses of World War Two. When I asked him, how much pressure it would take to make the bombs explode, he told me, it depended if the fuses were armed and ready to drop, by pulling the cotter pins. Well, we know Robbins pulled the pins as the bomber climbed to bombing altitude before it got to Saarbrucken. That left the propeller driven safeties still attached to the bombs. They would spin off as the bombs dropped through the air toward the target, arming the detonators. Some of the bombs might have had delayed action fuses to prevent repairs on the target for up to seventy-two hours. However, Christian told me, the bombs would still explode if they hit hard enough. At the time he was telling me this, he was showing me the latest fuses he had taken out of a World War Two bomb recovered from a farmer's field, since I last visited him.

With his knowledge of the pressures required, he thought the bombs would have broken loose from the bomb shackles and torn forward through the bulk head between the pilots and the bomb bay.

As the bomber's forward motion began to slow, the bomb's weight would have continued to want to move forward. They would have continued through the pilots and on through most of the bomber before they accumulated enough pressure to cause the fuses to detonate.

In that situation, any crew behind the nose of the bomber would have mostly been blown up and out of the hole made by the bombs, remember Metzger's I.D. bracelet being found outside the hole, as was Dunlap's wallet. A wallet that was supposed to have been left at the base in a locker until he returned. Metzger's bracelet was on his right wrist when the bomber struck. Of course, most of the bomber was also blown out of the hole, along with the men's remains. All would be in small pieces.

The three men closest to the bombs, Gott, Metzger and Dunlap, were literally blown to bits. Dunlap, fifteen feet behind the pilots was less damaged by the explosion, enough so his wallet, though badly damaged, survived. Krimminger, who was hanging under the tail was far enough way from the main blast to be blown into fairly large pieces.

At 15:30 on the afternoon of 11 November, 1944, the official remains of the four men[52] were buried side by side at the U.S. Military Cemetery, Limey, France:

KRIMMINGER, H. B., Grave Number 163,
    Row Number 7, Plot E.
    How were remains identified?
    Mark on undershirt "K-0339"
    Mark on underwear pants "K-0339"
    one identification tag
    Disposition of Identification Tags:
    Buried with body, YES
    Attached to marker, NO

DUNLAP, Robert A., Grave Number 164,
    Row Number 7, Plot E,
    Disposition of Identification Tags:
    Buried with body, YES
    Attached to marker, YES

GOTT, Donald J, in Grave Number 165,
    Row Number 7, Plot E,
    Disposition of Identification Tags:
    Buried with body, YES
    Attached to marker, NO, One identification tag, other removed by G.R. officer, 19th TAC

METZGER, William E., Grave Number 166
    Row Number 7, Plot E.
    Disposition of Identification Tags:
    Buried with body, YES
    Attached to marker, YES.

The Place of Death and Date of Death for each man was given as:
Hattonville, France, Coord. VU5346, Nord de Guerre Zone, 9 November, 1944.

The Cause of Death for each man was given as:
K.I.A. Burned in plane crash

The Limey Cemetery was located 16 miles east of St. Mihiel, France, near the World War One St. Mihiel Cemetery and 15 miles north of Toul. It was a temporary cemetery and all the men buried there were later transferred to other cemeteries in the United States and Europe in 1948 and 1949.

Each man's burial record was signed by Captain James T. Passman, Captain, Commanding, 609th QM Graves Registration Company. When I located him, I found that he had retired from the Army as a Colonel. Before his death in 1997, we discussed his work in France at this period in time and he was a great help in my research.

Each of the labeled Official Individual Remains now had an Official Grave. Most, if not all, of the remains in all four graves were the larger pieces recovered of S/Sgt. Herman B. Krimminger. Dividing the remains so that each man had an official grave never bothered me, finding that the rest of their remains had been hidden, did!

In S/Sgt. Krimminger's grave were the following remains:[53]

Disarticulated; all major bones fractured and /or missing except for lt radius and pelvic girdle.

In T/Sgt. Dunlap' grave were the following remains:[54]

Fractured: all major bones, skull & mandible; distal ends of rt radius & ulna missing.

In Lt. Gott's grave were the following remains:[55]

Body disarticulated; crushed skull, mandible & maxilla; fractured: lt humerus, radius, pelvis, femur, pelvis & femur; rt tibia & fibula missing.

In Lt. Metzger's grave were the following remains:[56]

Disarticulated. Multiple fractures throughout/.

Capt. Passman signed a copy of the form Inventory Of Personal Effects for one METZGER, William E., that day. The inventory consisted of one gold colored identification bracelet, no currency. It certified the effects will be forwarded by truck on 11 Nov., 1944.

On that same truck was the one other item of personal inventory forwarded that day. T/Sgt. Dunlap's wallet. Its inventory listed the following:

1. American Bill, Amount $5.00 ("Short Snorter") Ł 6. English
2. Certificate of Birth
3. Address Book
4. Wallet, Black
5. Social Security Card
6. Marksman H. P. Certificate
7. Money Order Receipt
8. WDAGO - Form No. 29

Money in amount of Ł 6 has been turned into Charles S. McCormick Jr., Lt. Col. F.D. 222-226.
Signed: Capt. James T. Passman

The Squadron History[57] for November, 1944, dated, 29 December, 1944, 729th Bomb Squadron, 452nd Bombardment Group (H), extracts provide the following information:

9 November : Seven (7) aircraft participated in combat mission to Saarbrucken.

13 November: Record of Events, 9 November 1944, amended to read: ... 1st Lt Donald J. Gott, 2nd Lt William E. Metzger, Jr., T/Sgt Robert A. Dunlap, S/Sgt. Herman B. Krimminger missing in action; 2nd Lt. John A. Harland, 2nd Lt. Joseph F. Harms, S/Sgt. James O. Fross, Duty to absent sick, 98th General Hospital, injured in action; T/Sgt. Russell W. Gustafson, Duty to absent sick. 98th General Hospital, injured in action.

26 November: T/Sgt. Russell W. Gustafson, duty to absent sick, 98th General Hospital, wounded in action, is amended to read, T/Sgt. Russell W. Gustafson duty to absent sick, U.S. Hospital Plant #4114, wounded in action.

On the same day that the men killed in the crash were buried in the first of their official graves, 11 November, 1944, a bulldozer was brought to Tincourt-Boucly. It pushed all the remaining bomber parts back into the hole and covered them over with dirt. *'The Lady Jeannette'* was also buried in a grave, though not forgotten.

At 12:08 hours[58] (Mission Time), the group crossed the Enemy Coast at 50-59 01-

59 at 9,400 feet. A let down started at 10:51 hours at 50-21 05-56. The English coast was crossed at 12:23 hours at 51-21 01-26. Base was reached at 13:08 hours and we landed at 13:15 hours.

As the returning bombers of the group began to line up for approach to Deopham Green, it was obvious to those on the ground that at least one of the squadrons had missing aircraft.

Before some of the returning bombers completed their approach to the runway, colored flares streamed from their cockpits, declaring that they had wounded crewmen on board and the ambulances rushed to meet them as they turned off the runway.

More and more bombers completed their approach, as the bombers in the air around the field thinned out. Finally, the last one made its approach, landed, taxied and rolled to a stop at its hardstand. The airborne part of the 162nd Mission of the 452nd Bomb Group (H), to Saarbrucken, Germany, had ended, it was time for debriefing to begin.

At several hardstands, there stood a forlorn group of men, the ground crew of a bomber that had not returned. Hope was not totally gone, perhaps their bomber and its crew had landed at another base. Perhaps, the bomber had too much damage to get to its home base, perhaps the engines had used too much fuel to get back to Deopham Green. Perhaps, perhaps, perhaps... Slowly, the ground crew began to disperse, the returning air crews--tomorrow or another day may tell.

The men of the returned crews collected their gear, dropped it out and swung down out of the bomber. Each acted out his own personal and private ceremony for being granted the opportunity of extended life, as their feet again touched the ground of England. Some shook each others hand and slapped each others backs in congratulation of another safe return, while other's with less shown emotion looked inward and counted the missions remaining to be flown.

Across all of Norfolk, bombers were disgorging their crews, across all of Norfolk ambulances were loading with the wounded, the dying and the dead. The crew's jobs were almost done, the hospitals and Graves Registration were just beginning.

As one man's feet touched the earth, he thought not only of himself, his mind was still partially out there! Out there, over Germany, where he saw a bomber buck and sway as it took flak hits and pulled out of formation and drifted to the west. On fire, smoking and still in control, his normal crew had flown out of sight toward the west. His crew, the men with which he normally flew, were missing, missing in action, how could he rest easy that night? He had to go back to the hut and face those empty beds and the lockers that would soon be emptied of personal effects. 2nd Lt. Gerry Collins was back, but would he ever see the flight engineer/top turret gunner again, the one who taught him how to play chess outside the barracks? How about the man he had sat beside in training, on the flight over and on so many missions, Don Gott?

Collin's mind ran through the crew list as each man's face and personality passed in front of his mind's eye, Gott, Penick, Harland, Gustafson, Dunlap, Fross, Robbins and Krimminger and Penick. He had only known them for a few months, but they had flown through the fire together, when he was the right seater. Unlike some crews, they were not a close crew, but they had grown into a good crew. He was going to miss those guys, sure hope they are all OK.

Later that afternoon, he met Lt. Penick and found out that he had missed the flight and that a new bombardier had flown in his place, a guy named Harms.

Each returning bomber crew boarded transportation and headed for debriefing. There they would tell what had happened during their mission. Had flak struck them, had a crewman been hurt, had they seen a bomber struck, had they seen its luck?

Many that day had a tale to tell, about the bombers that did not return. One was not seen after assembly had begun, two more were struck by flak, just minutes before the group's bombs burst on target.

One of them, number 904, was seen

heading west, badly damaged and losing altitude, it seemed in control, no chutes were seen, Lt. Collins would verify that.

The other, number 833, was seen damaged and going down over Germany, where it had disappeared from sight, supposed to have crashed and the crew M.I.A.

A/C number 931 was also unaccounted for that day.

On 1 December, 1944, the Unit History Report for the Saarbrucken Mission of 9 November, 1944, was written:

---

1. The 452nd Bomb Group (H) put up three Squadrons flying the 45th "C" Group. Thirty-five (35) plus four (4) PPF A/C were airborne to attack the German defensive strong point located 20 mile NE of Metz and 10 miles E of Thionville. However, because of the undercast they attack the secondary target which was the large marshaling yards located one-half mile NE of the center of the city of Saarbrucken by PFF means. No strikes were visible.
2. Flak over Saarbrucken was moderate, accurate and tracking. Eleven (11) A/C received minor flak damage and three (3) A/C received major from AA. A/C No. 904, Lt Gott and crew, was hit by flak on bomb run and left formation under control. Also A/C 833 and 931 are unaccounted for. No E/A was encountered.
Harold P. Thoreson
Major, Air Corps
Intelligence Officer

This book is about one of these three bombers, number 904. The following recounts the fate of the other two.

Aircraft number 833, slid into the position just vacated by '*The Lady Jeannette*,' to close up the bomber formation, as '*The Lady Jeannette*' continued its controlled descent toward the west. Within minutes the flak which had damaged 904, was bursting against the 833 and the number 3 engine received a direct flak hit about a minute before bombs away. Just after its bombs were toggled off with the group, the aircraft was observed sliding out of the formation. It left the formation smoking, appearing to be under control and no chutes were seen.

Unable to keep the bomber under control, the pilot called for the crew to bail out. All made it to the ground safely and the bomber crashed in the grapevine fields near Minheim.

Missing In Action Report, 452nd Group History, 9 November, 1944.

Aircraft B-17, Serial #43-37833
Bickford, Kenneth F. 1st Lt., Pilot
Reilly, John J., Jr., 2nd Lt., Copilot
Marquis, Robert S., 1st Lt., Navigator
Fannon, William W., 2nd Lt., Bombardier
Van Loozenord, Eugene E. T/Sgt., TTG
Srodawa, Max N., T/Sgt., ROG
Turner, Charles J., T/Sgt., BTG
Williams, Robert G., Jr., S/Sgt, RWG
Caldwell, Philip, E., Sgt., TG

The crew having bailed out safely into Germany were all captured immediately except for Lt. Fannon. He evaded capture for some time, having landed in a woods. Finally, after walking for a week, Lt. Fannon was captured trying to steal food from a farm house and joined the rest of the crew, in P.O.W. camps, for the remainder of the war. The officers went to the Beleria Compound of Stalag Luft III. All the men survived the war.[59]

Missing In Action Report - 452nd Bomb Group (H), 9 November, 1944.

Aircraft B-17, Serial #42-102931
Myers, Frances W., 2nd Lt., Pilot
Prado, Fred, 2nd Lt., Copilot
Hester, Robert L., 2nd Lt. Navigator
Valenzano, Aldo, S/Sgt, Bombardier
Long, Robert M.., S/Sgt, ROG
DeYoung, Harold, T/Sgt., TTG
Turman, Donald E., S/Sgt, BTG
Richards, Albert R., S/Sgt, RWG
Britt, Jackson C., S/Sgt, TG

It was later reported, that early in the

morning, about 07:30, a bomber was seen to circle over the city of Lowestoft. It headed out to sea and crashed two miles northeast of the city. Four chutes were seen to open, however only the body of Lt. Myers was recovered.

Missing In Action Report, 452nd Group History, 9 November, 1944

Aircraft B-17, Serial #42-97904
Gott, Donald J., 1st Lt., Pilot
Metzger, William E. Jr., 2nd Lt,. Copilot
Harms, Joseph P., 2nd Lt., Bombardier
Harland, John A., 2nd Lt., Navigator
Gustafson, Russell W., T/Sgt., TTG
Dunlap, Robert A., T/Sgt., ROG
Fross, James O., S/Sgt., BTG
Robbins, William R., S/Sgt., RWG
Krimminger, Herman B., S/Sgt., TG

The bomber was last seen damaged and smoking, It was lost to sight while under control, losing altitude, flying west and no chutes had been seen.

Early in the morning of 12 November, 1944, 2nd Lt. Gerry Collins remembers being woke up from a sound sleep by a distraught, Sgt. Robbins, who had just returned to the base from France.

Robbins wanted to talk to Collins, his crew's normal copilot, and tell him about what happened during the mission to Saarbrucken. "He (Robbins) was very disturbed and we talked for a long time about all the events leading up to his return," Gerry Collins has told me.

Robbins was the first to return and this was the first that Collins knew of what happened to his crew mates. Even after talking about all the events that Robbins remembered, Collins and Robbins could not be certain about what had happened to all the rest. Dunlap had been unconscious in the radio compartment and Krimminger's parachute had caught and he must have fallen to his death. Fross was clear of the ball turret and could have bailed out.

Robbins told Collins about the flare fire in the cockpit and the hydraulic fluid that had leaked out of the damaged cylinder. He told of Gustafson being wounded in the leg and having problem with getting his morphine shot in. He talked about the flak bursts, the missing number 4 engine, the flames flowing from its position and the damaged number 2 engine. He passed on everything that Metzger had told them, when they were in the radio compartment tending Dunlap's wound.

The conversation lasted for quite a long time and soon it was time for breakfast and for Robbins to report to the squadron H.Q. to repeat his story.

Already in Collins' mind, he was forming a determination to see that the two pilots were given the award that it would appear that they deserved. He would begin to lobby for an application for the award of the **Congressional Medal Of Honor**.

Collins went with Robbins when he gave his report about the flight and that afternoon Robbins was placed on a temporary assignment.

SO #311, HQ USAAF STA 142, APO 559, 12 Nov '44 (Contd.)

5. Sgt. William R. Robbins, 11051000, 729th Bomb Sq, 452nd Bomb Gp, WP fr this Sta to AAP Sta #524, rptng to CO thereof on 14 Nov '44 on TD for period of seven (7) days, excluding traveling time, for purpose of attending Rest Home...

Soon the other survivors began arriving back at the group. According to the Group's remaining records, on the 14th, S/Sgt. James O. Fross arrived and by the 16th, Lt.s Harms and Harland had returned to England by separate routes. Harms had been placed on a small observation plane and flown back to England, where he reported to the 98th General Hospital.

Harms remained at the hospital, under observation, for two weeks and when he did report to the Group, he was sent on to the Rest Home for seven days. That Special Order, SO #315, HQ USAAF, STA 142, 16 Nov '44 (Contd.), sending the men to the Rest Home, had been written, and therefore official, before the three men had actually arrived back at the base, i.e., Harms.

Fross had told me over 50 years later that he had spent quite some time at a hospital in England and never did return to the base. Mary, his wife, had found among his personal papers after Jim's death, his letter of recommendation from Colonel Batson and other papers of which she sent copies to me. The letter of recommendation seemed to disprove what he had told me. It was easy to question his statements because of his advanced Alzheimer's disease when we talked at his home in Texas. That is, until they were supported by my interviews with Harms.

Gustafson also arrived in England, via the hospital ship from Cherbourg on the 15th or 16th. He was assigned to the 98th General Hospital and later the 4114th Hospital Plant, where he spent the next several months in traction before being shipped back to the U.S. He had a large chunk of bone missing from his right leg bone, just above the ankle, and it would have to be allowed to grow back.

Robbins no sooner got back from the Rest Home, than he was given the orders he wanted.

SO #323, HQ USAAF, STA 142, APO 559, 24 Nov '44 (Contd.)

6. Sgt (612) William R Robbins, 11051000, is trfd fr 729th Bomb Sq, 452nd Bomb Gp to CP, 70th Repl Depot, AAF, and will report to CO at AAF Sta 569 w/o delay to await T to Z of I. (Auth: par 4 SO #328 Hq 3BD dtd 23 Nov '44)

In short S/Sgt. Robbins was to report to the Replacement Depot for shipment to the Zone of Interior, or United States. He should be home for Christmas.

Leaving right behind him, the following was prepared for S/Sgt. Fross. I expect that S/Sgt. Robbins had one in his file also.

Headquarters, Four Fifty Second Bombardment Group (H), Army Air Forces, Office of the Group Commander.

A.P.O. 559
New York, NY
26 November 1944.

SUBJECT: Letter Of Recommendation.

TO: Whom it may concern.

1. Staff Sergeant James O. Fross, army serial number 38462533, 729th Bombardment Squadron, 452nd Bombardment Group (H), has served in an operational capacity as a ball turret gunner and has flown 27 operational missions.

2. Awards recommended by reason of his diligent and courageous performance of duties assigned to him are: the Air Medal with 3 Oak Leaf Clusters.

3. The quality of Sergeant Fross' service has been excellent and extremely efficient throughout.

4. In view of Sergeant Fross' outstanding combat experience and superior ability, it is my opinion that he is well qualified for a position as a gunnery instructor in the zone of interior.

Signed:
BURNHAM L. BATSON
Lt. Col., Air Corps
Commanding.

S/Sgt. Fross rode back on a ship, his personal records[60] show his departure as Christmas Day, 25 December, 1944. He had flown 270 hours while in Foreign Service in the E.T.O. (European Theater of Operations)

As S/Sgt. Robbins boarded his ship for the voyage back over the Atlantic he carried back a lot more than souvenirs in his bag. He would carry in his mind for the rest of his life, the last hours of '**the last flight of *The Lady Jeannette***' and the men with whom he flew.

The officers who returned, except for Harms, were required to complete their full 35 missions, unlike the enlisted men who were allowed to go home at once.

Lt. Collins and Lt. Harland were no longer part of a regular crew. They had to make up their mission total on a standby status. They would only fly when a regular crew person could not make a mission. It took much longer for them, however by the end of the year, 1944, they could also go home. They missed Christmas at home, but they were alive and they were going to the Z.I.

Collins was able to leave for the States with a lighter heart, he had fulfilled his promise to himself to see that Gott and Metzger were rewarded for the supreme effort they had made during the Saarbrucken mission.

His personal drive had led the group to interview the survivors, including Gustafson in his hospital bed and in early December the Group submitted applications for both pilots, Gott and Metzger, requesting the award of the **Congressional Medal Of Honor** to each.

In July 24, 1995, I received a letter from a member of the 452nd Bomb Group Association. I am placing it here, a bit out of the stream of time, as I feel this is the best place in this book to set history straight. Irv's letter read, in part:

Dear Sam,

I was an intelligence officer in the 452nd BG (728th Sq), and was also the Awards Officer, in addition to regular duties. I wrote up the Gott, Metzger citations, which actually were the submissions applying for Medal Of Honor consideration. They were used word for word without alteration as the final citations.

This is <u>not to be misconstrued</u> as the <u>initiation</u> of same, merely a side note in the interest of historical fact.

Irving Math, Shaker Heights, Ohio

I was on the telephone to Irv within minutes of receiving his letter. Now, I had someone who could explain why the citations read *'The Lady Janet'* instead of the actual name, *'The Lady Jeannette.'* I was sort of expecting some real historical background when Irv told me, "Well, I was probably sitting there typing the first of the citations, when I reached the place I wanted to insert the bomber's name, I asked the name of the bomber and they probably said, '***The Lady Jeannette***.' My mind may have heard **Jeannette**, but it didn't automatically know how to spell it and type it, so it just typed **Janet**. No one corrected the citations when they read them over, so that the bomber name that became famous in the Gott and Metzger citations was and has always been wrong.

I also asked about the discrepancy in the statement in the citations, that the bombs had been dropped on target, when in fact they had not been.[61] Irv did not have an answer for that, other than as an experienced awards application writer he had found in his review of granted awards, that certain things really helped insure approval. One that really helped insure approval was for the reviewer to believe, that a bomber was held on course no matter what and that the bombs were delivered. This, they obviously believed, was heroic.

Gott and Metzger, it was felt by everyone in the group and its command, deserved the **Medal Of Honor** so much, that no chance should be left unused. So, they didn't die in an explosion of the bombs on board, the bombs had dropped on target. To set history straight, Gott and Metzger, along with Dunlap and Krimminger, were at the place where the bombs aboard '***The Lady Jeannette***' exploded, a short distance north Tincourt-Boucly, France.

I agree, and though I might face criticism for writing the truth, I believe that history deserves the full truth in this case. Especially, since most of the remains of those two men and two of their crewmen were hidden in a hole alongside a lonely road in France. It took all the courage and determination these two young men had to fulfill their promise, as much as they could. It was above and beyond the call.

One would think that all the events of the fatal plunge would have been known to the group. The name of the radio operator surely was, but he was not named in the citations. I think he should have been. Krimminger's death was a quirk of fate, so he was not listed as a fourth man aboard during the final plunge. There was not enough room to explain it all, I expect. So Krimminger's death was not recorded in the citations either.

I left that telephone conversation with Irv Math, somewhat smarter about the awards applications process. There had to be a very good reason that the 452nd Bombardment Group (H) ended the war with the most decorations of any group. I had talked to one of the best reasons.

The 452nd Group Historical Report for December, 1944, Award Report:

1. There were no Bronze Stars awarded due to the fact that a new division directive was published canceling the method of application. All Bronze Stars submitted after December 15th were therefore returned to Group and did not meet approval due to this reason.
Over 20 Distinguished Flying Cross applications for leadership and heroism are still pending at division. As yet, this group has not received their general orders.
2. On a statistical report received from third division, this group, since its arrival in this theater of operations, has submitted more awards and had more awards approved than any other group during this past twelve months.
3. During this past month, an application was submitted to the division award's board for the award of the Distinguished Unit Plaque for the 87th Station Complement Squadron, this station.
4. Two applications for the Congressional Medal Of Honor were submitted for Pilot Donald J. Gott and Copilot William E. Metzger Jr.

Signed
Ralph P. Goldsticker,
1st Lt., Air Corps
Awards Officer

Harms was transferred from the 729th Sq. to the 731st Sq. on SO #320, he received the orders when he returned from his seven days at the Rest Home.

After he returned from the Rest Home, Harms faced another 33 missions. He felt the fear of another combat mission closing in on him as they prepared to schedule him for his third mission. He had flown practice missions upon his return, but his guts clinched each time the bomber left the ground and until it landed safely he was very nervous.

Finally, he made a decision that was made even harder by the fact that he could be open to derision from his fellow flyers. He approached his commander and the flight surgeon and asked for a medical board.

Not that he was afraid to fly, it was that his nerves had been affected to a point that he was even more afraid that an error on his part might endanger others. For he was not just a fill-in bombardier on his second mission when '*The Lady Jeannette*' crashed, he was already a crash survivor.

Harms and his original crew had arrived in Iceland on their way to England, flying the new bomber they had been given to ferry to England. Their onward flight had been delayed for several days due to bad weather and the personnel in Iceland were wanting to get them on the way. Bombers and crews were needed in England.

They were alerted for flight, to leave the next morning. The weather stations in Greenland and at sea predicted that the current storm would blow through and there would be a break between it and the next one following.

Early the next morning, they were awoke in the middle of a dark and stormy night. Time to eat and be briefed and be ready to fly as soon as the storm passed over.

They sat there on the hardstand, the bomber buffeted by the winds constantly changing direction with the engines ticking over. As they watched, other bombers made their way to the runway and bore off into the murk, so bad, that some disappeared from sight before they left the ground.

The radio crackled and through the static the pilot was told to taxi to a runway and prepare for take off. They arrived and as they were going through their operational checks, the radio voice told them that the winds had changed and they must taxi over to another runway in order to take off into the blustery wind.

No sooner had the bomber arrived at the second runway when they were informed to move to another runway take off location. The crew began to get very anxious, especially when they were finally sent to a fourth location to begin their run to part with earth, the last of the departing bombers trying to beat the weather front that was coming. The winds were blowing hard as they began their take off run and the bomber swayed as they broke through various and fickle winds along the runway.

The pilot let it run out well and built up extra speed before pulling his stick back and forcing the bomber to break its hold with the ground beneath. As they gained altitude the crew were bounced around inside the bomber and each sought his safe place for the remainder of the flight to England.

Harms had gone to his position in the nose of the bomber and strapped himself into seat with the goldfish bowl view out the front. Soon, the bomber was in the clouds and the weather was rough, the next storm had arrived early. With all the runway changes the navigator and pilot were confused and there were no other bombers in a stream to follow. They were there, by themselves.

Suddenly, Harms could see through a blowing break in the clouds, a range of mountains and right in front of them was one with a large glacier. The clouds closed as quickly as they had opened and the glacier was lost from sight. The bomber was struggling for altitude, for the updrafts and down drafts were fighting it all the way.

Out front, Harms saw that glacier coming closer through the blowing and flowing clouds. He called over the intercom to make certain that the pilot had seen what he had just seen. However they continued to fly straight ahead. There were mountains on either side.

Suddenly, it was right there in front and before he could react, everything was happening at once. The bomber was bounced, jolted and slid to a stop on the surface of the glacier. One wing had broken and the plane had split--it was a mess.

Harms began to realize that he was awake and he was alive. He had to get out and do it fast, the plane was full of fuel. Quickly, he released his safety belt and as he turned to leave he saw the navigator starting to crawl back through the passageway to the cockpit. As fast as he could, Harms followed the navigator and as he scrambled along he could see the TTG, copilot and pilot making their way back along the bomb bay catwalk toward a break in the fuselage.

The crew found themselves in, what at any other time, would have been a winter wonderland. As they checked themselves and talked among each other, they found that most of them were unhurt, however a couple of the men were injured somewhat, but mobile.

Here they were, in the middle of a glacier in Iceland in the middle of a snow storm. Safe, somewhat unsound and a long way from anywhere. The crew discussed their situation and decided that it would be best to stay with the bomber and let the rescuers come to them. They had survival rations and a Gibson Girl portable emergency radio.

They thought that the people on the ground had heard their last minute emergency calls before the crash, so search planes should be coming soon.

The men searched the wreckage and each marveled at the luck that had ridden with them. With all that fuel on board, there had been no fire, so they were able to get out. Slowly they removed all the useable stuff and took an inventory. They had rations for a few days and there were gasoline and oil to make a fire to create heat and a beacon for the searchers.

For the next three days they managed to survive. They could hear what they took to be search aircraft flying around, but none came over the glacier. They kept trying to use the Gibson Girl to alert the close aircraft, however it was soon obvious that it was not working.

As the hours and then days passed, the

men discussed their situation again and again. One of the men told the rest of them about his climbing experience and he thought he could lead the crew down and off the glacier. In due time, as rations began to run out and hope of an over flying searcher dwindled, the crew decided to walk out.

They collected the items they thought they could use and they started their trek. Some hours later, with the knowledgeable man in front, they approached a cabin located just below the tree line. They had made it off the ice and partway down the mountain.

The cabin's occupants made them at home, filling them with hot drink and offering everything they could. As soon as the men were somewhat rested they started down the mountain. This time, guided by a local who knew exactly where and what they had to do to get safely off the mountain and back to the army air force base.

Finally, they were escorted back to the base they had flown from, just a few long days and one hazardous journey earlier. The first stop was the hospital where they were warmed, fed and checked in for rest and recuperation. The first thing Harms asked to do was to send a telegram to his pregnant wife, telling her that he was OK.

After being given a chance to somewhat regain their former selves, the crew was alerted for a flight on to England. They were to go as passengers aboard a C-47 cargo plane, one of a flight of several cargo planes.

As the C-47 rumbled down the runway and into flight, there was not one of Harms fellow crewman who did not worry about getting to England this time. Storm, after storm was passing in what seemed to be an unending stream. The flight of C-47s bumped, bounced and slipped and slid their way to England. Finally, the plane they were aboard touched down.

When the plane rolled to a halt in the staging area, everyone crawled out and looked around. There had been five C-47s in the flight and when they finished counting, they were one short. Where was the fifth plane?

It was gone, just gone. No one knew when, where or how. It had left Iceland in formation, it had not made it to England. On board was the flying crew and another load of personnel just like Harms and the others, gone without a trace.

Harms and his crew followed the replacement pipeline and soon found themselves at Deopham Green, members of the 452nd Bombardment Group (H).

His first mission didn't phase him, and he toggled his bombs when the leader dropped. The target seemed to be well hit and he was prepared for the second with his crew, However, he had been woke up to fly as a fill-in for a missing bombardier.

The medical board reviewed his records and agreed that the Army Air Force could use him in another position. They relieved him from flying status and assigned him to a finance noncombatant position.

Harms had completed three and one half years college before enlisting in the Aviation Cadets. He had been told, he would not be called until he had time to finish his accounting major. However, he had just bought his books when the greetings arrived and he was told to report. So, much for college then, but it came in handy now.

By end of January, 1945, the only people left in England who had flown aboard *The Lady Jeannette* were Gustafson in the hospital and Harms.

In late February, after three months in traction, the doctors authorized Gustafson's return to the Z. Of I. (Zone of Interior) via airplane. Upon arrival, he spent the next nine months at the Fort Dix Tilton General Hospital.

The 452nd Group Historical Report for April, 1945, Award Report:
(Partial)
3. Only one award ceremony was held at this station this month due to the shortage of medals in Third Division. Numbers of combat personnel were awarded DFCs at 45th Wing Headquarters.
4. A total of approximately 1,300 medals of every type were awarded during this month to combat and ground personnel.
5. This office was notified that the

Congressional Medal Of Honor for First Lieutenant Donald J. Gott, pilot of a B-17 who was killed in action, was approved by the theater commander, General Eisenhower.

Signed
Irwin Math
1st. Lt., Air Corps, Award Officer.

I never found a report on Lt. Metzger's Congressional Medal Of Honor being approved, however both of them were later approved on the same General Order.

In April, as the war in Europe began to wind down, Harms received orders to return to the Z. Of I., to report for further training as a finance officer.

One day, while looking at the paper Russell Gustafson read that Lt. Gott and Lt. Metzger had been awarded the **Congressional Medal Of Honor**. When his leg had grown together well enough, he was authorized recuperation leave at his home in Jamestown, New York. One night, he was in a restaurant and he saw an officer that he recognized from the 452nd Group. It was while talking to this officer, that he heard about Krimminger's death for the first time.

A short while after his return to the Fort Dix hospital he received a package of grapefruit from Fross, who had sent them from his home in McAllen, Texas. However, they had first gone to Fort Dix, then Jamestown and back to Dix. By the time he received them, they had rotted.

Those rotten grapefruit were his last contact with any of the crew for 50 years.

Sgt. Robbins arrived home and he and his wife spent some time at a rest center in Florida. Later, he was assigned to the base at Laredo, Texas, where he was a gunnery instructor.

In October, Robbins, his wife Shirley, and a friend decided to visit the Gulf of Mexico. On the way they stopped at the home of Sgt. Fross in McAllen, Texas, for a visit. Fross was home on leave and everyone enjoyed the short visit.

When they parted that afternoon, it was the last contact that either of these two crew members had with each other, except for Jim's later family, or any of the other crew for 50 years.

Jim Fross, Shirley and Bill Robbins
Jim's friend and Jacquelin, Jim' Sister

Lt. Collins returned, arriving back at the same depot as Robbins, the day after Christmas. Sgt. Robbins had lost all his money gambling on the ship coming back. He borrowed ten dollars for Lt. Collins and the last contact he had with Lt. Collins was when he sent him the ten dollars. Lt. Collins served with various transport commands in California and was the first original crew member discharged.

Once the war was over in Japan, the men with the highest points were selected to be discharged and Collins with his completed missions and twin boys had the lucky high numbers, permitting his discharge in August, 1945.

Lt. Harland came back to the States and also spent time at a rest camp in Florida before being reassigned. He was one of the first to be discharged, in October, 1945.

By the end of 1945, all the surviving personnel, except one, had returned to civilian life. Lt. Harms finished Finance Officer's school and was shipped to the Far East Command. He re-enlisted and remained in the service until 1947.

For each, **the last flight of 'The Lady Jeannette'** began to drift to the back of their minds as school, life, love and living took over for the next 50 years, as each went a separate path.

Chapter Seven

The French - After The Crash

The people of Tincourt-Boucly, France, watched in awe as the bomber rolled over into a vertical dive, exploded once and again when it hit the ground. Before the bomber hit the ground and exploded for the second time, the first person had started for the field where the man they saw bail out was going to land. Even from that distance, one could see that one of the flyer's feet was flopping around in the wind and knew that he had to be hurt.

It was a fairly long run from the village, up the sloping hill, into the open field to where he had landed. By the time the first Frenchman was part way there, one of the American soldiers, who were living in the village and another Frenchman was also running to the landing parachutist. He landed some distance from the road they had crossed and as they approached, he was being dragged along the field by his parachute that was being blown by the light wind.

The first thing they did was grab the parachute shroud lines to stop the parachute from pulling the airman. The American soldier started talking to the airman and he took a large knife from a holder on the airman's parachute harness. With this, he cut the shroud lines to separate the parachute from the parachute harness, so it stopped pulling the airman. Then while the Americans talked the French collected the parachute.

It was obvious from the look of the man's leg, that he could not stand and while they were standing there they heard an engine noise. Looking toward the village they saw an American ambulance start across the field toward them. To the west, beside the small wood, they could just see the crater edge where the bomber had crashed and the smoke still rose in a column. This American was very lucky, he had barely gotten out before the bomber crashed.

The ambulance pulled up to them and stopped. The soldiers inside got out, opened the rear door and removed a stretcher. They placed this next to the wounded American flyer and lifted him onto it. One of them tended the leg somewhat, however they seemed very anxious to drive off.

Just as they were loading the flyer in, another man came walking up across the field from further east. He seemed to know the man on the stretcher and the French realized that he was another of the bomber's crew. He must have bailed out just before the man they had helped. After the injured man was loaded aboard the other man climbed into the ambulance with him and it started to depart.

Once the ambulance drove off, the Frenchmen and American walked over to the still smoking crash site. By that time, many people from the village had started to walk to the large crater. Two young boys who had observed the bomber approach and crash half-walked and half-ran to the crash site. One, Mr. Cassel, would later become a Mayor of Tincourt-Boucly, the other was Mr. Chaulieu. All the Americans living in the village were soon there and another American ambulance had arrived and driven to the crash site in the field by the woods.

The two explosions seemed to have quickly destroyed all the burnable things on the bomber, because in just this short time since the crash, all the flame was gone and the smoke was disappearing fast.

The Americans from the ambulance started looking around the crater and one could see that they were finding something they were interested in. Looking at the ground around them, the French realized that there were small pieces of meat and bone lying all round them. It was with some horror that each of them came to the realization that they were looking at the remains of men who were not able to bail out of the bomber on time.

Death was not unfamiliar to these people. For in their small villages, parents and loved ones died at home. For most of these older people who were left in the villages at that time, the First World War was not so long ago that the men who served easily remembered what they had seen. And, it was only four year's ago, that soldiers and civilians were killed along the roads of France during the retreat before the German invaders.

However, what the French saw became an ingrained image in their mind's eye. Most of what they saw did not look like any human part they had ever seen. "It was, well, it was, it was just like sausage meat," I have been told by one Frenchman who was there and he continued, "it was just little bits and pieces. Just like the small pieces we made from the pigs, when we were preparing sausage." And, as he was telling me this, he demonstrated by making cutting motions with his left finger against his right arm and hand.

It took some time for the Americans to figure out what they were going to do. They had found a very large door that had fluttered to the ground after the first explosion and they began picking up some of the pieces and putting them on the door.

By this time, people were walking to the crash site from the other villages around. There was at least one person from Cartigny and, we know from the first chapter, about the two boys from Driencourt over the hill, Bernard and Claude Leguillier.

One family who watched the bomber come across the sky and observed its final dive was the Nuttens, who lived just over the small river, Cologne, in Boucly, the attached hamlet to Tincourt. They were lucky, they had a working vehicle and they could drive most of the way to the crash site.

The railroad station of Tincourt-Boucly had been bombed one time, when there was a German train on the siding. Most of the French had observed bomb damage, and yet they were amazed at the size of the crater left by the final explosion of the bomber.

As the newcomers reached the crash site, they asked the people of Tincourt-Boucly what happened and the villagers told and retold their story of the bomber that had streaked across their eastern sky and exploded, crashed and exploded again at the edge of their village.

The Americans must have realized that they could not complete their task before dark by themselves, for they asked all the people to gather and they explained what they wanted the French people to do.

"We all lined up, shoulder to shoulder, in a long line from one point alongside the crater, like the hand of a clock. In a line that must have been 100 meters (over 300 feet) long and we began to circle the crater,"

Bernard, as we already know, picked up the face of a man that fall afternoon. The skin of the face, beginning at the edge of one lip, up around the eye, above the eye brows, across the forehead and back down around the other eye to the other edge of the mouth. About what the mask might look like, that one might wear to a masquerade ball. The nose was there, the eyelids were there, but it was only the skin and some meat of some poor man's face.

Most of the human remains recovered that day, were small remains like we have read, however we now know, that someone did pick up larger pieces that day. It may be, that the reason no French person has ever told me about finding larger pieces, such as a crushed skull, part of a jaw, a shoulder in a tee shirt, a pelvis in a pair of shorts and other larger joints, may be that the Americans had recovered all those larger pieces as they were easier to find, before the French people were asked to join their search.

These large pieces of human remains may have been collected by the Americans and placed on a stretcher in the ambulance before the French began to place remains on the salvaged door and therefore most of the French would be unaware of their existence.

On my last trip to France in 1997, when Bernard and I were reviewing what had happened in 1944, he casually mentioned that the face was located near a somewhat crushed skull.

Even before the search was completed some people began to leave the crash site. Perhaps, they had farm chores that had to be completed. They left the way they had come, in the easiest, straightest line toward home.

Once the search had been completed and the door was stacked high with human remains, the Americans placed the door into the ambulance and drove off.

One Frenchman who had helped in the search was well along on his way home. He was walking through a woods when he heard the sound of an American vehicle coming along the road, not far from the woods. He soon heard the vehicle pull off the road and shut off its engine. Being curious, he walked to edge of the woods, the one closest to the road, and looked to see what the Americans were doing. It was obvious they had not seen him, so he continued to watch them.

He saw them shoveling out a hole alongside the road and he waited for sometime to see just what they were doing. It looked just like the ambulance from the crash site, but then all American ambulances looked alike. They worked for some time at their task and in due time he saw them remove something from the back of the ambulance and carry it to the hole. Soon they were shoveling the dirt back into the hole and when they were done they climbed back into the ambulance, started the engine and drove off.

The Frenchman waited until the ambulance had gone out of sight and then he walked across the intervening field to the roadside. Standing there, he looked around and realized that they had stopped in one of the very few places where the road was out of sight from any of the houses in the nearby villages. The dirt from the freshly dug and covered hole was obvious and he began kicking it aside.

Soon, he reached what he suspected he might find. He had found a collection of small pieces of scorched meat and bone. Meat and bone that looked exactly like the meat they prepared to make sausage. As he had thought while hiding at the edge of the woods, the Americans had actually hidden the human remains of their fellow American airmen. The very remains, they had just recovered at the crash site. The ones, he and so many French people had helped them recover.

As he studied the human remains the Americans had hidden, it must have placed a heavy burden on his mind. I can easily think of many of the questions he had to be asking himself. That is, other than the most simplest one, "Why?"

Did they, the Americans, plan on coming back for them? If so, why didn't they bury them alongside the road at the crash site, as the French had done with their aviators killed during the German attack in 1940? Why didn't they mark the grave, if they planned to come back? Are the Americans hiding their war dead instead of giving them proper burials? It was getting dark and he had his chores to do, he did all he could right then, he kicked the dirt back over the **American Hidden Grave**.

The '**Legends Of The Grave**' I have heard over the past years, gave several versions or routes along which the story passed. This is the one instance in this book that I will take a middle of the map approach and write what I prefer to think happened, instead of what might have happened in several of the legends. There is nothing to be gained by using a lower route, nor a higher route. The outcome of all the supposed routes lead to the same bit of earth along side a road in France, which contained the remains of the American flyers.

Two days after the bomber crashed, the French watched as a large American truck brought a bull dozer to the field at Tincourt-Boucly. It pushed all the bomber remains into the large hole created by the explosion and filled the hole with dirt. It didn't take all that long and the next spring the field and crash site was planted with the new year's crop.

Within the next few days, the leaders of the village of Cartigny, located about five kilometers from Tincourt-Boucly, learned about the hidden grave alongside a road located in their commune borders. All of the above questions had to have been discussed throughly in their many meetings about what to do with the American flyer's remains in the hidden grave.

There were no doubts in their minds who the remains belonged to, they had come from the bomber that had crashed at nearby

Tincourt-Boucly. But, what to do with them was a big question.

It seemed to them, that the Americans must be doing what they had heard the French had done during World War One. That is, hide some of the war dead so that the people will not realize just how many were being killed. It was common knowledge that some five hundred thousand, plus, French soldiers of World War One had never been accounted for. They left home and did not come back, that is all the families ever knew.

The French Unknown Soldier was selected and buried for just this purpose, to give the people with someone missing, someplace to feel that person might be. It helped get the people back to work rebuilding the country and to stop (what the French government considered) wasted effort in the searching for someone who no longer existed.

This village, as had the rest of this Somme region of Péronne, been liberated on the first of September, just over two months before. Most of the people left in the village at this time were either young, old, or infirm.

The young men had gone off to war and were now prisoners doing forced labor in Germany and the young women had been forced into factory jobs.

The village leaders consisted of the mayor, councilors, the policeman, and the one leader who knew all the secrets, the priest, CURÉ Étienne Serpette.

Today, over 50 years later, the village no longer has an active policeman, nor priest. In fact, as the old village priests of France have died, they have not been replaced in most villages. Though most of the French people are Catholic, they no longer support the small village churches, nor local priests. Many of the larger villages and towns still have active churches.

If the hidden grave had contained German aviator remains, most of these Frenchmen would have had a drink and made a decision to just leave them where they were. Hidden forever from the rest of the world.

However, though CURÉ Serpette died in 1960 and I never had an opportunity to talk to him, I think his calling would have been just as strong though even if he knew the remains to be German. Except this book would have never been written, as they would have assured the remains were transferred as soon as possible after the war.

One easy answer to the hidden grave was obvious to them. There was an American World War One Cemetery located at the village of Bony. They would go to the American Cemetery and ask them to bury the remains there.

When they arrived at the cemetery and told their story about the remains. They were told to, "Bring the remains and we will bury them in a grave for the unknown." As I wrote in Chapter Four, The Legends Of The Grave, such a burial was unacceptable to them. For to the French, such a grave means an Ossuary where the bones of many are placed into one mass grave.

To these Cartigny village elders, the American remains represented men who had died for their liberty from the oppressing Germans. In their collective minds, these heroes deserved a grave of their own.

Their biggest problem, they felt, was that a newly liberated people could not accuse their Liberators of hiding their war dead, even though they knew that they had. It could be a great insult to the Americans to accuse them of such a thing, so it was up to the people of Cartigny to provide the American war dead with an honored grave.

On the 23rd of November, 1944, a small group of citizens from Cartigny arrived at the site of the American hidden grave. There they began the task of uncovering the remains and transferring them to the village cemetery of Cartigny, where a new grave had been prepared next to the four French soldiers that had been killed nearby during the French armies retreat before the Germans, four years before.

The remains of the American airmen killed in the crash of the bomber at Tincourt-Boucly were placed in that grave that day, with a Catholic service read by CURÉ Serpette, the priest who had to answer to his calling and who could not let these American airmen lie in a hidden, unmarked grave alongside a small road in northern France. Above the grave, the villagers placed a small wooden cross as a marker, the same as over the French soldier's graves. On the cross was placed the usual medal plaque that stated:

American Avion
INCONNU
23 November 1944

That same day, the priest sat down and wrote out a statement about the grave, one that remained hidden away in the church archives for the next 49 years, 7 months. To protect the people of the village and their decision in the case of a future investigation into the new grave in the cemetery, he wrote the statement in such a manner as to reduce the actual fact, that **the Americans had hidden their war dead**.

Over the next seven years, whenever the Americans came through the area searching for the graves of missing Americans, the villagers kept quiet about the great American shame of hiding their war dead and the grave remained undiscovered by the Americans for 45 years.

On a cold and snowy day in January, 1945, an airplane's engines could be heard above the village of Tincourt-Boucly. It didn't appear to be very high and it circled several times. The noise was loud and it was obvious that one of the engines had problems. People came out of their homes and looked up at the low clouds, straining to see what it was. For they knew the airplane sounded very low and some of the hills around the village were fairly high.

The children and most of the adults listened to the engine sounds and recognized them as those of a B-26 bomber. There was a bunch of them at the Péronne air base and they were fairly used to hearing them.

The bomber continued to circle for around 15 minutes, getting slowly lower and lower. Each time it passed their hearts tended to stop each time an engine ceased to run, however it always seemed to start again. Some remember the last pass it made over the village, it seemed to appear out of the clouds and almost touch the houses as it passed over them for the last time.

Some time later, someone knocked on the door of a farm house near the village of Buirre. When the farm family answered the knock they found a man dressed in aviation clothing.

Unlike the bomber that had crashed a short distance away a few months ago, there were no Americans driving down the roads. Of course, there had not been a great explosion either.

The man asked to use the telephone and when he was done the family decided to call the Nuttens family, as they had the only operating vehicle at the time. Soon, the sound of approaching American vehicles were recognized and the man and family went to meet them. The man got into one of the vehicles and the family began to forget the event until almost 50 years later when the survivor of the B-17 crash came back to France.

Mr. and Mrs. Nuttens drove up the road, past the field where the B-17 crashed, toward Driencourt. When they reached the edge of the Bois de Buirre near the top of the hill, they started across the field alongside the tree-line. After bumping along for a while and looking for a sign of the crash, they saw smoke and a swath cut through the trees and several men. As Mr. Nuttens drove over to the men, the Nuttens could see the crashed bomber burning among the trees.

All the men seemed to be hurt and one had his hands and face severely burnt.

The men were loaded into the vehicle and the Nuttens took them to the hospital in Péronne where they left the men to be treated.

It didn't take long for the children to learn of another bomber that had crashed nearby and soon, they were crawling into and around the bomber.

After about two weeks, several Americans came to the area and talked to some of the men about what they owed for the damage to the woods. The French refused any compensation.

In due time, the Americans came by with a truck and hauled the airplane away and slowly it too faded into memory.

The war would soon end in Europe and all the men and women who had been sent off to prisoner camps and work camps would come home. They became much more interested in the future, than in the past.

After the war, the four French dead were removed and that small section of the cemetery was allowed to be taken over by the border hedge of the cemetery. In due time, the grave and its wooden marker were covered and slowly lost to most of the younger French villagers's memory.

One day in mid-1946 the villagers of Tincourt-Boucly heard several large trucks pull to the side of the road, near where the bomber had crashed two years earlier. One of the light vehicles continued into the village and asked to see the mayor.

The mayor was informed that they were a salvage company and that they had a contract with the United States government to dig up and remove the remains of the B-17, that crashed just to the north of their village.

Soon their large equipment was digging in the spot indicated by the field owner and others. As they dug, they separated the broken bomber parts from the earth and loaded them onto a hauler. They had to dig down fifteen feet before they were able to locate the three engines that had buried themselves that deep from the plunge of the bomber straight down. I expect they spent some time hunting for that fourth engine that had been blown off over Germany.

That day, most of the remains of '*The Lady Jeannette*' were removed from her temporary grave at the crash site to be reborn into coffee pots, skillets, radios and perhaps another airplane. She had served well, she had done her best to remain airborne and she would serve INCONNU (unknown) again and again. Perhaps, somewhere in the world today, someone will be reading this book and a reborn bit of '*The Lady Jeannette*' is within close reach.

Over the years, relic and metal detecting searchers have come again to the crash site, for bits and pieces of the bomber come to the surface yet. Reminders to the French of the terrible war that raged in the air above their homes so long ago.

The young people in the village of Cartigny were not told about the grave at the time and slowly the older people who knew the true secret began to die. If and when, one of the younger people heard of the grave, they were told one of the legends.

Over 20 years were to pass and the brush grew denser, the grave marker rotted through and fell over. However, the grave was not forgotten. One man, Emile Berger, once a member of the French Resistance, reached retirement age and as a member of *Le Souvenir Français* took on the association's task of looking after French war memorials and the graves of French soldiers.

This book would have never been written if Mr. Berger had not decided to honor and maintain the grave of the American flyer. He cut back the brush and found the broken cross lying upon the grave. After cleaning up the area around the grave, he carried in the material to make concrete, he made the forms and mixed and poured the concrete to make the berm that is around the grave today. Once that was done, he covered the grave with plastic to stop the weeds from growing, planted a rose at the foot of the grave and covered the grave with a layer of gravel. Through the *Le Souvenir Français*, he made arrangements with the French government to provide a new French military concrete cross and metal plaque for the grave. On this plaque was written the following:

Aviateur AMERICAIN
INCONNU
MORT POUR LA FRANCE - EN 1943

Correct, except that it indicates only one American aviator was buried in the grave and the date of death is stated as 1943, instead of 1944. It is probable, that even after 20 years, the people of Cartigny were protecting the Americans who had hidden their war dead. For they could always say, that the Germans made them bury the remains in their cemetery during the German occupation. And, if they were ever asked, the villagers had no idea how the Americans missed the grave during Graves Registration sweeps for such graves after the war.

From one Frenchman, I received the following explanation:

"The date was changed and the stories created to protect the village. Plus, to create a reason such a grave existed in a town, where the American Army Air Force was present during November, 1944."

On 11 January, 1980, Mr. Berger was decorated by the *Le Souvenir Français* for his ongoing effort in behalf of the organization's goal of Remembrance. Each year, he visited the grave several times, each time he would clean its surface, smooth the gravel and maintain the rose. He maintained this honored Remembrance of the American Aviators Grave until his death in 1988. He and his wife, are buried close by today.

At the end of another row of graves, not very far away, is the grave of the Priest, CURÉ Étienne Serpette, 1883-1960, who lived in the village under his charge, Cartigny.

When you visit Cartigny's cemetery someday, as we hope you will, to visit the honored grave of our American War Dead, take the time to visit these two graves. CURÉ Étienne Serpette and Emile Berger for they too, honored our dead.

Upon the death of Mr. Berger, another *Le Souvenir Français* member volunteered to take over the maintenance of the grave at Cartigny, even though he lived in another village a few kilometers away.

On Christmas Eve, 1991, he would invite an American and a Frenchman to visit his home, just so he could ask them to visit the grave on their way home. He also asked the American to try to identify the occupant of the grave, so the dead American airman's grave could be marked with his name and the French could especially honor the grave during the Anniversary of the Liberation in 1994.

On that Christmas Eve afternoon, 1991, the two streams of time which separated in 1944, started to merge again and the story of '**The Last Flight Of '*The Lady Jeannette*'**' began to be written.

January 11, 1980. Mr. Emile Berger is honored by his fellow members of the **Le Souvenir Français** with a medal for his service to the association.
Photo: *Le Souvenir Français*

Le Souvenir Français

As you travel throughout France, you will see these medal roundels on tombs and memorials. It is the sign that the **Le Souvenir Français** has accepted responsibility of maintaining that tomb or memorial. It has a red outer ring, white middle ring and blue center.

Chapter Eight
'On The Home Front' - After The Crash
9 November, 1944 - 4 April, 1949

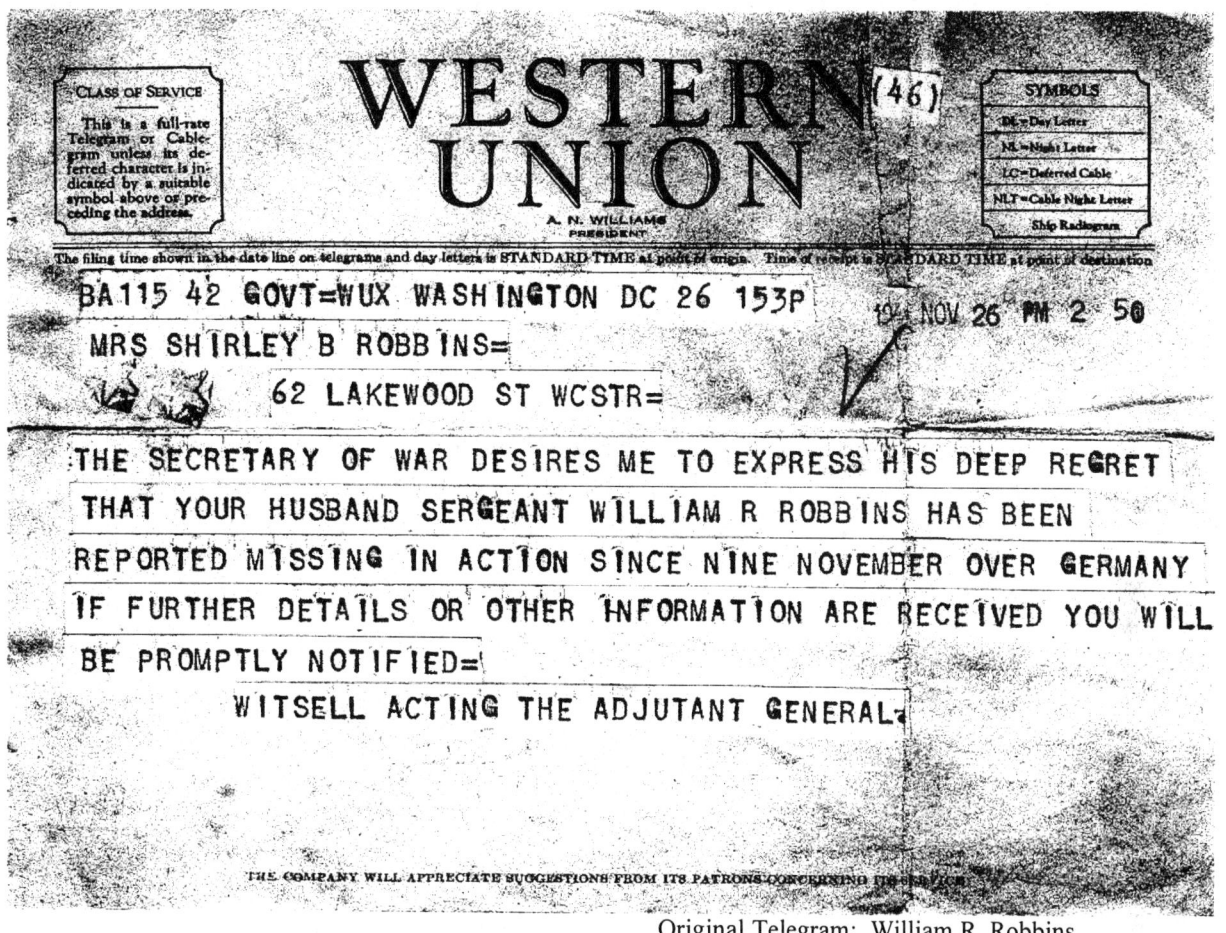

```
WESTERN UNION (46)

BA115 42 GOVT=WUX WASHINGTON DC 26 153P    44 NOV 26 PM 2 50
MRS SHIRLEY B ROBBINS=
    62 LAKEWOOD ST WCSTR=

THE SECRETARY OF WAR DESIRES ME TO EXPRESS HIS DEEP REGRET
THAT YOUR HUSBAND SERGEANT WILLIAM R ROBBINS HAS BEEN
REPORTED MISSING IN ACTION SINCE NINE NOVEMBER OVER GERMANY
IF FURTHER DETAILS OR OTHER INFORMATION ARE RECEIVED YOU WILL
BE PROMPTLY NOTIFIED=
    WITSELL ACTING THE ADJUTANT GENERAL.
```

Original Telegram: William R. Robbins

Neighbors up and down the street looked out and stopped what they were doing as they watched the bicycle move up the street. Many of them felt a catch in their chest as the bicycle approached their house and a great release when it passed. Many of them had someone in the military and the approach of the Western Union bicycle was usually bad news.

The ringing of a doorbell, or a knock at the door had become a dread for many. Several, in their neighborhood had already received such telegrams. Perhaps a loved one had been wounded, perhaps it was a report that they were missing in action and for some, it reported a death.

This time, it may pass them by. This time, their loved one may have had a rendezvous. The usual method of notification was the Western Union telegram, delivered via bicycle.

Many of the homes along the street were marked with in-service banners hanging in their front windows. Each star on the banner represented a family member in the service for their country. They knew this telegram might be for them.

A gold star on the window banner showed the world that this home had lost a loved one to the war.

At each home where the telegrams were delivered, people held their breath as they opened the envelope. Yes, the telegram was from the War Department and yes, it was bad. Still there might be hope, if their man was not reported dead they might breathe easier, as he had been reported as wounded or missing in action. The breath came back and the others present took the telegram in turn and read the words pasted onto the blank form.

On Saturday, the 25th of November, Sunday, the 26th of November, and Monday, the 27th of November, 1944, hundreds and perhaps, thousands of such telegrams were delivered across the length and breadth of the United States, a nation at war. Of those sent, nine went to families of men that were aboard A/C #904. 18 more went to the families of the crewmen aboard A/C 833 and 931.

Far too often, the telegram contained the news that their loved one would never burst into their home again. Home from the ball game, home from school, home from a date, home from the job, or home from the service. They would never come walking into the home again, for they had died while in the service of their nation.

I have been told by my readers that the foregoing is melo-dramatic for a book based on history, such as this. Well, I believe that is the way that the parents thought of their children gone off to war. They remembered the son who came home from the ball game and the daughter who came home from the high school prom. Wives remembered the husband coming home from work and they all remembered the last leave before the one they loved left for overseas. None thought of the loved one among exploding shells and bursting flesh, unless they awoke with panic from a deep, dark dream.

Shirley Robbins went to the door at her mother's call and as her mother's hand gripped her shoulder, Shirley signed for the telegram addressed to her. It was 4 p.m. on Sunday afternoon, the 26th of November, 1944, when the bicycle stopped in front of her parent's house, at 62 Lakewood, Worcester, Massachusetts. Had Bill met his rendezvous?

Shirley slowly opened the telegram as her mother's arm squeezed around her shoulder, providing close and loving support. Tears welled to her eyes as Shirley read the words "MISSING IN ACTION SINCE NINE NOVEMBER OVER GERMANY." Her Bill was gone, missing almost 20 days. She had received a letter just a couple of days ago and he had written of coming home for Christmas and now he was missing. And, he was missing over Germany, even if he had gotten down safely, he would be a prisoner of war.

Shirley's mother led her to the couch and her father gently took the telegram from her hand and read it. He too sat on the couch and holding her hand, told her Bill was a survivor and he would come back.

As Shirley took command of her grief the family prepared to go to Bill's parents house and bring them the sad news.

In Jamestown, New York, at 188 Virginia Boulevard, the home of Edith and William Gustafson, they were prepared when they saw the bicycle arrive and they met the deliveryman just as he started to knock on the door.

When their son, Russell W. Gustafson awoke from the operation on his leg, he found his leg in a full length cast and he was in traction. As he focused, he saw a doctor standing there observing him. The doctor asked him how he felt and presented him with the Purple Heart. Next, he was offered a V-Mail form and he checked the I'm OK message and added his parent's address. The date on his V-Mail message was a great assurance as his parents compared the date given on the telegram form and the V-Mail note.

Elsie Harms, who was Lt. Harm's high-school sweetheart and now his three-months pregnant wife, answered the door of 659 47th Street, Brooklyn, New York, and signed for the telegram. She was living with her parents while Joe was overseas and again, Joe had seen to it that she had been forewarned. Elsie had received her second telegram from him almost two weeks ago, telling her that he was OK and not to worry. The first was after the crash in Iceland, he had written her all about it from the hospital and then, so close after that letter she received his second telegram saying he was OK, again! How many more times, she wondered?

John A. Harland's mother, Ida Miller, read the telegram at her home in Chicago and gained hope in the fact that he was reported missing in action. But, he could be dead!

A few days later she received this letter.

---

29 November 1944
WAR DEPARTMENT
The Adjutant General's Office

In Reply Refer To:
AG 201 Harland, John A.
  PC-N ETO 254

Mrs. Ida Miller
863 Lill Avenue
Chicago, Illinois

Dear Mrs. Miller:

This letter is to confirm my recent telegram in which you were regretfully informed that your son, Second Lieutenant John A. Harland, 0723355, Air Corps, has been reported missing in action over Germany since 9 November, 1944.

I know that added distress is caused by failure to receive more information or details. Therefore, I wish to assure you that at any time additional information is received it will be transmitted to you without delay, and, if in the meantime no additional information is received, I will again communicate with you at the expiration of three months. Also, it is the policy of the Commanding General of the Army Air Forces upon receipt of the "Missing Air Crew Report" to convey to you any details that might be contained in that report.

The term "missing in action" is used only to indicate that the whereabouts or status of an individual is not immediately known. It is not intended to convey the impression that the case is closed. I wish to emphasize that every effort is exerted continuously to clear up the status of our personnel. Under war conditions this is a difficult task as you must readily realize. Experience has shown that many persons reported missing in action are subsequently reported as prisoners of war, but as this information if furnished by countries with which we are at war, the War Department is helpless to expedite such reports.

The personal effects of an individual missing overseas are held by his unit for a period of time and are then sent to the Effects Quartermaster, Kansas City, Missouri, for disposition as designed by the soldier.

Permit me to extend to you my heartfelt sympathy during this period of uncertainty.

Sincerely yours,
Signed

J. A. ULIO
Major General
The Adjutant General
1 Inclosure
  Bulletin of Information

Fross's family was busy at their dairy farm located just outside McAllen, Texas, that late fall afternoon, when the car bearing the Western Union deliveryman drove into the driveway. It brought them the news that their son was missing.

It would have been a friend and it may have been while he was at work, perhaps returning from a late run. It may be Alex was awakened early in the morning by a knock on the door. That friend brought the news of his son's death to Alex Dunlap.

Alex, a railroad conductor and union secretary, learned of his son's death and bore his loss only with friends. They were a close brotherhood of men and the Western Union would not have sent a delivery boy. They would have sent a friend with the grim news the telegram bore.

Alex and his wife, Martha, had separated after Bob had left for England.

He grieved deeply for the son that would no longer come home. Bob had been so proud of his radio skills and he had been planning his future in his letters and now Bob's life had been cut so short over Germany.

Each day Alex's trains carried soldiers, marines, sailors and air corps personnel across broad Montana on their way overseas and

```
WESTERN UNION

BC3 30 GOVT=WUX WASHINGTON DC 26 908P      1944 NOV 27 AM 7 46

ALEX DUNLAP=
SAN JAUN APARTMENT NUMBER ELEVEN CY=

THE SECRETARY OF WAR DESIRES ME TO EXPRESS HIS DEEP REGRET
THAT YOUR SON TECHNICAL SERGEANT ROBERT A DUNLAP WAS KILLED
IN ACTION ON NINE NOVEMBER IN GERMANY LETTER FOLLOWS=
      WITSELL ACTING THE ADJUTANT GENERAL.
```

Alexander and Robert Alexander Dunlap

back home. Alex spent a lot of time with them. Often, the ones returning had been wounded and he had heard many stories of heroism on the ground and in the air. And, Alex had heard the stories of death.

It would be even harder now as he watched the bloom of the youth of America going their ways, for the hope in his heart of looking up and seeing Bob's face at the other end of the car was gone forever.

Alex's wife, Martha, and Bonnie, his youngest daughter, had moved to California to live with his oldest daughter, Io Dunlap Hendron, at Bakersfield, California. Bob had been working there, and living with Io, when he enlisted in the Army.

All these years later, Bonnie Dunlap Owen's face still showed the pain and her voice caught in her throat, when she told me of the day she heard of her brother's death.

She was in school on a windy, cloudy, dark and very dismal Monday, when she was called to her teacher's desk. The teacher had

Bonnie Dunlap and Bob, Christmas, 1943.

Martha Schmitt Dunlap and son, Bob Dunlap.

just returned from the door of the classroom where the teacher had been quietly talking with the principal.

The teacher's face was troubled and in a soft and strained voice, she told Bonnie to collect her things and to go meet her sister at the school's front door. When Bonnie got to the entrance she saw her sister, Io, walking across the play ground toward the school and Bonnie hurried out to meet her.

As she approached Io, Bonnie saw how sad her sister looked and she asked, "Is it Bob?" Her sister could only nod. Bonnie asked, "Is he missing?" Io could only shake her head, as tears streamed from her eyes. Bonnie and Io, held tightly to each other in that school yard for some time and cried for their brother, Bob. After awhile, holding hands they walked slowly back home to share their grief with their mother, Martha.

Herman B. Krimminger's wife, Ida, a medical technician, was on duty at the base hospital when she was called to the front desk. The Western Union deliveryman who was waiting there for her, asked her to sign for the telegram he was holding.

Chemda Indritz, always known as Ida, was a young W.A.C. Private serving at the Sioux Falls Army Air Field, Sioux Falls, South Dakota, when she and Herman were married on Friday, April 14th, 1944.

As Ida read the telegram, her friends in the area began to gather around her, for they all knew what such telegrams meant. They had seen thousands of airmen leave for duty and they had learned of the injury and death of many.

Ida's first thoughts went to Herman's parents, Bessie Autrey and Hugh Carson Krimminger, she was that type of girl. She and Herman had so little time together before he left and now she was his widow.

On their sand and brush ranch, a few miles north of a small dot called Harmon on the Oklahoma map, Joseph and Mary Gott the parents of 1st Lt. Donald J. Gott, received the Western Union Telegram with its notification that their youngest son had been KILLED IN ACTION OVER GERMANY. It had always been at the back of their mind that they could receive such a telegram, but each new letter helped to build their hope of his return in time for Christmas.

Lima, Ohio, was a small city and many, including the Western Union people knew the Metzger family. They knew that Fran, one of the Metzger girls, would be at work at the jewelry store, so they delivered this telegram to her as they didn't want to give the telegram directly to her father. She knew it was bad news about her brother Bill when she signed for it.

She read it and began to cry, the store owner immediately told her to take the rest of the day off and Fran began what seemed to be the longest walk of her life.

The quiet of the day was broken by the grief of 2nd Lt. William E. Metzger, Jr.'s family, at 105 North Baxter Street, Lima, Ohio. His father, William Sr., for whom he was named, and his mother, Ethel, were supported in their grief by their two married daughters, Fran Fredericks and Jean Schofield. This was a home with three stars on the banner as both girl's husbands were overseas.

It had been such a short time ago that the two girls had given their brother the gold I.D. bracelet the day he left for England. Fran had been able to get the bracelet, even in these time of rationing, because of her job and now he was dead.

Each family, those of the missing and those of the dead, began to grieve for their sons, husbands and brothers. The friends and neighbors began to gather and keep them company. They brought food and helped with the chores as best they could. It was war time and these latest casualties, the families, needed their support.

There wasn't much they could do, but wait for the government to provide more information. The following days were hard as they waited. Some may have received letters that were mailed just before the crash. Others, perhaps, received V-Mail from the survivors releasing them from their fears.

Unlike Metzger's original crew, the Gott crew had not been a close crew. They

Jeanne Elizabeth Metzger Scholfield
Frances Louise Metzger Fredericks
The day the girls gave Bill a metal identity bracelet, just before he left home for England.

had not chummed around together and the men did not know the home addresses of all the other crew members. Usually they just knew, "Gus from New York State" or "Dunlap, the Montana cowboy". If they did talk of the crew when they wrote home or perhaps went on leave, it was the same. "Gus the engineer or TTG (top turret gunner)" was a great guy, he is from upstate New York and "Shorty or Fross, ball turret," is a Texan.

Some of the families who did know the address of other crew members, wrote letters to their families to see if they knew what may have happened. I found a letter

2nd Lt. William E. Metzger, Jr., Lima, Ohio. In late September, early October, 1944. Home on leave he took his family for an airplane ride. His sisters gave him an identity bracelet that he would wear to his death and it would return to his home.

STRATO BOWL STARTING PLACE OF WORLD RECORD BALLOON EXPLORER II REACHING 72,395 FT OR 13.71 MI

      Left, standing.   Photo: Sgt. "Tex" Burrell
T/Sgt. Harold E. Burrell "Tex"
      Left, kneeling.
Sgt. Albert E. Wyant, **K.I.A.**
      Right, standing.
2nd Lt. William E. Metzger, Jr., **K.I.A.**
      Congressional Medal of Honor
      Right, kneeling.
Sgt. Edward T. Gorman, **K.I.A.**

written by Mrs. Gott to the mother of Lt. Harland, Mrs. Ida Miller, in Harland's personal papers file. The letter was written two days after their notification of Donald's death and I believe, it well represents the anguish in Mrs. Gott's mind and all the questions those at home had when they received such notification with no supporting information.

     So began a period of longing for the families of the men. If they had received a missing in action notification and they had not received any further notification, they watched intently each day for the mail and less anxiously for the Western Union deliveryman. The next letter may prove their loved one alive, the next telegram may prove he is dead, or with luck, very much alive.

     It did not take the families of the missing men all that long to find out that their servicemen were alive, however it must have seemed an eternity, for they had been reported missing over Germany.

     Of the five men reported missing, Gustafson was the only one left with an ongoing physical problem. His family received a full letter from Russell within a short time, explaining just how bad his broken leg was and that he would be home after spending several months in traction in an Army Hospital, Plant Number 4114, in England. The others had quickly recovered from their physical wounds. However for some, their mental wounds would affect their memory of the event for the rest of their lives.

Within a few days after reading the missing in action telegram, a grieved, nearly heartbroken Shirley Robbins heard a knock on the door. It was the mailman and as all the local people knew about Bill, he was almost as excited as she became, when he handed her a letter from Bill, he had to be alive, the envelope bore a date after 9 November.

Calling to her parents, Shirley read the letter out loud. Bill's plane had come down in friendly territory and he was fine and back at his base. He had tested his rendezvous (death) and he had passed him, still he has his rendezvous. Four of the families received a letter from a man who had become too experienced at writing such letters. Almost every mission, if not every mission, placed such a burden on Chaplin Frank L. Whitney, the 452nd Group's Chaplin. He had to write to the families of the men who were known to be dead and tell them that their son had died. Note the grave reference.

The letters to the Gott, Metzger, Dunlap and Krimminger families were written on the 21st of November, 1944. However, the families did not receive them until after they had received the telegram, bearing the notification of their death over Germany.

During the time from delivery of the notification of death over Germany until the Chaplin's letter was received, they had to have thought their son, brother or husband, was lost somewhere in Germany, without a known grave. I had written this chapter and reviewed it many times, while I hoped to find a copy of the letter that had been saved by one of the families. Just when I had decided to write through the blank space provided for it, I talked to Bonnie Dunlap Owens who had found the letter, which she quickly mailed to me. It arrived, faded somewhat from time, but reproducible. Now I had to make a decision about it. Do I include the letter or not. Was it a valuable item in the history of the event this book is about, or not? I had hoped for a letter with small bits of the reality of the death and official burials of the men.

However, from this distance in time, I instantly see, what to me is obviously what we today we call, a form letter. The letter refers to future information about the location of a grave and the sending of personal effects, however it may be hedged by the restrictions of military security.

The families that received this letter quickly allowed their minds to fill in the blanks required in their personal grief. I decided to include it, as it an example of the non-informational communication with the families of those killed in action that seems to have been the norm.

These men were known to the 452nd Group to have graves in friendly territory at the time this letter was mailed. They were known to have not died *over Germany*, yet the families of these men would for months to come, be torn by the thought that a grave may never be found, or they had to use the reference to a grave in the Chaplin's letter to disbelieve the official notifications of death in the air over Germany. Any real knowledge to the contrary had to come from a friend of the deceased, then an illegal communication.

Alex Dunlap probably wrote his reply just as he received the letter from Chaplin Frank L. Whitney. For he chooses to believe his son, Robert, has a grave somewhere and that his effects would be forwarded. I would like to know how Alex was informed about this supposed burial with the usual military honors.

The Dunlap family has the most complete existing file, of any of the families, of letters, photographs, documents and all the papers the family saved of the events covering the death of T/Sgt. Dunlap, however after reviewing all the families files, I have found no communication which discussed such information being sent to the families by the government.

OFFICE OF THE CHAPLAIN
452nd Bomb Group (H)
A.P.O. 559

21 November 1944

Mr. Alex Dunlap
San Juan Apt. 11
Miles City, Montana

Dear Mr. Dunlap:

The War Department has notified you that your son, T/Sgt Robert A. Dunlap, ASN 39696406, was killed in action.

Pursuant to request from the Commanding General, Eighth Air Force, and in behalf of the officers and men of this station, I wish to extend heartfelt sympathy to you in your great loss. Let me assure you this would be a personal visit, not a letter, if that were possible.

Security regulations prohibit the mention of details, however, The Quartermaster General, ASF, Washington, D. C., will communicate information relative to the location of your son's grave and the disposal of his personal effects, as soon as military security permits.

We deeply regret that Robert was called upon to make the supreme sacrifice for our country and cause. However, we are very proud of his willing and unselfish attitude, in line of duty. The Lord of Life said "Greater love hath no man than this, that a man lay down his life for his friends." His many friends in this organization are determined that he shall not have died in vain.

The burden of sorrow and loneliness which is yours can be carried by no one else. There is one who was described as a "Man of sorrows and acquainted with grief" who is by your side in this hour of great need. He has promised "I will not leave you comfortless; I will come to you." Let us commend Robert unto His loving care, until that day when we shall all meet again in our eternal home, where there are no more partings.

Sincerely

Frank L. Whitney

CHAPLAIN FRANK L. WHITNEY

Arnett, Oklahoma
Nov. 29, 1944

Dear Mrs. Miller,

Your son, John, is navigator on the plane my son Donald was pilot. The have just received a telegram that he was killed on a mission over Germany Nov. 9. Have you any recent word of John. I sincerely hope he is allright. I have only your address and Mrs. R. E. Penick Star Route 1, Lawton, Oklahoma. Her son Earl was bombardier. Have you any address of the other members of the crew.

The last letter we had from Donald was of Nov. 3rd. At that time they had twenty

> five missions and was hoping to be home from there by Christmas. The boys were stationed about forty miles north of London.
>
> I will appreciate any information you might give me as we all want to know what happens to our sons over there.
>
> Sincerely,
> Mrs. J. E. Gott.

---

9 December, 1944
ALEX. DUNLAP, Secretary
1000 Knight St.

Miles City Montana

Brotherhood of Railroad Trainmen

Legislative Board Of Montana
Great Falls, Montana

Chaplain Frank L. Whitney
452nd Bomb Group (H)
A.P.O. 559

My dear Reverend;

I am very grateful for the information in your letter relative to Bob's death. (Robert Dunlap 39696406)

Like every parent I am interested in some detail as to how Bob passed on and where he is buried. I was informed that he was buried with the usual military honors. I am acquainted with most of his crew and if they have not passed on I should like to hear from them in due time. If possible I will have his body sent here after the war. I'm interested in his personal effects and should like to have them shipped home. Among those is a bicycle and an aviation jacket I sent to him a short time ago. If impossible to send all of the effects it may be necessary to dispose of the bicycle. In any case if there is to be an expense I will defray them. It was nice of you to give me the information and I am very grateful to you. It is a month today since he passed on and I have had a heavy cross to bear. My sorrow is deep and heart rending. It's hard.

Thanking you a lot for any information at a time when it is propitious, I am

Very sincerely,
Signed
Alex Dunlap

One can believe, each of the four men's families were reading and rereading the Chaplin's letter, trying to fill the emptiness they felt. The mention of the grave had to give all of them a grasp at a reality that had not been present since the notification of death had been delivered. On December 10th, the missing in action men's families received the telegram bearing the good news, that I'm sure most of them knew by then.

The Western Union deliveryman parked his bicycle near their porch and again rang the bell. Quite without fear, they read of what they knew, Bill had "RETURNED TO DUTY TEN NOVEMBER." And not only that, his latest letter told them he had cleared out of the 452nd Bombardment Group on 22 November, he was on his way home, perhaps by Christmas after all.

Poor Bill, he had been recommended for promotion to T/Sgt. back at the 452nd, however, since he had already checked out, his promotion recommendation of the 23rd of November, could not be favorably considered, by order of Lt. Colonel Batson. Bill would be discharged still a S/Sgt.

We must not forget that on those same days in November, 18 similar telegrams were delivered to the families of the men of the 833 and 931 aircraft. The men's families of A/C 833, including Bill Fannon's family in Connecticut, received telegrams telling them that their serviceman was missing in action on 9 November, over Germany.

Just which notification was sent to the families of the 931 aircraft crew is in question. Only the pilot's remains, Lt. Meyers, was recorded as being recovered. His family would have received notification of his death. The other crew members bodies were never shown in the group records as recovered, so their families may have received only a missing in action notification and they would have had to receive the news about what actually happened from someone at the group writing them. It was sometime after the war ended before many such missing in action were declared legally dead, so the insurance could be paid.

For this book, I have been able to trace the events which took place at the homes of the men aboard **_'The Lady Jeannette_**.' However, at each of these 18 men's homes a family went through the same agony and grief. Please, pause for a moment here and think!

There were so many thousands of families who experienced such anguish. Over 500,000 died before the war ended and the men and women of the United States Of America were home.

At the Fannon home it would be two months before they knew he was somewhat safe. They had received letters from a few of Bill's friends describing what they had seen over Germany as the 833 aircraft spiraled to earth with parachutes blossoming in the sky, Bill might have been one of them, he might be OK, he might not.

One day, Bill Fannon's father looked up from his work as a railroad track man and listened to the voice hollering in the distance. Each man in the crew strained to hear what the fellow was saying as he ran toward them. As the man approached, waving a slip of paper in his hand, Bill's dad recognized him as one of the fellows from the telegraphy office and with a leaping heart he heard the words, "Bill's a prisoner, Bill's a prisoner of war!"

Soon, the telegram was followed up by a letter from the Red Cross listing all the men's names who had been aboard the bomber with Bill and their next of kin's addresses. Letter writing criss-crossed among these families as they offered moral support to each other. A close crew to begin with, this communication of families helped Bill Fannon's crew continue their close relationships after the war.

I am touched, as I again contact all the people whom I have talked to over the years about the subject matter of this book. So few of the people alive in the United States today can fully understand the pressures that the families of service personnel were under when they received such notifications. The country went into World War Two almost totally unprepared to follow up on these notifications and long periods could pass before follow up information arrived.

When the Korean War started, there was a cadre of personnel in the services that were experienced in such matters and by the time the Vietnam War arrived, many of the experienced enlisted men of World War Two had received commissions and were available to help prevent much of the agony of not knowing-personnel, such as retired Col. Butte and Col. Passman, who has since met his rendezvous.

Reading through the family records and Individual Deceased Personnel Files of the four men killed in the crash of '*The Lady Jeannette*.' I found many saved letters and newspaper articles which helped me better understand the families need to find out what happened to their loved one. I have enclosed a selection of these letters, for they tell the story much better than I.

The friends of men killed in action might write the family of a friend and tell them the events around their loved ones death. Given the conditions of war and the friend's feeling for the family, these letters often painted the best possible picture instead of the grim reality.

The following newspaper article was provided to me, by Winona Derrick, a niece of Lt. Gott. It does not show in what newspaper it was printed or what date. I assume, it was a local paper, in December, 1944.

Mr. and Mrs. J. E. Gott received a letter from Lieut. Jerry Collins, co-pilot of the plane on which their son, Donald Gott, killed in action over Germany, lost his life. Donald gave his life in an attempt to save his radio man who was unconscious after others members of the crew had bailed out. The letter from Lieut. Collins follows:

Lieut. Collins O-771814
728 Sq-452 B. Gp
APO 559 %P.M. New York City
December 6, 1944

Mr. and Mrs. Gott
Arnett, Oklahoma

Dear Folks:

In case Don has never mentioned it, I'm the co-pilot on his regular crew. We flew through quite a few combat missions together, and I know what a great level headed pilot he was.

On the day the unfortunate accident happened, I was flying in a plane right next to Don's. When the crew returned, I found out that Don had sacrificed his life trying to land the plane after the others had bailed out.

The radio man was unconscious and couldn't get out, so Don with his great devotion to his crew tried to land the burning plane to save the radio man.

I'm writing this, because I thought you would like to know how it happened--and if there is anything I can do over here for you, let me know.

May I extend my sincere sympathy to you folks at your great loss.--Jerry Collins.

This is just one of the letters Collins wrote to crew member's families. Apparently, he was not supposed to write such letters, as you <u>will read</u> in Lt. Green's letter of May, 45.

The months passed slowly for the families. The war continued and every effort had to be toward helping bring the war to an end and to get the boys and girls home. Information regarding those who had been killed in action, often had to be pried out of the government.

Dear Sir: (Copy in record)   Dec. 14 (44)

About three weeks ago I received word from the War Department that my husband,

Sgt. Herman B. Krimminger, 34890339, A.C. was killed in action over Germany 9 Nov. Five weeks have now passed since the accident and I have received no more news other than the telegram and letter.

Today I received a package which I sent him with your name and the mark "deceased". I would appreciate very much if you would send me some additional information concerning his case. You see, I expected word from his crew as I was acquainted with them--but I received none. Or, I expected if the government was sure I would have received more definite word. Could you tell me as fully as possible what happened and how definite the proof is.

It is only natural that my mind is not at ease about the matter for no further news has been sent me. I realize that military secrecy & knowledge may be limited to some degree, but I would appreciate any material you could offer me.

Also, I should like to know about his possessions in the barracks--when and what I shall receive.

Thank you kindly and I hope I shall soon hear from you.
        Pvt. Ida Krimminger A-610423
        Section D, SFAAG
        Sioux Falls, S.D.

During my conversations with Robbins, he has told me about his trip home. "I didn't get home in time for Christmas, 1944, as I had hoped. I missed it by three days. The ship I boarded on the 19th of December, zig-zagged east and west and north and south. It seemed to go every way but toward the U.S. It seemed to take forever to get home."

Robbins followed up by saying, "The worst part was when I arrived on December 27th, I had lost all my money in a card game, that I'm quite certain now was rigged. I was lucky though, I ran into Lt. Collins at the depot. He must have flown back, because he arrived the same time as I did. Well, I hit Collins up for a loan and he gave me ten bucks. I got his address and I did send him that ten dollars later."

I left Fort Devon, Massachusetts, for home on the 28th of December and had a grand homecoming.

Sgt. Fross had a return trip that took even longer. His Honorable Discharge shows he got on a ship the 13th of December and he arrived back in the U.S.A. on Christmas Day, 1945. Well, he had made it back to the U.S. for Christmas, the only crewman to do so. Except he was two thirds the way across country from his home.

Second Lt. Harland was somewhere in the pipeline during the month of December, also on his way back to the U.S. I don't know what his schedule was.

December 31, 1944

Dear Sir:
        The 27th of November, I was informed that my husband, Sgt. Herman B. Krimminger 34890339, was killed in action over Germany the 9th of Nov.

I have since received no details concerning this accident nor any word from his crew. I am writing to ask if you would please tell me something about the matter and how definite the evidence for such a report you have in your records.

I realize the limitations in divulging any such military affairs at present and I would appreciate any small bit of information you would be able to supply.

I wonder also if you would let me know how to contact the members of the crew member's families in the States.

Thank you kindly,
Sincerely,
Mrs. H. B. Krimminger

Ida's letter of December 31, 1944, became very important in my being able to complete my research. When I had reached a dead end in each of my searches for several of the crew members, Ida's letter and the reply opened up new paths that quickly lead to success.

In newspapers around the country, there were articles printed about the men and the bomber. In all of the newspaper articles I have read, the name given the bomber is correct. In most instances the name is given only as the '**Lady Jeannette**' and not as '*The Lady Jeannette.*'

That scripted name, in red, across the nose is ingrained in the memory of T/Sgt. Gustafson. He distinctly remembers the word '*The*' in the name. Until I can disprove his memory, I will continue to use the full name of the bomber as, '*The Lady Jeannette*' (February 11, 1998).

Reading these articles introduces us to the effects of time and situation. There are some statements in the articles that are not true and others that are true--well known at that time and forgotten by most today. There was a B-17 in the 452nd Group called "**Snake Eyes**." Almost every saved article I have seen states the person written about flew aboard "Snake Eyes."

Apparently the person submitting these articles to the men's home town newspaper used that name as a standard name for a B-17 the men served on.

The following is a newspaper article given me by Bill Robbins. It does not have the name of the newspaper or date printed. It was released in England, over a month after Sgt. Robbins had left the group and he had already returned home to Worcester.

Fortress Gunner Tells Of Crash
An Eighth Air Force Base, England Jan 8

S-Sgt William R. Robbins, 24, of 62 Lakewood street, Worcester, Mass., waist gunner on the Flying Fortress "Lady Jeannette" has been awarded a third Oak Leaf Cluster to the Air Medal for "Meritorious achievement" while participating in bombing assaults against Nazi industrial installations in the toughest theater of aerial warfare.

The Worcester airman is a member of the 452nd Bomb. Group, a unit of the Third bombardment Division--The division that received a Presidential citation for its now historical England-Africa shuttle bombing of Messerschmitt aircraft plants at Regensburg, Germany.

Sgt. Robbins considers the attack against a vital marshaling yard in Saarbrucken, Germany, his toughest mission.

"We were getting along all right until flak caught us over the target," he recalled. "Two engines were knocked out and set afire, a third badly damaged, the electrical interphone systems destroyed and two of the crew, the top turret gunner (engineer) and radio operator wounded.

Badly Wounded Men

"The engineer's leg had been broken and the co-pilot applied first aid to his wound, but the radio man's wound was of an even more serious nature," said Sgt. Robbins. "His hand had been blown off at the wrist. The ball turret gunner and I tried to stop the flow of blood with a tourniquet and by applying pressure to the arteries of his arm. However, it did not help very much. Luckily, he was unconscious and not suffering any pain."

The pilot attempted to keep our plane in formation long enough to drop our bombs, but the one remaining engine wasn't sufficient to carry the load and 'Lady Jeannette' began to loose altitude rapidly. It was necessary to

Sgt. William R. Robbins

throw out every bit of moveable equipment to keep the fort airborne.

"Turning toward France, the pilot ordered us to prepare to bail out as soon as friendly territory was reached," said Sgt. Robbins. "Since the interphone was out, the co-pilot went from man to man giving him the instructions verbally. By this time we were down to 10,000 feet and as we crossed the German border, we were hit again by anti-aircraft fire."

"When the time came to abandon 'Lady Jeannette,' the co-pilot gave the top-turret gunner his 'chute' because the gunner's had been soaked with hydraulic fluid and was useless. He then helped him out through the nose of the plane. Both pilot and co-pilot chose to stay and land the Fort to secure medical aid for the wounded radio man."

Sgt. Robbins remembers the long trip earthward:

"It was like flying in a void - just a gray mist - you couldn't see anything. However, I didn't have to worry about landing in German lines.

I learned later that evening 'Lady Jeannette' had exploded as she was coming in for a landing," said Sgt. Robbins, "also that our tail gunner had been killed when his parachute caught on the tail of the plane."

The son of Mr. and Mrs Charles R. Robbins of 5 Freedom Terrace, Worcester, he was a shipping clerk for Coghlins, Inc., before entering the AAF in April, 1942. His wife, Mrs. Shirley B. Robbins, lives at the Lakewood Street home.

Among the few personal items that Bill Robbins brought home with him, along with the 'D Ring' that saved his life, was a small pocket notebook. Attached to the notebook with tape is a square paper tag with a large hole in it, written in ink in block type is the name Robbins. Despite the best of plans and having his stuff in his duffel bag aboard the bomber, he forgot to take the bag with him when the time came to bail out of the wounded bomber. In the book he has listed his missions. (The numbers are mine.)

* * * *

1. Aug. 27 - Berlin - (Recall) Lost
2. Sep. 2 - Frankfort - " Weather
3. " 9 - Dusseldorf
4. " 13 - Ludwigshafen
5. " 17 - Arnheim - Holland
6. " 19 - Weisbaden
7. " 21 - Ludwigshafen
8. " 25 - " (Col.)(No.5)
9. " 27 - Mainz
10. " 28 - Merseburg (Staff/Feather#4)

Merseburg, bombs on target.   Photo: S/Sgt. Robbins

11. " 30 - Bielefeld
12. " 2 - Kassel
13. " 3 - Nürnberg
14. " 5 - Münster
15. " 6 - Berlin
16. " 12 - Bremen
17. " 14 - Cologne (No Bombs)
19. " 18 - Kassell
20. " 25 - Hamburg
21. " 26 - Hanover
22. " 30 - Merseburg Recall)
23. Nov. 2 - Merseburg
24. " 4 - Neunkirchen
25. " 5 - Ludwigshafen
26. *" 9 - Saarbrucken*

(His list ends at 25, I added number 26)
At the bottom of his page is: "That's All Jack!!"

His last flight qualified Robbins for a membership certificate that declared him an official member of the Caterpillar Club given to all the men who used the company's parachute to save their life.

In January, 1945, 2nd Lt. Penick who missed the last flight was shipped back to the

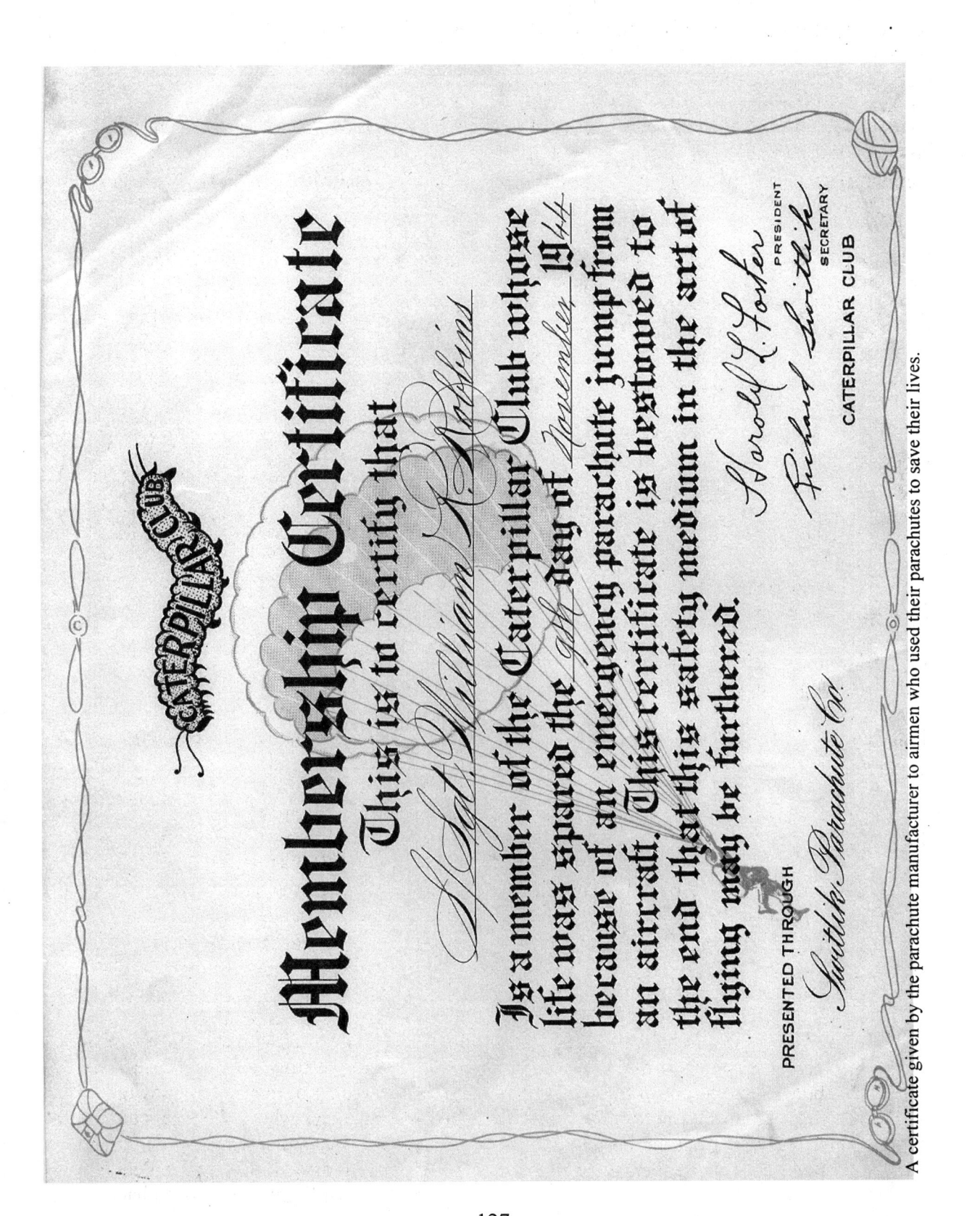

United States and he was soon discharged and returned home.

Membership Certificate

This is to certify that S/Sgt. William R. Robbins is a member of the Caterpillar Club whose life was spared the 9th day of November 1944 because of an emergency parachute jump from an aircraft. This certificate is bestowed to the end that this safety medium in the art of flying may be furthered.

Harold L. Foster, PRESIDENT
Richard Switlik, SECRETARY
CATERPILLAR CLUB

PRESENTED THROUGH Switlik Parachute Co.

A certificate given by the parachute manufacturer to airmen who used their parachutes to save their lives.

Arnett Okla.
Jan. 28. 1945.

Mrs Ada Miller.
　　Dear Friend -
　　I have heard some of the crew is coming home on a furlough anytime now. who was on Ronalds plane. and I wondered if your son has come home. if so would you write and tell me what he knew about Ronald and the way his plane went down. and was your son on plane at time it was hit. would be so glad if you would let us know. and what was the name of radio boy who lost his life. when Ronald did.? also the name of rest of crew. and if he knows the adresses of their parents.
　　We have heard no more from the Government about Ronald. but we

> would like to hear from you
> if you could tell us something
> about. However I did hear from
> Government they was sending
> us the Purple Heart.
>
> Thanking you for any
> information you can write us.
>
> Your Friend.
> Mrs J E Gott
> Arnett. Okla.
>
> I'm sending this to your old address
> I see you have a new address but it is
> blured on outside of envelope.
>
> And did your son say if he knew
> if Ronalds body was buried or not.

    Back in the Z.I., all the men were first assigned to bases where a combination of training and rest and recuperation occupied their time. After this training period they were shipped throughout the country.
Note: In England, after his first few missions, when he felt more comfortable with the missions and flak, S/Sgt. Robbins had volunteered to carry a group camera. Some pictures in this book are his proof copies of those photographs, explaining the damage to them. Several of his photographs are used in many aviation history books, credited to the 452nd Bomb Group.

Lawton, Oklahoma   Jan. 23, 1945
Mrs. J. E. Gott
Dear Friend:

    I will write a few lines this morning to let you know I haven't found out any more about Donald as Earl hasn't come home yet. But, we are looking for him right away & if he knows anything about it will let you know.

    I don't have the address of any of the boy's folks as Earl didn't talk about them much. The only thing I knew at all about any of the boys was how much he liked Donald & Jerry. Said, they went to London on pass several times. Said, one time it cost the three of them $16.00 a night for a room.

    You see, Earl was supposed to go across sooner than he did. But had sinus trouble and didn't pass the over-seas test and they told him they would treat him for it and than maybe he could go. So, that's why we didn't know much about Don and the crew he went over with. But, the other crew he trained with at Alexandria, La., we knew nearly all the boys, that is by him talking about them. I have a picture of all of them with their plane. But don't have anything of the crew he went over seas with.

    My second boy has gone over now and the last one will go into combat next month he tells me. He's the one in the Navy. Well, Mrs. Gott, I sincerely, hope you can find out more and if I can find out anything at all, I'll sure let you know. Just write anytime you feel like it and I'll be glad to answer you.

Sincerely, a friend,
Mrs. Penick

    It's almost the end of January, 1945, over two months since '***The Lady Jeannette***' went down and the families are still trying to find out what happened to their sons.

    Mrs. Gott is writing desperately to everyone she can, to find some shred of information to assuage the hopelessness she is feeling everyday. And, she is just one mother of the hundreds of thousands of mothers in the United States that were facing the loss of their sons and daughters.

    Apparently, the country was very busy winning the war and quick follow up could not be done. The soldier was called a G.I. (Government Issue) for good reason. They were replaced off the shelf with another issue coming up the line, item by item.

    Mrs. Gott and Mrs. Metzger were writing back and forth, however I have no preserved letters from Mrs. Metzger until much later in the year.

    By the end of January, 1945, Mrs. Gott was receiving bits and dabs of information, but still no direct communication that told her the Donald had died in France and that he had an official grave. She turned again to writing letters to the family members whose addresses she had.

    Two months after her last letter of December 31st, 1944, and still without any news of her dead husband, Sgt. Krimminger, Ida decided to improve her chance of getting the information she wanted so badly. Her brother, Phineas Indritz, was an Army Air Force Officer, and Ida thought that an officer writing might get an answer when a lowly enlisted person may not. So Ida contacted Phineas and asked that he write a letter in her behalf, requesting the necessary information.

---

8 February   C.D. AAF, ATSC
                              Box 1318
                              Detroit, 31 Michigan
Memorial Division Graves Registration Division
Office of the Quartermaster General
War Department
Washington, 25 D.C.

Gentlemen:

    My sister, a member of the W.A.C., received a telegram from the War Department about the end of November 1944 informing her that her husband, Staff Sergeant Herman Krimminger, 34 890 339, a gunner on one of the 4-engine bombing planes in the 729th Bomb. Sq., 452nd Bomb. Gp. (H), APO 559, New York, was killed in action on 9 November, 1944. None of us have been informed of the circumstances, his place of burial, or any other information.

My sister has been very broken up by this news, since she and her husband were very attached to each other. Her grief, doubled by the recent death of our Father, has been accentuated by the gnawing uncertainty and ignorance of the precise facts and circumstances of her husband's death, and his place of burial. I am therefore taking the liberty of writing this letter to ask you to assist in assuaging to some extent the deep anguish of my WAC sister by supplying some further information as to his place of burial and the circumstances of his death. In addition to his place of burial, I should like to know the details of my brother-in-law's death, including whether he was killed by flak, gunfire, drowning or crash; to what place was he on mission (if not restricted information); whereabouts did his death occur; whether he died of wounds previously received; and any other information concerning him or his death.

I shall certainly appreciate your help in alleviating, at least the extent of dispelling the constant uncertainty of lack of facts, our pain of bereavement.

Sincerely yours,
Phineas Indritz
2nd Lt., Air Corps

Three months have passed since the families of the dead learned about the death of their loved one. Yet, they are still grasping to find out what happened. I would have thought that the first thing any returning original crew member would have done is attempt to reach the families of the crew to either find out what happened to their loved one who survived or to tell the family of a dead crew member what they knew, this apparently did not happen.

Gustafson got home, but since he did not have the addresses of the crew, he was unaware of what was happening with them. Later, he remembers some communications. However, they seem to have been driven by Sgt. Krimminger's wife, Ida, when she later received the addresses of the crew and they did not remain in contact.

It is interesting for me, to see the men of the group at the 452nd Bomb Group Association reunions react to each other. One would not think, when observing them at the reunions now, that there were close crews and **unclose** crews 'over there.'

The Miles City Daily Star
(Sometime in late February, 1945)

* * * *

GIVES HIS LIFE IN DEFENSE OF COUNTRY

Under date of Dec. 28, 1944, Secretary of War Henry L. Stimson in his communication to Alex Dunlap, Apt. 11, San Juan Apartments, Miles City, advises him that President Roosevelt requests that the father of Technical Sergeant Robert A. Dunlap be informed that the Purple Heart was awarded to the Miles City soldier posthumously.

Accordingly, the Purple Heart was awarded posthumously to Sgt. Dunlap on Feb. 14th for military action and for wounds received in action on Nov. 9, 1944

Remembrances of the supreme

sacrifice made by Sgt. Dunlap were continued by the awarding of the Citation of Honor, U. S. Army Air Forces, to T-S Robert A. Dunlap, "who gave his life in the performance of his duty on Nov. 9, 1944, and signed by H. H. Arnold, General, U. S. Army, Commanding General of the Army Air Forces.

The record also shows that on Nov. 27, 1944, the War Department, through the office of the Adjutant General, James A. Ulio, forwarded a telegram to Alex Dunlap, father, advising that his son, Sgt. Robert A. Dunlap, was killed in action on Nov. 9, 1944, in Germany.

In mid-October last year Lt. Col. Burnham L. Batson of Manchester, Conn., commander of an Eighth Air Force B-17 Flying Fortress Group announced the promotion of Sgt. Dunlap to the grade of staff sergeant, radio operator and gunner on the Fortress "Snake Eyes." Sgt. Dunlap was a member of the 3rd Bombardment Division which was cited by the president for its historic England-Africa shuttle bombing of a Messerschmitt aircraft factory at Regensburg, Germany.

Shortly thereafter, announcement was made that Sgt. Dunlap was awarded the Air Medal for "meritorious achievement" while participating in numerous heavy bombardment attacks deep within the heart of Germany. The group flew in the toughest theater of aerial operations of the war, attacking such targets in such German cities as Bremen, Hamburg, Hanover and Frankfort.

A delayed item of information forwarded and received in Miles City after receipt of news of the death of Sgt. Dunlap, recited that he, as radio operator and gunner of "Snake Eyes," a B-17 Flying Fortress of the 452nd Bombardment Group was awarded a second Oak Leaf Cluster to the Air Medal for "Meritorious Achievement" while taking part in 8th Air Force bombing attacks on vital German targets and on Nazi military strong points in support of advances by Allied ground forces.

Flying in what was considered the toughest theater of aerial warfare, Sgt. Dunlap helped his bomber fight its way through severe enemy opposition to attack such objectives as the marshaling yards at Ludwigshaven and synthetic oil refineries at Merseburg, Germany.

On the 22nd of February, 1945, the longest overseas serving member of the crew of '*The Lady Jeannette*' was loaded aboard a hospital airplane to begin his trip home. Still in a full leg cast, but healed well enough to be brought home, T/Sgt. Russell W. Gustafson was heading home to the States.

On the 25th of February, he arrived at the Tilton General Hospital, Fort Dix, New Jersey, where he was to spend much of the next seven months.

Photo: S/Sgt. William R. Robbins
Don't drop on us, please! Compare to engravings on crash site and grave memorials.

Ida Krimminger was the first family member to find a grave location, thanks to the letter written by her brother. It must have helped to be an officer, for Phineas's letter was answered earlier than Ida's letter.

SPQYG 293　　　　　　　　4 May 1945
Krimminger, Herman B.
S.N. 34 890 339

Lieutenant Phineas Indritz
C.D., AAF, ATSC1318
Detroit 31, Michigan

Dear Lieutenant Indritz:

Your letter of recent date requesting information concerning your brother-in-law, the late Sergeant Herman B. Krimminger, has been received in this office.

The official report of interment received in this office reveals that the remains of your brother-in-law were interred in the United States Military Cemetery, Limey, France, Plot E, Row 7, Grave 163.

A copy of your letter has been forwarded to the Adjutant General, Washington, 25, D.C., for direct reply to you. That office has jurisdiction over information concerning the circumstances surrounding the death of military personnel.

Please accept my sincere sympathy in your great bereavement.

FOR THE QUARTERMASTER GENERAL:
Sincerely yours,
MAYO A. DARLING
Lt. Colonel, QMC Assistant

Approximately six months after Sgt. Krimminger's death, Ida's brother had forced out the information stating where Herman was buried.

The families must have received an accompanying explanation letter with the following pictures, however I have not located one. From letters I have read, between involved families, they seem to have been given the information as to who was buried on each side of their loved one, to make finding the grave easier in case of a visit.

Today, you will only get the grave location for the person of your inquiry with the name of the cemetery, the plot, row and grave number.

You can receive a picture of the grave of a loved one in an overseas cemetery and you can make arrangements to have the grave decorated with flowers on Memorial Day. Included in the cost of the flowers, is a picture of the grave with the flowers. Visitors do see the flowers and appreciate them.

Because Ida had known the original members of the crew and she had an inquiring mind, it appears that she followed through using all the information contained in the letter she received a few days later, in answer to her letter of December 31, 1944.

One which opened up the channels of communication which would help all the families learn just what had happened, even though it was still not to be an easy route. As near as I can deduct, Ida contacted every surviving crewman or their surviving family, including Sgt. Irving Hirsch.

Private First Class Ida Krimminger, A-610423
Section D, Sioux Falls Army Air Field
Sioux Falls, South Dakota

Dear Private Krimminger:

Your letters addressed to an overseas installation in which you request further information concerning your husband, Sergeant Herman B. Krimminger, have been forwarded to this office for reply.

The distress you suffered since you received the sad announcement of your husband's death is most understandable and, realizing your desire to know the attending circumstances, I wish to advise you that an additional report has been received in the War Department. This report states that Sergeant Krimminger was killed in action on 9 November 1944, when the aircraft of which he was tail gunner was hit by flak and made a crash landing in France. Five members of the crew survived, and in compliance with your request, their names and the names of their emergency address are furnished, as follows,

Mrs. Elsie Harms
659 47th Street
Brooklyn, New York
Wife of Second Lieutenant
Joseph F. Harms, 02056698

Mrs. Ida M. Miller
863 Lill Avenue Chicago, Illinois
Mother of Second Lieutenant
John A. Harland, 0723355

WILLIAM E. METZGER O-558834

DONALD J. GOTT 0-763996

Mrs. Cecille Fross
808 B.C. Avenue
McAllen, Texas
Mother of Staff Sergeant
James O. Fross, 38462533

Mr. Axel Gustafson
188 Virginia Boulevard
Jamestown, New York
Father of Technical Sergeant
Russell W. Gustafson, 12139229

Mrs. Shirley B. Robbins
62 Lakewood Street
Worcester, Massachusetts
Wife of Sergeant William B.
Robbins, 11051000

The following military personnel, associated with Sergeant Krimminger on 9 November 1944, were killed in action on that date:

Joseph Gott
Rural Route
Arnett, Oklahoma
Father of First Lieutenant
Donald J. Gott, 0763996

Mrs. Ethel Metzger
105 North Baxter Street
Lima, Ohio
Mother of Second Lieutenant
William E. Metzger, Jr,
0558834

Mr. Alex Dunlap
San Juan Apartment #11
Miles City, Montana

Father of Technical Sergeant
Robert A. Dunlap, 39696406

The Quartermaster General, Washington 25, D.C., has jurisdiction over all matters pertaining to the burial and to the personal effects of our military personnel who die overseas and I am, therefore, forwarding a copy of your letter to that official for direct reply to your inquiries regarding these matters.

I realize how futile any words of mine may be to assuage your grief but I trust that the knowledge of your husband's valiant service and heroic sacrifice in action may be a source of comfort and pride to you.

You have my heartfelt sympathy in your bereavement.

Sincerely yours,
Signed
J.A. ULIO
Major General
The Adjutant General of the Army
Copy for Quartermaster General.

Finally personal effects began to be returned to the home of the men. The first went to Alex Dunlap in Miles City, Montana.
ARMY EFFECTS BUREAU INVENTORY
12 May 1945   1 Package Tally No.7713

Robert A. Dunlap
39696406   T/Sgt.   304,746

1 package Box No. 10
Inventory - checked
Report - checked
GR label - checked
Billfold, book, short snorter bill
Inventoried by: Curley
shipped June 13, 1945

The billfold had arrived at the effects bureau in Kansas.

In May, 1944, the families of 1st Lt. Donald Joseph. Gott and 2nd Lt. William Edward Metzger, Jr. were notified that their

T/Sgt. Bob Dunlap's 'Short Snorter Bill,' signed by the men aboard their bomber as a "Lucky Piece" when leaving for overseas. They flew aboard a B-17G, Sn: 43-488184 on the North Atlantic crossing. Names and partial names visible: Bob Dunlap, Irvin Hirsch, Russell Gustafson, Earl L. Penick, Glenn T. Fuller, Herman B. K(rimminger), JA H(arland) and Bill Robbins. This is one of two surviving personal relics from the November 9, 1944, crash. It was found in the wallet of T/Sgt. Robert A. Dunlap, found at the crash site and returned to the family. The other pieces of paper and the wallet were lost over the years as the family did not recognize the importance of these items until I contacted Bonnie Dunlap Owens about them in November, 1997. The fate of the bomber, Sn: 43-488184, is covered in Chapter 12.

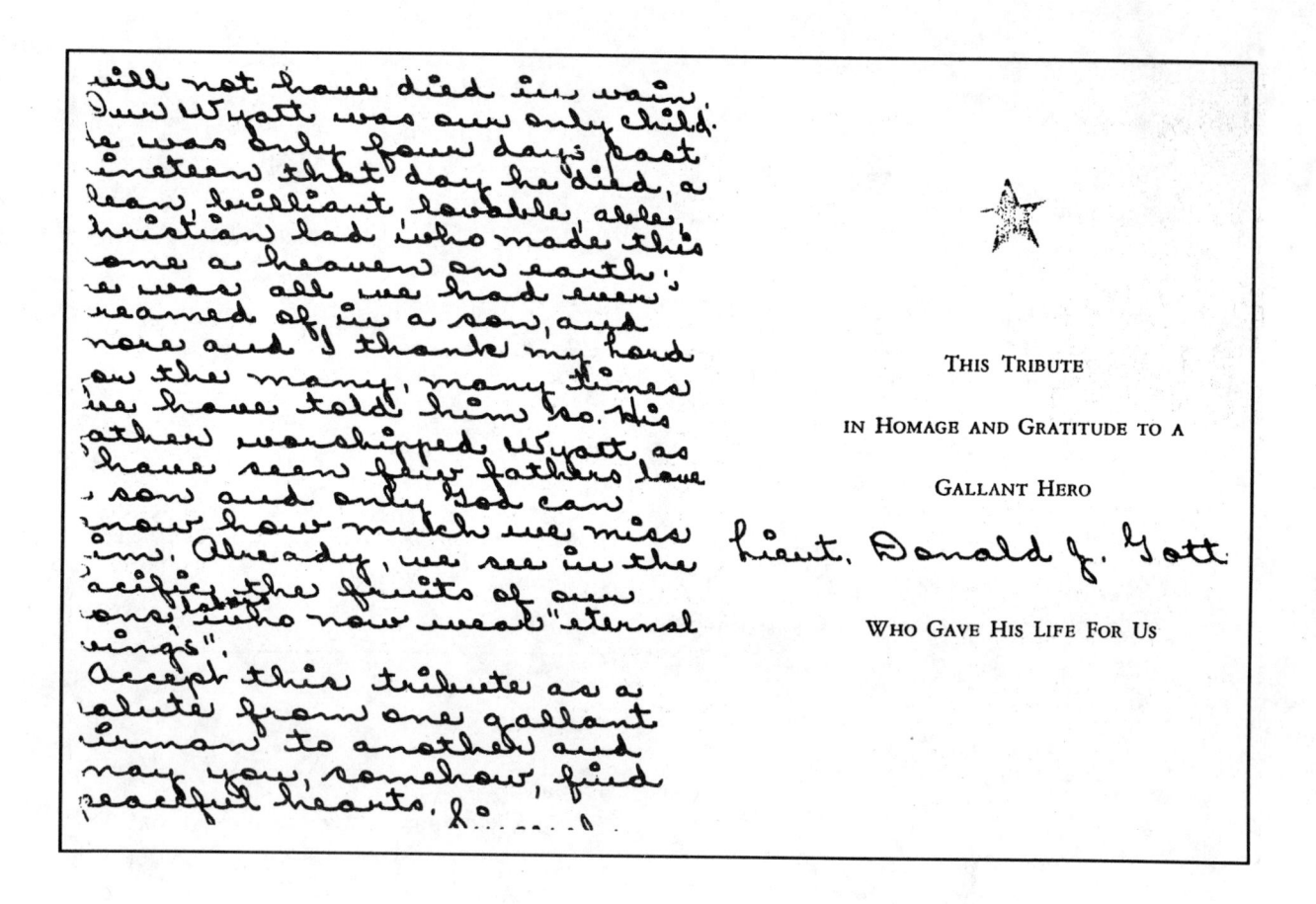

> ...will not have died in vain. Our Wyatt was our only child. He was only four days past nineteen that day he died, a lean, brilliant, lovable, able Christian lad who made this home a heaven on earth. He was all we had ever dreamed of in a son, and more, and I thank my Lord on the many, many times we have told him so. His father worshipped Wyatt as I have seen few father's love a son and only God can know how much we miss him. Already, we see in the Pacific the fruits of our son, who now wears "eternal wings".
> Accept this tribute as a salute from one gallant airman to another and may you, somehow, find peaceful hearts, too......

THIS TRIBUTE

IN HOMAGE AND GRATITUDE TO A

GALLANT HERO

Lieut. Donald J. Gott

WHO GAVE HIS LIFE FOR US

sons had been awarded the **Congressional Medal Of Honor** on General Order 38, 16 May 1944, for their devotion to duty during **'the last flight of 'The Lady Jeannette.'**

Though the medals were awarded on orders of 16 May, 1944, the knowledge they had been approved was forwarded earlier to the 8th Air Force Headquarters in England and made available to news organizations.

The following newspaper clipping, was sent to Sgt. Robbins. It was printed in the **Miles City Star**, on May 12, 1945.

DUNLAP, MILES CITY IS ALSO INCLUDED

U.S. 8th Air force Hdqs. May 11-(AP)

The Medal Of Honor has been awarded posthumously to two pilots of a Flying Fortress who gave their lives trying vainly to save a crewman.

Recipients were Lt. Donald J. Gott, 21, Arnett, Okla., and Lt. William E. Metzger, 22, Lima, Ohio.

The fliers died last Nov. 9 after their bomber 'Lady Jeannette' was ripped by flak over a rail yard at Saarbrucken.

Gott the pilot, ordered the crew to bail out. One whose leg was broken used the parachute of Metzger, the co-pilot, because his own was damaged. The radio operator-gunner lost his right hand at the wrist and was hurt too badly to parachute.

The pilots elected to stay with him and try to land.

The plane blew up a few hundred feet off the ground, killing Gott, Metzger and the gunner.

The other crewmen--except the tail gunner who was killed when his parachute caught on the tail of the plane and ripped off his back - now are back in the United States.

They include Sgt. Robert A. Dunlap, Miles City, Mont., radio operator.

Again the name of the bomber does not include the leading 'The.' Apparently cutting of the article by the newspaper tends to show that Sgt. Dunlap had returned to the

IN MEMORY
OF
LIEUT. WYATT F. HUNDLEY
BOMBARDIER
U. S. ARMY
AIR CORPS

KILLED IN ACTION
NEW GUINEA
JANUARY 7, 1943

There's a picture I see, 'tis a fair-haired boy,
It's engraved on my heart today
And the prayer I breathe to the Maker of men
Is a prayer that the image may stay.

May the wounds grow less sharp and my grief allay,
May the skies grow fair and as blue
As the eyes of my lad, in khaki clad
Who rests in New Guinea today.

May my spirit grow in service to those
Who have given their sons, and may
The pain fade away and the picture stay
That's engraved on my heart today.

RUTH FAHN HUNDLEY (MOTHER)
April 18, 1943.

---

17 May 1945

Dear friends; You have lost a heroic dear one, Donald, and my heart aches for all you who loved him. I know what it means to lose a beloved so and I know, too, what it means, months afterward, to face each day anew, standing guard over the portals of my heart lest I betray to the world that the pain and the anguish have never lessened. You have laid a costly sacrifice upon the altar of freedom and while the grief is singularly your own, to do with as best you can, the loss is not yours alone; it is all America's loss; it is mine; it is my next door neighbor's. May I, now any free American, never prove unworthy of the great gift of life itself that Donald has given. Perhaps if we do not live in vain, he

---

U.S., instead of being among the four dead.

The following article, from the Bill Robbins collection, would have been printed in a Lima, Ohio, newspaper. Probably the local newspaper, today named, *The Lima News*.

LT. Metzger Eighth Ohioan To Win Highest Award   (May 13)

The Congressional Medal Of Honor, the nation's highest military award for heroism, has been awarded posthumously to Lt. William E. Metzger, Jr., 22, Army Air Forces co-pilot, son of Mr. and Mrs. William E. Metzger, Sr., 105 N. Baxter-st, who was killed in action Nov. 9 over Germany.

Lt. Metzger is the eighth Ohioan to win the award. Pvt. Roger W. Young, Fremont, infantryman, was posthumously awarded the medal last February.

The action for which Metzger received the award occurred last Nov. 9 when his bomber "Lady Jeannette," was ripped by flak over a railroad at Saarbrucken, Germany, and Metzger gave his life trying to save members of his crew.

The bomber, with two engines afire, a third damaged and the plane's interphone and electrical system destroyed, was ablaze from nose to tail by the time it got over friendly territory.

Metzger and Lt. Donald J. Gott, pilot of the ship, of Arnett, Okla., ordered the crew to bail out. A crewman whose leg was broken used the parachute of Metzger because his own was damaged. The radio operator, who lost his right hand at the wrist was hurt too much to parachute.

The pilots elected to stay with the ship and try to land.

The plane blew up a few feet off the ground, killing Metzger, Gott and the gunner.

Metzger was on his third combat flight since joining the 452nd Bombardment Group.

"This example of valor above and beyond the call of duty is the tradition established by the sacrifices of countless combat airmen and reflects the highest credit on themselves and their country," Col.

Burnham L. Batson, Manchester, Conn., said.

The other crewmen - except the tail gunner who was killed when his parachute caught on the tail of the plane, now are back in the United States.

Lt. Gott also was awarded the Congressional Medal of Honor for the heroic action.

Metzger entered service in October, 1942, and received his basic training at Camp Young, Cal., Santa Ana, Cal., and the Lancaster Air Academy, also in California. He was graduated from Central High School in 1940 and formerly had been employed at the Lima Electric Motor Co.

As of March 9, there were 100 Congressional Medals of Honor presented in the United States.

It is interesting that this article, like the first, refers to Lt. Metzger giving up his parachute and yet that action was not included in his medal citation. In fact, Lt. Metzger gave away two parachutes. One to Gustafson and one to Harland. Unlike the first article, no reference is made to the radio operator's name, Sgt. Dunlap. His name had already begun to be lost to history for the next 50 years.

Others knew and shared the sorrow of the Gott's. The forgoing note to Mrs. Gott from Ruth Fahn Hundley, the mother of Lt. Wyatt F. Hundley shows how one mother developed a way to reach out to other mothers who had lost their sons or daughters.

On 21 May, 1945, 1st Lt. Walter R. Green wrote the following letter to the Metzger family. As you read it, you can better understand how each little bit of input can change what I thought had happened and you can understand, as I have, how so many different stories of the same event exist.

I was told by one top turret gunner, that his was the best position in the bomber, "I could see everything but what was right under me, for I was the flight engineer/top turret gunner. I could see where we were going, what was alongside us and where we had been. I just couldn't see where we were."

He continued, "We were like nine blind men touching the elephant. Each of us saw everything from quite a different view. The people up front could only see where we were going and a bit to each side. The waist gunners only saw one side, the ball turret couldn't see up and the tail gunner had a great view of where we had been. When we got back and were debriefed, we each might have a different story of the same event, and we were each right."

---

21 May, 1945
Dept. Of Training, Box 28
Hendricks Field
Seabring, Fla.
Dear Mr. and Mrs. Metzger:

Will write this long put-off letter now as I have your address. I was pilot of the crew Bill went over on and may be able to furnish a few details you would like to know. Would have written when he went down but the censorship rules forbade it.

Mrs. Green sent your letter of May 6th on to me so first I'll tell you just what happened that day and then explain a few points from your letter.

On Nov. 9th we drew Saarbrucken, Germany, as our target. Bill rode with another crew that day and a new co-pilot rode with us to get experience. About four minutes from the target we ran into very heavy and accurate flak. They kept it on us until a couple of minutes after bombs away - about five or six minutes. Seven ships from our squadron went down. Bill and Gott were in a position I could see and I saw them go out. Just before bombs away they took a direct hit in the bomb bay and radio room and another shot number two completely away and knocked two more out of operation. The gas in the left wing was on fire and burning pretty bad. I saw them go down a few thousand feet and then get the ship under control and start for the battle lines and France. I had to stop watching then as I had some trouble myself. Later I talked to members of the crew who bailed out and got the rest of the story there. It probably isn't entirely correct but should be very near what happened. After that, I am certain, at least, of the final outcome. Here's the story as I pulled it together from the ones who got back.

The radio operator had an arm shot away; two or three other men wounded, and the ship a pretty thorough wreck. I believe (although the version accepted officially disagrees with me) that Gott was most certainly wounded by the shell exploding in the engine room four feet away. They lost use of interphones and most other equipment. So as soon as they got the ship under control Bill checked the damage and gave first aid to the injured. He decided it could get them to the lines and into friendly territory, which it did. They came out very low but safely behind the lines. Bill then started bailing the men out. One man was killed by his damaged chute. Others had damaged chutes also and Bill, having decided to crash-land because of the very serious wound of the radio operator and, in my belief, the wounds of Gott, the pilot, gave his chute to the bombardier who was last to leave the still burning ship at less than 1,000 feet. He had almost completed his approach to the attempted landing when the fire which was still burning in the wing, ignited the main tank and the ship exploded. All on board were killed instantly by the blast and the ship completely destroyed. (The official version says Gott was not wounded which is the only difference. I disbelieve that it is possible for a shell that size to make a direct hit on the engine nearest him and not wound him). Bill and Gott were recommended for, and believe were to get, the Congressional Medal of Honor. And no man deserves it more.

Falsey is Bob Falsey, who was our engineer. We agreed that if any of us had the chance we would see the parents or wife of any of us who didn't get home. He was going to Buffalo to visit the parents of our tail gunner, Al Wyant, who was killed on a later mission. We had two other men wounded during our missions.

Capt. Stiles was mistaken about the target. It was Saarbrucken. I realize I can't say anything to erase the pain of what happened and I'm terribly sorry I can't offer any hope, but I feel you had rather know exactly what happened and how it happened. Therefore, I've been frank - almost brutally so. All I can do is offer our sympathy - the entire crew. And add that I've never known of a braver man in an outfit where bravery is commonplace. He was devoted to duty and took a keen interest in all our work; he looked after those under him and died in an effort to give a badly wounded man a chance to live. I believe his is the third Medal of Honor in the 8th Air Force. We can't bring him back, but we can honor him and feel sure that the story of his sacrifice has inspired other men over there to stick with damaged ships and save a great number of other lives.

If I can answer any questions or clear up any points you may wonder about, just write and ask. I'll be glad to answer anything I can.

In closing, may I again offer my sympathy on your loss, I remain,

Sincerely
Signed
Walter R. Green. 1st Lt. AC

It is obvious from his position in his bomber, Lt. Green did not fully understand the two flak strikes and their damage. The engine shot off the plane was the number 4, the far right engine. The fire was not actually in the wing, but under it from the gas streaming from the broken number 4 engine's fuel line. The second shell did not hit the number 2 engine directly as the first shell had directly hit the number 4 engine. The second shell did not hit in the bomb bay. It exploded between, below and perhaps a bit back from the two engines, number 1 and number 2, on the left side of the bomber. It stopped the number 1 engine and damaged the number 2 engine. It was also the shell that broke Gustafson's leg, damaged the electrical and hydraulic system, wounded Dunlap's leg and almost cut off his hand, and it was the concussion from that shell that "rang Fross's bell" and its fragments were lodged in Fross's head as he sat in his ball turret.

As Gustafson never got back to the squadron, Green never talked to him to find out what happened in the cockpit and that Gott was not wounded. He does write that Harland received a parachute from Metzger, which does verify Harland's family saying that their father had always told them, "They owe their life to Lt. Metzger." That was, in fact, the second parachute Metzger had given away. And he would have known that Harland was the second to last out, for Gustafson was the last.

All aside, 1st Lt. Green's letter verifies so much more. It is the longest letter I have found written about the event within somewhat the same time period. All the rest I have learned, came from the survivors and families 50 years later and newspaper articles of the time.

Russell Gustafson had told me the story of meeting an officer from the 452nd in upstate New York in early 1945. From that officer, Gustafson had heard about Krimminger falling to his death with a damaged parachute. I wonder to this day, if it wasn't Falsey that Russell had met at the restaurant in the story? For Falsey could have passed on that erroneous information.

The telegrams and telephone calls flowed quickly back and forth as the military and the local authorities planned the ceremonies for the presentation of the two posthumously awarded **Congressional Medals Of Honor**, G.O. 38, 16 May, 1945.

As one of the very few dual awards of the **Medal Of Honor** these award ceremonies were to be carried out very specially. The country may have ended one major part of the war, however the war with Japan was still raging and recognition of such men was of great importance.

A letter to Alex Dunlap, dated June 9, 1945, notifies him that a package of personal effects is being forwarded within the next few days. They were shipped on the 13th.

One wonders if they sent the damaged wallet, as is. Bonnie Owens, Bob's sister, does not remember her father ever mentioning receiving this shipment. He may have kept the condition of the contents to himself.

---

12 June, 1945
ARMY SERVICES FORCES
KANSAS CITY
QUARTERMASTER DEPOT
601 Hardesty Avenue
Kansas City 1, Missouri
In reply refer to 304048

Mr. William E. Metzger, Sr.
105 North Street
Lima, Ohio

Dear Mr. Metzger:
The Army Effects Bureau has received from overseas some personal property of your son, Second Lieutenant William E. Metzger, Jr.

I regret to advise that the property belonging to your son consists of an identification bracelet which is damaged, apparently by fire. Please say whether you want this item forwarded to you. It is our desire to refrain from sending any article which would be distressing; at the same time, we do not feel justified in forwarding the item without your consent.

For your convenience, there is inclosed a self-addressed return envelope which needs no postage.

Yours truly,
Signed
P. L. Koob
2nd Lt. Q.M.C.
Officer-in-Charge
SJ unit
1 encl -- Envelope

---

14 June, 1945
SHIPMENT CLERK
Lima, O

2nd Lt. P. L. Koob
Kansas City Quartermaster Depot
601 Hardesty Ave.
Kansas City, 1, Mo

Dear Sir:
Re: 304048
In reply to your letter of June 12,

regarding personal property of my son, 2nd Lt. William E. Metzger, Jr., please be advised that I do wish to have all of it sent to me, including the damaged identification bracelet.

Thanking you for your interest in this matter, I am

Very truly yours,
Signed
William E. Metzger, Sr.
105 N. Baxter St.
Lima, O.
WM/OS

The families had mostly received the funds of their loved ones and the personal effects were slowly making its way through the pipeline from England to home.

I have chosen these communications regarding the identity bracelet, as it was the one personal relic returned as having been recovered at the crash site.

The bracelet left the Temporary American Cemetery at Limey, France, on a truck on the afternoon of 11 November, 1944, forwarded to the Effects Depot. It had taken eight months to travel from crash site to home site.

---

15 June 1945
Krimminger, Herman B.
S. N. 34 890 339

Private First Class Ida Krimminger, A-610423
Section D, Sioux Falls Army Air Field
Sioux Falls, South Dakota
Dear Private Krimminger:

Acknowledgment is made of your letter of recent date requesting information concerning your husband, the late Technical Sergeant Herman B. Krimminger.

The official report of interment received in this office reveals that the remains of your husband were interred in the U.S. Military Cemetery, Limey, France, Plot E, Row 7, Grave 163.

In view of the fact that the Army effects Bureau, Kansas City, Quartermaster Depot, 601 Hardesty Avenue, Kansas City 1, Missouri, has been designated to receive and ship the personnel effects of our deceased military personnel, I am forwarding a copy of your letter to that office for a direct reply.

Please accept my sincere sympathy in the loss of your husband.
FOR THE QUARTERMASTER GENERAL:
Sincerely yours,
Signed
MAYO A. DARLING
Lt. Colonel, QMC
Assistant

As two families prepared to receive their nation's honors for their sons, two others were just trying to find out exactly what had happened and where their loved one's effects were.

Even as they received the honors so justly due, the families of the two dead heros did not know where they were buried. They most certainly, in their deepest nightmares, would not have dreamed that most of their loved one's remains had been hidden in an unmarked grave in France after the crash and later moved to a grave marked:

Aviateur AMERICAIN
MORT POUR LA FRANCE

Again, I believe, a newspaper article and a letter from Mrs. Gott to Mrs. Metzger tells of the award ceremonies much better than I can, 50 years and more later. The presentation of the **Congressional Medals Of Honor** were made to both the Gott and Metzger families on the same Sunday, June 17, 1945.

This article appeared in the Daily Oklahoman.

FARGO MOTHER GETS HIGH U. S. HONOR FOR SON CONGRESSIONAL MEDAL GIVEN STATE OFFICER WHO DIED FOR CREW
BY: CULLEN JOHNSON
(Daily Oklahoman Staff Writer)
FARGO, June 17. -- The nation's highest award, the Congressional Medal of Honor, was awarded posthumously Sunday in Fargo to Lieut. Donald J. Gott, Ellis County

Major General Robert B. Williams attaches 1st Lt. Donald J. Gott's posthumous **Congressional Medal of Honor** around the neck of his mother, Mrs. Mary Lucy Hanlon Gott, observed closely by Lt. Gott's father, Joseph Eugene Gott and Lt. Gott's older brother, Otto James Gott, on left.
June 17, 1945

bomber pilot who died trying to save the lives of injured crewmen during a raid on Saarbrucken, Germany, last November 9.

The medal was presented to Mrs. Joseph Gott, mother of the 21-year-old Lieutenant, by Maj. Gen. Robert B. Williams, commanding general of the Second Air Force in a simple but impressive ceremony in the Fargo High School auditorium where four years ago her son had stood as valedictorian of his graduating class.

Friends and neighbors crowded the school auditorium to witness the presentation, the first ceremony of its kind ever held in Oklahoma.

Flak Alley Needs Courage

"One who has never flown down the enemy flak alley or met enemy fighters cannot conceive of sustained courage, day after day, our fliers such as Lieut. Gott," Gen. Williams said. "He truly lived up to the tradition of the air forces--mission completed."

And, as he prepared to place the beribboned medal about the neck of Mrs. Gott, the second air force commander, himself a veteran of the European air war, remarked "I consider it a great honor to have been selected by Gen. H. H. Arnold, army air forces commander, to represent the president of the United States in paying this tribute to Lieut. Gott." As the audience which overflowed the auditorium stood reverently, Capt. John E. Jordan, Catholic chaplain from Will Rogers Field, prayed and a Will Rogers Field bugler sounded taps, many eyes were moist in memory of the farm youth who chose to fly his crippled B-17 bomber back from enemy territory in an attempt to make a crash landing that possibly would have saved the life of a badly wounded radio operator.

"We are here today to pay tribute to a gallant flier," Chaplain Jordan said, "Lieutenant Gott rose above the call of duty so conspicuously that our nation has bestowed upon him its highest honor."

Major General Frederick L. Anderson presents the **Congressional Medal of Honor**, awarded posthumously to 2nd Lt. William E. Metzger, Jr., to his mother, Mrs. Ethel V. Metzger, observed by Mr. William E. Metzger, Sr.
June 17, 1945

The Ellis County youth flying his 28th mission over Germany territory, "was piloting a bomber over the Saarbrucken marshaling yards when enemy fire disabled three of the four motors," a citation by President Truman said.

The craft was damaged beyond control and was on fire. The engineer was wounded in the leg and the radio operators arm was severed below the elbow.

Knowing that the wounded radio man could not be parachuted to safety, Lieutenant Gott and the co-pilot decided to fly the flaming aircraft to friendly territory and attempt to crash land. Other crew members bailed out. Then with their goal in sight, the plane exploded, crashed and burned. The pilot, co-pilot and radio operator were killed.

With the mother on the auditorium stage were the fliers father, Joseph Gott, Ellis country farmer of the Harmon community; his brother O. J. Gott, Los Angles aircraft plant mechanic and two sisters, Mrs. Lucille Compton of Arnett and Miss Hazel Gott of Los Angeles. It was a proud day for Fargo, a farming community that has felt the war deeply, and at the same time it was a sad one. Donald, popular as a student and a leader in his classes was a favorite here.

Pray for Other Boys

After the presentation, other gray-haired mothers came to press Mrs. Gott's hand briefly.

"I pray every night that no more of our sons will have to go," one said.

After the ceremony, the parents and other relatives drove to the Woodward Army Airfield where they inspected the B-17

Left to right: Frances Louise Metzger Fredericks, Mrs. Ethel V. Badeau Metzger, Major General Frederick L. Anderson, Jeanne Elizabeth Metzger Scholfield, Mr. William E. Metzger, Sr., view the **Congressional Medal of Honor** posthumously awarded to 2nd Lt. William E. Metzger, Jr.

bomber which brought General Williams here from Colorado Springs. The visit to the field was at the request of Mrs. Gott who was eager to see the big bomber, similar to the one Donald piloted.

Mother Views Plane

The plane, an overseas veteran with patched flak holes along the fuselage, was piloted by General Williams on the trip here.

Taking off from the field, the general wagged his wings at the crowd.

"Donald always said he would do that if he flew over our place," Mrs. Gott said, "But, I told him not to."

The Gotts and their children will go to Oklahoma City next Tuesday for a second ceremony at Tinker Field. There, they will receive the Air Medal and Oak-Leaf Clusters, awarded posthumously to their son.

City Luncheon Set

They will be guests at a luncheon at

1st. Lt. Donald Gott's mother and father sit in the cockpit of a war torn warrior, B-17.

noon Tuesday at Will Rogers Field, with Col. John E. Bodle, Commanding Officer, as their host.

Colonel and Lieut. William M. Silbert, public relations officers at Will Rogers field, arranged the ceremony here Sunday.

In General Williams party were Col. B. L. Wilson, Second air force flight surgeon,

Left to right: Raymond Compton with daughter, Patricia Corinne Compton Gann, Theron Eugene Compton, Gary Joseph Compton, Winona Colleen Compton Allard Derrick, and Donald Max Compton.

Lt. Col. Robert F. Hamilton, Capt. Jack R. Ginter, and Lieut. J. J. O'Hara.

June 30, 1945, Arnett, Okla
Dear Mrs. Metzger and Family

I received your letter today, and think I neglected to answer your other one. But, I've been very busy and had some relatives from other states here until after the presentation and I was busy and worn out with worry and all.

We had our program to start at three o'clock as the general said it should be so they would be at the same time. But, guess it was alright the way it was, as delays do happen.

We had a lovely day here and was a large crowd for a thinly settled country. Largest crowd ever known at Fargo they couldn't all get in, some thought 1,500, and everything was so nice, but very sad.

The General Williams flew a plane from Colorado to Woodward Air Field was a flying fortress B-17 like our boys flew.

All was so nice to us. They really treated us swell. Taken a large number of pictures, size 7 x 9 in and then mailed them to us this week. Also 13 pictures of that size of Donald. Was 22 different views sent all together. Had several taken of the plane, as we went to Woodward to view the plane. Had our picture taken in plane, if you haven't been in a B-17 plane, would advise you to, then we have an idea about them.

We went to Will Rogers Air Field at Okla. City the following Tuesday and they served us a swell dinner. Then taken us to see more planes, then to Tinker Field about 20 miles from there to view the B-29 plane, then was presented the Air Medal and Oak Leaf Clusters, then to radio station to broadcast 15 minutes of which they made a record.

We have heard from several of the crew, in fact Donald's regular co-pilot wrote us how Donald sacrificed his life, soon after it happened. But guess he wasn't supposed to. He was flying another plane to the left of Donald's the day it happened. When he came back home to Los Angeles. My daughter and son visited him he told them all that happened.

I asked Lt. Col. Van Der Wolk if he would find out if Donald was buried, so when he went back to Washington, he phoned across to find out and he wrote me, they gave him the following information.

Donald was buried at Limey Cemetery, France. Grave number 165, Row

7, Plot E, that is the grave next to Robert Dunlap and I got a letter from the tail gunner's wife said her husband was buried by Robert, so I'm sure Billy was buried there to. Write to Lt. Col. Van Der Wolk and he will find out for you. He said it would be confirmed by a letter from Colonel Darlings office. But, haven't received it yet.

Hazel and Otto came by plane from Los Angeles their way paid. Stayed one week. I didn't get to visit enough with them as we had so much company all time. And some know things are not right since we know Donald can't come back. But, we are so proud those boys have prove to be real hero's however our home are so sad. Sometimes I wonder how we can go on. And, I feel so sorry for Otto. He tries to cheer us up and so broken hearted himself.

Earl Penick was Donald's regular bombardier. We got to meet him at Kearney, Nebr., before they flew across - was from Lawton, Okla, the reason he wasn't with them the day of the accident, (--- see following note ---), so Donald's regular copilot told Hazel and Otto. (--- Following her wishes, I have edited these sentences, as Mrs. Gott wrote "..say nothing about it.."). ...he was 19 years old.

Well it is bedtime and tomorrow a funeral. Our neighbor, an invalid for 13 yrs. passed away Tuesday, her son arrived today from France. Too bad he couldn't come in time to see her before she died. They have another boy across also.

I think the folder of the presentation and Citation of the President you had made was so nice. We didn't have any. Will send a clipping from paper.
Signed: Mrs J. E. Gott

Hope we may sometime see you folks. Have you heard anything of Billy's personal things, we haven't.

---

5 July 1945
ARMY EFFECTS BUREAU

On this date, an order of shipment was filled out and the shipment authorized. At the same time, a cover letter was sent to the family notifying them of the shipment of personal effects.

The army moved at speed and the item actually was placed in the mail, in a franked envelope on 16 July, 1945.

The families of all the dead were waiting out there, grief strong in the hearts and minds and it was taking over one month to sort and forward personal effects. The bureau must have been heavily loaded with work, as one cannot imagine such a delay being based upon a slow work ethic. So many dead, so many grieved, so many waiting.

The remarks section contains the following remarks:

ARMY EFFECTS BUREAU INVENTORY
No information (rechecked)
Inventory of Effects
1 Burial Report
1 GR. Label
DAMAGED * Bracelet is Slightly Blackened
appears to have been Burnt
and bent.   N.K.

In Ohio, at the Metzger home, around the 18th of July the mail contained a heavy shipping envelope, within the envelope was a relic so dear. A surviving relic that had to bring home more than anything at the time, that their son and brother was dead.

I have held the bracelet, with its broken chain, and it saddens one's heart and sneaks a tear to dampen a cheek, in spite of mental will. Though the bracelet is damaged from the bombs great blast, it is the smoky soot still staining the gold that brought it home at last.

For, that bracelet was on Bill's wrist the second before he ceased to be the Bill they knew. And, it flew from Bill in that great flash, to find its way home to them. Back to the house where sisters still, hoped for Bill. Now they knew, no more questions, no doubt.

The grief had to well, as tears and sobs surfaced again that day. For before, it was somewhat remote... this gift they gave the day he left, brought the message home in no uncertain way, Bill was gone. In the smoke and soot that covered it well, their heartbreak dwell. Goodbye son, goodbye Bill, brother, they think of you still.

The time stretched out, in time they came, the personal effects, just bits and pieces of Bill and his life, now past. The other families received this history too, at long last.

It took a personal request to the army officers presenting the **Congressional Medal Of Honor** for this family to learn of their loved one's burial location. Apparently, the military was not prepared to tell a survivor much unless they wrote letters or managed to question the right person.

July 24 - 25
Bureau of Graves Registry
Washington, D.C.

Dear Sirs-

I am Mrs. Wm. E. Metzger, Sr. and would like to know where my son, Wm. E. Metzger, Jr. is buried and about the services. Someone told me I could write to you & you would know it.

I have a son-in-law & a nephew over there who maybe could go there before they come home. The pilot's mother told me where her son was buried & 2 of the others & Billy must be there too. At Limey, France, they said.

Billy's number, 2nd Lt. Wm. E. Metzger, Jr., 0558834, 729th Bomb Sq., 452nd Bomb Group.

Thanking you in advance, I am,
Sincerely,
Mrs. Wm. E. Metzger
105 N. Baxter St., Box 758
Lima, Ohio

- -

This letter was written over two weeks after the family was presented with their son's **Congressional Medal Of Honor**. It baffles me still, why the army personnel who attended the presentation did not make certain the Metzger family knew where 'Billy' was buried. Surely, the parents had asked them where he was buried. Mrs. Gott's letter had provided a probable where, but eight months later this family still had no real knowledge of their son's burial place.

Aug. 10, 1945

Dear Mrs. Gott,

I have waited in answering your letter, thinking I might be able to say, had received Billy's effects, but so far nothing except that identification bracelet which was sent to them separately, they said. Have you received Donald's yet? The Chaplain back in May said the two boxes of Billy's things has arrived in Liverpool in January. That seems like a long time to wait if only they are not lost. Never got letters, boxes or anything back except my Xmas card and one letter. What I wonder is - where are they?

The trains are going all the time now loaded with soldiers and I have to cry knowing Billy will never come.

Can always see him on the back

platform waving as long as he could see us.

The longer it goes the worse it gets. They were so young. Frances's husband (Cecil Fredericks; author) is leaving Le Havre for America today, so he will be home soon.

Jeanne's husband (George W. Scholfield; author) is in Luzon. I do hope this war is over soon, so no more boys than necessary have to die.

Got a lovely letter from Mr. Dunlap. He says the Robbins boy from Worcester, Mass., who was in Laredo, Texas, was the last one off and saw the plane explode. So, I wrote to him as he must have been the one Billy gave his parachute to. But, haven't had an answer yet. I wrote July 31 -- I suppose it is hard for him to write.

Got such a lovely letter from the bombardier, but he wasn't the one with the broken leg.

I wrote to Graves Registry Bureau and they said Billy's grave #166 - Row 7 - Plot "E" so he is beside Donald.

Col. Vander Wolk wrote to me too after I said you had found out where Donald was and I supposed Billy must be there too. They said the National Cemetery at Limey, France, is 16 miles east of St. Mihiel and 15 miles north of Tours, a little west of Nancy.

I found out too late to tell anyone over there. Except a friend of ours whose husband is there yet and wrote he had been to Limey, France, so she wrote right away to see if he could go back and maybe take some pictures of the graves. I hope he got her letter and of course he may not have the chance to get back.

I am glad you had such a nice day for the Presentation and got to see so much. They sure did a lot for you.

Did you get our pictures? Col. Van de Wolk said was going to send some to you and of yours to me but I haven't received it yet. He had me send Billy's picture and they would take off of it and keep what they wanted and send the rest back to me with yours.

Coal moving slow but am here everyday taking care of what comes.

Best wishes - Mrs. Metzger

My birthday in several days and no flowers or telephone message will come Billy like last year.

"...the worse it gets." The pain of watching all those boys going home and knowing her boy was not coming back is so clear in this letter to Mrs. Gott.

Ida Hoff Krimminger was not waiting, as before, she was going to push.

September 1, 1945
16469 Van Buren Ave.
Detroit 10 Michigan

Office of the Quartermaster General
War Department
Washington 25, D.C.

Concerning:
Sergeant Herman B. Krimminger, A.S.N. 34 890 339
Killed in action November 9, 1944, on bombing mission over Saarbrucken, Germany. Interred in U.S. Military Cemetery, Limey, France, Plot #, Row 7, Grave 163.

Gentlemen:

My sister, AAF WAC Pfc. Ida Indritz Krimminger, the widow of Sergeant Herman B. Krimminger, Air Corps, has asked me to write to you.

She desires that the remains of her husband, my brother-in-law, be returned to the soil of the continental United States. Could you please (1) send whatever documents or forms which must be submitted to your office; and (2) indicate what the cost would be and when, or how long it might be until, her request can be fulfilled?

She has also mentioned that she has received only a $25 money order from his personal effects. Could you please check for her as to when she may expect the remainder of his personal effects?

Thanking you for your kindness to my sister in this matter,
Sincerely yours,

WE FLY THE HEAVIES, Bill Metzger's "Short Snorter Bill" sent to his family with the rest of his possessions. Signed by: Robert Falsey, Walter Jankowski, Paul Tickerhoof, Harold E. Burrell, William E. Metzger, Albert E. Wyant, E. Elirn Gerard, Walter R. Green, Don E. Roberts, Edward T. Gorman. The name of the right end is mostly unreadable, James E. Mic., 2nd John.

Signed, Phineas Indritz
2nd Lt., Air Corps

On 5 Sept. 1945, the Army Effect Bureau shipped a 2nd package of personal effects to Alex Dunlap. It contained the effects of his son, that had been boxed at his barracks at Deopham Green.

The inventory consisted of:
Misc. Laundry
1 muffler
1 writing folder
7 ties
1 razor and case
1 envelope personal papers
1 pr shoes
1 pr tennis shoes
1 bag brass buttons 7 charm bracelets
no funds
signed: Carlton F. Messinger, 1st Lt.

The final shipment of the personal effects Robert A. Dunlap returned home.

Dear Mrs. Gott,   Sept. 15 - 45

Sept. 6 - I received from Col. Vander Wolk the pictures of your presentation and 4 large pictures taken off of Billy's and one of Donald's enlarged from yours - you seem more real when can see your pictures. Was so nice to get them.

He says he is going to try and get a set of ours and send to you. I hope he does it.

He had said if I sent Billy's they would reproduce and keep what they wanted and send the rest to me. I got 4. I don't know how many they kept.

I was at a Gold Star Mother's Tea given by the Lady's Auxiliary of the Vet. Of Foreign Wars this p.m. in the Memorial Hall.

They want me to belong and then they will give me a gold star to wear. They presented 4 this p.m.

But, I don't like to belong to anything and feel I have to go if I don't want to and so I had not joined yet, tho they asked me back in June.

We are home people and prefer to stay at home when can instead of having to go here, there and yon. We do go to the Coal

Conference Meetings though. They have them on Tues. night every other week and we talk over our problems, etc.

Every Mon. night we go out about 4 miles in the country after our milk and eggs and cream. Have gone for over 20 years. We also take gallon jugs of well water. The city water is so full of chlorine and tastes horrid.

The one girl's husband has just sent word last week that she shouldn't write anymore and that means he will be coming home. He said in the letter before that had located the place where Bill and Donald went down and he had something to tell me. I don't know whether he got to go to the cemetery or not. I hope he did.

Also the girl that stays at our house went down to the reservoir to see a cousin of theirs that she hadn't seen for several years. He is discharged and been back several months but was over in the 8th Air Force in England and she said where the boys was killed over Saarbrucken and he said he remembered Saarbrucken real well and when she told who it was, said he didn't know him personally but heard the fellows that got back talk about him and what he did and how he could bailed out and gotten back with the rest but he wouldn't but stayed with the other two to help.

In Robbins letter he said they all owed their lives to Billy for what he did releasing the bombs by hand to lighten the plane and they got back and he helped bring it out of the fatal spin they went into when first hit. Donald must have been hurt too.

They gave the sketch of Billy over the air last Wed. night at 10:30 eastern Standard Time. Lowell Thomas program "Congressional Medal of Honor Awards." C.M.H. Awards it is called. Gives one every week. Our station here WLOK sent it in and they did it.

I was to send one of the pictures of Billy to you and I sent it off Sat. a.m., so I thought that had better get this written quick so you would know it was coming.

The coal is coming but our truck had to be fixed and the man couldn't get at it. Been 5 days now. Everybody's cars and trucks are giving out and having to be fixed. Am so glad gas rationing is over.

I wrote to the Effects Bureau at Kansas City, and they finally answered and said had not received anything to date of his- Funny.

Today, the one woman whose boy was killed Nov. 18 - had his effects and another one whose son sent down over Greenland 2 years ago and they just recently got his things. They have never heard anything for so long after their first notice. They belong to our church too.

I have never heard from Gustafson the Flight Engineer. Maybe he wasn't in shape to write. I should have sent it to his father instead and if safe he would have sent it on. Got such a lovely letter from a boy Billy knew when in Indio, Calif. In Ordinance before he got into the air. He didn't know Billy was dead till I wrote and told him. They had planned to meet each other after the war was over and I came across his letter and wrote to him. He is still in France and he said Billy had done so much for him.

I see the Gen. placed the Medal around your neck. Mine just handed it to me. Vanderwolk had said before that some do one way and some another and he didn't know how this one would do it.

Well it is getting late and I must get to bed.

      With best wishes,
      Mrs. Wm. E. Metzger

Thought had better read over your letter and see if questions to answer.

V.J. Day was sad for us too tho I was glad for the rest that were saved. Some one sent the bracelet separately. We haven't thought about the bringing back of Billy yet. I think it would nicer to have them where you could see their graves once in a while. You would feel they were not so far away. Billy was such a home lover.

Still Foundry and Westinghouse on strike here, thousands out of work.

That ptomaine poison is terrible. It often leaves after effects if a bad case. Yes, a women from near Pittsburgh wrote me she saw it in her magazine paper. She had just heard the day before about her son who had been missing and she hadn't heard from him. The boy told her he was killed and on what date. A terrible long time to wait for a letter and not know.

Well Will is waiting on me and I must shut up. We go after our milk tonight.
Best wishes for everyone
Mrs. Wm. E. Metzger.

It appears that Mr. William E. Metzger, Sr. went by Will and not Bill. I have seen him also referred to as Ed.

This letter does tell fairly well the problems in the fall of 1945 that the men were coming home to. The vehicles were in sad condition, but gas was now available. Strikes were on across the country and the future was wide open. The G.I. Bill would send hundreds of thousands of soldiers to school, their education would become the foundation of the future growth of the country. The movie, **The Best Years Of Our Lives**, undoubtably is the best visual presentation of the lives of returning service men.

On the 22nd of September, 1945, Phineas Indritz was mailed what was basically a form letter that all the families received about this time, in request to their inquires. They were told: "Now that Japan has been defeated immediate plans are being formulated with a view to returning to the next of kin the remains of their loved ones. This sacred duty will be carried out by the Government at its expense and insofar as practicable in accordance with the expressed wishes of the legal next of kin, who will be notified by this office well in advance of the actual return of the remains."

It was to be three more years before the remains in the official graves were repatriated to the United States.

On 18 December, 1945, an ex-T/Sgt. limped out of the Tilton General Hospital entrance and boarded a bus to the train station. Russell W. Gustafson may have been in uniform, but he proudly displayed his 'ruptured duck' discharge pin. A pin given to discharged service personnel to indicate they were now civilians. He would be home for Christmas, it was just one Christmas later than he had planned. Russell was the last survivor to be discharged, except for Lt. Harms who reenlisted.

In due time, the military insurance of the men killed in action was paid to the designated beneficiaries.

Ida (Chemda Indritz) Krimminger was quite a girl, she did not accept the insurance that Herman had set aside for her. She allowed the full amount to be paid to the family of her deceased husband.

It was almost two full years before Ida received another communication about the return of Herman. The government was now ready to prepare for final disposition of their family member's remains. In July, 1947, The four men's next of kin all received a cover letter, a copy of "Disposition of World War II Armed Forced Dead" and a form: OQMG FORM, 14 Nov 1946, 345 MILITARY: REQUEST FOR DISPOSITION OF REMAINS

The form listed the man's rank, name, serial number, grave location and cemetery. The next of kin were offered a choice of four methods of disposition.
1. Be interred in a permanent American Military Cemetery overseas.
2. Be returned to the Unites States or any Possession or territory therefore for interment by next of kin in a private cemetery. (With a blank line, to list upon the name and location of cemetery.)
3. Be returned to (Blank-Foreign Country), the homeland of the deceased or next of kin, for interment by next of kin in a private cemetery located at: (Blank - Location of cemetery selected).
4. Be returned to the United States for final interment in a National Cemetery located at: (Blank - Location of National Cemetery).

Three families requested that the remains be returned to the United States for interment. The Gott's requested that Lt. D. J. Gott, be interred at the Fairmont Cemetery, just down the road toward Harmon, in Ellis County, Oklahoma. The Metzger's requested interment in the family plot at Woodlawn Cemetery, Shawnee Township, Lima, Allen County, Ohio. Ida Krimminger, after fully discussing the matter with Herman's family, chose interment at Arlington National Cemetery, Arlington, Virginia.

Alex Dunlap thought about it very much and thought back to all those boys who had ridden on his trains during the war. Even as he thought, he rode trains that continued to carry military personnel from post to post and even home. Most of them were veterans and each time he saw an air corps man, he thought of Bob.

At this point, one must remember his letter of 9 December, 1945, when he was so determined to bring his son's remains back to the United States for interment. Something had to have changed his mind since he wrote that letter.

He had certainty heard by now, much of what happened the day Bob died. He knew about the bombs on board and the two explosions. He certainty had heard, what would have happened to someone in the middle of the explosion of 6,000 pounds of bombs. He thought and thought about Bob's reburial and later he told his daughters and ex-wife, that Bob could not be in that grave in France.

His youngest daughter remembers her father saying, "No grave in France could hold the Bob they had known. Not when the bombs on board had exploded." In the end, he made his decision and he checked the box for interment in an overseas cemetery. There he thought, the remains as they are, in the grave in France will rest forever with others who had died in Europe during World War Two.

I believe his decision was partially affected by his remembering the pictures and full descriptions of the care of World War One cemeteries when the Gold Star Mothers of World War One went over to visit them in the early 1930s. There his son could be remembered as he was and never questioned in the mind again.

On 19 April, 1948, a crew of Graves Registration personnel disinterred the official remains of the four airmen buried side by side at the Limey Temporary American Cemetery.

Much of this work was supervised by men who had been in Graves Registration during the war, who had been offered the option to rejoin the service with a commission as an officer, for they knew the business.

The report of this disinterment, a temporary form, QMC Form 11(unreadable) 4, DISINTERMENT DIRECTIVE had to have been run on a spirit duplicator, as the form wording is almost unreadable, while the typed-in information is quite clear. Each lists the complete personal information for the remains removed from the grave and their condition. And, each man's form also states that the remains were placed in a transfer box on 22 April, 1948.

Another Disinterment Directive, a permanent form QMC Form, 1194, REV 15 Mar 46, was later prepared, as the remains were readied for transfer. On the 8th of May, the men's official remains were placed in a marked casket and the casket placed in a well marked shipping box. From the Limey Cemetery, the travel of the casket and shipping box were documented on a Record Of Custodial Transfer.

The remains returning to the United States were first shipped to the OIC Casketing Point, at Antwerp, Belgium. The remains left the Port of Antwerp aboard a ship on 22 June, 1948. They cleared the New York Port Of Entry on the 9th of July, 1948.

Sgt. Krimminger's official remains were shipped on the 14th of July, from the NYPE to DC03, apparently a reshipment point. QMC Form 1193, 15 Nov 46, states that his remains, along with 50 more, were received at the Arlington National Cemetery on the 3rd of August, 1948.

The last entry in his file is a notification to Mrs. Ida Krimminger, C/O Biological Div., John Hopkins Hospital, Baltimore, MD.

It states that the information to be inscribed on the government headstone of the general type will be as follows:

Herman B. Krimminger
T/Sgt AAF - U.S.A.
1720 Section 12

The next of kin could fill in the following information:
State desired: North Carolina
Religious emblem desired: Latin Cross
Date of birth: August 29, 1923

The date and address verification of next of kin was required. Ida had penned a note on the side, "Was out of town when this arrived. Probably no change is necessary as the same is shown in the Official Records. Thank you."

Though Krimminger and Dunlap had been promoted one grade upon death, the T/Sgt. showing above as Krimminger's rank was never inscribed on his grave marker. Both markers list the rank at time of death, S/Sgt. Krimminger and T/Sgt. Dunlap. Apparently, it was later decided that such promotions would be disregarded.

2nd Lt. Metzger's official remains were shipped on 14 July, 1948, to D.C.#07 and received on the 15th of July, by Major A. A. Smith, TC.

The Metzger family and friends, along with Mr. E. M. Soward of Soward's Funeral Home, Lima, Ohio, met the Baltimore and Ohio train number 56 at the Lima train depot at 12:35 p.m. on Friday, the 20th of August, 1948. The remains of Lt. Metzger were received by Mr. Soward. The escort, 1st Lt. Dudley J. Allen, USAF, was greeted by the family and they told him of the arrangements of Bill's burial.

I was provided newspaper articles about Lt. Metzger's burial by Bill Robbins, Hank North and the family. Most would have been printed in **The Lima News**.

HEROS' BODIES WILL ARRIVE FRIDAY

The body of the only Lima man to receive a Congressional Medal of Honor in World War II will be among three scheduled for arrival from overseas Friday for reburial services.

Servicemen returning are Lt. William E. Metzger, Jr., 105 N. Baxter-st, Pfc. Robert B. Wallace, 1041 N. McDonel-st, and Jack E. McBride, Route 2, Delphos. Scheduled arrival time is 12:36 p.m.. at the Baltimore and Ohio station.

Headed by Mayor William L. Ferguson, a delegation of city officials will meet the train. Lima veteran's associations also are planning to be at the station, Thomas Galagher, Allen-co Soldiers and Sailors Relief agent said.

Lt. Metzger, Jr., Army Air Forces co-pilot, son of Mr. and Mrs. William E. Metzger, Sr., was killed in action Nov. 9, 1944, over Saarbrucken, Germany. He died in a bomber crash, after giving his parachute to an injured member of his crew, who bailed out safely.

Entering the service in October, 1942, he was stationed at Camp Young, Santa Ana and Lancaster air academy, Calif. before going overseas. Metzger was on this third combat flight with the 452nd Bombardment group when killed.

A graduate of Central High School in 1940 he formerly had been employed at the Lima Electric Motor Co. Recently his parents received a letter from Mayor William O'Dwyer of New York City, who expressed sympathy to the family and commended Lt. Metzger for his honorable action.

In addition to his parents, he is survived by two sisters, Mrs. George Schofield, Vaughnsville and Mrs. Cecil Frederick, Columbus.

Sowards Funeral home will be in charge of the arrangements.

PFC. Robert B. Wallace
18, was killed in action Mar. 15th, 1945, at Blyes river, Germany. He was born Oct. 21, 1926 and a former employee of the Lima Tank Depot.

Surviving are his father, Dewey, Lima; his mother, Mrs. Irene Hirn, 1041 N. McDonel-st; a brother, Charles and a sister, Mrs. Charles Greenland, both of 549½ S. Main-st.

Services will be 10 a.m. Monday in Davis-Miller and Son Cathedral chapel with the Rev. E. J. Penhorwood officiating. Burial will be in Memorial Park Cemetery. The body will remain in the funeral home.

* * *

PFC JACK E. McBRIDE, 20

Route 2, Delphos, was killed in action at Metz, France, Nov. 18, 1944. He was born near Delphos, June 18, 1924.

A brother, Pvt. Paul Allen McBride was drowned accidentally in 1945 near Keesler Field, Miss., in a stream adjacent to the air field.

Survivors include his wife, Eleanor McBride Protsman, a son, James, both of Route 1, Elida; his parents, Mr. and Mrs. Levi McBride, Route 2, Delphos.

Reburial services will be at 2 p.m. Sunday, in Davis-Miller and Son Cathedral chapel. The Rev. Peter Weaver, Spencerville, will officiate, and burial will be in Allentown. The body will remain in the funeral home until burial.

8-27-1948
FINAL RITES
SUNDAY, MONDAY
Trio To Be Reburied With Military Honors

Final rites for three Lima Area servicemen, whose bodies arrived here Friday for reburial, will be held Sunday and Monday in Lima.

Services for Lt. William E. Metzger, 21, of 105 N. Baxter-st., who posthumously was awarded the Congressional Medal of Honor, will be at 2 p.m. Monday in Sowards funeral home with the Rev. Paul Graser officiating. Burial will be in Woodlawn cemetery. The body will remain in the funeral home.

William P. Gallager, Post 96, American Legion and Edward J. Veasey, Post 1275, Veterans of Foreign Wars will conduct military rites at the grave.

Pallbearers will be Floyd Dew, Richard Hulliner, Carl Phillips, Harry Otstott and Robert Patton, all of the VFW,; Harold Snyder, Louis Wolfe and William Spencer, all of the AMVETS.

* * *

Rites for Pfc. Jack E. McBride, 20, Delphos, Route 2, will be Sunday in the Davis-Miller Cathedral chapel. The Rev. Paul Weaver, Spencerville, will be in charge, with burial to be made in Allentown Cemetery. American Legion and Veterans of Foreign Wars will be in charge of miliary service.

Funeral services for Pfc. Robert B. Wallace, 18, 1041 N. McDonel-st, will be at 10 a.m. Monday in Davis-Miller and Son Cathedral chapel with the Rev. E. J. Penhorwood officiating. Burial will be made in Memorial Park Cemetery. The body will remain in the funeral home until burial. American Legion and Veterans of Foreign Wars will conduct military service at the grave.

* * *

CITY OF LIMA
Public Water Supply
METZGER LAKE
RESERVOIR
CONSTRUCTED 1946
CAPACITY 1,200,000,000 GALS
NAMED IN MEMORY OF
LT. WILLIAM E. METZGER, JR.
KILLED IN ACTION OVER GERMANY
NOVEMBER 9, 1944
AWARDED
CONGRESSIONAL MEDAL OF HONOR

A MEMORIAL
TO ALL VETERANS OF WORLD WAR II

* * *

From bronze plaque picture-Not reproducible.

On Monday, August 30th, 1948, 2nd Lt. William E. Metzger, Jr. was laid to rest in the family plot at Woodlawn Cemetery. His grave location is Plot 17, Grave 29. 1st Lt. Donald J. Gott's remains were signed for at the Woodward, Oklahoma, train station by Franklin Stecher of the Stecher Mortuary on Friday, the 27th of August, 1948. The remains had arrived on the Santa Fe Train Number One, at 6:55 p.m. that evening. The transfer was witnessed by, 1st Lt. Marshall R. Duncan who had escorted Lt. Gott's remains on his final trip home and burial. 1st Lt. Donald J. Gott had met his rendezvous in the air over France and now he was home, forever home. For his parents and many friends who were present when the coffin was transferred from the train to the hearse, Donald Gott had

1st Lt. Donald J. Gott, home at last.
Congressional Medal of Honor

returned. Many years later, the surviving nieces and nephew came to learn that was not necessarily true.

The home again filled with friends and neighbors. For Donald had come home, home for the last time. Donald had sacrificed his life, so others might live. Don Gott had come home for evermore, a hero.

Dad and Mom Gott. Sad, so sad.

They left the house together again, the father, the mother, the son. No joy lay upon their journey, a final rendezvous the goal.

The trip was slow, just down the road, a place of memories. A journey they had taken together many times before, to share the grief of family and friend. Men and women and children made the trip too. Those, who will join them in Remembrance at that rendezvous, were much the same as they, a relative buried here beside and over there a friend. It was sad, ever so sad, a son, a great lad, was joining the past today.

The services done, the rifles had fired, tap's echoes have died in the wind. Don's mother accepted her nation's last honor, a flag in exchange for a son.

1st Lt. Donald J. Gott
Congressional Medal of Honor
Air Medal, 3 Oak Leaf Cluster
Purple Heart

The Individual Deceased Personnel File of three of the four men killed in the crash of '*The Lady Jeannette*' files were permanently closed by the end of 1948. Gott's, Metzger's and Krimminger's interments were completed in August and final interment expenses compensated for. It was months later, in April, 1949, before the last entry was made in T/Sgt. Dunlap's file, it is a letter to his father, Alex Dunlap.

----

4 April 1949
T/Sgt Robert A. Dunlap, ASN 39 696 406
Plot C, Row 23, Grave 19
Headstone: Cross
St Avold (France) U.S. Military Cemetery
                Mr. Alex Dunlap
                715 Woodbury
                Miles City, Montana
Dear Mr. Dunlap:

This is to inform you that the remains of your loved one have been permanently interred, as recorded above, side by side with comrades who also gave their lives for their country. Customary military funeral services were conducted over the grave at the time of burial.

After the Department of Army has completed all final interments, the cemetery will be transferred as authorized by the Congress, to the care and supervision of the American Battle Monuments Commission. The Commission also will have the responsibility for permanent construction and beautification of the cemetery, including erection of the permanent headstone. The headstone will be inscribed with the name exactly as recorded above, the rank or rating where appropriate, organization, state and date of death. Any inquires relative to the type of headstone or spelling of the name to be inserted thereon, should be addressed to the American Battle Monuments Commission, Washington 25, D.C. Your letter should include the full name, rank, serial number, grave location and name of the cemetery.

While interments are in progress, the cemetery will not be open to visitors. You may rest assured that this final interment was conducted with fitting dignity and solemnity and that the grave-site will be carefully and conscientiously maintained in perpetuity by the United States Government.
Sincerely, yours,
Signed, H Feldman
Major General, The Quartermaster General

T/Sgt. Robert A. Dunlap's remains had been stored in Europe from the date of his disinterment, 19 April, 1948, until his reburial on the 26th of January, 1949, in Plot C, Row 23, Grave 19, USMC, St. Avold, France. On his right is John T. Bodwell, Pvt. Sn: 14131815. The name of the person on his left is not visible.

A notation states that his father had been sent a flag, on January 31, 1949.

I HAVE A RENDEZVOUS WITH DEATH
(World War Two -- Aviation)

I have a rendezvous with Death
At some disputed target there
When God brings back weather fair
And flak blossoms in the air
I have a rendezvous with Death
When he brings back blue skies and dare

It may be he shall take my hand
And lead me into his dark land
And close my eyes and quench my breath---
It may be I shall pass him still
I have a rendezvous with Death
On some scarred slope of battered hill
When we cross the enemy's fear
And the first flak bursts appear

God knows 'twere better to be deep
Pillowed in silk and scented down,
Where Love throbs out in blissful sleep,
Pulse nigh to pulse, and breath to breath
Where hushed awakenings are dear...
But I've a rendezvous with Death
At midday in the flak filled air
When fragments whistling, I hear
And I to my pledged mission am true,
I shall not fail that rendezvous.

Willis S. Cole, Jr.
In Remembrance: Alan Seeger
Adapted 1915 poem to flak and the American Aviator of W.W.II.

Today, the American Cemetery at St. Avold is always carefully and conscientiously maintained. T/Sgt. Dunlap's grave is one of thousands lined upon the gently rolling slopes below the memorial and chapel.

The years passed and the surviving men of '*The Lady Jeannette*' went on with their lives and slowly the events of 9 November, 1944 were remembered less often.

The families of those who died also went on, the fire of life had dimmed greatly in the parent's breasts. Sisters and brothers came to tell their children about their uncles who were killed in action during World War Two and a young wife had to find a new route along the road of life.

In a small hill and valley town in Ohio, a little boy was growing up. His roots to this book, I found almost as the book was completed, go back to the spring of 1944, when this small boy watched a tall soldier leaving for war, saying goodbye to his aunt and cousin, standing like a giant on the porch above the steps, tall and pink, the hat with the eagle under his arm. I know, for that little boy was me.

Chapter Nine

Remembrance - 1994

When I arrived home in the evening of July, 11th, 1994, Carol picked me up at the airport and it turned into a long night as we discussed what had happened in France and the information she had been able to provide to me there. We were now certain of the names of two of the men in the grave and the awards they received, it seemed that the name of the radio operator, who also had to be in the grave should be easy to find.

On the way back, I had a layover at Dulles International Airport outside of Washington, D.C., and I spent some of the time on the telephone talking to Ryan Arthur, the Air Force Historian. Sally McDonald, of ***The Seattle Times*** had given Carol Ryan's telephone number so I could talk to him directly. It was time well spent, as Ryan showed an immediate interest and promised to get me some information as soon as he could.

I was full of confidence that we would soon have all the information to fully identify the three men in the grave and to have them honored by the French and the United States before the 50th Anniversary of the Liberation of France ended.

Pierre Segers, Bernard Leguillier and I had discussed the possibility of having a memorial service at the crash site and grave on the 9th of November, 1994. That would be exactly 50 years from the date of the men's death and within our original goal of **Remembrance-Souvenir** during the 50th Anniversary of Liberation.

Early on the morning of the 12th, I received a FAX from Ryan Arthur that provided the foundation upon which I would be building for several years. One was the Missing Air Crew Report, 3BD (17-7-44), 9 November, 1944, and the other was the Battle Casualty Report, 10 November, 1944.

Both provided the names and positions of all the crew of the bomber that crashed and the Battle Casualty Report provided the full serial number of the B-17 bomber, plus the men's ranks and serial numbers. One of the more important items of new information, I thought, was the name of the radio operator who had died in the crash, T/Sgt. Robert A. Dunlap.

As far as I knew at that moment, only three men had died in the crash and six had survived.

That day, I took the first step in tracing the men listed. I started my computer and opened the national telephone directory and began a name by name national computer search for a telephone number.

Gott and Metzger were first and I found that having their full names was not going to be of much use. There were many people with the same last name and none with the first. With no geographical location to separate out some of them, it was going to take lots of telephone calls and letters.

Within the hour, I tried the third name on the list. I found only one listing for John A. Harland and when I called it, a man's voice answered. When I explained the reason I was calling, he told me that I had the right telephone number and that his name was Scott Harland and that he had lived with his father, until his fathers's death the month before, on June 3rd. Lt. John Harland had been buried on the 6th of June, 1994. The D-Day 50th Anniversary of the Normandy Invasion. A date already logged into my research, as that was the early morning that I challenged some of the **COMMEMO-RANGERS** to find the truth of the grave. I had missed talking to the first survivor I had located by one month.

Scott told me, they had talked many times about the bomber that his father had been aboard so long ago. He told me that his father had carried a picture of Metzger in his billfold until his death, for Metzger had given his father a parachute to replace the damaged one he had. I was beginning to learn about **the last flight of '*The Lady Jeannette*.'**

3BD (17-7-44) MISSING A/C REPORT
(See reverse side for A/C to be reported)

A/C No. 904   Squadron: 729   Group: 452   Date A/C Missing: 9 November

27 Pilot	Gott, Donald J.	1st Lt.	26 B.T. Fross, James O.	S/Sgt.
2 CoP	Metzger, William E.	2nd Lt.	26 T.T. Gustafson, Russell W.	T/Sgt.
19 Nav	Harland, John A.	2nd Lt.	22 T.G. Krimminger, Herman B.	S/Sgt.
1 Bomb	Harms, Joseph F.	2nd Lt.	25 R.W. Robbins, William R.	S/Sgt
26 RadOp	Dunlap, Robert A.	T/Sgt.		

Targets   Attacked   Attacked
Assigned: Saarbrucken   by Group: Saarbrucken, Ger   By this A/C: none

A/C was lost to: (use X)   Position of A/C in Group   1
Fighters   Rocket   (Circle number)   3   2
AA Fire XX   Collis   Position of Group in   1   (4)   1
Air Bomb   Other   formation: 3   2 6 5 3   2
Combinations   Lead Sqdn of 45th   4   4
                            "C" Wing

A/C sustained initial damage at (co-or) Bomb Run Time   No. of chutes: none
A/C was last seen at (co-or) 4913-0700   Time: 1004 Altitude 23,000 Hdg. 208T
(Give a complete narrative, citing all known facts not covered in above answers,
using reverse side if necessary. If weather was a contributing factor, describe
briefly. Bear in mind that a ship which "blew up" cannot continue to fly and
that an explosion aboard an A/C is not necessarily a ship "blown up").
This A/C hit by flak on bomb run, left formation under control.
12/11/44 Waist gunner - William R. Robbins bailed out of A/C #904 and landed near
Verdun. He relates that #4 engine was knocked off A/C and #1 was hit by flak and
they couldn't feather it. He saw one chute from front of A/C, TT had a broken leg
(couldn't find any morphine), RO had flak wounds in his hand and leg, the BT was
clear of ball and could have escaped and there was one chute from the tail section.
Interphone was out and he never receive any word to bail out. WG bailed out at
1t00 feet. They could not drop or jettison bombs and he was A/C crash.
Info. from crew of A/C 615 Group 452 interrogating Officer Lt. Taylor
(Errors are same as in report - read 1,200 feet and saw Aircraft crash, author)

BATTLE CASUALTY REPORT
452ND Bombardment Group (H)
APO 559

Aircraft B-17, Serial #42-97904   10 November 1944

                    ARM OR TYPE OF   FLYING   PLACE OF
ASN-NAME-RANK-SQUAD-SERVICE-CASUALTY-DATE-STATUS-CASUALTY-MOS

O-763996	GOTT, Donald J	1st Lt.	729th B Sq AC	MIA 9 Nov 44	Pilot	Oper Mission-Saarbrucken 1091
O-558834	METZGER, William E Jr	2nd Lt	729th B Sq AC	MIA 9 Nov 44	CO-Pilot	Oper Msn-Saarbrucken 1091
O-723355	HARLAND, John A	2nd Lt	729th B Sq AC	MIA 9 Nov 44	Navigator	Oper Msn-Saarbrucken 1034
O-2056698	HARMS, Joseph F	2nd Lt	729th B Sq AC	MIA 9 Nov 44	Bombardier	Op Msn-Saarbrucken 1035
12139299	GUSTAFSON, Russell W	T Sgt	729th B Sq AC	MIA 9 Nov 44	TTG	Oper Mission-Saarbrucken 748
3969406	DUNLAP, Robert A	T Sgt	729th B Sq AC	MIA 9 Nov 44	ROG	Oper Mission-Saarbrucken 757
38462533	FROSS, James O	S Sgt	729th B Sq AC	MIA 9 Nov 44	BTG	Oper Mission-Saarbrucken 612
11051000	ROBBINS, William R	S Sgt	729th B Sq AC	MIA 9 Nov 44	RWG	Oper Mission-Saarbrucken 611
34890339	KRIMMINGER, Herman B	S Sgt	729th B Sq AC	MIA 9 Nov 44	TG	Oper Mission-Saarbrucken 611

For the Commanding Officer:
CARL F EMINGER,
Capt., Air Corps
Adjutant

I learned there were six children from his father's and mothers's marriage and that most of them lived within a short distance of each other.

He told me that his father had a fairly large collection of papers from those days, however they were stored in the basement and it would take some time for him to locate them and look through them. Scott gave me the name and telephone number of a sister, Debbie, who lives in the same building, so I could call her and get further information.

It was exciting to know that I had found the first person, even though he had recently died and it was his family, that I had contacted. It seemed, that I should be able to find the rest without too much effort.

Of course, that was before I had spent over two years and many thousands of dollars in my effort to locate, or account for every name on the list.

It was time to take a break for a few minutes. Several of my American Legion magazines had come while I was in France and I sat down to look through them. When I got toward the end of the first one, I looked at the reunion section where I had once located the 735th AC & W Squadron Association through a listing there. I had served with that outfit in 1957/58 in Morocco and I was quite pleased to attend their first reunion.

It seemed like fate was working for me that day, for there was a listing for the 452nd Bomb Group. That was the unit's name given on the two reports I had received that day.

Within minutes, I had called the magazine's reunion line and received the telephone number of the Group. Soon, I was talking to John Witte of the 452nd Bomb Group Association.

John told me, that I could join as an Associate Member and there was a reunion in October, in California. I got the address and told him my check would be on the way in the next mail. I went on to talk about '**The Lady Janet**' and my search for the crew.

As I read out the crew's names, he suddenly said one of them sounded familiar. He asked me to hang on for a minute and when he came back, he told me that he had been right. He had been called by Gustafson the week before. He said Gustafson had told him that he had been watching a television show about the 8th Army Air Force. At the end it gave a contact number and from it, Gustafson had managed to locate the Group he had served with and make arrangements to join the Association.

John passed on Gustafson's telephone number and told me he didn't have any information on the other men. However, I might contact Hank North, the Lost Souls Committeeman. Hank spent a lot of his time looking for people who they knew were in the Group, but had no contact with.

I called the number that John had given me and when the fellow answered at the other end, I told him that he didn't know me, however, I knew a lot about him. I went on to describe a man bailing out of a B-17 bomber, called '**The Lady Janet**' over France. That the bomber was flaming from the far right engine, with smoke boiling from the engine next to the pilot. He was the last one to bail out and the villagers could see that his leg was broken as he fell to earth. Also, that the bomber had rolled over and dove toward the earth, exploding once in mid-air and again when it hit the ground. Later, the pilot and copilot had been awarded the **Congressional Medal Of Honor**. I also told him of the Radio Operator, T/Sgt. Dunlap, who had been killed in the crash.

He sputtered a couple of times and then said, "I'm that fellow and everything you said is right, except the name of the bomber was '**The Lady Jeannette.**'" I asked him if he was sure of that, and he replied, "I stood right under the name written in red script on the nose as I prepared the Flight Manifest." Besides that somewhat shocking information, Russell went on to tell me that the bombs had not been dropped as the citations stated. They were the major part of the second explosion as the bomber hit the ground.

We discussed what happened to him that day and agreed that we would keep in touch and that I would keep him informed as I found out new information. We also talked about the other men on the crew and he gave me some idea of where he thought they lived.

Russell told me that he had thrown away all his relics about 10 years before, as he had figured that part of his life was gone and best forgotten. However, the 8th Air Force story had piqued his interest again and he was happy to belong to the Group Association and that I had called him.

Russell told me, that he had not seen any of the men since Lt. Harland and he split at the hospital. With his bad leg, Russell was in the hospital for over a year and except for a person who came to interview him once about the crash, he did not know what happened to the other survivors.

He had once met a fellow in a restaurant, in Jamestown, New York, that he recognized as an officer from the Group after the war. He had told Russell, that Krimminger had been killed when he had opened his chute in the bomber by accident and gathered it up in his arms and jumped out the door. The wind had whipped it away from him and it caught on the bomber and ripped off. He had fallen to his death without a parachute.

Now, I knew that another crew man was dead, falling to his death. I knew, I had another search to locate where he fell.

Russell told me about a box of grapefruit he had once received from Fross while he was in the hospital at Fort Dix. He had been on recovery leave at home when it came and they forwarded the box of fruit to his home. By the time it arrived at Jamestown, Russell had reported back to the hospital, so the box of fruit took the trip back also. By the time Russell actually got the box all of the grapefruit had rotted. That was the last he knew of any of the crew until I called.

Before we hung up we discussed one very surprising thing, that I have written about. Russell told me that the crew was not a close crew. He continued, "You have never seen nine people who had so little in common. When we got back from a mission, we each went our own way." That's why he wasn't sure of where the other crewmen were from.

The next day, I called Hank North about the men I had not located. When I read the names of the men, he told me that the **Medal Of Honor** winner, Lt. Metzger was from Lima, Ohio, but he couldn't help me with any of the other survivors. None of them were accounted for in the TAPS listing either. The Group's TAPS list is all of the men who are known to have died since the war. I told him about Lt. Harland being dead, so he could add his name to the TAPS list.

Using Russell's idea of where the other men lived, I again started my computerized directory to search for them. I quickly found there were a lot of William Robbins in the country and there were many people named Harms scattered around, as well. I thought that finding Krimminger's family would be fairly easy and I found quite a few in the southeast. However, telephone calls to the ones with close first names hit a dead end. I found the same for Robbins, Fross and Dunlap.

Russell had said, he thought Gott might have been from Oklahoma, perhaps the northeast part. He also told me, that he lived in Oklahoma now, having moved there from New York State with the company he worked for selling bearings. While the telephone book had some listings for Gott, it didn't provide any who knew of the bomber's pilot, I tried another method.

I have found, that when you are somewhat sure of where a person is located and you have a very, very good reason to locate them, the Mayor's office of the towns are a good place to ask. You explain exactly who and why you are hunting them and they will often help.

I called the mayor's office in ten towns in northeast Oklahoma and had no luck until the tenth. The person to whom I was talking, told me that she had heard of some people named Gott in the western area of Oklahoma, down near the pan handle area.

My first call to a town in that area, Arnett, got the town Clerk. I had just started to go into my lecture when she started to fill in information gaps for me, I had hit pay dirt. She told me, that I was really talking to the wrong person because the niece of Lt. Gott was the County Assessor and she was working with the county to have a special memorial dedicated to him during the Arnett Rodeo on the weekend of August 27th. She gave me Winona Derrick's home and work telephone numbers and the whirlwind began.

When I reached Winona, she was as excited as I was. Of course, I had to tell her that I had something to tell her, that might be very upsetting.

I went on to tell her about the grave in France, the priest's statement and what we had found about the soldiers hiding the remains. I went on to tell her about the reburial and that the priest had performed the Last Rights and Burial Services.

Her reaction was surprising to me, she said, "I am so glad that he was buried with Catholic services, Uncle Donald was a devout Catholic." However, Winona quickly added to the confusion of the hidden grave by telling me that her Uncle Donald was buried at Fairmont Cemetery, near a crossroads east of Arnett called Harmon.

If the soldiers hid what they recovered how did the men get a grave back home? It would take many months to figure out the truth.

Winona told me quite a lot about her grandparents, Donald's mother and father, and how much his death had affected their lives.

We talked about the presentation of the **Medal Of Honor** and her plans for the memorial the next month. Of course, she said, you are invited, please come.

During the next few days, we had several conversations and she told me that the younger members of the family at the time of Donald's burial really didn't feel that he was there. Between the medal citations and various letters and other information they had received, they knew all about the explosions.

During one conversation, she asked me to be a speaker at the dedication of the memorial to Donald that was to be mounted on the porch of the Ellis County Courthouse on August 27th, of course I agreed.

Within a few days, I followed up on Ryan Arthur's contact, Total Army Personnel Center searching for the men's burial files. I managed to talk to an assistant director and he told me, as an outsider, I would have to get a letter of permission from a family member to have such records released to me.

I had been keeping the people in France up to date via FAX messages and when I told them about the memorial on the 27th of August, they asked if some of them could come and represent the **COMMEMO-RANGERS**. I thought it was a grand idea and so did Winona.

I was also writing letters to people in France I had met, who lived back along my projected flight line. I asked them to ask around and see if they could find anyone one who might remember a body falling from the air. Several put ads in their local papers, but we received no leads.

I also wrote letters to some village

I soon received back some of my pictures and this one became a fixture on my desk to remind me, what it was all about.

On July 10, 1994, I was able to tell two of the men in the grave their names. Now I knew the third man's name and was working on achieving recognition of the grave. Three years, seven months later, that is still the goal.

mayors along the route asking them if they had any bodies fall out of the air around their village. I didn't get any leads from them, but I did hear about several other bomber crashes in their areas. These contacts would continue through 1994, to October, 1995.

Winona and I had talked about Russell and we agreed that we would invite him to attend the memorial for Donald.

When I talked to him about it, he wasn't sure he would come, as he felt he might become upset by the old memories and such. He had lost a year in the hospital with his hurt leg and the memories were not all good. And, if he did come, he wasn't sure he would want to talk about it.

In the end, he agreed to come and I arranged to meet with him and discuss what I had found, and see if we could work it out.

In one of my conversations with Winona, she told me she had found an article about the radio operator who had died with Donald, that must have been sent to her grandmother. It listed his home town as Miles City, Montana.

Now that I was getting more information, the people in France were really working on having a memorial service exactly 50 years after the crash, at the crash site. I told Winona and Russell about their plans and that they were invited to attend.

I looked for the listing of any one named Dunlap in Miles City, and couldn't find one. I called information and got the Mayor's office number and called him. Mayor George Kurkowski told me, he didn't know anyone by that name but promised to look around and see what he could find.

It appeared, that there must not be any surviving family there. On the 21st of July, 1994, I called the V.F.W. Post in Miles City at 8:30 p.m. and I asked if someone there might know something about the Dunlap family? They told me, they would check around and on the morning of the 22nd I got a call from Keith and Phyllis Johnson. Bob had been one of Keith's best friends in school. He told me that the family was dead, except there was one sister somewhere. But, he would collect any information he could and send it to me.

On the 28th, I received a letter from Keith, telling me more about Sgt. Dunlap's family and he was sending me a picture of Bob Dunlap, cut from a high school year book showing the Senior Class of 1942. He told me, that Bob's father, Alex, and mother, Martha, had both died. Also that his older sister, by 5 years, Io was dead. However, there was a younger sister, Bonnie, by about 15 years, who was believed to be alive, somewhere.

I decided to take another approach and wrote a letter to the **Miles City Star** newspaper telling them of my research and asked if they would put an article in the paper about my research.

Within a few days, I received a letter from Bob Bautcelmess, telling me that he had seen the article and that he had lived next door to Bob when they were young. He verified that Bob's older sister, Marsha Io was dead and that his younger sister, Bonnie Mae was alive. She had visited the museum where he volunteered the year before and he had talked to her. He wrote that she lived in Augusta, Georgia, but she had been divorced and he didn't know her married name now. But, if he heard anything, he would let me know.

On August 10th, I talked to the Mayor Kurkowski again, telling him what Keith had sent me and again asked his help in locating Bonnie Dunlap.

On the 11th, I received a letter from the Department of the Air Force Historical Research Center at Maxwell Air Force Base in Alabama.

They notified me, that the bomber B-17G-35VE, Sn: 42-97904 had been written off to battle damage in England on the 18th of November, 1944, even though it had been lost eleven days earlier, in France. They could not locate any other records for the aircraft or incident. Also that they did not have a listing of any serial numbers of equipment on the aircraft.

Now isn't that the pits. If the Air Force records don't show where it crashed, how do I prove it crashed at Tincourt-Boucly. It was going to be eleven months before I figured out how to do it.

The following article ran in ***The Lima News***, on Wednesday, August 17, 1994, under the byline of Mike Lackey. I had been in contact with him and had sent him an information package.

WWII hero received due 50 years late

For 50 years, the people of a small French village have tended the grave of a nameless stranger, a grave marked with a cross and the words "Unknown American aviator, died for France."

The grave is off the beaten path, in the cemetery at Cartigny, a village of 600 people in the Somme region 60 miles north of Paris. Few Americans visit the site, which is not listed in meticulous graves registration records kept by the U. S. military during World War II.

But after four years research, a military history buff has concluded the grave holds remains of three American fliers, including 2nd Lt. William E. Metzger, Jr. Congressional Medal of Honor winner from Lima.

Now researcher Willis S. "Sam" Cole is planning a hometown memorial service for one of Metzger's comrades and hopes to arrange a similar service in Lima.

Metzger, a graduate of Lima Central High School was 22 years old and flying his third combat mission Nov. 9, 1944, when his B-17, the Lady Jeannette was ripped by anti-aircraft fire on a bombing run over Saarbrucken, Germany. With the plane on fire and three of its four engines knocked out or damaged, the pilot 1st Lt. Donald J. Gott turned back toward France, hoping the crew could bail out over friendly territory.

The radio operator Technical Sgt. Robert A. Dunlap, his arm severed below the elbow, was unable to jump. Gott determined to stay with the plane and attempt an emergency landing in a bid to save Dunlap's life.

Co-pilot Metzger, who had given away his parachute to replace one that had been damaged also volunteered to stay.

Six crew members jumped. One was killed when his parachute caught on the tail of the plane and was ripped off. The other five survived.

Gott and Metzger kept the crippled plane in the air an hour. Cole believes they were attempting to reach an American B-26 base several miles from Cartigny, but with only one engine the plane pulled to the right and drew them off course. As they attempted to maneuver back toward the landing site, fighting to hold the Lady Jeannette, 100 feet off the ground the plane exploded, crashed and exploded again.

Both Metzger and Gott were posthumously awarded the Medal of Honor. Metzger's parents accepted the award June 17, 1945, in a ceremony at Market Street Presbyterian Church. The following year, the city of Lima named Metzger Lake reservoir in the flier's honor and dedicated it as a World War II memorial.

Cole, who operates a military museum in Kirkland, Wash., first visited Cartigny while doing World War I research. He spent four years sifting and sorting local legends about the anonymous grave before connecting it to the crash of the Lady Jeannette. The break-through came in June when Cole, in France for the 50th anniversary of D-Day, charged his French friends to return to Cartigny and "wring that town out" for solid information.

They found a statement dated Nov. 23, 1944, by the parish priest. The priest said remains of one or more American fliers from the crash had been found in a makeshift grave outside of town. The priest insisted they be reburied in consecrated ground. Keepers of a cemetery in nearby Bony offered to place them in a common grave with World War I casualties. But the priest thought the fliers deserved their own resting place, so he had them buried in Cartigny.

Cole believes the remains were buried in a temporary grave immediately after the crash, then either abandoned or forgotten. All three men who died in the Lady Jeannette have marked graves elsewhere -- Gott near his hometown of Arnett, Okla.; Dunlap in a military cemetery in France; and Metzger in Lima's Woodlawn Cemetery, where a committal service was held in 1948. But Cole believes those graves contain only fragmentary remains when the crash site was excavated after the war.

Now Cole and his French colleagues are raising money for a new monument at the grave at Cartigny.

These American aviators aren't unknown anymore.

As you have read, further research has provided a somewhat different end to the story concerning the crash and grave.

This article provided the first real public access to the story of '**The Lady Jeannette**.'

I received notice from the **COMMEMO-RANGERS** saying that Mike Vieillard and Jocya Charlet were going to come over for the memorial at Arnett.

When it was set that they were going to come, I got back in contact with the Mayor Kurkowski, of Miles City, and asked if they could have some type of memorial service for Sgt. Dunlap which the French could attend. He agreed that it would be a good idea, and since the time was short, he would see what he could do.

Within days, Mayor Kurkowski came though for me. He had located Bonnie Dunlap Owens and called her, telling her about my research. He had also sent her a copy of the newspaper account of my request for information about her brother.

He also told me, that he had arranged a small memorial service to be held at the Miles City, City Hall on September 2nd. I told him that we would be there.

On August 24th, 1994, the **Miles City Star** printed the following article as a follow up to the first article telling about my research and search.

Sister Looks Forward To Ceremony For Fallen Aviators
John Halbert, Staff Writer

Bonnie Mae Dunlap last saw her brother Robert when she was 9 years old and he was home on furlough from the Army Air Forces. The Dunlap family lived at 1005 Knight St. at the time.

About a year later, she and her family, then in Bakersfield, Calif., learned that Robert had died during a bombing attack on Germany.

"**I remember it vividly**," she recalls, now Bonnie Owens of Augusta, Ga., she is the sole survivor of Staff Sgt. Dunlap's family.

She was the object of a search by military historian Willis "Sam" Cole, Jr., who has a great interest in military memorials. Cole recently discovered evidence that the remains of Robert Dunlap and two Medal of Honor winners are contained in the grave of an unknown aviator in northern France.

"It's very, very bizarre to me," Owens said in a telephone interview Wednesday. She said letters from the Army to her father, Alex Dunlap, arriving at different times indicated that Robert had graves in three different cemeteries in France. The unknown aviators' grave makes a fourth location.

On Nov. 9, 1944, the B-17 bomber "Lady Jeannette" was taking part in an attack on Saarbrucken, Germany, when it was hit by anti-aircraft fire. The blast knocked out three engines, started fires, broke the leg of the flight engineer and severed radio operator Dunlap's arm below the elbow.

Because Dunlap was unconscious and could not parachute, pilot Donald Gott and copilot William Metzger, Jr. decided to try to fly back to friendly territory in France rather than bail out over Germany.

On reaching friendly territory Gott and Metzger ordered the rest of the crew to jump. The plane blew up about a hundred feet above the ground about three miles from an allied field, killing all three men.

Gott and Metzger won posthumous Medals in trying to save Dunlap.

Owens said she plans to go with her daughter to a Nov. 9 memorial ceremony Cole is organizing in the village of Cartigny, about 60 miles northwest of Paris, where villagers have tended the grave ever since.

Owens said she returned to Miles City after the war and attended Custer High School as a member of the class of 1951. She married and left town in 1950 but made up her senior year credits later and received a CCHS diploma.

Since then, she has lived in the South with her husband Frank. She returned to Miles City for the first time in 1991 to attend her 40th class reunion and plans to attend future reunions here.

Owens got a call from Mayor George Kurkowski Tuesday morning and has received a copy of the newspaper article about it.

"Everybody has been so super-nice," she said, "I really appreciate it.

As soon as Mayor Kurkowski gave me her number and obviously before the article was written, I called Bonnie Dunlap Owens-I had located Dunlap's little sister.

She told me a lot about her brother and the fact, that her father had made the decision to have Bob buried over there. After hearing about the two explosions he felt there could be nothing in the coffin that was the Bob they knew. It would be best if he were buried side by side with others who had died overseas during the war.

Bonnie also confirmed my research actually helped her and she felt much better knowing that Bob did have a real grave. And when I told her about the planned memorial service for the men in France in November, she immediately said she would make arrangements to go to it and that her daughter Angela would go also. Angela had been studying French and doing well, so she would really enjoy the trip. Bonnie agreed to send permission for me to request Bob's records.

She told me Io had two boys, Don and Mark Cyr Herndon, married to Leigh.

The days seemed to rush by, as I searched for other survivors and made arrangements to get to Arnett, meet the French and plan to be in France for the memorial services.

After several calls to France, Pierre Segers sent me their schedule and I made arrangements to fly to Denver and meet the French. We would drive from there to Arnett and back. In the end, we determined that Jocya wouldn't be able to attend the memorial at Miles City, but Mike would fly on to Seattle with me, after we left Jocya at a Denver hotel, near the Airport, so she could catch her flight back to France.

They told me that our friend, Richard Boniface, had taken his equipment to the field and started excavating the site where the bomber crashed. He had dug down about 15 feet and located some burnt earth which indicated the engines had stopped there and scorched the earth. He had found nothing big. However, he is going to go back and they were going to pick up whatever they could. It appears the site had been salvaged earlier.

Mike, Carol and I, would rent a car in Seattle and make a flying trip from Seattle to Miles City for the service there and back to Seattle, where Mike would leave for France.

During that month, I sent out over two hundred letters to people on a random basis for each of the men I had not yet located. I got some replies, but they were just wishing me good luck and telling me that they were not the person and they had not heard of them. The telephone bill continued to grow, as I tried every 25th name and later 15th name and 10th name in the directory trying to locate the men.

I was having some luck though. I had written David Berger, the Mayor of Lima, Ohio, after Hank North had told me that Metzger was from there. I told him what I had found and reminded him that this was the 50th Anniversary of Lt. Metzger's death and asked if the city was going to have a memorial or anything for it?

Interesting, that the mayor has the same last name as the Frenchman who restored the grave, Emile Berger, pronounced quite differently.

When we talked on the telephone, Mayor Berger told me that the city had been looking for something to do special for the 50th Anniversary of 'D-Day.' It would be a good time to do something for Lt. Metzger and the other veterans. The city had named a reservoir in honor of him after the war and they had decided to refurbish the memorial and have a memorial service and rededication at the reservoir on the 11th of November,

1994. As a result of my telephone call, he later sent a very nice letter and the following proclamation.

Office of the Mayor
Proclamation

Whereas: Lt William E. Metzger, Jr. a Lima native son was killed on November 9, 1944, aboard the U.S. Army/Air Force B-17 Bomber, ***The Lady Jeannette***, of the 452nd Bombardment Group operating in France; and

Whereas: Through Lt. Metzger's deliberate actions, two men survived because Lt. Metzger chose to give two parachutes to others rather than use one himself; and

Whereas: His actions on that day earned him this nation's highest military medal, with President Harry Truman awarding Lt. Metzger the "Congressional Medal of Honor" in June, 1945; and

Whereas: Through the research efforts of Willis Cole, Curator of the Battery Cpl. Willis S. Cole Military Museum of Kirkland, Washington, the remains of Lt. Metzger and several other previously unidentified persons now buried in a common grave for Unknown Aviators in Cartigny, France, have now been identified and are being awarded their due respect.

Now Therefore: I, David J. Berger, Mayor of the City of Lima, Ohio, do hereby proclaim November 9, 1994, as

2nd Lt. William E. Metzger Jr. Day

throughout the City of Lima, Ohio, and urge all citizens to join me in memorializing Lt. Metzger on the 50th Anniversary of his death in service to this nation and his fellow service men and women.

In Witness Whereof, I have hereunto set my hand and caused to be affixed the
Seal of the City of Lima, Ohio, this 9th day of November, 1994.

Signed: David J. Berger, Mayor
City of Lima, Ohio

Grand Seal, Lima, Ohio

Things were happening and the flow was speeding up. On the morning of August 24th, I located Sgt. Krimminger's grave in the U.S. He is buried at the Arlington National Cemetery, but I didn't get the location. I left later that morning for Denver and met Mike and Jocya and we headed south. Winona had made arrangements with her brother, Max Compton, who lived in Springfield, in the southeast corner of Colorado, for us to spend the night at his home.

The drive from Denver to Springfield began to show the French some of the distances involved in travel in the United States.

Max prepared an excellent steak barbecue dinner for us. And, before we went to bed, his son and his wife came to visit with us after going out to dinner to celebrate their anniversary. They had driven 95 miles, one way, just to have dinner. My, oh, my.

The next morning we started out for Arnett, with a stop at a fort to see the way it was in the real old west. On our way east on the pan handle of Oklahoma, Jocya suddenly talked to Mike, she only speaks French, and Mike told me to quickly pull over. Jocya had seen some long-horn cattle just a bit back from the road and she wanted some pictures.

We arrived at Arnett that afternoon, found our motel, got settled down and contacted Winona to let her know we were there. I checked and found that Russell had arrived and I called his room and made arrangements to talk to him in his room for a while. Mike walked over with me and we made our introductions. Mike left and Russell and I started taking about his experiences.

He was hesitant to talk about it, as he told me, "he had always seemed a bit guilty." I told him, that I understood. Survivors guilt is quite standard in a situation such as that. It has come to be a very accepted psychiatric condition.

Besides, he needed to talk about it and

he should feel proud of his six kids. For Lt. Metzger had given him that parachute to save his life, and in his life Russell has also been carrying on Lt. Metzger's life. As long as he and his children remembered Lt. Metzger, he would be alive, if only in their minds.

As we talked, Russell began to accept me and we started what I consider to be a very good friendship.

Winona had invited us all up to her house for a picnic that night and we had a grand time. She showed us all her pictures and I copied many of them with my camera which can take very good shots of other photographs and letters.

That night, after the picnic, Jocya, Mike and I walked around Arnett. It wasn't a very long walk.

We did find the '**Longhorn Bar**' and enjoyed the company of the people. Mike made the acquaintance of a legend of the county.

I was honored to be a speaker at the 50th Anniversary Memorial Service in Arnett to 1st Lt. Donald J. Gott, **C.M.H.**

The next day, Saturday, August 27th, 1994, we participated in the:

Memorial for Donald Joseph Gott, Ellis Country Courthouse, Arnett, Oklahoma.
    Memorial Honoring
    Donald Joseph Gott
    Medal of Honor Recipient.

Emcee   John D. Miller
    Commander Am. Leg. Post #313
Vance Air Base Drill Team
    Posting of Colors

Invocation   Dr. Jene Miller
    Arnett Methodist Church
National Anthem   Glen Dorr
Introduction of Guests   Cordell Taylor
    Vice-Comm Am. Legion
U.S. Congressman   Frank D. Lucas
    Cheyenne, Oklahoma
State Senator   Don Williams
    Balko, Oklahoma
Wing Commander Vance AFB
    Colonel James N. Soligan
    Enid, Oklahoma
Rep. Museum   Willis (Sam) Cole, Jr.
    Kirkland, Washington
Surviving Crew Member
    Russell W. Gustafson
    Oklahoma City, OK
Ellis County Commissioner
    District # 3   Earl Mitchell, Arnett
Ellis County Commissioner
    District # 2   Tom Starbuck, Shattuck
Ellis County Commissioner
    District # 1   Dwight Pugh, Gage
Comments   Lowell (Pete) Black
Unveiling of the Memorial.

The Memorial to Lt. Gott, now mounted on the Ellis Country Courthouse wall, Arnett, Oklahoma.

Winona had a memorial display box prepared which contained the flag that was on Donald's coffin along with a description of the citation and various pictures.

After the memorial was unveiled, the family and Russell Gustafson were in the leading float of the Arnett Rodeo Parade. The Rodeo was being held that weekend, which helped account for the large crowd.

There wasn't a large crowd on the sides of the street watching the parade, the large crowd was in the parade, as almost everyone in town participated.

That afternoon we traveled around to see all the places where Don's life took place, the cemetery, the home where I collected some dirt from the front yard, and the high school where he graduated and where his **Congressional Medal Of Honor** was presented to his parents.

Winona Derrick and Russell Gustafson at the official grave of 1st Lt. Donald J. Gott, **Congressional Medal of Honor**.

Early the next morning we began the long drive back to Denver to catch our flights. We drove straight north into Kansas and passed mile after mile of nothing but more miles. When we finally got far enough north to turn west, we ran into a thunderstorm bank, one that looked perfect for spawning tornados. I tried to get Mike and Jocya to look out for them, but they didn't seem to understand the danger. We were blown all over the road but we finally got clear of the storm.

Arriving in Denver, we found a hotel for Jocya to stay in until her plane left for France, and Mike and I boarded our plane for Seattle, where Carol met us at the airport.

Mike, Carol and I, left Kirkland, Washington, on the morning of the September 1st and drove to a point about a third of the way across Montana. We spent the night and the next morning, we went to the Little Big Horn, or now the Greasy Grass, Battlefield of the 7th Calvary and General Custer fame. Knowing the area well, we gave Mike a real good tour and headed on to Miles City where we spent the night.

We were at the city hall early for the planned 10:00 a.m. memorial to T/Sgt. Dunlap, being presented by the Veteran's of Foreign Wars and The American Legion.

We were happily surprised to find Don and Diana Herndon. He is the son of T/Sgt. Dunlap's sister, Io. Bob was staying with Io in California, when he enlisted. That is why so many records show California as T/Sgt. Dunlap's home state.

I will use the words of Mayor George T. Kurkowski, issued in the following statement, on November 8, 1994, to describe the ceremony when there was some doubt if Cartigny would permit a service at the grave.

CITY OF MILES CITY
To Whom It May Concern:
I wish to take this means of communications to acknowledge that I firmly believe that the research conducted by Mr. Cole regarding the dead American airmen is valid. We had a prelude to the European service here in our town honoring the one airman from this city, Sgt. Dunlap on Sept. 3rd. Attached is a press release of that service. **I URGE ALL PARTIES CONNECTED WITH THIS CEREMONY TO CONTINUE ON WITH THE MEMORIAL AS WAS THE ORIGINAL INTENT OF MR. COLE.**
Sincerely,
Signed
George T. Kurkowski, Mayor

Press Release:
At 10 o'clock, September 3rd in City Hall Council chambers a special memorial service was held for T/Sgt. Robert Dunlap, a Miles City native whose remains were found

in a shallow grave in France. Sgt. Dunlap died in the crash of his B-17 after being hit with flak during an air raid over Germany in November of 1944. The recent discovery of the remains of these flyers prompted a memorial to be erected for them near the grave site by the grateful people of France. Willis "Sam" Cole of the Cole Museum is the American liaison person spearheading this drive in the U.S., which through his efforts, a sister and nephew were located. Sgt. Dunlap's sister will attend the ceremony in France, in November. The sister Bonnie Owens of Atlanta, Georgia sent a picture and plaque to Mayor Kurkowski for the local ceremony, Saturday. Present from the local VFW and American Legion to receive the award were; Jess Erickson, Commander of Post 1579, VFW; and Ray Sirup, Past Commander of The American Legion. Members of the color guard were: Jess Erickson, Keith Johnson, Ray Sallgren and Roman Lala. Ray Glover videotaped the program. Representing the Dunlap family were Sgt. Dunlap's nephew and his wife, Mr. & Mrs. Don Herndon of Billings.

The Memorial at Miles City, Montana. The picture and shadow box for display at the V.F.W.
L. to R.: The author, Mike Vieillard, Ray Glover, Diana and Don Herndon, T/Sgt. Dunlap's nephew and Mayor George Kurkowski.

After the ceremony, we spent some time talking to each other and during my discussion with Mayor Kurkowski, I learned about his own great loss.

Two years before, his son who had graduated from West Point and was a captain in the Army, when the helicopter he was riding on in Texas crashed with all aboard killed. He personally knew the deep hurt the Dunlap family had felt.

Mike and Jocya had brought shadow boxes containing a recovered piece of '*The Lady Jeannette*' with a picture of a bomber flying over a woods behind it. I have box number one. Mike presented one of the boxes, to the V.F.W. to mount on the wall to represent Sgt. Dunlap. He had also given one to Russell and Winona.

That afternoon, we started our flying trip back home to Kirkland, so Mike could catch his flight in time and we could return the car with over 2,500 miles on it during a four day weekend rental.

Before he left, Mike and I discussed the planned Memorial in France on the 9th of November, exactly 50 years after the crash. Russell had committed himself to attending the memorial while in Arnett and Bonnie Owens and Angela were coming. Though, I had their addresses, I was having no luck in contacting the Metzger sisters, to invite them.

'Montana' Mike Vieillard checking my map and the markings for the 452nd Bomb Group's flight path on November 9, 1944 and my projected path of the final flight of '*The Lady Jeannette*.'

Thanks to a frequent flyer ticket and reduced overseas travel in November, I was able to get reservations to go to France for the memorial, myself.

After showing Mike a bit more of Seattle, we got him to the airport in time to head back to France.

During the month of September, I found that the 452nd Bomb Group was going to hold its annual reunion in Palm Springs, California, at the end of October, so I made arrangements to attend the reunion. My travel agent, Pam Farrow, got me a very special return ticket to Palm Springs and the cheapest car rental I've ever had.

When Russell and I next talked, he decided that he would also go and meet me there.

The month of October was taken up in chasing leads to locate more of the men, with little or no luck. I began to think, that I would never find the others.

On the 13th of October, I sent a follow up FAX to Mayor Berger, of Lima, Ohio. I told him that I was leaving November 4th for the memorial in France and asked him to send me some dirt from Lt. Metzger's grave so I could scatter it on the grave in France.

He accomplished that, with the help of Mr. James E. Bourk. He also informed me that the city was going ahead with the plan to use this opportunity to restore the Metzger Reservoir.

They were going to have the rededication for Lt. Metzger, Jr., and a memorial service for the rest of Lima's veterans on the 11th of November, 1994.

Carol and I talked it over and decided that we really needed to be represented there. So, she asked for a few days vacation and we made reservations for her to fly to Columbus, Ohio, rent a car and attend the ceremonies at Lima. She would then drive down to New Concord, Ohio, and visit my mother and family. She would return home, before I would return from France.

When I arrived at Palm Springs, California, I met up with Russell and we attended all the events together. We were standing out in the lobby talking one time and a fellow walked up and introduced himself. He told us, his name was Harold 'Tex' Burrell and he had been the waist gunner on Lt. Metzger's original crew. He then told us how Lt. Metzger had told the crew the day before they left for England, "That he would never leave a bomber with a wounded crewman on board." It has been this type of find that has kept my research alive and exciting.

Russell and I spent a lot of time together, I learned about his service life and the flights over Europe. We also discussed his life before and after he was in the service.

I met a great bunch of people and was a speaker during the business meeting. Before I left Palm Springs, I had become a life member of the Group Association.

One of the Group made it big time and has many restored war planes in his museum in Minnesota. He had flown in his B-17 for the reunion, so we could go out and tour it.

Russell and I spent a long time in the bomber discussing just what had happened and determining where the second flak shot had to have burst to do the damage it did. We left the bomber with me having a greater knowledge of the B-17 bomber and what it took for the men to fly them.

The last night of every reunion is the dinner dance and I found that old flyers, at least Russell, seems to have a hidden magnet for younger women. I was almost ashamed of myself, but I did have to cut in when he was dancing with the band's beautiful singer. You know, I did it for his health. I wouldn't want the rush to cause a heart attack. Russell hasn't forgiven me yet.

Russell managed to get ticketed on the same United Airlines flight from Chicago to Paris, that I was going to be on. So, we said goodbye and I'll see you in a few days.

I returned home on my birthday, the 30th of October, to find a large pile of messages and event scheduling. Everything was set with us, I was going to be in France and Carol in Ohio. For, we had succeeded in having memorials for the three men killed in the crash, in both the United States and France.

I left Seattle early on the 4th of November and met Russell in Chicago. We lucked out, as he was in the seat behind me and we were able to get talk about our lives and continue to cement our friendship.

We arrived in Paris and something must have been on the plane that shouldn't have been. The luggage was delayed over two hours before it started to spit out of the chute. The person who was to have picked us up was waiting outside customs and after a while, left without checking to see why we were delayed.

When we contacted Pierre Segers and explained what happened, he said he would be right down. Now, you must understand that right down means about 80 miles from where Pierre lives.

It wasn't quite an hour and he was there. We loaded in a rush and off we flew. Pierre had been a road race driver when he was younger and in effect, he still races. I think, that is the only trip I have made from the airport to Péronne that no other car passed us.

As it was Russell's first trip to France since his sudden arrival on November 9, 1944, Pierre took us to the grave first, so Russell could visit the grave of his comrades.

Russell Gustafson returns to France to visit the 5th grave of the men with whom he flew.

The first crewman to return to visit the grave of those killed that day.

We left the grave and drove past the crash site on our way to Driencourt, where my car was located.

When we stopped at the crash site Russell expressed that he still had some doubts. He still wondered, if that is where they actually crashed? He would still have lingering doubts, just like the Village Elders of Cartigny until I could solve the problem of finding an official way to prove '*The Lady Jeannette*' crashed in the field at Tincourt-Boucly.

The next day, Russell and I left for eastern France with the goal of visiting T/Sgt. Dunlap's (official) grave at the Lorraine American Cemetery, at St. Avold.

We arrived in Verdun that afternoon, found a hotel, checked in and toured the city.

Early the next morning, we left Verdun for St. Avold. The closer we got, the more tense Russell became.

When we arrived at the Lorraine Cemetery, I went in to the office and talked to the Superintendent about our quest. At my request he printed out the entire list of all the men of the 452nd Group who were buried there, and made preparations for Russell's visit to the grave.

The staff will check the grave marker to make certain it is clean and place damp sand in the letters on the cross to make them stand out for photographs.

Though Russell was trying to hide his emotion, it was obvious to me, when they found the cross marking the (official) grave of T/Sgt. Robert A. Dunlap. His friend, the radio operator of '*The Lady Jeannette*.'

We spent some time at the grave and then Russell left for the car because his knee was hurting. Russell's knee had been bothering him the past few years and he was finding it more difficult to walk any distance. The V. A. later traced his knee problem to his leg bone being allowed to improperly grow back together after the crash of the '*The Lady Jeannette*.'

I walked around the cemetery for a while and observed the beautiful setting. One can never stand in an overseas American Military Cemetery without feeling proud of the way our country takes care of the graves of our military men in those cemeteries. The chapels and walls of honor for the men with no known graves are always well done and they bring forth your emotions.

As we left the cemetery, we drove around St. Avold awhile, and found a marché (a good purchase grocery store) where we bought the makings of sandwich jambon, potato chips and pop, or soda, as a New Yorker says.

On our way back to Verdun, we pulled over at a nice roadside park and made our French bread, butter, ham, cheese and mustard sandwiches. They are excellent and you have

ROBERT A. DUNLAP
T SGT 729 BOMB SQ 452 GROUP
CALIFORNIA NOV 9 1944

Visiting Chatel-Chéhéry's memorial to Sgt. York of World War One fame. He won his **Congressional Medal of Honor** for an action just outside this village in the Meuse-Argonne Battle.

try one to know just how good real French bread, butter and ham are.

We talked about the grave and I told Russell that many of the men in that cemetery would have been found by T/Sgt. Wilmer Henderson, of the 606th Graves Registration Co., while on their sweeps in search of lost American aviator graves. They went from town to town asking people if they knew where such a grave might be. When they found one, they marked their maps for the follow up retrieval of the remains.

We arrived back in Verdun and we spent the rest of the afternoon touring the museum, forts, ossuary and the 'Trench of the Bayonets' along the battle line of Verdun.

On our way to Fort Vaux, I stopped at the sign I had visited with Carol and my son, Willis (III), a few years earlier and got Russell to stand beside the sign where Will had posed for a good photo

The next day, we headed back to the Somme, touring through the Meuse-Argonne area so Russell could see the World War One American battle area.

We stopped at the Meuse-Argonne American Cemetery to visit the grave of PFC Robert Leach. When stopped at the office to sign in, the Superintendent gave us a French and an American flag to place upon the grave for our photographs. Nearby there is a grave of a **Medal Of Honor** awardee and I placed the flags on it for a short while. Just two days

172

John Middleton Brodin, 1748 Private, 5th Battalion Inf., 25 July, 1916, Age 25.
His family selected the following: "A HERO HE LIVED, A HERO HE DIED, PEACE PERFECT PEACE,' Carol Cole's Australian Cousin.
Buried: British Pozières Cemetery.

Madame Josiane Brihier and husband, greet an American hero. This café has changed but the old is not forgotten. See cannon picture on shelf above stove on right.

later, I placed the flags at the new memorial at Tincourt-Boucly for the ceremony and later that day, I placed them on the grave at Cartigny where they flew until I replaced them with new flags on our next trip to France, when I brought the old flags home with me to decorate my desk.

When we got back to the Somme, people were beginning to arrive from the States. Arrangements had been made at the hotel at Rancourt for them to stay. On the 8th, I took Russell for a tour of the Somme 1916 Battle Field, visiting all the special spots.

We often stopped alongside the road in the middle of fields and I told Russell who and what had happened '*Right out there.*' We met many of my special friends and we stopped at the Pozières British Cemetery where we visited Pvt. John Middleton Brodin's grave in **Remembrance-Souvenir**.

By the end of the 8th, the hotel had Americans and ***COMMEMO-RANGERS*** at the evening dinner.

That day, I had been surprised when Russell and I drove past the Tincourt-Boucly crossroads to find a base for a monument. I had thought the ceremonies were going to be held where we would later place a memorial, not already have a memorial in place.

However, thanks to the men and women of the ***COMMEMO-RANGERS*** and the people of France, we were going to actually have an memorial in place to be unveiled on the anniversary of the crash.

Late on the morning of 9 November, 1994, 50 years to the day and hopefully to the hour from when '*The Lady Jeannette*' came from the east with fire and smoke darkening the sky behind, people began to gather for the memorial.

As I drove from Péronne to Tincourt-Boucly, on my way to the ceremonies, I stopped at the top of the hill with the crossroads in sight and sat for a long while and thought of the past few months and years of my life. And, I especially thought of that day, so long ago.

It had started so simply three years before on Christmas Eve, 1991. I stood before the grave at Cartigny, with Bernard Leguillier, and I really could not believe, what I saw. I had passed so many graves marked unknown on our trips to France. British, French, Russian, Italian, German and American graves, and at every one, perhaps for just a split second my mind felt the pain of the family of the man therein and how he would have felt if he had known that he would remain forever **<u>Unknown!</u>**

I had made a promise to that man in that grave that Christmas Eve. If I could, I would. If at all possible, his name would replace the word INCONNU (Unknown) and his family would know.

Today, in just a short while, part of what I promised would come to be. Their families knew, even if I couldn't replace the Unknown name today. And, today, for two, it would come true. A sister and niece would be there for one, and two nieces and a grand-nephew for the other.

I had been helped by so many people. Each had believed in my quest and provided unselfishly time and effort to make this special day. There was much to do yet. The grave was still marked unknown and not with the men's names. But, I would find a way to prove officially that the men were there.

Looking in the distance, I could see the new memorial and the **COMMEMO-RANGERS** around it. What a group of people, they could have dismissed me so easily at Normandy, instead they really took up the torch and they can be very proud of themselves.

Just four months ago, I identified the first two of the men in the grave. Today, we were going to dedicate a memorial on a new memorial site and we are going to hold memorial services at the grave.

Four months and nine days before, I had been assured by several people who knew, that it would take as much as five years to have such a memorial approved. Thanks to my French friends, today we dedicate one.

With a sigh and a tear in my eye, I started the car and drove down the hill to the crossroads of Tincourt-Boucly, France.

It was a typical November day in France. It had rained, but the clouds were breaking and it appeared the weather was also going to be a repeat of that afternoon so long ago.

When I arrived, the **COMMEMO-RANGERS** had draped the new memorial with an American Flag in preparation of the unveiling.

Each village, town and city has its **Souvenir (Remembrance)** associations. Each association has it Souvenir flag. Throughout the year, the different associations, such as the *Le Souvenir Français,* hold their special memorial days

The Souvenir flags and crowd approaches across the crossroads from Tincourt-Boucly to the new memorial site.

T/Sgt. Russell W. Gustafson and Mayor Madame Yvonne Gronnier, Tincourt-Boucly, unveil the memorial to '*The Lady Jeannette*' and the men killed (we only knew of three at that time.). Fifty years almost to the exact hour of the day the bomber crashed.

Russell W. Gustafson, crash survivor, with Maire Michel Boulogne, Roisel and Maire Yvonne Gronnier, Tincourt-Boucly.

and each association honors the other unit by attending with their flag, in Souvenir.

As I stood there, I heard a drum and bugle corp coming up the road from Tincourt-Boucly. Behind them was a parade of flags, I realized that I had never seen more flags and that we were going to have quite an aisle of honor for the memorial.

Arrangements had been made for a loud speaker system and Jacques Notebaert and Pierre Segers were running around making certain everything was correct.

Due to a misunderstanding in the schedule, the Americans were late in arriving, however they did arrive and the memorial service began.

Those in attendance from the United States were:

Russell W. Gustafson - Survivor
Winona Derrick - Niece - Lt. Gott
Kevin Allard - Grand-Nephew - Lt. Gott
Pat Gann - Niece - Lt. Gott
Jim Gann - Lt. Gott
Bonnie Owens - Sister - Sgt. Dunlap
Angela Owens - Niece - Sgt. Dunlap
Willis S. Cole, Jr.   Battery Corporal
                        Willis S. Cole
                        Military Museum
                        2nd Lt. Metzger, Jr.

Russell Gustafson was asked to unveil the new memorial with Maire Madame Yvonne Gronnier of Tincourt-Boucly, with the assistance of Mr. Michel Boulogne, Maire,

I presented to the Mayor's of Tincourt-Boucly and Cartigny a set of photographs of the three known men to be hung in the Mairie of each village. The frames and metal identity plaques were donated by Bonnie Dunlap Owens.

Conseiller Général, Roisel.

The crowd stood some distance away from the new memorial at the head of the funnel of Souvenir flag holders which formed an aisle of honor on each side leading to the memorial. Perhaps at the same hour, exactly 50 years after he had parachuted into the field just to the east, T/Sgt. Russell W. Gustafson and Maire Gronnier, paid homage and honor to '*The Lady Jeannette*' and to the three men of Russell's crew, as they removed the draped American Flag and unveiled the new memorial to the three men that we knew had perished in the crash of '*The Lady Jeannette*,' just 300 meters behind the new memorial.

Needless to say, a large round of applause rose from the crowd and camera shutters contributed. The unveiling was video taped for French television news.

After the memorial was unveiled, a round of speeches was held. They spoke of the occasion and of their feelings about the sacrifice of the men who died so close. Some of the speakers were:

Mrs. Yvonne Gronnier
        Mayor, Tincourt-Boucly
Mr. Michel Boulogne
        Mayor, Roisel
        Conseiller Général
Mr. Bernard Leguillier
        Local Historian
        Friend
        For the families.

Proud **COMMEMO-RANGERS**
Jacques Notebaert, Willis S. Cole, Jr. "Sam"

Mr. Willis S. Cole "Sam"
    Battery Corporal
    Willis S. Cole Military Museum

During my presentation, I thanked the Americans for coming so far to the memorial services and I thanked all the French for their

L-R: Bonnie Dunlap Owens, Angela Owens Whitesell, Gustafson, Pat Gann, Jim Gann, Kevin Allard and Winona Derrick.

grand help in making the memorial services possible. I also, presented the mayors of Tincourt-Boucly and Cartigny, with a set of framed pictures of the three men to be hung in the village hall, the Mairie, of each village.

As the ceremonies came to an end, the Souvenir flag men lined up and marched back down the street to the Fête hall, led by the drum and bugle corp.

The Americans gathered together for pictures and a visit to the actual crash site marked by a pole with a large American flag on it.

As Russell stood at the site of the crash of '*The Lady Jeannette*,' I recorded it for posterity. We went into the village where there was a reception for all. On the way, we had to stop by the home compound of a man who had what he thought were two pieces of '*The Lady Jeannette*.' He insisted that Russell sign both.

As I have written elsewhere, the propeller tip is from '*The Lady Jeannette*.' The propeller hub is from the B-26 that crashed in the Bois de Buirre two months later (see Chapter 12).

When we arrived at the village Fête hall, it was so crowded we could hardly get in the door. Russell was in great demand as every French person wanted to be introduced.

One of the **COMMEMO-RANGERS** had arranged a display of various items recovered from the crash site. All small broken bits of the bomber.

When it was to time to go, the Souvenir flag bearers lined up on both sides of the walkway and we all left through them.

T/Sgt. Russell W. Gustafson stands at the place his bomber, '*The Lady Jeannette*' crashed 50 years before. The spot where 1st Lt. Gott, 2nd Lt. Metzger, T/Sgt. Dunlap and S/Sgt. Krimminger ceased to be on November 9, 1944.

Russell with the largest known surviving piece of *'The Lady Jeannette'* to his right and the hub end of a propeller from the B-26 *'Where's It At?'*

Mr. Roland Ringenbach, at the time, President, *Le Souvenir Français*, Somme (80) Department, presents the Association's respect and honor. A grand man of the Somme region and France.

The **COMMEMO-RANGERS** loaded all the Americans up and took them to Buirre, to show them the farm where a survivor of a bomber crash had walked up to. That event is explained in Chapter 12.

As I went to the cemetery to prepare for the ceremony, they went off to a woods to see where the radio control center had been.

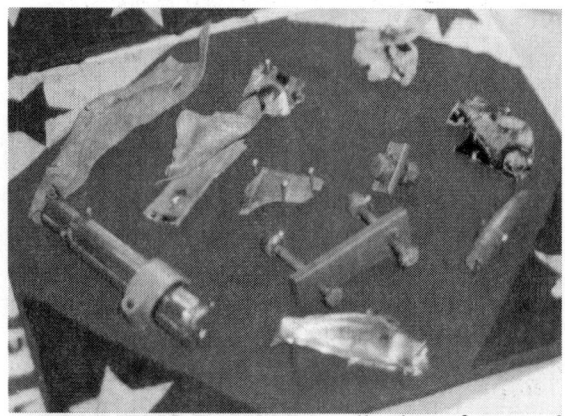

A **COMMEMO-RANGERS** collection of parts of *'The Lady Jeannette'* from the crash site. One can imagine the results on the men aboard the bomber.

Russell later told me, that the French told them the bomber had crashed, on part, because the radio men were drunk. You will discover the truth in Chapter 12.

Soon, a group of Souvenir flag bearers arrived at the cemetery and Bernard Leguillier showed up, enabling all of us to talk. I learned that the **COMMEMO-RANGERS** had gotten another memorial to mark the grave, but the Mayor of Cartigny would not let them install it, as I had been unable to find an official paper that would state where the bomber crashed. Therefore, proving who was in the grave. They had, however, agreed to permit the memorial services at the grave for the family members.

When everyone arrived, we had a simple service and I asked Winona Derrick and Bonnie Owens to place the dirt from the men's homes, that I had brought with me, on the grave. When they were finished, I placed the dirt, I had been sent from Lt. Metzger's grave at Lima, on the grave. We also laid wreaths and flowers for each man. A small amount of dirt from the United States made this just a little bit of America. In due time, perhaps Congress will make it official.

Jacques Notebaert, President of the **COMMEMO-RANGERS** had arranged for a second wreath and when we finished with the memorial ceremonies at the men's grave we went to the grave of the village priest. And,

Winona Derrick was asked to place the wreath upon his tomb.

During the memorial at Arnett, the memorial at the crash site and the memorial at the grave, Winona may have looked a bit teary, but as she placed the wreath upon the Priest's tomb, the tears began to flow. And, I remembered the first conversation I had with her in July, when she told me that she was so glad to hear that Donald had been buried with Catholic services, as he was such a devout Catholic.

This was the man's tomb who had lived to his calling and performed the services. Winona's emotions surfaced.

Before leaving, I took the family members by the tomb of the Emil Berger and we spent a moment thanking the man who helped make this all possible.

With the ceremonies complete, it was getting very dark and the attending people left the cemetery. I was among the very last and as I left, I stopped by the grave and told the men, that I would not stop my quest to see that their grave would be accepted by the United States, as it had been by the French.

That evening, many of those in attendance at the memorials gathered at the hotel for a wonderful dinner arranged by the **COMMEMO-RANGERS.**

Russell and I were asked to sit at the head of the table. It was an excellent end to an excellent day. A day that I had been working toward since Christmas Eve, 1991. And yet, I still have so much to do to complete my promise.

Placing dirt from Lt. Metzger's grave. Winona Derrick will place dirt from Lt. Gott's home and Bonnie Dunlap Owens will place dirt from T/Sgt. Dunlap's home.

Wreaths laid in honor at the grave of the last Priest of Cartigny.

Well Done!

Chapter Ten

Remembrance 97

On the 10th of November, 1994, the morning after the dedication, memorial service and dinner, most of the attendees left to travel around France. However, Bonnie and Angela Owens took me up on my offer to take anyone who wanted to go, on a tour of the Somme 1916 Battle Lines.

Bonnie Owens and Angela Whitesell at the Beaumont Hamel Newfoundland Park, with the great Newfoundland Caribou looking out over the preserved World War One trenches.

We had a fairly good tour until we ended our quick visit to the Newfoundland Memorial Park and I found a tire was going flat. Normally, that would not have been a problem, but I already had a flat spare tire in the trunk.

I made the quick decision to find the English lady running the B&B that I heard was in Auchonvillers, just up the road.

We arrived at the village crossroads and I asked a Frenchman who was by his tractor, where the English woman lived and he pointed up the street to the right.

About a block up the street, next to the water tower, we found the Tea Room, Bed and Breakfast of Avril Williams.

As we pulled into her yard, Avril came out to meet us and I told her what was wrong. She invited us in and made a telephone call to a person who said he would be right there and get the tires.

As it was still cold and damp, a typical November there, Avril offered us tea and cookies and we started to talk. It wasn't long before the fellow came to get the tires. He told Avril he would take an hour or so and off he went.

Avril told us we were welcome to stay in her dining room-bar-lounge while we were waiting. While Bonnie and Angela were talking to Avril and her daughter, Kathy, in the kitchen, I went into the combo-room and looked at the relic and book collection. Kathy's baby, Sebastian, was lying on the couch with their large golden retriever dog. It was quite a sight as the baby cuddled deeper into the warm stomach hair of the dog. Watching Sebastian grow the past few years has been one of the enjoyable benefits of visiting Avril. I believe, Sebastian is the most independent child I have ever seen.

I found Avril's books to be most interesting as were all the relics, pictures and letters. Mark, her son, is an avid collector.

As I read the newspaper articles, mounted in frames on the wall, I read about the basement of her home. It had been a dressing station during World War One and the articles told of the carvings on her basement wall and the research she had done to find out about them. She believes one carving is the initials of a man who was '**Shot At Dawn**' by his own British Army. He is buried at a nearby British military cemetery.

It didn't take much to convince Avril to take us for a tour of the basement. She hadn't been living there for long and the basement did look like it dated back to World War One. The carvings were very interesting and over the years, famous historians have had a look and some have even written about them.

When the fellow came back with the tires, we got them mounted and were soon ready to go on. Well, before we could leave, Avril insisted that we enjoy another cup of tea. During our visit, Avril had told us of her plans and I had to admit to myself, that I was jealous. Though, myself, I would rather have had a café.

As we left, I promised Avril that I would be stopping by before I left. I was going to stay another week before going home. No use letting a perfectly good frequent flyer mile ticket be used in five days, instead of two weeks.

Bonnie and Angela had made reservations at the Hotel Residence Marceau in Paris for the 11th, Armistice Day. The evening of the 10th, their ride to Paris told them, that he would be unavailable and all of a sudden they were without transportation to Paris on the morning of the 11th. So, I told them I would be at their hotel early the next morning and I would run them into Paris.

I had made prior commitments to the **COMMEMO-RANGERS** and the French soldier's associations to be at their November 11th memorial services at Roisel, which started at 10:30 a.m. Church services were to start at the same hour and day, that the World War One Armistice had gone into effect.

On the morning of the 11th, we made my fastest trip to Paris. Thankfully I had become somewhat used to driving in Paris and knew exactly where to go. Boy, did I go.

We reached the circle road exit and as we started east, up the avenue toward the Arc de Triomphe, I noticed police and soldiers everywhere. As we progressed up the avenue, the police started pulling barriers across the road behind us.

They were preparing for the parade that started at 11:00 a.m. and we were the last car allowed up the avenue. Wow, that was close.

I got to the hotel and quickly helped Bonnie and Angela into the hotel, bade my goodbyes and got the heck out of there.

Now, I had to figure out how to get back to the circle road without crossing the barricade line. As I waited at a corner, I noticed several cars shooting up and around one of the side streets. They looked to me like they knew where they were going. When the light changed, I scooted right along behind them. Sure enough, I was right. They turned this way and that way and other cars joined the caravan as we worked our way to another entrance to the circle way.

I hit that ramp speeding up, which is what you must do if you are ever going to merge on the circle road. Since, it was a holiday and there was a big parade in Paris, it was just like home. Everyone was going into the city and not so many out.

I beat it up the pay way to Exit 13 at Assevillers and headed toward Roisel on the Amiens, St. Quentin Road. Soon, I passed the Péronne Airport, the old A-72 air base, and turned left toward Péronne on D-44. I quickly turned on the next road to the right and started threading my way through small villages toward Roisel.

I arrived in Roisel at 10:20 a.m., with minutes to spare. I started to worry I had heard them wrong concerning the time the memorial services started, as there were no **COMMEMO-RANGERS** vehicles around. I had just finished putting on my World War One uniform and adjusting my gear, when the roar of engines sounded, in the distance and around the bend in the road came the convoy.

They had wanted all the Americans to attend and I didn't know until the day before that they were not. However, I had promised and I was there.

Roisel presented an extended, well planned Souvenir service. It started with a short march to the town war memorial with wreaths being placed on the memorial by various military organizations and civil representatives. A choir of children sang as the wreaths were place.

The laying of the wreathes at the Roisel War Memorial.

At 11:00 a.m., there were services in the church which ended in time for the 12:00 noon march to the town cemetery for a wreath laying, followed by a service at the attached Roisel British Military Communal Cemetery.

At 12:30 p.m. we marched back to the Mairie for a reception, reminding me of the memorial at Cantigny on July 4th.

Following the reception, everyone retired to the town Fête hall, where we found the large auditorium filled with tables joined together to form a square around the center for the dinner beginning at 1:30 p.m.

It was a combination gathering of all the veteran's groups, Souvenir groups and others celebrating Armistice Day.

The first thing that happened, was the wine started to flow. I was happy they had beer and I can get along on that.

As I was the only Yank that did come, I was treated very well indeed and was introduced to everyone. Some I had seen before, a few I knew and others I met for the first time. However, by day's end, we were all fast friends. It was not a short event.

It was grand time though and as the toasts were made, I realized that it was partially sponsored by the **Union Nationale Des Combattants En Afrique De Nord**.

They were the French veterans who had served in North Africa. Claude Leguillier was one who stood up for the toast. I pulled at his arm and told him, that I was also a Veteran of North Africa, in 1957 and 1958. Enough people knew enough English to get it across and from then on, I was an honorary member of their group and each time they got up, so did I.

We ate a fine meal and drank fine wines, except for me it was beer, and at 3:00 p.m. the dancing and singing began. I enjoyed it all. It wasn't long, before I figured out that Jacques Notebaert was a party animal. He was a natural, as he took the lead in getting people up to do their thing.

Jacques and I ended up performing on stage together, as I did my '*Over There*' rendition and he led a group songfest. All in all, it was a great beginning for me to this chapter.

At 5:00 p.m. there was a great circle dance with almost everyone participating. Couples met and kissed in the middle of the circle. At 6:00 p.m. there was a drawing for prizes and I won a seat cushion and commemoration cup. By 6:40, we were starting to clean up, however the dancing continued for some time as Jacques Notebaert sold **COMMEMO-RANGERS** *'The Lady Jeannette'* shadow boxes to help support the memorial expenses.

As I left, I thought of the two days of Souvenir I had been a part of and I so realized how much better the French are at Souvenir, or Remembrance, than we are.

I spent another week in France, visiting all my special places of interest and visiting my collector friends who introduced me to new W.W.I locations.

I spent one afternoon with Christian Kowal, the bomb disposal man, one of about

112 men in that elite unit. Christian told me about the latest World War Two American bombs he had defused, since I last saw him.

He also had samples of some bomb fuses to show me how the fuses worked. Later, we discussed the crash of '***The Lady Jeannette***' and what would have happened to the bomb load, with the in-flight safeties still in place.

Christian is one of the men of the Bomb Disposal, North France, who teaches the new members of his organization how to safely handle the goodies and when he speaks, I listen.

It was his opinion, that the bombs would have broken loose as the bomber crushed and drove their way through the bulkhead and through the pilots before the bombs would strike hard enough to overcome the safeties.

The recovered I. D. tags, wrist bracelet and wallet tend to prove out his theory.

One of the sample fuses he had, came from his latest escapade with one of our 1,000-pound bombs.

It had hit in a farmer's field, and it had hit at a very shallow angle. In the muddy field it skidded along, finally came to a halt and began to sink into the field.

Around 50 years later, the Frenchman plowing the field hooked onto the bomb and snagged it to the surface. Not wanting the bomb in his field, he got his front loader, picked the bomb up and hauled it out to the main road which passed his farm. There, he dumped the bomb into the roadside ditch, filled with water. The bomb ended up with one end up and the other buried in the mud at the bottom of the ditch. When the farmer got back to his house, he called the police, who called the Bomb Disposal Squad to come and get it.

When they arrived, the five bomb disposal men looked at the situation and shuddered. This was a big problem, a real big problem, for they had no way to know if the bomb was a true dud, or one that had a delay system screwed into it. They didn't know how hard the farmer had handled the bomb getting it to the road, or if he might have dropped it hard enough, into the ditch, to start a time delay fuse cooking off.

The time delay fuses, if I remember right, came with different time delays, running in 8 hour increments up to 72 hours.

Normally, if the farmer had left the bomb where he found it, they would have blocked off the area and let the bomb sit for well over 72 hours before they attempted to defuse it. That way, if it was cooking off, no one would be near it, when it exploded. However, since the farmer had dumped the bomb at the side of a major road between cities, they could not shut down the road for a long period. They had to defuse the bomb and defuse it quickly, for there was no way to know if the fuse was cooking off.

The time fuses used an acid bath on a spring loaded wire. When the fuses were off safe and they hit the ground hard enough, a glass vial would break, releasing the acid to start eating on the calibrated thickness wire. Depending on how thick the wire was, the acid would eat through the wire, at a known rate determining how long it was before the wire broke. When the wire broke, the spring loaded firing pin was released to strike the initiator detonator which exploded, exploding the detonating charge which detonated the bomb's main explosive.

The delayed bomb action kept the Germans from repairing a bombed place until after all the bombs went off. If they didn't realize there were delayed bombs in a drop, all of a sudden holes would open up and Germans would fly through the air. By mixing the bomb load of instant detonation bombs with varied time delayed bombs, you can imagine the result if you tried to repair a railroad yard.

When the bomb squad started to work on the bomb, the fuse at the upper end of the bomb broke loose, unscrewed easily and was soon removed.

The fuses were usually booby trapped in a way as to make the bombs explode if you didn't know exactly what to do. You may have to unscrew them a bit, lift and unscrew again, and follow several other secrets of the trade to remain safe.

To get to the bottom of the bomb so

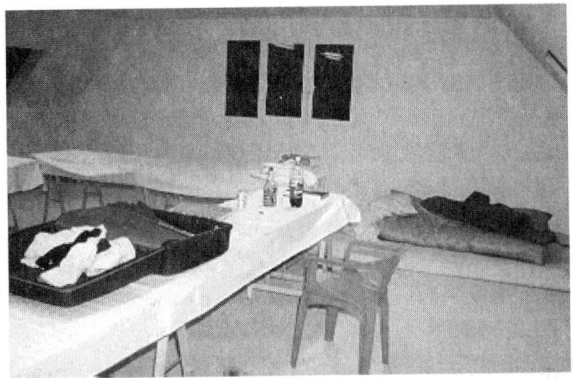

My Paris loft? I used my evenings here staying warm and starting this book.

they could work on it, they had to dam up the ditch on each side of the bomb and dip all the water out of the ditch.

Once that was done, a squad member got down on his knees and working upside down and up inside the tail flanges he began to release the fuse. He couldn't see what he was doing and he had to do it all by feel.

It didn't take long and he was able to slide the fuse out and take the secondary detonator explosive container off the main fuse. When that was done, they put the fuses in a tray in their truck and had the farmer lift the bomb into the back of the truck with his tractor's front lift.

When they were finished cleaning up the site and opening traffic flow again, they drove off to their compound at the west end of the Somme District (80).

They took the now very safe bomb to the bomb dump and then they got the fuses out of the truck and took them into the workshop. Like little kids, they wanted to see how they ticked.

When they took a close look at the fuse the squad member had taken out of the bottom of the bomb, they found that the initial detonator had gone off. It had been a timed fuse after all, and the farmer had dropped it hard enough to start the acid eating the wire. It had fired sometime between the time they put the fuse in the truck and when they got back to their depot.

As Christian finished his story about the bomb, he lifted his hand into the air and made a motion, rubbing his thumb in his cupped fingers. He looked up and told me, that this was one time five Frenchmen owed one to the big guy up there. It had been luck and skill, and he was not so sure which was which.

The question was, did that thing go off five minutes after they put it in the truck or an hour later. No matter, it was close enough.

On the evening of November 12, 1994, I started this book, sitting at the arbor table in my loft at Bancourt. The loft wasn't heated except for what worked its way up. My bed was a warm sleeping bag on a pallet on the floor. It was well lit and there was only one permanent item in the very large room, the toilet standing in the open, along with a large arbor table which had been set up for a **COMMEMO-RANGERS** banquet.

I'm certain that large room will be the closest I will ever come to having a garret in an attic in Paris. But it was a great place to start a book. Pierre was going to fix it up and make an apartment for himself. I keep meaning to ask him if he ever got it finished.

I worked with finger-less gloves. A heavy coat was often necessary. I had my long underwear on and a little bit of Old Kentucky and Pepsi Max combined to warm my innards every so often.

Before I left, Pierre and I talked about the grave and crash site and discussed what we hoped to see in the future. I thought, a separate memorial at the crash site should be put in place for Krimminger, once we determined where he had fallen to his death. Pierre agreed. We also decided to work together to make certain the crash memorial and the grave continued to be honored and improved.

When I arrived home, I continued talking to the people at the Total Army Personnel Center to work on getting the Individual Deceased Personnel Files of the dead men. When I received the authorization from the men's family survivors to act in their behalf, I sent in my requests for the records.

Since, I thought the Mayor of Cartigny might soon approve our request to mark the grave with the men's names, I had taken the measurements of the mounting holes for the Unknown Aviator plaque on the grave's

Before I left, Pierre and I sealed up my next shipment of scrap metal home. Notice section of tank track stretching the length of the box. The box in the far corner is the tool kit of a large German mortar, found by Richard Boniface while digging a hole.

marker cross. By the end of November, I had designed a temporary brass plaque for the grave which listed the three men's names and all the information required to duplicate my research. As soon as it was produced by a local trophy company, I sent it to the President of the *Le Souvenir Français*, Mr. Roland Ringenbach, so he could put it on the grave when we got the approval.

I had been talking with Mr. Doug Howard at the T.A.P.C. in regards to obtaining the men's records, along with the Director, Mr. John Manning, and once they had the family's authorization, they promised me fast action. Doug Howard later became the Deputy Director of the Mortuary Affairs Center at Fort Lee, Virginia.

One afternoon, in mid-February, 1995, I opened the mail box and there was a very large envelope from T.A.P.C. Soon I was sitting at my desk exploring the Individual Deceased Personnel Files for three of the four men killed during the last flight of '**The Lady Jeannette**.'

There was a note with the three files, stating that the file of Sgt. Krimminger had been misplaced and that they would keep my request on record and send it to me, if and when they found it.

Blast! That was the one I really needed. I knew what had happened to the three men whose records I received, I didn't know what had happened to Krimminger.

Each record was almost a half inch thick and as I read the first one, 1st Lt. Donald J. Gott's, it became apparent what a wealth of information the records contained. Each and every contact with the men's families, in both directions, were recorded. I now had a copy of every communication that the families sent to the army and a copy of every family communication sent back, except for the telegrams sent to the families notifying them the men were missing or killed in action.

The most surprising thing I learned, shot down my theory that the men's remains in their official graves had come from the excavation of the crash site in 1946. Their official Burial Record showed they were buried at the temporary cemetery at Limey, France on the 11th of November, 1944, just two days after the crash. The most frustrating thing was that their place of death made no sense. It looked like a map reference, but when I scanned my maps the references did not fit anything on them.

I made copies of the Burial and Disinterment records of each man and laid the copies side by side for comparison. The burial reports allowed me to determine the number of I.D. tags (Dog Tags) recovered and to whom they had belonged. One very strange thing, was an entry on Lt. Gott's Burial Record, stating that the G. R. Officer of the 19th TAC had kept one of his I. D. tags. The really big question was and still is, why?

It was not a standard practice to do such a thing. Graves Registration rules said that both I. D. tags were to be transmitted with the remains. One was buried in the grave with the remains and the other was attached to the temporary cross above. Well, it was a lead to who had recovered the remains. It must have been someone attached to the XIX TAC. As I read the disinterment reports, it became obvious how the men had each received an official grave and what remains had been hidden along the road. Larger skeletal pieces had been kept and divided into three parts to create three official remains.

As the year continued, I maintained my contact with the men's families and filled them in on what I had found. I also continued trying to make sense of the map coordinate listed as the place of death for the three men.

I decided, that I had better get some of my cartographer friends involved. Soon, I had written to some World War One cartographers in France and England, hoping they could help.

I sent another 20 letters to people I knew in France, including the map references and asked them if they would let me know if they could determine where the location was. The entry was a very cryptic:

Hattonville, France, Coord.
VU5346, Nord de Guerre Zone

Each of the three men's records listed the same information, including:
K.I.A. Burned plane crash.

During my final reviews of this chapter, I found another new detail that I had overlooked before, even though I had checked and rechecked the files, I continue to find hidden details. Just two days ago, I realized that Sgt. Dunlap's wallet had been found the day of the crash, as was Lt. Metzger's identity bracelet.

Until this review, I had overlooked the signature of Capt. Passman on a personal effects inventory form, indicating Dunlap's wallet had been sent in from the Limey Cemetery. The recovered wallet was not marked as damaged and the Personal Effects Bureau did not contact the family when they sent the wallet back, as they did the Metzger family about the damaged I. D. Bracelet. The returned inventory report lists two wallets with some money, including a 'short snorter' bill and a book, probably a flight record notebook. A 'short snorter' bill, often a two-dollar bill, was a souvenir bill signed by everyone present, often the entire aircrew of a bomber, when the bill was declared a 'short snorter.' The wallet had to have been in Dunlap's heavy leather flight jacket pocket to have come out without much damage.

Now back to my narrative of 1994. While talking to Bonnie Owens about the files of the three men I had just received, she told me that she just had found a reference to Sgt. Krimminger. Going through the papers the

The family Boniface, the children grow so fast when you only see them once year or so. Author, Peter, Richard, Romain and Michelle Boniface, with Carol Cole on right.

family kept, she had found that Sgt. Krimminger had signed her brother's will and his hometown was listed as Marshville, North Carolina.

Finally, a lead to where Krimminger lived before he went into the army. The telephone just rang and rang at the mayor's office at Marshville, so next I tried the high school listed there. The office didn't seem very interested in helping and I didn't expect much when I finished talking to them.

A few days later, I managed to contact the Mayor of Marshville, and I promised to call him back to see what he had found. That afternoon, he told me that a Darren Krimminger lived nearby and that he was Herman Krimminger's nephew.

On the 20th of February, 1995, I was able to write a letter to Darren Krimminger furthering the discussion we had when I contacted him via telephone.

In part, my letter states: "As of now, I have contacted family members of five of the nine crew men and one directly, Russell

Gustafson. Only three to go, but they are proving very hard to locate."

I went on to tell him that I thought perhaps Herman's remains were picked up around Hattonville. It was under my projected flight route from Saarbrucken to Tincourt-Boucly. My reasoning was simple, but not correct as I later discovered.

The Burial Record shows who is buried on each side of the person. From the three records I received, I was able to determine that all four men had official graves at the Limey cemetery and that they were buried side by side.

This was surprising to me, as I had a good idea of how many remains the cemetery were burying each day and what were the odds of Krimminger falling to his death along the flight route and still being buried beside the three that had remained with the bomber?

I had spent a lot of hours making a model of a B-17, damaged to look like '*The Lady Jeannette*' must have looked just before it rolled over and exploded. My model of Russell Gustafson even had a twisted broken leg, as he cleared the bomber when bailing out. You have seen pictures of it in Chapter 5.

I tried to make the damage match the location of the second flak burst, as Russell and I had determined it must have gone off about midway between the two left engines, the number 1 and number 2, and about 15 feet under them. When I sent Russell a set of pictures of the model, he wrote back that it looked like, "a good job."

It was soon the end of March, 1995, and still no help from the map people, the map coordinates just didn't fit anywhere in Europe. One fellow told me, it was somewhere out in the North Pacific if it was a good coordinate.

One Sunday, while out looking for World War One relics in 2nd hand and antique stores, Carol and I stopped at a military collector's store in Edmonds, Washington. I found a book for sale there that I thought would solve the problem:

Manual For Instruction In Military Maps And Aerial Photographs
Norman F. Maclean and Everett C. Olson

The family Leguillier, Bernard, Valerie, Gérard and Régine. Always one of our first visits when in France.

The Institute of Military Studies, The University of Chicago, Harper & Brothers Publishers, New York : London, 1943

I spent a lot of hours with the book and the place of burial location. I thought I became fairly good at doing what the book said, but I couldn't figure it out. I didn't feel bad about it though. Neither could anyone one else.

Back in February, when I got the burial location, I called Captain, now Colonel Passman, retired, (since deceased) and asked if he had any idea of how they had plotted the place of death.

Col. Passman told me, that they had been assigned a shell shocked artillery man and that he prepared all the reports and he, Passman, had no idea of how he did it. Thinking it would have been a standard system of reporting, I contacted several old Graves Registration men. No, they said, it was not a standard thing.

It was getting close to when Carol and I had planned our vacation. I had not been able to determine the place of death of the men so that I could prove it was them in the grave at Cartigny.

Meanwhile, I continued my stream of letters, telephone calls and fax mail to my friends in France and to the many people who were becoming part of the network of '*The Lady Jeannette*.'

As I was preparing to leave for the midnight shift late on June 19th, 1995, I walked past the maps I have pinned on the walls in my office and hallway. That afternoon I had also been working with a World War One map out in the museum, doing research for my public access television show which I hosted in Seattle for two years. As I walked down the hall to leave, something I had read in the map reading instruction book and seen on the maps that day, jogged my memory and suddenly matched, I knew how to prove the place of death using an official document.

The author at the large map with the 162nd mission flight route and estimated bomber flight path, as shown in an article in ***The Seattle Times*** in the summer of 1994. Up to this date we had been searching for the place S/Sgt. Krimminger had fallen to his death, now I knew.

I ran out to the museum and checked the World War One trench map, where I had marked the place where the bomber had crashed a long time before. Then I went back in and checked the big map, I knew it was close, very close.

However, I had to leave for work and I was on pins and needles all that mid-night shift. As soon as I arrived home in the morning, I put the maps together and laid out what I thought I had discovered.

As I had walked down the hall, the night before, I had suddenly remembered the book discussing back azimuths and that zeros were often dropped when writing down coordinates. What I had also remembered, was a triangular concrete pole just outside of Nurlu, a village on the road from Péronne to Cambrai. Bernard Leguillier had once told me that it was a survey zero point. The survey points had been established by Napoleon many years ago when France was first surveyed. Bernard also remarked, this one represented 50 degrees north, 03 degrees east.

Seeing the trench map had brought back to mind, the concrete tower I had seen at Nurlu and what it meant and walking down the hall, I had looked at the location of Hattonville on my large wall map. Then it struck me. If I laid an azimuth line between Hattonville and the concrete tower at 50:03, the line went right over the crash site. If I came back down the line from the tower, 4,600 meters it had to be close.

As I laid out the line that morning and measured back, I always came up wrong. I was close but usually a half mile or so off. Then the subconscious started worked again and I thought of the trench maps. They were not laid out in meters, that came later. They had to be in yards. So, I worked the math out using 4,600 yards and came closer, but not close enough to convince the people in France.

Putting it aside for a while, I went on with the daily search for those not found and maintained network contacts. As usual, within a short while, a brilliant thought popped up. Check the trench maps. Were they set up on a mile standard? When I checked, I found they were set up on 1,000 yard grids. Instead of looking at 4,600 yards or meters, I should try 4.6 miles on the 1,000 yard scale. When I laid it out on the map, I was within 94 feet of where I had put an x on the map to reference the crash site.

My next contact was with Russell Gustafson, I told him what I had figured out and that I could now prove it was he who landed in the field that November afternoon. I could also tell him what happened to the woods he remembered seeing next to where the bomber crashed. The World War One trench map showed a small woods right where Russell remembered seeing it.

Looking at the map, I could remember the first time Bernard had shown me the spot where the bomber crashed. He had pointed at a bank running from the crossroads toward the crash site and mentioned that a small woods used to be there, but it had been cut down when the big farm tractors had arrived in the early 1980's to permit larger fields. Russell agreed that I must have it right now.

I could now use the Official Burial Record of each of the three men to prove that the United States Army, on 11 November, 1944, had listed the crash site at Tincourt-Boucly as their place of death.

That evening, I sent out several faxes to the Mayor and **COMMEMO-RANGERS** in France and the next day, follow up information packages went to each one in the mail. Enclosed, were copies of my maps and instructions on how to lay out the back azimuth line and how to measure back along it to pin point the crash site.

That same afternoon, I followed up my fax to the U.S. Army Casualty and Memorial Affairs Department and they agreed, the crash at Tincourt-Boucly was the one in which the men died.

Carol was leaving on the 23th of June for two weeks in France. This was one trip we would not be able to share as I was not free to travel at that time as we had planned earlier in the year.

When Carol left, she carried duplicate

Bernard Delsert, Huguette and Jean-Jacques Gorlet. French collector, notice Jean-Jacques crutch. In 1997, Jean-Jacques took us on an excellent tour of W.W.I tunnels. He has a collection of excellently carved grave stones from small German cemeteries that were later combined into larger cemeteries. The individual's stones were thrown away.

information packages for the mayors, plus several baseball caps I had designed, that pictured the bomber just before it crashed, with each man's name and fate next to his position. She gave the mayors their caps and the copy packages before the end of June.

I had included a copy of the Burial Records, reduced in size maps showing the azimuth line and instructions on how to transfer them to a large size map. Just in case the small size map was not a large enough scale for them.

While Carol was there, Kim Sasaki, a friend from Carol's work, joined her and they went to the British and American memorials on the 1st and 4th of July.

Carol returned soon after the 4th and told me that the village elders of Cartigny had held a meeting on the 4th of July, American anniversary, and voted to permit us to take off the Unknown American Aviator Plaque and exchange it for one with the men's names.

By now I was free to travel and it did seem very opportune. Carol and I discussed the situation and I was lucky to find a cheap, short trip, one week ticket to Paris. I would go and change the name plate myself.

I arrived in France on Friday, July 21nd, and was picked up by Bernard and Claude Leguillier. I told them that I was on very limited time and that I was going to change the plaque at noon on Sunday.

Since I had liked Avril's so much when I had visited there before, I had made arrangements to stay at her B&B during my visit. After arriving at Avril's, I quickly contacted all my friends and made arrangements to visit them during my short stay.

That Saturday night, the other guests, Avril, Kathy and I, with Sebastian in a baby stroller, left the B&B about 9:00 p.m. for one of Avril's famous walks. No problem because it doesn't get totally dark in that part of France until 10:30 p.m. or so. It was a beautiful, warm summer evening.

We walked along the sunken road from Auchonvillers down around to where we could walk up the sloping field to Hawthorne Crater. You can see the soldiers leaving the trenches and beginning their attack walking up the field after the Hawthorne mine was blown in the movie made of the July 1st, 1916, morning attack. They were slaughtered.

After walking around part of Hawthorne Crater, we crossed to the sunken road which was between the lines the day of the attack, but occupied by the British that had dug a tunnel to it. However, as fast as they climbed the bank to rush the Germans, they were cut down. The small cemetery, just down the hill, shows the effects of the German machine guns that day.

We walked up and around to Jacob's Ladder, the place where the camera was located that morning when it took the pictures of the explosion and later, the men. We discussed the camera man's work and went on up the road to White City, so named that because of the chalk spoil from the dugouts and tunnels.

It was after midnight when we got back to the B&B. It was grand and if at all interested in World War One military history, a walk that you should take with Avril one night.

The next day I was at the cemetery just before noon. I set up my camera and video camera and prepared to exchange the plaques. As everyone had said they would be busy, I proceeded alone. At noon, on the 23th of July, 1995, I removed the Unknown American Plaque and replaced it with one with three names on it.

1st Lt. Donald J. Gott
    Congressional Medal of Honor
2nd Lt. William E. Metzger, Jr.
    Congressional Medal of Honor
T/Sgt. Robert A. Dunlap

A few days later I flew back to the United States. Knowing I had made a great advance and that, I still had so far to go.

By now the families and I had decided that under no circumstances did we want the grave disturbed. They had come to accept what had happened and felt that the French who had preserved the remains and created the grave would care for the grave better than any one here in the United States. We felt that a shared responsibility with the American Battle Monuments Commission and the *Le Souvenir Français* would be best.

From all my conversations with people in Washington, D.C. I had become aware that the only way to accomplish what we wanted was to achieve an Act of Congress that would recognize the grave as an Isolated American War Grave. I have been told there were several official Isolated War Graves in France. We would prefer the grave at Cartigny become another.

I came home and settled into trying to find out what had happened to the tail gunner, Sgt. Krimminger, and locating the missing men of the original Gott crew: Fross, Robbins and of course, Joseph Harms, the bombardier. He was on his second mission filling in for the bombardier who failed to show up for the flight.

There are hundreds of Harms around the country, as well as Robbins and people called Fross. I continued to make calls and write letters, skipping through the list using a

The grave at Cartigny, France, marked with the names of three of the men in the grave, July 23, 1995.

set number to skip each time, in the hope I would find the right one by straight luck. But as with my lottery tickets, I had no luck finding them.

I had sent in a request to the V. A. to try to locate Lt. Harms, as I had his full name and serial number. In August, 1995, I got an answer back from them that he was still alive. So, I took the next step of sending a Priority Mail letter to the V. A. containing another Priority Mail letter with his address blank. They are supposed to forward it to the last known address and if the person wants to get back to you they can.

After several months passed, I knew that had not worked out. For some time I tried to think of various reasons why he had not answered my forwarded letter, as it had not been returned by the post office.

Thursday afternoon, October 5, 1995, I came home and when I opened the mail box, there was a package from Total Army Personnel Center. When I ripped it open, I found the Individual Deceased Personnel File for S/Sgt. Herman B. Krimminger, with a note saying they had found where it had been misfiled.

I literally ran inside and sat down at my desk to study the file. I was amazed at what I found. It had all changed, for there it was, just as it had been typed almost 51 years ago. I didn't have to search for where S/Sgt. Krimminger had fallen to earth any longer.

Place of Death:
Hattonville, France, Coord.
VU5346, Nord de Guerre Zone

The exact same place of death as the other three men, they had all died together at the crash site. This was explained under Cause of Death: Chute caught on plane.

I also noticed, his recovered I. D. Tag did not contain his full name, so he was buried as H. B. Krimminger and the name Herman had been penciled in later. It had to be much later, as his 1948 Disinterment Directive still carried his initials only.

As Dunlap's personnel file had shown Krimminger on his right, Dunlap was shown on Krimminger's left. Interesting also was the fact that he was shown as a T/Sgt. when he was a Staff Sgt. I suspect that some larger clothing pieces had been found and that another crewman's, probably Dunlap's, clothing, had been placed in the mattress bag with the pieces of Herman that were buried. He was the only one with some of his own body parts identified, as you have read, and actually put in his own grave.

A bit further into the file I found something that I could hardly believe. To date, I had spend hundreds of hours and a lot of money searching for crew members and/or families of crew members such as Sgt. Krimminger. If this file had arrived with the first three, I would have been so far ahead.

For there was the answer to Ida's letters. A full listing of all the men who were on the bomber with Herman and their next of kin's mailing address.

Within an hour, I had contacted the right waist gunner, Sgt. William R. Robbins and the ball turret gunner, Sgt. James O. Fross. Now, I had witnesses to what exactly happened in the back of the bomber from the time of the first flak strike to when they bailed out.

I struck out on the bombardier though, there was no Harms listed with either his or his wife's name in the Brooklyn, New York, borough.

I have learned one important lesson when interviewing people about the past. Remember well, their first response, before they have had an opportunity to screen their reactions.

It isn't that someone will try to hide something. However, after reviewing the answers in their mind, they will often change their story somewhat to fit what they think you want, or to smooth over and protect themselves or someone else involved.

As I have often told all the people I have talked to about what happened that day, "I want to know the truth, however I will not purposely include something to hurt anyone, living or dead, unless it is absolutely necessary."

When I called the Worcester, Mass.,

information operator, she gave me the telephone number of a Mr. William R. Robbins and when the lady answered, I told her that I was hunting for a Sgt. William R. Robbins who had been aboard a B-17 bomber that crashed in France on November 9, 1944. Without missing a beat, Shirley said, "just a moment, I'll get him, it's for you Bill."

Bill was the second survivor I had found. He was very surprised that I had located him and we talked for some time. When I asked him to describe what happened in the back, I was surprised how much he had compressed in time all the events that took place, in comparison to how long it actually lasted.

It was his report that had included the remark that he had bailed out near Verdun and he was surprised when I told him how far they were away from Verdun when the bomber crashed.

When we talked about Sgt. Krimminger, Bill told me what happened and I remembered it well. He also told me that he had bailed out when he saw a chute go by from the front of the bomber.

Talking to Bill, I became aware that the crew had not been gathered together after the crash. Bill was walking the avenues in Paris the same afternoon and except for Fross whom he visited once in Texas, in 1945, he had never met with any of the crew again.

When I called the number in McAllen, Texas, that the operator gave, Mary Fross answered, she verified that I had the right Fross, however Jim was having a problem with Alzheimer's disease. There was no problem talking to Jim, but she warned me not to expect too much.

Jim came to the telephone and we talked about his experiences aboard the bomber and about Sgt. Krimminger.

When Jim and I finished, Mary came back on the line and we discussed my research and the fact that the remains of all four men were in a grave in France, as well as each having their own official grave.

I promised to keep her and Jim informed as things progressed and as I had with Bill, I promised I would come visit sometime in the future.

The next person I talked to was Darren Krimminger and we had a long discussion about his uncle, Sgt. Krimminger. We had heard that he had opened his parachute in the bomber and now that I had talked to Robbins and Fross there was no longer any doubt.

By the November 27, 1995, I had to write a letter to the Total Army Personnel Center declaring that the families, the French and myself did not want any of the men's graves disturbed in any way.

By unconfirmed telephone conversations with me, I had been told the only way our country would recognize the 5th grave was to destroy it. They suggested that the families sign a request that all 5 graves be dug up, with what ever remains found being sent to the Hawaii identity center for D.N.A. testing. Of course, the families would have to provide D.N.A. samples.

Instead of recognizing the unique situation of the grave with its hidden American war dead, the government people were suggesting a way to cover it up. When I told the families, they immediately requested that I write a letter stating their official request to not disturb the any of the graves and restating their desire that the government recognize the 5th grave and the situation under which it came to be.

In early February, 1996, Mary Fross and I talked about Jim's condition and she told me that Jim was going deeper into Alzheimer very fast and if I was going to come visit, perhaps I should do it soon.

I had been talking to Russell Gustafson all along, always keeping him up to date with what was going on, so I called Russell and we discussed Jim's condition.

We determined that Russell would fly to San Antonio directly from Oklahoma City and we could meet there and rent a car to drive on down to McAllen, as connecting flights were hard to make and expensive.

I flew the United Airline's red eye to San Antonio on the last Friday in February and met Russell there on Saturday morning. We rented a car and headed for McAllen.

When we arrived at the Fross home, I

had the pleasure of watching two men meet for the first time since the crew split up to enter their separate parts of '*The Lady Jeannette*' story over 50 years ago.

James O. Fross "Jim" - Ball Turret Gunner
Russell W. Gustafson - Flight Engineer
It's been a long 50 years.

Jim's wife Mary, and his daughter, Kimberly, made us feel right at home and Jim seemed to open up as more and more memories of the period came back to mind.

We had an excellent evening, enjoying a barbecue and good Texas company. My talks with Jim did help me understand more about what happened in the back and it supported Robbins' statements about Jim having his bell rung.

He told us about his bailing out and that he saw Krimminger hanging there. He remembered going to a hospital and his trip back to England and the United States. It was obvious that Jim has suffered greatly with the loss of Krimminger.

Russell and I spent the night at a motel in McAllen and we were on our way back to San Antonio the next morning. I was back in Washington State late Sunday evening.

For the next six months or so, I'd call Jim at home during the daytime and we would have short conversations. He would always recognize me and each time I learned a bit more about what really happened back there after the flak hit.

I had now talked with both survivors from the back of the bomber and yet, exactly what happened there remained somewhat fuzzy to me. After our first conversation, Bill Robbins said he had bailed out when he had seen a chute from the front go by the escape hatch where they were standing. I knew only three men got out from the front and Harland jumped just before Gustafson. As Robbins had landed further away than Harland, it would had to have been Harms' chute that Robbins claimed to have seen before he jumped.

Harms, the fill-in bombardier, was up front where Gustafson could not see him, so there was no way, without talking to Harms, to tell just when he bailed out.

But at that time, it would seem that the men's bail-out order was: Harms, Robbins, Krimminger, Fross, Harland and Gustafson.

I continued hunting for Harms, but still no luck. No letters came back from my sample mailings and I had talked to every Harms I could find in the New York City area and even some distance to the north. None of them had ever heard of the fellow I was hunting for.

As Memorial Day weekend, 1996, got closer, Carol and I decided that it would be a good time to fly to Boston and visit Bill and Shirley Robbins at their home in Worcester. We would combine a trip back to our Nation's history with a visit to a living source of more modern history.

We had an excellent visit with Shirley and Bill and enjoyed staying two nights in a very quaint, old fashioned motel near Worcester.

Bill and I discussed the events he had participated in, but I still felt what had happened in the back had to be different than what it appeared. It seemed a lot would depend on finding Harms.

After we got back, I called Jim and Mary Fross and it was obvious that Jim was getting worse and that soon he would not be able to be home alone or even answer the telephone.

On one of my very last talks with Jim, he said hi to me and as usual we discussed what had happened, this time Jim told his story somewhat differently. Krimminger had opened his chute in the plane and he was pulled out, they couldn't hold him. He, Jim, had to bail out while Krimminger was hanging there under the bomber's tail.

The use of, "They couldn't hold him," also had to mean that Robbins was still in the bomber. That would switch the back end bailout order to Krimminger, Robbins and Fross last.

That matched what Bill Robbins had told me during our first conversation. During our later conversations, Bill still had Krimminger in the bomber when he bailed out. The problem with that was it just didn't match the report from the front that was in the records. "One was gone and the other two were bailing out," was Lt. Metzger's last report on what he had found in the back. Lt Harland had to have been the one who relayed that report back to the group, after being given the report by Metzger just before Harland and Gustafson bailed out.

During the summer, I was contacted by Mr. Steve Snelling of the Eastern Daily Press of Norfolk, England, and asked to submit a chapter for a book he was preparing for the newspaper. To be titled, '***Over Here, The Americans In Norfolk.***' The book was to be about the Americans serving in the Norfolk, England, area during World War Two. That area had been called 'Little America' because of all the Americans there at the time. When the book was published by Breedon Books[62] in October, 1996, the chapter titled: **Above and Beyond** was mostly taken from Chapter 5 of this book, with additional information provided by Russell Gustafson.

The Group's reunion was held in Tucson, Arizona, and Carol and I attended. Our special group attending the reunion was growing. Shirley and Bill Robbins attended, as did Russell Gustafson. Several more were going to attend, however problems came up preventing them from coming.

Max Compton, Lt. Gott's nephew came to represent the Gott family. Mary Fross had been planning on bringing Jim, but he had progressed to a point where it was not possible. Harold and Florine Burrell were also there and I was very surprised, for I had been told by Russell, that he had heard that Harold had died.

One thing was very special though, Winona Derrick had made arrangements with the Oklahoma Aviation Hall of Fame for Lt. Gott's **Medal Of Honor** to be loaned so it could be on display at the reunion. Russell had picked it up and brought it with him. I had been hoping to have Lt. Metzger's medal present, but it had not worked out.

For the first time in years, Carol and I did not go to France. We had always wanted to go to Australia and visit her Australian branch of the family tree.

It was going to be the 80th Anniversary of the 1916 Battle of the Somme, where so many Australians lost their lives. Carol had the great idea of our planning our vacation to attend the Australian Armistice Day memorial services at the Australian Canberra War Memorial.

We left aboard United Airlines in time to arrive in Australia and attend the Memorial and it was well worth attending, as all the Australian leaders were present.

Just before we left home Barry Brodin called. Barry is a long distance runner, and Australian cousin of Carol's who had stayed with us for a while a few years earlier. Barry is the grand-nephew of John Middleton Brodin buried at the Pozières British Cemetery. He travels the world running marathons in such places as Boston, Spokane and New York. Barry had called to tell us he had made arrangements for us to have a special tour of the Canberra War Museum Annex. This is where all the large equipment is stored on the outskirts of Canberra.

It was a grand tour, we were the only people there with one guide. And, I got to crawl on two more KRUPP 210 mm cannons like ours. I was very pleased to see a set of girdles, which were large wooden blocks attached together to circle the wheels of the cannon so it could be pulled across soft ground. We had seen many of them in pictures but this is the only existing original pair we know of.

From there we went to New Castle and saw another KRUPP 210 mm cannon which belongs to Monty Wedd, at Williamstown. He has an excellent war collection and was building a museum building in which to display it at the end of the runway of the Australian Air Force Base.

After visiting Monty, we toured the Australian Air Force Museum located on the base. Interesting and worth visiting if you are the aviation type.

On the way north to Carol's cousins, we spent two nights with Marge and Jim Dawson. We had taken them on a tour of the Somme Battle lines a few years before and they made the mistake of telling us if we were ever in Australia to stop by.

When we arrived at Barry's parents home at Mullumbimby, the family had a great dinner for Eric's birthday and everyone was there. Eric Brodin, is the nephew of John Middleton Brodin who is buried at Pozières, France.

After we left the Brodins, we drove north to Childers to visit another 210 mm cannon. From there we drove into the 'outback' and circled back to Sidney and our flight home. All in all, a great trip covering 2,500 miles of Australia in two weeks.

The end of 1996 came and still no closure with '*The Lady Jeannette*.' There was not a lot to find out, but what was missing was what it would take to finish telling the story as it actually happened.

As I reviewed my research, it was apparent none of the men were intentionally trying to change what happened. It was more like the parable of the blind men touching the elephant. Each had remembered something, sometimes very different. It was obvious that all of their minds had come to believe what was comfortable but not necessarily the truth.

There was still no effort by the government agencies I had contacted to get the grave recognized by the United States. The grave was still marked with the temporary plaque I had put on it.

I made up my mind, that my research was going to be done by the end of 1997 and my book would be finished.

In February, 1997, around the same time as our visit with the Fross family a year earlier, I answered the telephone to hear Mary Fross at the other end. "Jim," she told me, "had died." He had been in the nursing home for some months and seemed to be holding his own, however he suddenly took a turn for the worse and had died within a few days. In its own way, a blessing.

Mary had taken Jim's medals and such, had them framed for display in his room and she had given him the '*The Lady Jeannette*' cap I had sent. "He was so proud of his display with its medals and his hat, he wore it everyday," she told me.

Like Margaret Siegfried Schinz, my World War One Nurse friend, I was pleased that I had gone to visit Jim and Mary and get the story while the story was still somewhat able to be told. Unlike Lt. Harland, of whom I know so little, Sgt. James O. Fross will live for many years in this book and in our memories.

Always at the back of my mind was the lack of information on the memorials at the crash site and grave. A problem that sort of solved itself one evening at my American Legion Post 161, of Redmond, Washington.

Our post is building a memorial and Kelly Farnsworth had donated several 28 inch by 36 inch by 1 ½ inch marble pieces to be engraved for the facings of the memorial.

The post commander, Blue Trenbeath, suggested Kelly might donate two more to the post, who in turn would donate them to our museum so we could use them for the grave and crash site informational memorials in France. I soon had the two marble pieces at home. With them at hand, I was ready to design what I wanted displayed upon them and to seek donated engraving and transportation to France.

Our local '*The Lady Jeannette*' display.

Just after the first of the year, United Airlines had a special priced ticket to France at the end of February. It was the lowest price to France, I had ever seen. Carol agreed that I could go for two weeks.

It had been my intention for a long time, to visit France during each season so that I would be familiar with the climate when it was described in the books I was reading.

Besides, it was time to renew old acquaintances and strike up some new ones. One result of the this trip was the renewed determination to visit France in May and June.

A couple years before, I had been told of a person who was interested in purchasing our cannon, a Mr. Didier Boniface, no relation to Richard. When I knew I was going to France, I had asked Bernard Leguillier to contact him and make arrangements for us to visit. I had heard that he had several cannons and when Bernard and I visited him, we found that to be true. I was most impressed and asked if I could bring Carol to visit when we came back at the end of May.

One of Didier Boniface's French 75 mm cannons. One of several cannons his museum owns.

While in France, I visited everyone I could and took measurements of the base of the crash site memorial at Tincourt-Boucly. I wanted the marble to be the right size to fit on the memorial and grave without problems.

I came back from France feeling much better and prepared to try to get the marble engraved and shipped in time for us to install on the United States Memorial Day in late May.

The memorials as existing, only had the names of the first three men and there was no room to add a fourth. Besides, I wanted all the information at the crash site and grave to allow someone else in years to come, to be able to duplicate my research.

When I got back, I completed my designs for the two memorial plaques and started working with Mr. David Quiring, of Quiring Memorials, Inc., Seattle, Washington. I had talked to him several times in the past few years about the memorials in France and we had discussed his firm doing the work at a reduced cost.

At the same time, I contacted Ms. Sue Zorn, of United Airlines and told her of our project to properly identify the American airmen involved. She asked me to prepare and submit a request and she would take my request into consideration.

Russell and I had been talking about what he was doing the summer, of 1997, and he told me that he was going to visit his son, Michael, in New Jersey. We started to discuss the people of '*The Lady Jeannette*' that I had been in contact with, but had not met as yet. It seemed that perhaps I could meet Russell in Washington, D. C., when I came back from France, and we could go visit them together. We decided to think it over.

The day I took my designs to show David Quiring, he looked it over and said his firm would do the engraving as a full donation to our museum.

When David and I had removed the two marble pieces from my vehicle, he pointed out some marking on the back of them and told me, that those were the marks of his father. His father had supplied the marble for the store when it was applied in the 1930's. It was a very rare Alaskan white marble that was no longer quarried after the war. I left Quiring Monuments, Inc., that day, a very pleased fellow.

With that problem solved so nicely, I contacted Ms. Zorn, and she told me that United Airlines would transport the memorials to France for us at no charge. All I had to do was to safely crate them and deliver the crate to the United Airlines Freight Terminal at the

On 9 November 1944, The Lady Jeannette, a B-17G-35VE Bomber, SN 42-97904, was on a mission to Saarbrucken, Germany. Just 4 minutes before bomb drop they were struck twice by FLAK. The Pilot and Co-Pilot kept the bomber in the air for over 90 minutes. Just 8 km. from the emergency A-72 Airbase at ESTFÉS-EN-CHAUSÉE they crashed 330 meters behind this memorial. For their effort to save a wounded crewman, the Pilot and Co-Pilot were awarded the United States highest military medal, the Congressional Medal Of Honor. GO 38, 16 May, 1945

* 1st Lt. Donald J. Gott, Pilot, Harman, Oklahoma, *Medal Of Honor*, Air Medal, Purple Heart
* 2nd Lt. William E. Metzger Jr., Co-Pilot, Lima, Ohio, *Medal Of Honor*, Air Medal, Purple Heart
* 2nd Lt. Joseph F. Harms, Bombardier, New York, New York, Air Medal, Purple Heart
* 2nd Lt. John A. Harland, Navigator, Chicago, Illinois, Air Medal, Purple Heart
* T/Sgt. Russell W. Gustafson, Flgt Eng/Top Turret Gunner, Jamestown, New York, Air Medal, Purple Heart
* M/Sgt. Robert A. Dunlap, Radio Operator, Miles City, Montana, Air Medal, Purple Heart
* S/Sgt. James O. Frost, Ball Turret Gunner, McAllen, Texas, Air Medal, Purple Heart
* S/Sgt. William R. Robbins, Waist Gunner, Worcester, Massachusetts, Air Medal
* T/Sgt. Herman B. Krimminger, Tail Gunner, Marshville, North Carolina, Air Medal, Purple Heart

* These four men were killed in the crash, most of their remains gathered that day are buried in their common grave in the Village Cemetery of CARTIGNY, 5 km. southwest of this memorial.

729th Bombardment Squadron (H), 452nd Bombardment Group (H) at Deopham Green, England. 45th Combat Wing, 3rd Bombardment Division, 8th Air Force, United States Army Air Force

Alaska Marble - Donated by the American Legion Post 161, Redmond, Washington, U.S.A. and Kelly Farnsworth
Carved by Quiring Monuments, Inc. Seattle, Washington
Transportation by United Airlines

Willis S. (Sam) & Carol L. Cole Jr. – 1997
Battery Corporal Willis S. Cole Military Museum

The informational memorial installed on the base of the **COMMEMO-RANGERS** memorial at the crash site of '*The Lady Jeannette*.' Listing the entire crew with all the information required to duplicate my basic research. It is the hope of the people, of France, that the United States will work to make the crossroads memorial park into a memorial park that other units and men of the United States can memorialize their service in France.

DONALD JOSEPH GOTT
First Lieutenant. SN: O-763996
United States Army Air Force. Pilot
Congressional Medal Of Honor G.O. 38, 16 May 1945
Air Medal, 3 Oakleaf Clusters
Purple Heart
28 Missions
Harmon, Oklahoma, U.S.A.
Born 21 June, 1923
2nd Grave, Harmon Cemetery

WILLIAM EDWARD METZGER, JR.
Second Lieutenant. SN: O-558834
United States Army Air Force. Co-Pilot
Congressional Medal Of Honor G.O. 38, 16 May 1945
Purple Heart
3 Missions
Lima, Ohio, U.S.A.
Born: 9 February, 1922
2nd Grave: Lima Woodlawn Cemetery

ROBERT ALEXANDER DUNLAP
Master Sergeant. SN: 39696406
United States Army Air Force. Radio Operator
Air Medal, 3 Oakleaf Clusters
Purple Heart
28 Missions
Miles City, Montana, U.S.A.
Born: 26 October, 1924
2nd Grave: C-23-19 American Cemetery. St. Avold, France

HERMAN BRUCE KRIMMINGER
Technical Sergeant. SN: 34890339
United States Army Air Force. Tail Gunner
Air Medal, 3 Oakleaf Clusters
Purple Heart
23 Missions
Marshville, North Carolina, U.S.A.
Born: 29 August, 1923
2nd Grave: 1720 Section 12, Arlington National Cemetery

Crew members of 'The Lady Jeannette.' B-17G-35VE Bomber. SN: 42-97904
729th Bombardment Squadron (H). 452nd Bombardment Group (H) at Deopham Green, England.
45th Combat Wing, 3rd Bombardment Division, 8th Air Force, United States Army Air Force

This common grave contains most of these crewmen's remains recovered from
the crash site of the bomber at TINCOURT-BOUCLY on 9 November, 1944.

The families of these men will always remember the people of CARTIGNY for honoring
their fallen sons and granting them a place of honored rememberance among their own

The Congressional Medal Of Honor is the United States' highest Military Honor.

Alaska Marble-Donated by the American Legion Post 161, Redmond, Washington, U.S.A. and Kelly Farnsworth
Carved by Quiring Monuments, Inc. Seattle, Washington
Transportation by United Airlines

Willis S. (Sam) & Carol L. Cole Jr. - 1997
Battery Corporal Willis S. Cole Military Museum

The new informational memorial plaque for the grave at Cartigny, France. For the first time, all four men's name and personal information is shown, as well as their second official grave site. As with the crash memorial, this one references the other so that the two sites tie together for future generations information. As of this writing, the Unites States still does not recognize the 5th grave in France.

Seattle Airport, and, of course, provide the necessary paperwork at either end.

It began to seem that this might be the year I would be able to complete my promises to the men in the grave. I promised myself before the year would end, I would forward a request to Congress to recognize the grave. Of course, knowing how slow that process might take, we shouldn't expect an Act of Congress for months afterward. At least I would have all their names at both sites and that would be a major step.

Interest was growing though, I had started to get requests from people researching the **Congressional Medal of Honor** for help in their research and I had given several talks about my research to various veteran's groups. All of them had offered their support when it was needed. Still, I had a lot of unanswered questions before I could finalize a request.

One day, I received a letter in the mail from the Veterans Administration. I had sent in another request for Lt. Harms' address, quite some time ago and this reply gave me his last known address in New Milford, New Jersey.

I immediately got on the telephone and found that Harms had an unlisted number. I tried the library and the mayor's office, but no one would give me his actual telephone number or address.

I was running out of time and really needed to reach him before we left for France. Russell and I had made most of our arrangements, but we could still visit Harms while seeing the other people. That is, if I could get in touch with him and set it up.

Since I was going to install a memorial that was going to have his name on it, I wanted him to know it before I left. Besides, it was almost two years since I first knew his name. I could think of one last effort. I wrote him a letter and placed it in an unsealed, stamped, partially addressed envelope. I wrote a cover letter to the post master of New Milford telling the post master about the memorial and why I needed to get in touch with Mr. Harms. I left it up to the post master to forward the enclosed envelope.

A few days later, I came home and found a message on my answering machine. Hi, I'm Joe Harms - - I had made contact at long last. It took another day to reach Joe, but I found out a lot from him. Without a doubt, he was the third from last to bail out of the bomber. He had walked toward the crash site and was almost to it when he was picked up and taken to a hospital.

I told him about my planned trip with Russell and asked if we could meet with him. No problem, just call when we knew exactly when.

The week before we left for France, I manufactured a crate for the two marble pieces and David Quiring helped me slide the beautifully carved memorial stones into the crate. I took the crate out to the airport, where Schenkers International Air Freight Forwarders donated the preparation of the shipping documents and I delivered the crate to the United Airlines Freight terminal.

The next Thursday, Carol and I boarded United Airlines for our trip to France.

If you notice, I shamelessly use the United Airlines name in this book. It is because of their donation of transportation of the Memorial stones to France. Without this transportation, the grave would still have temporary markers. And, they have been my airline of choice for many years.

We arrived at the Charles De Gaulle airport and found out just how much ground it covers. Finally, we asked a semi-truck driver who was parked along the road where to go. It turned out, he was going to the same building and had us follow him. Once there, he asked questions and located the exact room I was to go to. Myself, I have always found the French very helpful.

The Jules Roy-Schenkers International Freight Forwarders at Charles De Gaulle Airport, worked hard to process the paper work and personally walked me through the clearing process. They donated the processing of the clearance paper work and we got our memorials into France without duty.

Carol and I felt quite good when we had the crate loaded in our poor rental car and were on our way Péronne. The donations had made it all possible and so far, the museum's only outlay was the cost of the crating material.

Our first stop was at Avril's to check in and get a cup of tea. Then we went by Pierre Segers to let him know our plans and finally arrived at Richard Bonifaces. Richard, an excellent friend, has a large shop and plenty of tools. Richard was out at a job site but, Michelle, Peter and Romain were around.

We used Richard's tools to take the crate lid off and inspect the memorials. Both had survived the trip well. As we were getting ready to leave, Richard drove up and we were able to show him the memorials. I also made arrangements with Richard to use some of his tools to mount the marble memorials.

On Monday, the U. S. Memorial Day we drove to Richards and picked up the two memorials and took them to the crash site and grave. All set, we thought to install them on the two **COMMEMO-RANGERS** memorial bases.

As luck would have it, the portable drill I got from Richard decided to have a low battery problem and we were unable to permanently mount the marble memorial. We had to prop it against the base of the memorial and plan to come back and to do it right.

When we arrived at the grave, we didn't have any better luck. We found the base of the new **COMMEMO-RANGERS** grave memorial was different in size than I had been told. The new memorial stone we had brought was too big for the flat surface of the base.

There was nothing to do but also prop the new marble memorial against the new **COMMEMO-RANGERS** memorial and figure out a way to mount it.

Carol and I decided that we would have to make a concrete base for the new memorial that would fit between the grave and the hedge behind it.

However, we had achieved our purpose. For the first time, both sites had all the information about the incident and all of the men's names were listed correctly at each site. At the crash site were all of the crew's names, and at the grave, all four men now had their full personal information. The grave was

Romain, Peter and Richard Boniface with the author and the two memorial plaques.

referenced to the crash site, as the crash site was referenced the grave.

When we arrived back at Avril's, she was busy outside the B&B fixing up her front approach steps. Working with her was a good friend from Albert, Freddo.

Freddo, Frêdêric Loyer, is a musician and stage manager who visits with Avril to enjoy the country and he had helped a lot improving the B&B. We discussed the fact, that I would have to make a concrete form out of the shipping crate and find the makings for concrete. Then we would have to mix and pour the concrete to make a base for the new grave memorial. I also had to find a hand brace in order to drill the concrete base of the crash site memorial to be able to install the mounting anchors that I had shipped along with the memorials.

Freddo stepped in and told us that he would be happy to help us buy the concrete materials and do the mixing. Avril told us to use her tools and mixing container and with Freddo's help it should be easy. I've learned enough not refuse such an offer of help and Freddo, in effect, saved the day.

One thing I have not located in France is premixed concrete base in bags, the

Mr. Leguillier, *Le Courier Picard* reporter
Claude Obert   Author and Freddo Loyer

standard add water to the mix and stir that we use for smaller jobs. The next morning, after picking Freddo up in Albert, we started out and picked up the basic materials on the way to Richards. We tore the memorial crate apart and constructed the required form. It was a tight fit in the small car, but we all got in and we were soon at the crossroads.

Freddo had brought his hand drill and soon was drilling the required holes. As we worked, a truck pulled up and Claude Obert got out and volunteered to help. Claude is the local President of the **Union National Combatants**. It is like our veteran's organizations all combined. I expect, it gives them a larger voice for veteran's affairs in government. I remembered Claude from the 1994 memorial services and Armistice Day celebration.

Before long, the new informational memorial was attached and sealed. We visited Claude at his home in Tincourt-Boucly for an aperitif, before going to work on the grave memorial base.

Freddo insisted on mixing the concrete, which I helped pour and tamp into place. Between mixing, I worked on realigning the berm of the grave and cleaning it of leaves and such. While we were working, Bernard Leguillier stopped by to see how we were doing and we talked about the times we had been to the grave together.

Twenty-two months after I placed the temporary plaque listing the first three men's names on the cross, I could remove it and for the first time all four men's names and personal information were listed on their 5th grave at Cartigny, France.

When all the concrete was poured, we left. Carol and I would have to come back in two days to remove the form and permanently mount the new memorial. When we got back, I removed the concrete form and Carol and I lifted the new memorial into place and sealed it. Then we began cleaning up. As I was working, a French soldier walked into the cemetery and passed me to go up the aisle behind me.

He stopped at one of the tombs up the aisle for a while and then came and talked to us. He told us that he was Marc Berger, the grandson of Emile Berger, the man who had

The **COMMEMO-RANGERS** memorial to the left with author and Freddo pouring concrete into the base form, with Bernard Leguillier observing.

A promise kept. Their names for all to see.

Marc Berger, grandson of Emile Berger.

restored the grave and cared for it for so long.

It seemed to Carol and me that perhaps fate had brought him here that day, visiting from his helicopter unit. It somehow seemed very fitting as we completed permanently marking the grave with the four men's names to have the grandson of Emile Berger present.

Fort Duhdux, Seclin, France. Commander Didier Boniface.

I have always thought of our work to identify the men in the grave, and the improvements we hope to see made, as an extension of Emile's beginning.

The following Sunday, we drove to Cornay, at the edge of the Argonne Forest to visit Vincent Bentz for lunch. Vincent was my guide for the tour of the German tunnels in Vauquois some years earlier.

When lunch was completed we walked up over the hill upon which Cornay is built and Vincent showed us the area where Sgt. Alvin York won his **Congressional Medal of Honor**, during World War One. We were on the next higher ridge to the north from where [63]Sgt. Alvin York earned his medal, and Vincent explained the whole sequence to us from this great overview of the area.

I can't finish this book without introducing you to Didier Boniface.

I have written of visiting Didier with Bernard Leguillier earlier and Bernard had made an appointment for Carol and me to visit and have lunch with the Boniface family.

Didier and his family, like ourselves, are intent on saving military history. The Boniface family of Lille, France, has recently embarked on a great journey to provide a museum that will always preserve cannons.

Didier has leased Fort Duhdux, at Seclin, a village just south of Lille, for 99 years and I am jealous. Located just off the pay-way, exit 19, the fort is a very large, old style brick construction fort. The family plans to move into the fort, to live and work to make the fort a living museum and a bed and breakfast.

Didier's cannon collection will be there along with lots of other military relics

Casements soon to become museum display rooms and bed and breakfast rooms for your enjoyment.

An angel carved by a warrior of World War One.

dating from early French military periods to about 1920. The planned opening is in late 1998 and Carol and I hope to be there, to be among the first official visitors.

If Didier manages to make his dream into the living history fort, I expect, that one day he will find a very large cannon arriving at his fort's gate. A large German KRUPP 210 mm Lange Mörser.

If all goes well, the fort at Seclin will become one of the must visits for people touring the World War One lines of France. When the B&B is in place, you will be sleeping in the large casement areas of the fort, as did the original garrison.

During the summer months, various reenactment groups are going to be invited to set up their camps and you will be able to see the periods as they were. The passion of their reenactment groups is equal to any here in the United States.

A mostly underground quarry with many underground rooms. Throughout the quarry are carvings on the walls.

Among Didier's many cannons is a complete French 75 mm cannon, with all the harness and equipment, just as it was issued to the French army during World War One. It has been stored inside and greased the whole time and I love it.

The week after we installed the new memorials, we were called, along with Bernard Leguillier to act as interpreter, to meet with the mayors and councils of Tincourt-Boucly and Cartigny, and the mayor of the major commune, Roisel.

After we explained the new memorials and our future goals, the meeting turned into a planning session for future events to honor the two sites. Before it ended, many decided to join the 452nd Bomb Group Association as Associate Members and several expressed an

On one wall of the quarry is this carving depicting the two types of women the men might know. One, is a woman dressed for an evening in Paris and another dressed as the mother or wife at home. Hidden war art of a war long ago.

When Jean-Jacques points down and says, "Sam, down." It is best to head down. The author emerging from the entrance of a French dugout located about 30 feet down. The hole led to a large underground room about 10 feet across, 20 feet long and 7 feet high. The shaft was full of dry sand and I was having a hard time getting back out.

interest in attending the reunion in October, to which I had invited them.

Before we left the meeting, I promised to research the B-26 crash in the Bois de Buirre, so that a future memorial could be installed for the bomber and its crew at the crossroads along with '*The Lady Jeannette*' memorial.

We discussed the 80th Jubilee of the end of World War One being held in the fall of 1998 and what might be done to incorporate that celebration with the crash site and grave, including a rededication of the crash site and a dedication of the grave.

Hopefully, including recognition of the grave by the United States, which I had promised myself to pursue further in the fall. I told them, that if my previous efforts continued until after the reunion without any results, I would prepare a direct appeal to the Senate asking for official recognition of the grave. Perhaps, by working directly with the Senate, official recognition can be obtained in time for the United States to participate with the villages during their 80th Anniversary.

One of my long term wishes was met this trip when Jean-Jacques Gorlet took us to visit quarries and tunnels used by both sides during World War One.

When we returned to Dulles Airport in Washington, D.C. Carol continued the flight to Seattle and I met Russell Gustafson at the main terminal.

We left the airport and drove to Roanoke, Virginia, where we visited with Jeanne and George Schofield the next morning. Fran Fredericks had driven up from her home to be there during our visit.

Jeanne, Lt. Metzger's older sister, had many of the pictures and letters sent and written to the Metzger family after Bill's death. Several of which, are included in this book.

We left there late that morning and drove back to Washington, D.C. where Russell and I went to Arlington National Cemetery to visit S/Sgt. Herman B. Krimminger's official grave. We spent that evening with 2nd Lt. Gerry Collins. Russell had visited Gerry several times before when Russell was back east. It was interesting to ask questions about the crew and get two views.

The next morning Russell and I went to the National Archives to see the Army Air Force Photographic Collection, only to be told again, the transfer of files had not been accomplished. If I wanted to see them, I had to make an appointment two months in advance with the National Air and Space Museum in Washington, which was still holding onto the collection.

We left there and headed to the Jersey shore where Russell's son Michael had a bicycle shop in Long Branch. I had met Michael at the Phoenix reunion the year before. Later, I did my washing while Russell visited with his daughter, Lee Marie, who also lives in the area. So far we were making real good time. We were now a full day ahead of schedule.

I had called Joe Harms when we arrived at Long Branch to make arrangements to visit him in New Milford and he said that he would be happy to drive down and visit with us the next morning. That way, we would save several hundred miles going to and from his place.

The next morning when I arrived at the lobby somewhat early, there was a gentleman sitting on one of the sofas in the lobby. I looked at him, and he at me, and I knew I was face to face with the last man I had to find from '*The Lady Jeannette,*' 2nd Lt. Joseph F. Harms.

Before Russell arrived, we discussed how Joe had been assigned to the bomber and what happened before he bailed out. From what he told me, I now had the basis to set out the correct bail out order, which did differ from what everyone had said. You have read about the true order in Chapter 5. Joe also told me he had been in another crash on a Glacier in Iceland on his way over to England and he gave me a quick recap of his life after the service.

Russell arrived and I listened to them reminiscing that day so long ago. For other than Lt. Harland, Russell was the only crewman of '*The Lady Jeannette*,' Joe had

T/Sgt. Russell Gustafson meets the Bombardier, 2nd Lt. Joe Harms. Fifty-two years, 7 months after sharing several hours of history.

seen that day. He arrived at the bomber late, gave his name to Russell and climbed into his position up front with Harland and later bailed out over France. Joe had not known anyone on the bomber when he got on it and he had not met anyone from the bomber since the day it crashed.

We left New Jersey that day and drove to Ohio. The next morning we stopped by New Concord to visit my mother, Luella Claire King Cole Rice and my stepfather, Lawrence E. Rice, for a short time before heading to Lima, to visit the grave of Lt. Metzger. We arrived in Lima at lunch time and three days ahead of schedule so we didn't get to meet Mayor Berger, who had been such a help. However, we did visit the Metzger Reservoir and the rededicated war memorial.

At the Woodlawn Cemetery, I found their records didn't even show Lt. Metzger as having been in the service or having been awarded the **Congressional Medal Of Honor**. I penciled in all that information in their record before I left their office to visit the grave.

As Russell and I stood at the official grave of 2nd. Lt. William E. Metzger, Jr., **Congressional Medal of Honor**, though at the time the gravestone did not show the medal, I realized, that we had completed one of my major wishes. Both Russell and I have visited all the graves of all four of his fellow crewmen. Both the official graves and the unofficial one at Cartigny.

Across from the cemetery as we left, I saw the location of a monument provider. After I got back, I contacted them to find the cost of removing Lt. Metzger's head stone and engraving the medal award upon it. Of course, I can not do it, it takes a family member. Fran Fredericks has promised to see that it is done so that future generations can visit the grave of this American hero, her brother, and know the honor that was bestowed upon the man that the official grave represents.

Our trip was way ahead of schedule. We left Lima and drove to the edge of Indiana, near Chicago, to spend the night.

I called the Harland family from the motel and told them that we would be there fairly early the next day. At the same time, I made arrangements to leave early the following day from Midway Airport for Seattle. Russell was happy that we were ahead of our schedule, as he had to get back to Oklahoma City to complete some business.

Scott Harland made us feel at home and two sisters also came to meet us, Debby and Kathy. Kathy volunteered to take me to the airport and after a short visit Russell left for home, a two day drive away. Russell has been such a support in my research. We had driven almost 2,000 miles in the past few days, miles that for Russell were unnecessary, but for my research so important and thanks to Russell, I was completing a major step this day.

Scott got his father's boxes out of the basement and they had quite a bit of his military history in them. The most important find for me was two letters from men Lt. Harland had served with. Those two letters, along with a letter from Mrs. Gott, provided the links to locating the last two men I had been searching for so long.

Kathy invited me over to her house and put together a picnic dinner for several of her family and me, and I told the story of '***The Lady Jeannette***' to many of Lt. Harland's grandchildren. Late that evening, Kathy took me to Midway Airport where I spent the night and left early the next morning for home.

I arrived back to another stack of letters and inquires. Among them was an invitation to the first Graves Registration - Mortuary Affairs reunion at Fort Lee, Virginia, to be held in mid-September. It was time to contact Gail and Charles Kettlewell and ask if I could stay with them for a few days, again?

The e-mail reply was a terse, come on. I immediately sat down, wrote and sent my advance request for an appointment at the National Air and Space Museum to see the Army Air Force photographs. Then I sent my fee to attend the G/R reunion.

My next job was to call Chicago and see if I could get a number for an Irving Hirsch, which I did. When I started talking to the fellow at the other end, I knew I had reached the guy who was air sick every time the bomber went up. Irv Hirsch, the missing 10th original crewman. He told me they sometimes called him Cracker Jack because he carried empty Cracker Jack boxes to vomit into.

During our telephone conversation, I filled Irv in on the crew and gave him the numbers of Gustafson and Robbins and told him the news of Fross.

Next, I called the Oklahoma City operator for the number of Earl Penick, as he had written his letter to John Harland from there. There were two Penick's listed, but a call to them found them not to be relatives, nor had they heard of him.

In the letter from Mrs. Gott to Lt. Harland's mother, you have read the letter, it referred to Lawton, Oklahoma, as Penick's home. I called the operator there and found that there was a Penick listed.

When I called the listed number, a lady answered and I asked if she knew of an Earl Penick. She told me he was dead. However, she was the wife of his brother Carlton, and if I would hold for a minute she would get him.

From Carlton, I heard the other side of the story of the night of November, 8, 1944 and the morning of November 9th. Yes, Earl had lived in Oklahoma City for many years but had moved back to Lawton some time earlier. Carlton told me Earl had been dead since the late eighties.

That one day within an hour, I had located the last of the missing original crewmen of Lt. Gott's crew.

The next day I started to get caught up with the work around the house and began to finish this book. The one I had started so long ago at Pierre Segers at Bancourt, France.

There were no more excuses. There were no crewmen left to find. I now knew what happened during the last flight of '***The Lady Jeannette.***'

At the end of June I mailed out chapter five to each of the survivors, enclosing a stamped, self addressed envelope. I wrote that I would like them to read it and make any corrections needed.

Within ten days, I had received each copy of the manuscript back. With each was a note.

(Sgt) William R. Robbins wrote:

"Sam:
I read this chapter and it is very well done and accurate. One small change on page 5, line 15 is - my middle initial is R.
See you in October
Bill R."

Verifying what I thought had happened in the waist of the bomber, just as you read in Chapter 5.

As much as I wish I could end this book, writing that everything was set and that the grave had been recognized by the United States government, I knew it was not going to be so. But I wanted a place and time that gave a natural closure to the time period I was writing about.

As I contacted the families and reminded them of the 452nd Group reunion at Savannah, Georgia, on the weekend of October 19th, 1997, I realized that the reunion was the proper place and time to close the story.

I told them of my plan and I hoped that they would come. Most had responded that they would be there. Winona Derrick and Fran Fredericks both agreed to bring the **Congressional Medals of Honor** awarded to Lt. Gott and Lt. Metzger. The first, and perhaps the last time the two medals would ever be displayed together.

Mid-September soon arrived and I was

off to Washington, D.C., and the Graves Registration - Mortuary Affairs reunion.

Gail and Charlie Kettlewell made me welcome and introduced me to the light rail system into Washington.

I got my day at the National Air and Space Museum. Mostly it was a large disappointment, but I had some luck as you will read in Chapter Twelve.

I spent one afternoon visiting the offices of each of the four men's home state senators and the office of my home state Senator Slade Gorton. I talked to people in each office to find out how best to begin the request for an Act of Congress to gain official recognition of the grave at Cartigny. I left with a plan in mind.

When I left for the reunion a few days later, I had found enough on our very large KRUPP 210 mm cannon to call for another trip back some day in the future to the Photographic Archives at College Park, Maryland.

The Graves Registration - Mortuary Affairs reunion was very enjoyable. I met many fellows who had been in the same areas as Will Henderson and I learned more about the work of the men in those organizations from World War One through today.

During the business meeting, they discussed a joint association of the older Graves Registration Association and the newer Mortuary Affairs people. When it was agreed, I asked if they were going to have associate members, as did the 452nd Bomb Group and many other such organizations? When it was voted to do so, I became the first Associate Member of the Graves Registration-Mortuary Affairs Association.

Back home, I worked to complete this book and I began the research on the B-26 bomber of the Bois de Buirre, reported in chapter twelve.

Through my constant communications with Bernard Leguillier, in France, I had heard that four French associate members of the 452nd Bomb Group Association were going to come to the reunion and that one other member of the **COMMEMO-RANGERS** was also going to be there.

First Graves Registration-Mortuary Affairs combined reunion at Fort Lee, Virginia, September, 1997. From World War Two to present, these are the men and women who served our military dead with respect.

They were coming for three reasons, one was to establish stronger Franco-American ties with the Group members, another was to establish a strong relationship with the Group for planning future Souvenir (Remembrance) both in the United States and France, and finally, to invite all the members of the Group to attend their 80th Jubilee of the end of World War One in the fall of 1998 and the planned further recognition of the crew of '*The Lady Jeannette*' and the men in the grave at Cartigny.

Carol and I left for the 452nd Bomb Group reunion and the "*The Lady Jeannette' Remembrance 1997*" with a prepared display and a new research project, you will also read about in chapter twelve.

We arrived in Savannah late on a Wednesday night. Found and checked into the DeSoto Hilton Hotel, where the reunion was being held. We had two real goals, one was the reunion and the planned closure of the period covered in this book. The other was the necessity to see two houses at the edge of one, of the many, of Savannah's beautiful squares.

The first would take a couple of days, the second, a walk around Savannah to please Carol and her quest-one of those trade offs I have mentioned.

Carol and I had just got our display set up in the hotel's atrium when a couple came in to see the display. When Carol started talking to them, we found they were a couple of 452nd Bomb Group members who we had

Author showing Lt. Metzger's sister, Fran Fredericks, the **Remembrance 97** display with both **Congressional Medals of Honor**.

Two **Congressional Medals of Honor** on display together for the first time since they were presented to Lt. Gott's and Lt. Metzger's families on Sunday, June 17, 1945. With Lt. Metzger's damaged identity bracelet still stained with the smoke of the explosion.

been wanting to meet for the past two years.

Just to prove the world is a small place, they were from eastern Washington State and we had traveled to Savannah, from Washington, to meet Paula and Bob Lorenzi.

Four of the French arrived late Thursday evening and Pierre Segers told me that Mike Vieillard was coming also. During the next two days more and more of the special attendees associated with '*The Lady Jeannette*' arrived.

I had made arrangements with everyone that Friday evening was to be '*The Lady Jeannette*' night. Saturday night, the night of the dinner dance, is always so busy and the tables so small that we would not be able to mix, so Friday night was our night.

The Group holds it reunions at different locations across the United States each year to make it easier for those who live in different regions to find a reunion in their general time zone every few years.

Ed Hinrichs wall of honor for the 452nd Bomb Group.

There would not be another Group reunion in the east where most of the people connected to '*The Lady Jeannette*' live for several years. We are growing older and finding travel difficult. I thought that this was the year to do it and do it right.

Everyone had been located and everyone knew about the reunion. We hoped every crewman would be represented, however we knew that everybody has their own lives and something might have to take precedence.

On Friday evening many of the Group attended a dinner on the river boat. The ones who had signed up for that trickled in a bit late, however, quite a few showed up for our special night.

Darren Krimminger, the nephew of Sgt. Herman B. Krimminger, had told me that he had a new job and that he would not be able to come to the reunion. I talked to him more about it and he said he might be able to make it one night. I suggested that he try to make it Friday night as he would have time to talk to everyone.

As the people started to gather, I heard a familiar voice call my name and turned to see a man that I did not recognize. Irv Hirsch, took my hand and introduced himself and immediately we became fast friends.

That evening we missed two of the crash survivor representatives.

Joe Harms' brother had the nerve to get married 50 years earlier and the family had an entire weekend of excellent anniversary entertainment planned. Our Bombardier, 2nd Lt. Joseph F. Harms, would not be present to represent himself. Lt. Harland, the Navigator, was also unrepresented I had been hoping one family member might have made it.

I heard someone else call my name and when I turned around I found two big guys and it took me by surprise to find Darren Krimminger standing there. He introduced me to his friend Scott Love, who had made the trip from Monroe, North Carolina, with him. They had driven over six hours to get to Savannah and they had to leave in a couple of hours to start back to be there in time for the new job. I was proud of Darren for his effort and later I saw him sitting with Irv Hirsch for quite a while, learning about his Uncle Herman, who had died so long before Darren was born.

It turned out that the portable bar in the atrium closed at 8:00 p.m. and it seemed that the night was going to dry up and end early.

Suddenly through the door swept an entourage consisting of Mary Fross, daughter, Kimberly and son, Michael. She came over to me and asked if it would be OK for her to serve her '**Texas Buttermilk**,' a McAllen, Texas, concoction. Saved by the family from Texas.

We had discussed the drink a couple of times over the telephone and I told her I could see no reason we wouldn't enjoy a sip or two or three or more.

Within minutes, Mary, Kim and Michael had set up their spot. Michael had brought his blender from home to crush ice and they had a cooler full of ice along with all the mixing.

Soon, we were enjoying Texas Buttermilk and it really smoothed out the evening.

We had a grand get-together and throughout the night all the special attendees came and went, the French were there and many of the Group came in for a while to visit. Mr. Ringenbach and Angela Whitesell had become good friends during her visit to France for the 1994 memorial. Through Angela, who speaks good French, he told me that he had just been on French television for restoring his 200th War Memorial, the grave at Cartigny.

I don't remember just what time it was, but the Buttermilk finally gave out and we were getting ready to leave when the hotel security came in and asked us when we were going to leave. The Sgt. James O. Fross, Ball Turret Gunner, family had stood Jim proud.

Saturday, 334 people gathered in the ballroom of the DeSoto Hilton Hotel for the 1997 reunion of the 452nd Bomb Group Association. A large group of them was associated with '**The Lady Jeannette' Remembrance 1997.**'

For the past two days the two **Congressional Medals of Honor** had been with our display in the commons room. Included in the display was the identity bracelet that Lt. Metzger had on his wrist when '*The Lady Jeannette*' crashed.

For the dinner part of the evening, I had made arrangements for a small table to be placed in front of the band in the center of the ballroom. It had two place settings, with the **Congressional Medals of Honor** display at the middle-back of the table. Standing behind the table was the American Flag. One empty place, represented the men of the Group who had died during the war, the other was for the men of the Group who have transferred since the war ended.

It also seems to be our lot in life that our good camera, which had served faithfully for years, had to pick this night to stop serving and we had to use our standby pocket and one time use cameras.

Just before dinner was served, I was called to the front, along with the five Frenchmen who had come so far to meet this gathering of the 452nd Bomb Group.

Bill Roche, the Association President introduced us and I was asked by the French to read a prepared statement for each of the men. They had given their statements to Bernard Leguillier who had translated and faxed them to me.

Pierre Linéatte, Councillor General, du

canton de Péronne, provided the following statement which, I believe, truly tells the feeling of the French of today for the men of the United States who fought for their Liberty during World War Two.

L .to R.: Mike Vieillard, Pierre Segers
Roland Ringenbach, Claude Obert
Pierre Linéatte, Author
Representatives of France to the United States to thank the men of the 452nd Bomb Group and the people of the country for their sacrifices during both World Wars.

Dear Friends:

I am very proud to greet you on behalf of the people of the Somme and particularly the people of the eastern part of the Somme I am representing here.

Our Province of Picardy suffered a lot during the two World Wars and we will never forget, that thanks to the help of our allies and their sacrifices, we have recovered the freedom our country is so proud of. More particularly, you, Americans participated in both wars with all your military power for the Liberation of France. What would have happened to us without your help.

I was a young boy, aged 6, when the small town where I lived, was liberated by the Americans. The Souvenir of those wonderful days is still very alive in my mind. I remember the good relationship between the American soldiers and the inhabitants. So, I am very grateful to you, Americans, even if later, some difficulties appeared in the policies of our two countries.

But, in this very special day when you are welcoming us, I would like to thank you on behalf of the General Council of the Somme for your invitation to participate in your annual congress.

Of course, we should first think of those who lost their lives in France. That's why, with my friends representing patriotic associations, we are willing to improve and develop the links started by our friend, Sam Cole, between you and us. We would like, in the future, to meet you in the States and in France as well on the very places where your fellow Americans lost their lives. The main purpose of our visit is to create a good relationship around our common memories and we are willing to find the best conditions to welcome you and your families, the friends of the missing who will wish to visit us.

Let our visit be a good opportunity to prepare the private or official ceremonies that will take place in the future.

REMEMBRANCE-SOUVENIR

Thanks again for your warm and friendly welcome and I would like, once again, to wish you all the best from the Somme and France.
Pierre Linéatte, General Councellor

It was an excellent night, we dined and danced and the French and the Group came to know each other.

Attending "'*The Lady Jeannette*' Remembrance 1997" were the following:

1st Lt. Donald J. Gott, Pilot
  Congressional Medal of Honor
  Patricia Gann, Niece
  Nadine Ware

2nd Lt. William E. Metzger, Jr., Co-pilot
  Congressional Medal of Honor
  Frances Fredericks, Sister
  Cecil Fredericks
  Harold Burrell, Metzger original crew
  Florine Burrell

T/Sgt. Russell W. Gustafson, Flight Engineer
  Russell W. Gustafson, Himself

T/Sgt. Robert A. Dunlap, Radio Operator
  Bonnie Owens, Sister
  Frank Owens
  Angela Whitesell, Niece
  Noah Whitesell, Grand-Nephew

Sgt. James O. Fross, Ball Turret Gunner
  Mary Fross, Wife
  Kimberly Fross, Daughter
  Michael Fross, Son

Sgt. William R. Robbins, Right Waist Gunner
  William R. Robbins, Himself
  Shirley Robbins

T/Sgt. Herman B. Krimminger, Tail Gunner
  Darren Krimminger, Nephew.
  Scott Love

Sgt. Irving Hirsch, Left Waist Gunner,
  Irving Hirsch, Himself
  Original Gott Crew

Willis S. Cole, Jr., "Sam" and Carol L. Cole
  '**Remembrance-Souvenir**'

The men of '*The Lady Jeannette*' and the 452nd Bomb Group, from France.

Mr. Pierre Linéatte, Conseiller General
Mr. Roland Ringenbach, President
  Le Souvenir Français
Mr. Claude Obert, President
  Union National Combattants
  all of the de canton de Péronne
Mr. Mike Vieillard
Mr. Pierre Segers
  COMMEMO-RANGERS

'Remembrance-Souvenir'

1997

Frances and Cecil Fredericks.

Bill and Shirley Robbins

Most of our group at Savannah, **Remembrance 97**

The reverse side of the 1997 reunion display.

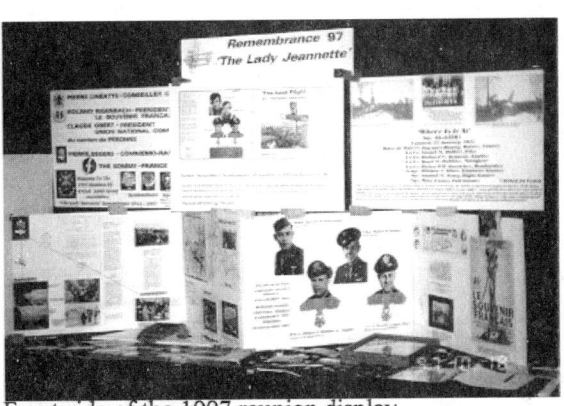

Front side of the 1997 reunion display.

Table of Remembrance, 1997, with **Congressional Medals of Honor** and identity bracelet.

Kimberly and Michael Fross with the 452nd Bomb Group Memorial Plaque installed at the 8th Air Force Museum at Savannah during the 1997 reunion.

Frances Fredericks, author, Carol Cole and Claude Obert find out that 'Texas Buttermilk' is smooth.

Carol Cole being shown the French way of dancing by one of our French visitors, Claude Obert.

Author, Mary Fross and Irving Hirsch.

Mary Fross, Irving Hirsch and Frances Fredericks in front of the **Remembrance 97** display.

Many a new friendship was made during the reunion, with all of us looking forward to the reunions to come.

Kimberly Fross heard so many talking about 'taking to the silk' she went home and tried it. I don't think daddy, S/Sgt. James O. Fross, had that big of a monkey on his back when he got out of '*The Lady Jeannette*.'

Angela Whitesell, Roland Ringenbach.
Kimberly Fross, Pierre Linéatte
Claude Obert, Carol Cole

Michael Fross   Mary Fross   Kimberly Fross
James O. Fross, Ball Turret Gunner
Bill Robbins peeking from the rear, about the same position he was at, in relation to S/Sgt. James O. Fross who was hanging under '*The Lady Jeannette*' when it was struck by flak.

My special thanks to Frances and Cecil Fredericks and Mary, Kimberly and Michael Fross for sending copies of their reunion pictures that I have used here.

Deep in an underground quarry, Jean-Jacques took our picture in front of a World War One German artillery unit's carving.

It is not all work and no play!

Russell W. Gustafson
Survivor

Irving D. Hirsch
Original 10th Crewman

William R. Robbins
Survivor

'The Lady Jeannette'

9 November, 1944 - 19 October, 1997

The rivers of time of '*The Lady Jeannette*'
had combined to flow into the future
Joined in Remembrance and Souvenir.

The Grave at Cartigny, France, October, 1997.

Mr. Roland Ringenbach, *Le Souvenir Français*, was presented on French national television in early October, 1997, for restoring his 200 memorial. The 200th restored memorial was the grave of four American Aviators of World War Two.

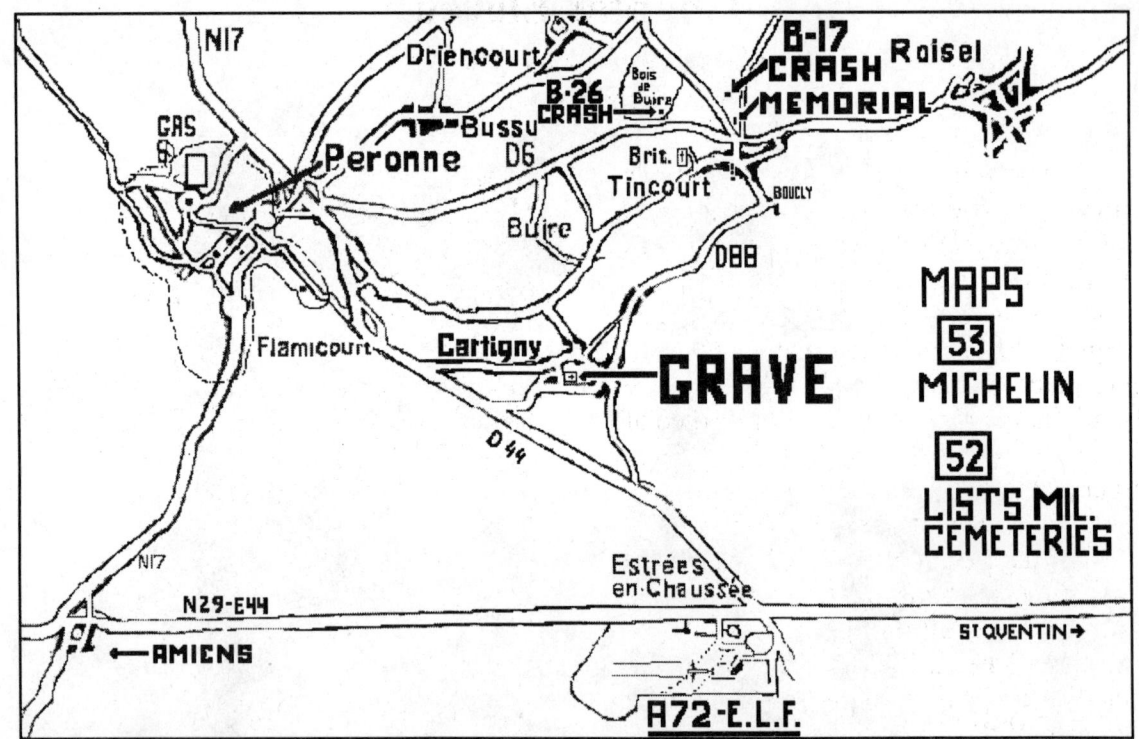

Map 2: Péronne area of France showing the four main locations mentioned in this book. The crash site and memorial to '*The Lady Jeannette*; the Isolated World War Two **Congressional Medals of Honor** grave at Cartigny; the Péronne A-72 World War Two air base and the crash site of the B-26, '*Where's It At?*'

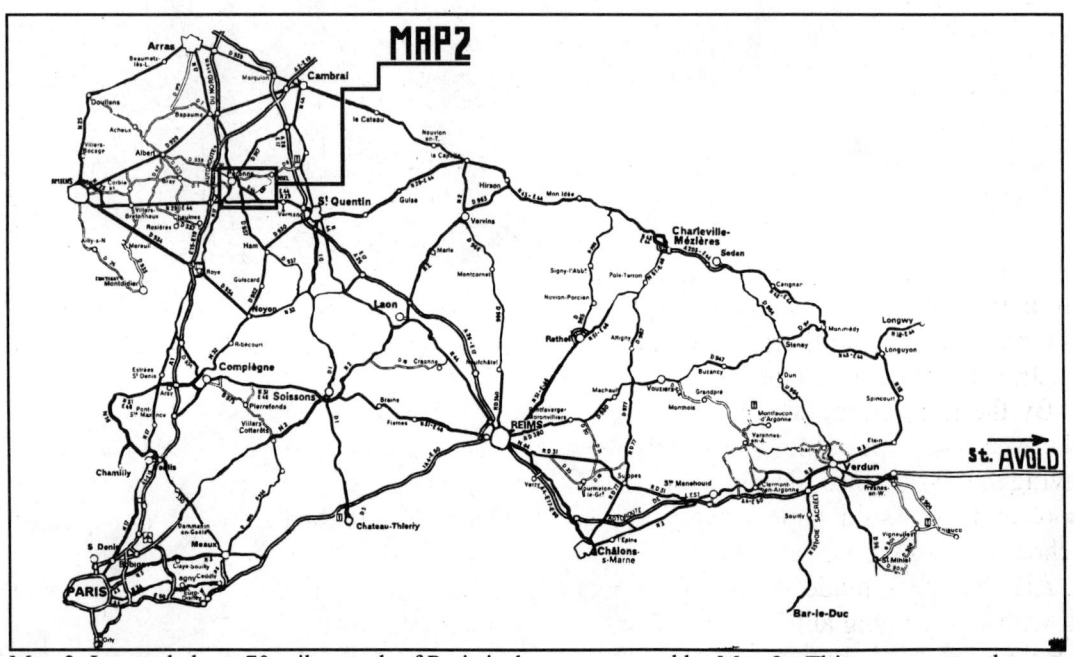

Map 3: Located about 70 miles north of Paris is the area covered by Map 2. This map covers the area of our travels written about in this book.

Chapter Eleven
The Men Of *'The Lady Jeannette'*
And The 452nd Bombardment Group (H)

The original crew of *'The Lady Jeannette,'* as we have heard from Russell Gustafson, was as diverse a group of ten as one might find. But, just who were they?

Over the past few years, I have been privileged to meet four of the five survivors of the men on board the day of the crash and five of the original Gott crew, one of whom died of Alzheimer's disease during my research. Another of the crash survivors had died, just weeks before I located members of his family.

Having read hundreds of books about military subjects, it has always seemed to me that a reader had little opportunity to know much about the actual people involved, especially their families. This chapter is about the ten men of the original Gott crew and the Group to which they belonged. Most were board *'The Lady Jeannette'* during her last flight on 9 November, 1944.

Gerald W. Collins
October 23, 1919----
Born: Canon City, Colorado
Serial Number: O-0771314
2nd Lieutenant, Co-pilot
United States Army Air Force
Original Gott Crew Co-pilot

Gerry was born to **Hazel A. Builderback Collins** and **Harold Collins**. One of three boys, his brothers being Harold Collins, Jr. and Don Curtis Collins.

By the time Gerry was 10 years old, his father was gone out of their lives and they were living in Los Angeles. The boys were all in school and they sold papers every night after school to help the family budget.

All the boys made it through high school, with Gerry being able to play football on the Belmont High School team, while still selling papers at night. He did have a long term girl friend, she later became his wife.

After graduation Gerry was able to find employment with the California Public Utilities Commission as, to use his words, "a flunky."

In June of 1941, Beverly Grace Bergstrum and Gerald. W. Collins were joined in marriage. In mid-1942, Gerry's brother, Harold, left for the Air Cadet program and pilot training. After completing his training and receiving his commission, he served in the Pacific Combat area as a B-25 Pilot.

Both Don and Gerry put in for the Cadet Program and were accepted into the service program in January, 1943.

Completing their required ground training they reported for primary and basic flight training at Oxnard, California. Upon completion, Don went on to fighter training and Gerry reported to Marfa, Texas, for his multi-engine heavier aircraft training.

In due time, both completed their training and became commissioned pilots. Don went on to fly P-38 fighters out of England and in France. During February, 1944, Beverly became pregnant and at his graduation from multi-engine school, on March 12, 1944, Gerald W. Collins became a 2nd Lieutenant.

Gerry then reported to Rapid City, South Dakota, to become the co-pilot on the Gott crew as they prepared for overseas duty.

After November 9, 1944, and the loss of his operating crew, Gerry went on to complete his full 35 missions before leaving the 452nd Bomb Group at the end of January, 1945. The length of time this took, illustrates a major problem of being listed as a fill-in crew member.

Also, during November, 1944, Gerry received word that he was the father of identical twin boys, Ronald and Donald.

Upon his return to the States, he was first assigned to the Air Transportation Service at Long Beach. Later, he was transferred to Bakersfield, serving there until he was discharged in August, 1945. He was the first of the original crew to be discharged.

Gerry went back to work for the California Public Utilities Commission for a while and soon got a job with the Chamber of Commerce in Los Angles where he worked until being transferred east to the National Chamber of Commerce office in Washington, D.C. in 1955. Gerry was exceptional at this type of work and he later accepted the position of President of the National Defense Transport Association, at which he served until his retirement.

Gerry's wife, Beverly has since passed on. The twin boys married two girls who were best friends in high school and both now have families of their own.

Ronald and Pamila are the parents of three children, Ashley, Angie and Bryant.

Donald and Lauri are the parents of two children, Scott and Beverly.

Russell Gustafson and I stayed with Gerry at his home in Bethesda, Maryland, one night in June of 1997, and we enjoyed a nice visit with him. It is always enjoyable to get two old friends together like this and see what pops up in their minds. What one forgot, the other one remembers.

Gerry is very active in his golf club and was helping host a professional golf tournament the day we left.

ROBERT ALEXANDER DUNLAP
October 26, 1924 - - November 9, 1944
Serial Number: 39696406
Technical Sergeant, Radio Operator
United States Army Air Force
Killed In Action, Tincourt-Boucly, France
9 November, 1944
'The Lady Jeannette'
B-17G-35VE, Sn: 42-97904
452nd Bombardment Group (H)
729th Bombardment Squadron
Mission: Saarbrucken, Germany
Buried: Cartigny, France
2nd and Official Grave
Plot C, Row 23, Grave 19

Lorraine American Military Cemetery,
St. Avold, France

Alexander Dunlap, who was born at Sheffield, Montana, April 29, 1888, and died at Miles City, Montana, May 2, 1953, and **Martha Schmitt Dunlap** born at Eureka, South Dakota, on February 4, 1898, and who died December 30, 1967, were his parents.

Bob, as he was called, grew up and attended school in Miles City, where he graduated from Custer County High School.

During his youth, his rough and tumble outdoor activities fetched him a broken arm when he fell off a horse at his grandmother's ranch and a brain concussion when a bicycle wheel broke during a hard ride.

He greatly enjoyed riding his bicycle, spending many hours discovering Miles City and the surrounding area with his friends, Ray Glover and Keith Johnson.

Ray told me, "We were typical kids, an inseparable trio, growing up in Miles City. We started first grade together and graduated in 1942. It was typical depression times and you had to make your own fun. We might have snuck a few smokes, but we never got into serious trouble."

Keith lived across the alley until his family moved. He remembers playing marbles with Bob and Ray and later going hunting with Bob and his dad.

All the boy's dads worked for the Milwaukee Railroad, Bob's dad was a conductor, Keith's dad was a foreman on the repair crew, and Ray's dad was an engineer.

"Alex, Bob's dad was a fine gentleman," Ray told me. During Ray's first job as a brakeman on the railroad, a job he had taken right out of high school, he often worked for Alex. Ray later went into the navy and saw action aboard a 110-foot sub chaser in the Pacific. His ship was sunk during the first typhoon at Okinawa. His brother who was on another ship there, came to his aid and gave Ray, "A duffle bag of clothes and a fist full of money," as all of Ray's things, except for the clothes on his back, went down with the ship."

Ray worked with Alex a lot after he returned from the war and Alex often talked of Bob. Ray told me, "I remember Alex telling me that he had gone up to the Great Falls Army Air Force Base, where he had been presented with Bob's medals." He was proud of Bob and missed him a lot.

Ray Glover remembers his bicycle well. Our dads bought us Ranger bicycles made by Meade Bicycles, manufactured in Chicago. They were the best bicycles at that time, mine cost around $40.00 and Bob's Dad, Alex, got him one that cost $50.00. That was a lot of money during the depression.

Later, when we got to high school, we went our different ways, I was interested in sports and Bob never did show much interest in sports.

Keith Johnson remembers the last time he saw Bob. Keith also attended the radio school at Rapid City for a time and he heard that Bob was there, so he went to visit him. Bob was working the night shift and was sleeping in a barracks that was kept dark during the day. Keith told me about how surprised he was when Bob started to get up. "He seemed to unfold as he got up," Keith continued, "Bob had grown tall, since I last saw him."

Keith later got into the Aviation Cadet program and after completing his training he was commissioned and became a pilot on C-47's and later flew C-46's throughout the Pacific.

After school, Bob took to 'riding the rods' for a while and he later stayed with his older sister, Io Dunlap Hendron, who was living in Bakersfield, California.

Bob enlisted in the Army Air Force at Bakersfield, on March 19, 1943, hoping to be a pilot. However, like so many others, that did not come to be and he attended radio school at Rapid City, South Dakota.

Unlike many who were in the service, Bob's radio school was fairly close to home and he was able to go home on leave for Christmas, 1943, and several other times, before he left for England.

Bonnie Owens, Bob's youngest sister remembers, "He enjoyed being outdoors, one well remembered trip that he told me about was a fishing trip to Yellowstone National Park with Dad and our brother-in-law." "Bob," Bonnie said, "was especially close to his older sister, Io, and his father, Alex. He also had a girl friend, Virginia and on his last furlough home, he gave her a cashmere sweater." She also remembers the last time she played the piano for Bob. He asked her to play a tune on the piano. Bonnie remembers to this day, playing, '*I Dream Of Jeannie With The Light Brown Hair.*'

T/Sgt. Robert A. Dunlap
729th Bomb Sq. 452nd Bomb Gp
Plot C Row 23 Grave 19, November 7, 1994
Lorraine American Military Cemetery
St. Avold, France
A beautifully maintained American World War Two cemetery.

James Olin Fross
16 March, 1925 ---- Feb. 17, 1997
Born: Davenport, Iowa
Buried: Roselawn Cemetery, McAllen, Texas
Serial Number: 38462533
Staff Sergeant, Ball Turret Gunner
United States Army Air Force
Wounded In Action
'*The Lady Jeannette*'
9 November, 1944
B-17G-35VE, Sn: 42-97904
452nd Bombardment Group (H)
729th Bombardment Squadron
Mission: Saarbrucken, Germany

He was the son of **Glen Charles Fross** and **Cecille Ling Fross**. The family lived at 808 B.C. Ave., McAllen, Texas, when Jim entered the service on 14 June, 1943. He was 5 ft. 2 in., 121 pounds at the time. He spent 2 years, 4 months, 16 days on active duty, separating on November 1, 1945.

Jim had a sister, Jacquelin Fross Hamilton, married to W. Martin (Marty)

Hamilton, the parents of a niece, Elizabeth Dawn, and nephew, Joe Martin. Clair, Jim's brother, was in the navy during the war and was killed in a truck accident in West Texas while driving for Mayflower Van Lines. Clair's wife, Norma survives him along with his children Derrell, Dorothy and Valerie. Clair's son Jeffrey, also died in a vehicular accident.

Jim's mother Cecille died in 1982 and his father died in 1992, at the age of 97. His father was a veteran of World War One, and active in the local V.F.W. chapter until his death, a member of the last man's club.

The family had settled in McAllen after Jim's father had visited McAllen during one of his sales trips for the Home Comfort Stove Company.

Jim received his draft notice one week after graduating from McAllen High School.

Upon returning from the service, Jim attended Pan American Junior College in Edinburg then he joined the family as owners of a large dairy farm; they were also in the orchard care business.

When the dairy and orchard care operations were sold, Jim purchased a Phillips 66 service station and operated it for several years. He then became a licensed meat inspection for the State of Texas Department of Health. He retired from the State of Texas in 1987. Shortly thereafter, he was diagnosed with Parkinson's Disease, and later diagnosed with Alzheimer's Disease. It was during medical tests to determine this problem that the metal fragments from this long-ago wound were found in his head.

Jim married Mary June Alderman, on July 17, 1955. They had three children. Their oldest son, James Olin Fross II, disappeared one evening from South Padre Island on the Gulf Coast. His car was found there with his personal items, it appeared he went for a swim and was swept out to sea. Their daughter, Kimberly is a pert young college girl who quickly reminds one of her mother and father. Their son, Michael, lives in San Antonio, Texas, and works in hotel management. He is surely his father's son, with mom's sprite personality showing through as well.

Jim loved to build airplane models - he was very proud of all his B-17 models. He also worked at a coin collection, pieces of which are still being found in his belongings. Jim was very active in his church, the First United Methodist Church, of McAllen, where he served many years as a Sunday School Superintendent. He was also a youth sponsor, accompanying the young people's groups on trips far and wide. He was a fine example to these young people and his friendships with some of them endured to his death.

Jim was stuck with one of the ususal nick names for ball turret gunners, he was called 'Shorty' by the crew.

Jim did not talk much about his time in the service, and after his death, Mary was quite surprised to find a box with various papers, such as his Caterpillar Club Certificate and the telegrams stating he was missing and returned to action. He also kept his monthly flight records and other papers of interest to a historian:

8:10 Hr. + 5:15 + 12:3 = 25:55 = Overseas.

Jim's personal notebook contained the following flight log:

Date	Logged Time
Aug. 27 - Berlin (Recall)Keil	6:30
Sep. 2 - Frankfort (Recall) (Weath)	8:15
Sep. 9 - Dusseldorf	7:00
Sep. 13 - Ludwigshafen	3:40
Sep. 17 - Arnheim-Holland	5:30
Sep. 19 - Weisbaden	7:30
Sep. 21 - Ludwigshafen	7:30
Sep. 25 - Ludwigshafen (Col. No.5)	7:15
Sep. 27 - Mainz	6:30
Sep. 28 - Merseburg (Feather #4)	8:40
Sep. 30 - Bielefeld	7:15
Oct. 2 - Kassel	8:00
Oct. 3 - Nurnberg	8:15
Oct. 5 - Minster	6:30
Oct. 6 - Berlin	8:30
Oct. 7 - Merseburg	8:45
Oct. 12 - Bremen	3:00
Oct. 14 - Cologne (No Bombs)	6:10
Oct. 15 - Heligoland	7:45
Oct. 18 - Kassel	9:25
Oct. 25 - Hamburg	7:45
Oct. 26 - Hanover	8:00
Oct. 30 - Merseburg (Recall)	6:10

Nov. 2 - Merseburg   8:00
Nov. 4 - Neukirchen   6:50
Nov. 5 - Ludwigshafen   8:15
Nov. 9 - Saarbrucken   Est: 6:30
No. 4 shot off & #1 & #2   Total 176.15
running away. Para-   Combat Flight
chute over France   Hours.
Pilot, Co-pilot, Tail,
Radio, went down
with plane. Home on 14th to base.

His last Individual Flight Record showed a total of 280:20 hours flight time.

His Honorable Discharge, filed with Hidalgo County on November 20, 1945, gives the information that he received $212.90 in separation pay and that he was eligible for the following Battle and Campaign ribbons:
Northern France GO33WD45
Rhineland GO40WD45
Decorations and Citations:
EAME Ribbon
Purple Heart GO56-10Nov44
    Hq 109th Ev Hos.
Air Medal, 3OLC
    GO701-25Sep44
OLC GO756-5Oct44
    Hq 3 AD
OLC GO874-22Oct44
    3BD

Mary told me, she was working as a car hop at a drive-in when she met Jim. He came in for lunch one day and left a whole nickel tip. He came back again and again, even though she told him he was a cheap tipper.

Psychic income is very important in my life, especially when I receive a letter from someone like Mary who wrote to me stating, "I cannot tell you how much it meant to Jim and to me to have you travel all that way to visit with Jim--I do hope you were able to learn some concrete things, and the trip was somewhat beneficial to you. I know Jim enjoyed it greatly, although he was not overly demonstrative, we can attribute that to his illness. I will say he seemed to remember more than I thought he would, and it was fun for me to watch him blossom, even for a moment.

Again, how can we thank you enough for your attention. Our prayers are for the very best for you, and yours, you are a very special man."

I'll leave Jim's life with a statement by Mary, "My, he was some handsome, darling dude then!"

Donald Joseph Gott
June 3, 1923 ---- November 9, 1944
Born: Family Farm, Harmon, Oklahoma
Serial Number: O-763996
1st Lieutenant, Pilot
United States Army Air Force
Killed In Action, Tincourt-Boucly, France
9 November, 1944

'The Lady Jeannette'
B-17G-35VE, Sn: 42-97904
452nd Bombardment Group (H)
729th Bombardment Squadron
Mission: Saarbrucken, Germany
Buried: Cartigny, France
    2nd and Official Grave
    Fairmont Cemetery
    Harmon, Ellis County, Oklahoma

I have visited the farm where Donald Gott was born to **Joseph Eugene Gott** and **Mary Lucy Hanlon Gott**. The house is now deserted and weather-beaten, as the years have taken their toll. Vandals have destroyed much, including the room where Donald's coffin was displayed with much honor, now strips of wall paper hang from the wall.

The address when it was a viable home, full of growing children and hard-working ranchers, was Route 1, Box 26, Arnett, Oklahoma. Located just south of where the panhandle juts out and a bit east.

It wasn't a big house and the house is located on what has to be called 'hard scrabble land.' As we drove north from Harmon, a little crossroads village with a few buildings, most which were empty, the more the area around us reminded me of Eastern Washington. It is flat and windblown, and an image of Carol's grandfather jumped into my mind. Some distance north of Harmon, Winona stopped at the Fairmont cemetery.

As I thought of the country, Carol's Grandpa Smith, was also in my thoughts, he was over 90-years-old when he died. He still lived on the original family homestead, a place of canyons and trees with every bit of farmable ground fought for and well earned, but still hard scrabble.

Grandpa Smith once told me that his grandson, Carol's brother, would have a hard time making it during the depression. "Bill is a large crop grower, grandpa Smith said, "wheat and barley, but he isn't a farmer." In effect, he's a grain manufacturer.

During the bad times the farmers on the good ground had to depend on dry land cropping, with little rain, while grandpa was able to grow everything a family needed on his broken ground with water here and there. He even had some excess to sell in town to get some ready cash for what he couldn't grow or make himself. He would haul his vegetables, pigs and chickens into Spokane, Washington, and sell them in the neighborhoods.

The evening we got to Arnett, Winona Derrick, the Gott's grand-daughter, had shown us many pictures of the family and Donald. I was struck by the face of Mr. Gott. Here was a man for whom life did not come easy. He had met it head on, depression and all. And, he suffered the greatest crop loss of all, his youngest son.

I'm certain that grandma and grandpa Smith and grandma and grandpa Gott could have sat down on the front porch swing and talked for a long time about what it took to carry a family through the bad times. The other fellows might be best off in good times, but the hard scrabble farmer knew how to survive in the bad times.

On November 9, 1944, Donald J. Gott knew that he could not desert the fight, he had to bear up, even in the bad times. It was ingrained.

Don had two older sisters and an older brother. They were able to keep much of the load of the farm work off Don and he was the 'apple of everyone's eye,' the one they all sacrificed for, the one who was to be the real family success later in life. One brother had died as a baby.

Hazel Cathryn Gott Peil Born: June 2, 1910
    Died: Jan. 27, 1991
  Married: August Peil Born: Dec. 3, 1910
    Died: May 1, 1997
  Buried: Fairmont Cemetery.

Clarence John Gott   Born: Feb. 23, 1912
    Died: Aug. 3, 1913
  Buried: Fairmont Cemetery

Lucille Magdalyn Gott Compton
    Born: June 14, 1914
    Died: June 2 8, 1986
  Married: Raymond Compton
    Born: Dec. 9, 1910
    Died: June 29, 1975

Children
Donald Max Compton
    Married: Joan Brooks Compton
    Children: Terrie Lynn
             Lorrie Ann
             Donald Max, Jr.

Winona Colleen Compton
    Married: Bert Allard, Jr.
    Children: Kevin Eugene
             Kenneth Cleo
             Starla Kay
             Cheri Denise
    Married: Calvin Eugene Derrick
    Died: Dec. 25, 1991

Patricia Corinne Compton
    Married: Jimmie Lee Gann
    Children: Krista Dawn

Gary Joseph Compton
        Died: May 29, 1969
    Married: Bonnie Pauline New
    Children: Brent

Theron Eugene Compton
        Died: Jan. 13, 1976
    Married: Sammie Rude
    Children: Troy Theron

Monte Ray Compton
    Married: Patricia Ann Ryan
    Children: Chad Ryan
             Jared Monte

Otto James Gott, Died: Aug. 10, 1983
    Married: Ione Donoghe
    Children:
      Kenneth James Gott
      Married: Alice Fincham
      Children: Peter James
               David William
                 Married: Kurstin

The Gott family to which Donald was born were devout Catholics and they drove to Shattuck, Oklahoma, 25 miles away, to attend St. Joseph Catholic Church. Donald is especially remembered for his faith and straight forward living.

The family was fair, but strict and Donald never took on the vices of smoke or drink. He was known for scholarship and honesty.

His first schooling was in the proverbial, one-room school at Kennebec Country School, where he graduated from 8th grade. Though Arnett was closer, the Gott children attended high school at Fargo, a 16 ½ mile straight shot north.

Fargo High School, 1940-1941 -
First String: #6 Kenneth Chalmers, Center; #1 John Allen, Forward; #8 Donald Gott, Forward; #9 W. B. Catlin, Guard; #4 Ralph Persons.
Subs: Leroy Zigler, Billy Wayne Calhoun, Earl Lee Hartley, Raymond File, Clarence Hokweiler, Coach A. A. Tuck

As one drives up the road to Fargo you are struck by the abrupt change of ground, from hard scrabble, blowing loose sand range to large cropped fields.

Otto, Don's five year-older brother, drove the school bus and was ever so proud of Donald. Donald blossomed in school getting excellent grades, enjoying baseball and basketball and became valedictorian of his class.

The family worked the harvests in the summer, doing custom harvesting and Donald pitched in helping the family business as he could. However, some jobs like pulling broomcorn, convinced him he liked school better. He was said to have a good sense of humor. I met several class mates when I visited Arnett, they told me that Don was a good friend, liked by all and surely missed.

When Raymond Schneider and his bride Lucille were married in 1935, cousin Donald presented them with a rolling pin. As a boy of 12, he must have been a reader of the 1930's "funny paper's Katzenjammer Kids" Ma Katzenjammer always displayed the rolling pin to bring her family into line. Donald must have had this gift in mind as a weapon in his delight to tease cousin Raymond. Mrs. Schneider still uses this precious gift, over 50 years later.[64]

After graduation, he chose to attend a technical school at Enid, Oklahoma. At that time, recruiters from companies all over the country were looking for young people to fill positions being vacated by drafted men and openings created by the need to expand to meet war demands.

Don Gott
Graduation Picture

Leaving behind his girl friend, Earline Mann (Barton), Don rode a bus cross country to take a war production position with the U.S. Aluminum Company in Bridgeport, Connecticut. On the way across the wide country, his mind must have thrilled as he watched the many aircraft speeding across the country as the bus crawled along.

About this time, Don's brother and his brother's wife moved to California and sister Hazel soon followed, all to participate in the good times of war production in California with long hours and good wages.

Otto Gott ended up living in Washington State, not far from where we live, however we never met him. One of his boys still lives across Puget Sound from us and perhaps someday, we will meet him and his family.

As with Russell Gustafson and Herman Krimminger, the thought of being a pilot was a driving force and Don soon signed up for the cadet program, on September 21, 1942. He left Bridgeport for active duty as an Aviation Cadet on March 22, 1943.

It would be over a year before Don prepared his Crew 33-c (Crew AC-72, FV900CJ/16349CJ-4/4) to depart the United States, via the northern route to join the 452nd Bombardment Group (H) on August 17, 1944.

On the way, he attended pre-flight school in Santa Ana, California, going on in June, 1943, to Primary Flight Training at Glendale, Arizona. Basic pilot training followed in September at Gardner Field, California. Followed by advanced twin-engine flight training school at Stockton Field, California.

On January 6, 1944, he became an officer and a gentleman when he was authorized to pin on his gold 2nd Lieutenant bars.

He completed his four-engine B-17 transition training at Hobbs Field, New Mexico on March 24th, 1944, and his graduation ceremony was attended by his parents.

Donald had been told by his cousin, Loren Schneider, that he could use Loren's 1940 Ford whenever he wished. However, before Donald went home on his final furlough, he had his mother contact his cousin, now serving in the Pacific, to ask specific permission for Donald to drive it. Donald had become a 'by-the-book' flyer and that included asking official permission.

It was a fun furlough, he and Earline dated in style, however Donald was uneasy about his future. He had a premonition and when he left, he gave his sister a two-dollar bill on which he stated he did not expect to return.

While home, Don saw a friend waiting at the bus stop and stopped to talk to him until his bus came. The friend, Kenneth Sherrill, another Air Corps man was heading for Europe. When Don's (official) remains were returned, Kenneth honored Donald as one of the pallbearers who carried Don's casket to the grave.

Russell Gustafson visiting the official grave of his pilot, 1st Lt. Donald J. Gott, **M.H.**. August 27, 1994

Russell William Gustafson
11 August, 1922 ----
Born: Jamestown, New York
Serial Number: 12139299
Technical Sergeant, Flight Engineer/Gunner
United States Army Air Force
Wounded In Action
9 November, 1944
'*The Lady Jeannette*'
B-17G-35VE, Sn: 42-97904
452nd Bombardment Group (H)
729th Bombardment Squadron
Mission: Saarbrucken, Germany

Russell, a 2nd generation American Swede, was the son of **William Axel Gustafson** and **Edith Gustafson**.

Growing up in the 1930s and 40's airplanes were fascinating and a subject of great adventure to Russell. After graduating from Jamestown High School in 1941, he attended Elmira Aviation Ground School, with the intention of becoming an aeronautical engineer. During a weekend trip home he heard the news of Pearl Harbor. The news immediately altered his life's direction, as he now knew what his future held.

He completed the semester at Elmira, obtaining the "A" part of the "A&E" course, returned home and started the process of enlisting in the Army Air Corps Cadet Program. Russell completed his enlistment process by August 29, 1942, but he was not called to active service until February 26, 1944.

Air Cadet Russell Gustafson.

Russell completed the cadet program primary flight training, but "washed out" and as many of the "washed out" men were, he was soon assigned to the Amarillo, Texas, B-17 Mechanics School. From there Russell went through the pipeline to gunnery school at Las Vegas. Upon completion of gunnery school, he was assigned to a combat crew and entered transition training as the Flight Engineer on 2nd Lt. Donald J. Gott's crew.

After escaping, just in time to see the bomber crash right in front of him, Russell spent the next 13 months in army hospitals getting his leg put back together. They placed him in traction for months so that the missing inch of bone could grow back in. However, as he aged, he began to have knee problems which can be traced directly back to a poor setting of the bone position in his wounded leg. Russell says, "how and why I survived that fatal day have often been in my thoughts".

On December 20, 1945, he was discharged with a medical disability and subsequently entered Fairleigh Dickinson College in New Jersey. He graduated, in 1950, with a B.S. in business administration. He then went to work for the Marlin Rockwell Corporation, which manufactured ball bearings.

The company was later purchased by TRW, Inc., Bearing Division. Starting in the New York area, he later moved to the Boston area for the company in 1959.

At the 452nd Bomb Group's reunion, after meeting up with the right waist gunner Bill Robbins for the first time since they boarded the bomber the day of the crash, Russell figured that they had been around each other several times and just missed meeting back then. In 1976, the firm asked Russell to transfer to Oklahoma City.

Over the years, Russell acquired two wives and six children.

His first wife was Joanne Campbell and they had two children named, Lee Marie and Michael.

His second wife was Phyllis Williams and the four children were: Robin Ann, Amy Elizabeth, Kerry Ann and Erick William.

In 1985, he retired from TRW, Inc. and remained in Oklahoma City where he has lived since 1976, near several of his children.

Since I first personally met him at the Gott memorial in August, 1994, Russell has been a steadfast supporter of my research and we have spent much time together.

Russell's life was greatly changed by one man, a man who really knew none of the men aboard *The Lady Jeannette,* 2nd Lt. William E. Metzger, Jr., **Congressional Medal of Honor**, who without a second thought, gave his parachutes and his life so others may live. One of those parachutes carried Russell safely to earth and today six Gustafson children can directly trace their being back to that day in the air over France, when Bill Metzger had no greater love for a crew member, than to give his life to save their father.

John A. Harland
Unknown ---- June 3, 1994
Serial Number: O-723355
2nd Lieutenant, Navigator
United States Army Air Force
Wounded In Action
9 November, 1944
'The Lady Jeannette'
B-17G-35VE, Sn: 42-97904
452nd Bombardment Group (H)
729th Bombardment Squadron
Mission: Saarbrucken, Germany

The first *'The Lady Jeannette'* survivor I accounted for, Lt. Harland. I know the least about Lt. Harland. He grew up in Chicago, I believe, in what is called the north side. Apparently the depression was hard on his family and he left high school early and started working in order to help the family through the tough times.

He was the son of Mrs. Miller, for which I have two names, Ada or Ida. Mrs. Gott's letter of January 28, 1945 is written to Mrs. Ada Miller, while the army letter sent to Ida Krimminger, on 8 May, 1945, lists Lt.

Harland's mother's name as **Ida M. Miller**, which has to be the correct name, the one I will use when referring to Lt. Harland's mother. I have no information, at this time, as to his father.

Lt. Harland was born and lived his life in Chicago, Illinois, except for his service.

Lt. Harland was always known as Jack to his family. He joined the Aviation Cadet Program and took courses on a college campus in Ohio. When he completed his on-campus courses he went through the training schools to qualify as a navigator and he received his 2nd lieutenant's commission. Upon completion of his schools, he joined the Gott crew for final overseas training.

During his time in the service he was called Johnny by those who knew him.

After his discharge, John attended De Paul University, before taking a job at a major Chicago newspaper, working in the roll paper department. When he retired, he was the union steward and in charge of roll stock at two locations.

John maintained his reserve status for some years, during which he was promoted to captain. He was married and had six children, four of whom live in the same block where they grew up.

Kathy Greinier
Dianne Kowar
Elizabeth (Liz) Harland
Scott Harland
Debby Harland
Judy Galloway

The children maintain a tight family relationship, often visiting each other and taking care of the children of the siblings.

John purchased and lived in a fairly large apartment house, so his children could always have a place to live.

He died just a month before I located his family, on June 3, 1994, and he was buried exactly 50 years after '*The Lady Jeannette*' arrived in England, 'D-DAY,' 1944. I would have like to have talked to him and learned everything that occurred to him aboard the bomber.

Joseph Francis Harms
February 12, 1922 ----
Born: Brooklyn, New York
Serial Number: O-2056698
2nd Lieutenant, Bombardier
United States Army Air Force
Wounded In Action
9 November, 1944
'*The Lady Jeannette*'
B-17G-35VE, Sn: 42-97904
452nd Bombardment Group (H)
729th Bombardment Squadron
Mission: Saarbrucken, Germany

The son of **Ernest Edward Harms** and **Mary Justina Rigney Harms**, Joe was the eldest of the three children. His brother was named Gerard Vincent and his sister, Regina Delores. Joe's Dad, was a foreman for Western Union Telegraph.

Joe participated on the debating team and the orchestra while in high school. He enjoyed building model airplanes and was a flying enthusiast. Upon graduation from St, Michael's High School, Joe immediately entered St. John's University. He was in his senior year, finishing his accounting major, when he signed up for the Aviation Cadet Program with the assurance that he would be allowed to graduate before being called up.

Joe went ahead and signed for his final semester and purchased his books. No sooner had he done that, when he got his call to leave at once.

In January, 1943, Joe entered the Cadet program. The next month he married his high school sweetheart, Elsie Gray, on February 19, 1944.

Though he had requested navigator school, he was assigned to pilot training. As I have heard in several cases, the instructor was one who felt uneasy with students in control and he telegraphed his feeling to his students, resulting in washouts, Joe being one.

Unlike many who were sent to engineer/mechanic school as enlisted men, Joe was sent to bombardier school. He completed his aerial gunnery school at Harlingen, Texas, and his bombardier training at San Angelo, Texas, on May 20, 1944, when he was commissioned a 2nd Lieutenant.

When Joe left for Europe, Elsie was pregnant with their first child. Back in the States, she delivered their daughter, Janet Lynne Harms, on February 22, 1945. A second child was born November 7, 1950, Karen Jean Harms.

After training with his original crew, they left for Europe and their exciting visit to a glacier in Iceland.

When the crew arrived in England they were assigned to the 452nd Bomb Group (H) per Par 15 S) #287, HQ 70th Repl Dep, dtd 13 Oct '44, and having rptd this sta 16 Oct '44, are asgned to orgns indicated and will report to respective CO there for dy, per SO 285, HQ 452nd Bomb Group.

729th Bomb Sq, 452nd Gp
Crew 28-B (Cr78, APO 16403 BJ 78)
2nd Lt. C. J. McCollum
2nd Lt. Frederick W. Hardin
2nd Lt. Steven A. Mem

2nd Lt. Joseph F. Harms
S/Sgt. Richard Weemes
Cpl. Marley R. Conger
Cpl. Edward L. Polick
Cpl. Oscar B. Lane

Interestingly, the other crew assigned on the same orders to the same squadron is Crew 20-C (Cr178, APO 16500 AF178). The crew on which 2nd Lt. William E. Metzger, Jr. was the copilot. Though they were in the replacement pipeline together, he had never met Lt. Metzger.

Upon returning to the United States Joe completed the Army Finance Officer school at Fort Benjamin Harrison and was shipped to the Pacific for a year's duty at Clark Air Force Base, in the Phillippines. While there, he enlisted for a second tour of duty. Upon returning to the states the family was stationed at Greensboro, North Carolina, until Joe was discharged as a captain in May, 1947.

Joe established his own business and became a manufactures representative when he was discharged and took on lines of plumbing and heating goods. He lives in New Milford, New Jersey, and still puts in time calling on accounts and he continues to expand his coin collection.

His two daughters married and Elsie and Joe have four grand-children:

Jean Lynne Harms Witte and her husband Richard Witte have two children:

>Richard, a West Point Graduate, is now in civilian life.
>William lives and works in the Washington, D.C. area.

Karen Jean Harms Wood has two children,
>Christine, married to Mark Ianello.
>Brooke Wood

Joe was the last survivor of the crew I located and he provided the input required to know what happened in the nose of the bomber and from him, I was able to figure out the exact order of bailing out.

Irving David Hirsch
June 11, 1925 ----
Born: Chicago, Illinois
Serial Number: 36698607
Staff Sergeant, L. Waist & Ball Turret Gunner
United States Army Air Force
Original 10th member of the Gott crew.

Irv, as he is called, was born to **Charolette Winkler Hirsch** and **Joseph Hirsch**, who was an upholsterer. Irv had one brother, Edward Hirsch, who is deceased.

He wasn't that big, but Irv played baseball and football at the Tulely High in Chicago, a school that no longer exists. While in school, he met his future wife and life-long partner.

I located Irv, in June, 1997, using a letter that he had sent to Johnny Harland on January 10, 1946. Irv had found Harland's address in some papers he had from crew training. However, Harland never followed up, though he saved the letter, they never met again. When I contacted him, he got in touch with some of Harland's children and plans to visit with them sometime in the future.

In that letter, Irv writes that he had been contacted by Ida Krimminger who had been discharged a couple of weeks earlier. This proves that Ida was the person behind the flow of letters between families once she had gotten the list of survivors and families from the Army.

Irv does remember going to Herman and Ida's wedding.

Irv was another of the amazing number of men on the Gott crew that had participated in the Air Cadet Program. However, he wasn't even given a chance to wash out, or take any training.

Upon reporting, the entire class was pulled out of the air cadet program and put in gunnery school, as the Army Air Force had just suffered several huge losses and the higher-ups decided they needed gunners more than officers. Remember, that Irv was removed from his original combat crew and sent to Italy because of an excess number of gunners when he finally got to England.

Irv married his high school girl friend, Ruth Schwartz, and they have three children and five grandchildren.

Sharon Allison married to Lee Hogeorges, the parents of one
    Bryan Wolf

Cybil Adel Miller, the mother of two children:
    Tracy Miller
    Ryan Miller

Robert Allen Hirsch married to Jill Schmidt, are the parents of two children.
    Chad Hirsch
    Scott Hirsch

Irv used the G.I. Bill when he returned from the service to take a course in jewelry manufacturing and had his own wholesale jewelry manufacturing business in Chicago for many years. He has enjoyed it so much, that he still works to this day.

His major hobby is the enjoyment of fishing. Irv would greatly enjoy meeting many of my French fishing friends, they do it with a passion.

Irv has provided vital information on the crew from the time they assembled in South Dakota until he left the crew for service in Italy.

Herman Bruce Krimminger
August 29, 1923 - - November 9, 1944
Marshville, North Carolina
Serial Number: 34890339
Staff Sergeant, Tail Gunner
United States Army Air Force
Killed In Action, Tincourt-Boucly, France
9 November, 1944
'The Lady Jeannette'
B-17G-35VE, Sn: 42-97904
452nd Bombardment Group (H)
729th Bombardment Squadron
Mission: Saarbrucken, Germany
Buried: Cartigny, France
2nd (Official) Grave
    Grave: 1720, Plot 12
    Arlington National Cemetery

Herman was a tried and true North Carolina boy. Described to me, as a slow mover and talker, a typical southern boy. He was born and raised around Marshville, just a bit east of Monroe, North Carolina.

Herman was the 1st of three children born to **Bessie Autrey Krimminger** and **Hugh Clifford Krimminger**.

Hugh had served in World War One, where he was gassed during the Meuse-Argonne campaign. He died early in life, from ongoing complications of being gassed. Hugh died in 1930, three months before their second son, Hugh Carson Krimminger was born. Leaving Bessie with two young sons, Herman and Hugh, and a daughter, Elizabeth, to support, as the depression raged.

When Herman left for service in the army, his mother, sister and brother were living at Rt. 1, Box 128, Marshville N.C.

Herman's sister, Mary Elizabeth who was four years younger, married Otis Riggins. Otis served in the Army as a crew member on 155 mm 'Long Tom' artillery during World War Two. He landed in France a week after 'D-Day' and served with Patton's Third Army. His unit was participating in the attack on the Metz-Thionville German defense zone, the 452nd's primary target, the day Herman was killed. Otis had a confirmed kill of a Panther German tank with the 155 mm cannon and a confirmed kill of a BF-109E German fighter with a 50 cal. anti-aircraft machine gun to his credit. It sounds like Otis, was one of those backwoods type of boys, who could shoot the eye out of a squirrel. You don't want to spoil the meat, when supper depends on what you shoot. My uncles, Gerald and Charles King, were the same type of backwoods boys, only from southeast Ohio.

Herman's brother, Hugh Carson, now deceased, married Betty Jo Rowell and they had two sons, Michael Hugh Krimminger and Darren Neil Krimminger. Michael is married to Deborah Phillips and they have two girls, Lauren and Kristen, the family lives in the Washington, D.C. area. Darren is married to Ginger Louise Martin, and they still live in the Marshville area. Ginger and Darren have two children, Amber Michelle and Haley Nicole.

Darren has been a constant and enthusiastic help in my research and when I visited with his family, he drove me up to Frances Metzger Fredericks' home for a visit with the sister of the copilot who died in the same bomber crash.

Herman graduated from Union High School and worked around the area until he was accepted into the Naval Aviation Cadet

Program on November 13, 1942. When he was 'washed out,' the Navy standard was to release the person from service. Herman was discharged from the program on June 11, 1943.

On August 14, 1943, Herman enlisted in the Army and went though basic training at Fort Knox, Kentucky. He was serving in an armored battalion when he was selected for gunnery school in the Air Corps. Herman wanted to fly, up front or in back.

Herman completed his gunnery courses and reported to Rapid City, South Dakota. While on duty there and assigned to the Gott crew, he met and courted a young Chicago gal, who later became his wife at a ceremony attended by most of his fellow crew members.

Mrs. Ida Chemda Indritz Krimminger, wife of S/Sgt. Herman B. Krimminger

Herman's wife, Ida Chemda Indritz Krimminger turned out to be some lady. A Chicago native, she had three years of college when she entered the service at Fort Des Moines, Iowa, on 8 September, 1943.

When she was discharged on the 16th of December, 1945, after Herman's death in France, she was a Private First Class Medical Laboratory Technician.

Ida is responsible for much of my research proving out. For without the letters she and her brother, Phineas Indritz, wrote, the references I used to find many of the men would never have existed. This book owes a great debt to that fine lady.

Phineas Indritz was living in the Washington, D.C., area when I contacted him about his sister. He graciously gave me Ida's husband's telephone number so I could continue my research.

Just a slip of a girl, at 5 feet, 1 inch, she had brown hair and brown eyes, even then she had her future somewhat planned. We know that she was working at Johns Hopkins Hospital in Baltimore, Maryland, when she had to fill out the papers requesting the return of Herman's official remains in 1947.

We also know, that Ida released all claims to Herman's insurance to his family back home in North Carolina and that she attended the services at Arlington National Cemetery, with Herman's parents, when he was interred in his (official) grave, in August, 1948.

Hugh Carson Krimminger   Photo: Irwin Hoff
Bessie Autrey Krimminger
Mary Elizabeth Krimminger

Later, Ida finished college, became a micro-biologist and married Irwin S. Hoff, with whom she had two boys, Jonathan and Ken. Irwin, was a lawyer and both boys became lawyers. Ken lives in the Los Angeles area, while Jonathan, his wife Judy and two children live in Harrison, New York.

Later in life, a tireless worker for social good, Ida was honored before her death for her good works, by having the field house of the Fulton Street Playgrounds, in San Francisco, named after her. Irwin Hoff is retired and still living in the San Francisco area, at this time.

San Francisco, Fulton Street Playground Fieldhouse.

2nd Lt. William Edward Metzger, Jr., M.H.
February 9, 1922 ---- November 9, 1944
Born: Lima, Ohio
Serial Number: O-558834
2nd Lieutenant, Co-pilot
United States Army Air Force
Killed In Action, Tincourt-Boucly, France
9 November, 1944
Congressional Medal of Honor
'*The Lady Jeannette*'
B-17G-35VE, Sn: 42-97904
452nd Bombardment Group (H)
729th Bombardment Squadron
Mission: Saarbrucken, Germany
Buried: Woodlawn Cemetery, Lima, Ohio
       2nd Grave, Cartigny, France

    Born to a coal merchant, Bill was the son of **William E. Metzger, Sr.** and **Ethel Badeau Metzger**. He had two sisters, Jeanne and Frances.
    As with most families, times were hard for the Metzger family during the depression years of the kid's early life. Ed, with his own business was at least employed and people

had to have coal to heat their houses at that time. However, collecting the bills was a major problem with so many unemployed. To earn spending money, Bill distributed a weekly magazine of the times.

As with many of his fellow crew members, Bill was very interested in airplanes as a youth. So much so, that he and his sister Frances used to ride their bicycles out to the local airport to observe the planes flying. Frances remembers her first airplane flight well, for Bill had saved his route money and used it to purchase the flight. Her last flight with Bill was when he took them flying just before leaving for England.

The early years of Bill's life, he shared with his parent's Presbyterian church. But the loss of a very good friend at a young age, left Bill feeling the need for a more active church and he began attending the Church of Nazarene, he became a very active member.

During his school years, Bill became interested in playing the harmonica and he became very good. Later letters to his parents often mentioned his skill and how much the men in the barracks enjoyed listening to his playing.

The William E. (Ed) Metzger Family
Jeanne, Ed, Bill, Ethel and Frances

Bill graduated from Lima Central High School in 1940 and obtained employment at the Lima Electric Motor Company. During the next few years, he became very involved in his church, so much so that he contemplated entering the ministry.

Before Bill left for England, both of his sisters were married and their husbands were in the service.

Jeanne married George W. Scholfield who after the war worked for the Norfolk Southern Railroad maintaining inventory, they lived in Ohio for many years until they were transferred to Roanoke, Virginia. George was sent his draft notice to report for duty on March 28, 1942. He and Jeanne were married on February 1, 1942, and on the 28th of March, George left for basic training at Fort Hulen, Texas, on the gulf coast. Upon completion of basic training he was assigned to the 693rd Airborne Anti-Aircraft Battalion at Fort Bliss, Texas.

I know Fort Bliss well, my daughter, Rebecca Lynn Cole Willsey first visited life there on the 27th of June, 1962, thanks to Nancy Carol Gibson Cole, my first wife. I was in technical school training to be a Nike Fire Control Maintenance Man in the United States Army at the time.

By the way, Nancy Carol Gibson Cole and Carol Lorraine Reinbold Cole, my second wife are very good friends. When my second wife, Carol, won two free trips to the Rose Bowl football game in 1991 (while I was in France learning about the grave), she took, Nancy, my first wife, with her to the game!

George Schofield left with his unit aboard transport to arrive at Port Lyautey, Morocco, for the invasion of Africa. I visited the beach upon which he landed when I was stationed in Africa.

The 693rd was first assigned as anti-aircraft protection for two bridges, a railroad and a road bridge near Port Lyautey.

Their weapon was a single 50 Caliber machine gun mounted on a tripod and George, now a Corporal, was the lead gunner. Their method of transportation was aboard C-47 aircraft, thus the airborne designation. Their main duty was the defense of air bases. They would be loaded aboard a C-47 and transferred to forward air bases to provide aerial defense against raiding German aircraft.

George's outfit participated in the invasion of Sicily, arriving for their second D-Day on another ship. They left Sicily via a short boat trip across the narrow straight to Italy. For some time, the unit provided aerial defense for trains transporting war material to the front. They had mounted 20 mm anti-aircraft guns on one end of rail gondolas with a covered shelter at the other. Every time a train left for the front, two or more of these specially equipped gondola cars were mixed in with the regular railroad cars. George had to admit that he did not ride the gondola Ack-Ack cars very often, as his commander said, 'he couldn't afford to loose any Sergeants." So, he sent the Lieutenants to command the gondola cars and kept the Sergeants back at the unit.

George introduced me to another thing I did not realize about World War Two, early rotation for enlisted men. George was rotated back to the United States in 1944, after 19 months in Africa, Sicily and Italy. He spent a year in the States and was transferred to the 25th Field Artillery. The 25th Field Artillery was shipped to the Philippines in May, 1945, to be prepared for the invasion of Japan. I believe, you might find him a soldier of the time, who would believe the dropping of the Atom bombs on Japan, might have saved his life.

George saw a lot of the world during those years. "And, all for free," he told me when we discussed his service.

Jeanne and George are the proud parents of 3 children and the Metzger family roots continue to grow:

Stephen Wayne
  Children: Stephanie
    Daughter: Christina
Phyllis Lynn
  Married: Frank Prado
  Children:
    Magan
    Krista
Thomas Eugene
  Married: Ginger Segal
  Children:
    Tess
    Samuel

Frances married Cecil Carr Fredericks, who was in the 13th Airborne Glider Division, during the war. Luckily, Cecil's unit was in reserve most of the time, which reminded me of the World War One history of Willis S. Cole, Sr. and the 6th Division and their long walks through the French countryside. After the war Cecil worked for Westinghouse selling electronic gear to the Air Force for military aircraft. They lived for some time overseas in England. They had 4 children:

Deborah Lou Fredericks Coate
  Married: Wendel B. Coate "Bud"
  Children: Lisa Mc.,
Dian Sue Fredericks Rubiera
  Married: William J. Rubiera
  Children: Cecilia Marie
    Alexander Wm.
Betsy Ann Fredericks Intellini
  Children: Lynely Intellini
    Kristen Intellini
    Lauren A. Intellini
Laura Jane Fredericks Creer
  Married: Rosco Bradford Creer
  Children: Rebecca Morgan Creer
    Lauren Alexandra Creer

On October 5, 1942, Bill Metzger left his job at Lima Electric Motor and enlisted in Toledo, Ohio, and began his service at Camp Perry, Ohio, and he later served with an ordinance battalion at Camp Young, California. In March, 1943, a dream accomplished, he was accepted into Aviation Cadet Program. He entered the pipeline, serving at Santa Ana, Twenty-Nine Palms and Lancaster, California. He took his two engine multi-engine training at Douglas, Arizona, obtaining his wings and flight officer status. Further training followed at Kingman Air and was assigned to Rapid City, South Dakota where he received his commission as 2nd lieutenant on August 21, 1944.

Assigned to the 2nd Lt. Green Crew they completed final training before leaving for overseas, via the northern route, as Crew 20-C(Cr178, APO16500, AF178). In England, they were assigned to the 729th Squadron, 452nd Bombardment Group (H).

Harold "Tex" Burrell told me about the meeting the crew held the day before they began the trip to England. It was during this meeting that the Co-Pilot, 2nd Lt. William E. Metzger, Jr., told his assembled crew, "I will never leave an aircraft with a wounded crew member on board." The original crew consisted of:

2nd Lt. Walter R. Green, Pilot
2nd Lt. William E. Metzger, Jr. K.I.A.
2nd Lt. Elmer E. Gerard
2nd Lt. Donald E. Roberts
Cpl. Harold E. Burrell "Tex"
Cpl. Robert J. Falsey
Cpl. Edward T. Gorman
Cpl. Walter Jankowski
Cpl. Paul F. Tickerhoof
Cpl. Albert E. Wyant, K.I.A.

When reviewing the families records, letters and pictures of Bill's life, I found the following high school composition. I know few of us who have thought so much about how we should be living our lives as Bill Metzger did. In this school report he laid out a way of life that he followed through to the last second of his life. He gave up two parachutes so that others might live. He lived his life as he believed and ended it with the "wounded crewman on board."

A LITTLE PHILOSOPHY
Wilhelm Metzger
(A play on the German course he was taking at the same time.)

The fact that a man knows what is right does not mean that he will do what is right. Often you will see men who have had good training and whose minds are active do things which they know are harmful to themselves or to others.

Once in a while you meet a person who tells you that he has a right to do what he wants to do without any regards to what others may think or say. Such a person is very likely to be left to go his own way; he will have few or no friends. If you want to live a rich and full life, you need to think of others as well as yourself.

Knowledge cannot be stolen from you; it cannot be bought or sold. You may be poor, and the sheriff may come to your house and sell your furniture at auction, or drive away your cow or take your lamb, and leave you homeless and penniless; but he cannot lay the hand of the law upon the jewelry of your mind.

How shall I live? How shall I make the most of my life and put it to the best use? How shall I become a man and do a man's work? This and not politics or trade or war or pleasure is the question. The primary consideration is not how shall one get a living, but how shall he live; for if he lives rightly, whatever is needful he shall easily find.

Do not let envy tempt you to do things for which you are not fitted. Be yourself.

Long words get into the minds of men; short words get into their heart. When we wish to talk of the things that lie at the roots of life--birth and death, youth and age, joy and pain--we use the short words that have come down to us through the stream of time. They are words that touch and move us.

The only way we have to set out our ideas is by our words. If we wish to make those ideas clear, we shall do well to learn the right use of the short words in our tongue.

Long words may be all right when we want men to know; but when we want them to act, short words are the ones to use. Keep in mind the fact that we act when we feel, not when we know.

Tell me what you do in your off time, and I can tell you what sort of person you are. The way in which a man spends his leisure is a good index to his character and his habits of thinking.

The man who really lives, in the best sense of the word, tries all the time to broaden his interests in a wholesome way. He sets apart a time for reading good books, so that he may learn to commune with the great masters of prose and poetry; he develops a sport or a hobby--something to which he can turn his mind and his thoughts in his off time.

A philosophy of life to which a young man of Lima, Ohio, was true to the last. One wonders just what this man would have accomplished if he had lived.

I have read letters that the family received after his death. No matter where Bill went, he attended and was active in the church. People who knew him for only a short time, wrote his mother to tell her of the difference he had made in that short time.

At Wright Patterson Air Force Base you can drive down the street named in his honor. While there visit the Air Force Museum and see his picture and his citation on the Wall of Honor.

He waved goodbye to his mother from the end of the train and for the rest of her life she saw him there each time a train passed.

On May 11, 1953, 2nd Lt. Metzger's father died, just 9 days after T/Sgt. Dunlap's father, Alexander Dunlap died in Miles City, Montana. Lt. Metzger's mother lived for another 13 years. His parents first child, Robert, died as an infant.

2nd Lt. Earl L. Penick
Deceased
Born: Lawton, Oklahoma
Serial Number: O-755039
2nd Lieutenant, Bombardier
United States Army Air Force
Original Gott Crew Member

Through a letter written by Earl Penick, on December 29, 1948, to Lt. Harland, thanking him for sending a Christmas card, I was able to locate the brother of Lt. Penick, Carlton Penick who lives in Lawton, Oklahoma, with his wife, Willene.

From Carlton, I learned that Earl Penick had died some ten years ago. He had moved back to his home town of Lawton after retiring and had lived there for some time before he died.

Apparently, Earl and John Harland did not maintain contact after the first Christmas card and follow up letter in late 1949.

From the letter to Mrs. Gott from his mother, we know that the Gott crew was not Lt. Penick's original crew. He had trained with another crew for overseas shipment and had been removed at the last moment due to sinus problems. Air crew had to be able to stand using oxygen when at higher altitudes and they had to have clear passages due to changes in air pressure.

In his letter, Earl said he was a parts manager for a large firm. He asked if Jhonnie, had heard from any of the other fellows and asked if Jerry is still in California, referring to Lt. Collins. He also said, that he was thinking of going for a visit to California and he would like to look Jerry up if he knew his address. Collins does not remember Penick ever coming to see him, so we have to assume that they did not meet again after both left England.

Based upon these two letters, it would appear that perhaps Lt. Harland may have associated with the enlisted crewmen more than the other officers.

Earl was married twice, with a son, Michael with his first wife. He lived in the big city right after getting out of the service, but decided to move home to Lawton, Oklahoma later.

Michael entered the United States Air Force and made a career of it. He is now retired and living in Arizona.

The Earl Penick family taken in 1970 at mother's 50th Wedding Anniversary.
Lavona, Lee's 2nd wife.
Michael Lee Penick, Son U.S.A.F. Ret.
Earl Lee Penick

William Russell Robbins
May 6, 1920 ----
Born: Worcester, Mass
Serial Number: 11051000
Staff Sergeant, Right Waist Gunner
United States Army Air Force
Only survivor not wounded.
9 November, 1944
'*The Lady Jeannette*'
B-17G-35VE, Sn: 42-97904
452nd Bombardment Group (H)
729th Bombardment Squadron
Mission: Saarbrucken, Germany

Bill is one of those people that makes you think, if the war had not come along when it did, he would not have ventured more than 40 miles from home for many years.

William R. Robbins was born to **Helen Josephine Robbins** and **Charles Russell Robbins**, who were married in 1919.

He was hardly ever late to school, as he grew up next door to the school. Bill has one brother, Howard Frederick Robbins.

His father was a World War One veteran, a member of the 104th Infantry, 26th Division. While serving in France he had been gassed. Later, he would become a Commander of his Veteran's of Foreign Wars Post.

Bill graduated from South High School in Worcester and after the service, upon his return to Worcester, he took night courses to obtain an Associate Electrical Degree.

Bill, the 2nd oldest member of our group, enlisted in the army on April 20, 1942, took his basic training and was shipped to a Military Police outfit at Fort Dix, New Jersey. There he took a physical and a mental battery that qualified for the Air Cadet Program. Upon acceptance, he was sent to San Antonio for classroom training and upon completion he was transferred to primary training at Cimmeron Field in Oklahoma. Having completed primary training he began basic from which he was washed out after ten hours.

He was transferred to gunnery school

Shirley and Bill Robbins, May, 1996.

at Wichita Falls, Texas, then to Scott Field, Illinois and on to Rapid City, South Dakota, to join the Gott crew.

Bill had left behind his high school sweetheart Shirley and they decided to get married before he left for overseas. So Shirley joined him in Rapid City where on May 29, 1944, they were married.

After a short time at home, when he returned from England, he and Shirley went to Florida for his rest leave and then on to the Laredo Army Air Force Base in Texas where he was an gunnery instructor until he was eligible for discharge on October 15, 1945, with 3 years, 20 days service.

Upon return home, Bill returned to work at Coghlins, Inc., electrical distributor, where he worked until retirement. Beginning in the shipping department, Bill retired after 49 years, ending as an outside salesman.

Shirley and Bill are the parents of two children and currently the proud grandparents of five and great-grandparents of one.

>William R. Robbins, Jr.
>Children:
>>Tracey Ann Robbins
>>Todd Andrew Robbins
>>Tami Marie Robbins Dumphy
>>>Married: Kevin Dumphy
>>Wendy E. Robbins Bosse
>>Children:
>>>Derek Matthew Lambert
>>>Lisa Marie Lambert Blodget
>>>>Married: Scott Blodget
>>>>Children: Derek Joshua Blodget

Shirley and Bill are living in enjoyable retirement in Worcester and we have enjoyed visiting their home and meeting with them at the 452nd Bomb Group Association reunions.

* *

The 452nd Bombardment Group (H)

The following is from *The 452 Bombardment Group (H) History*. The Group's Squadrons were the 728th, the 729th, the 730th and 731st Bombardment Squadrons, Third Edition, 1980. Compiled by S/Sgt. Marvin E. Barnes, greatly supported by his wife, Opal. Published by The Delmar Printing Company, Charlotte, N.C.

Marvin died on May 13, 1980, soon after he completed assembling the book. One of the many members of the Group who have transferred since World War Two ended.

The 452nd Bomb Group was part of the United States Army's Eighth Air Force, consisting, in part, of 22 B-24 Heavy Bomber Groups, 24 B-17 Heavy Bomber Groups. Totaling 2,760 bombers when at strength.

The 452nd Bomb Group was initiated on the 1st of June, 1943, at Geiger Field, Washington. It was temporarily disbanded in August, 1945, to be reconstituted for the Korean War and it is still serving as a Transport Group at March Field, California.

Their last base in the United States was at Walla Walla, Washington, from which they proceeded, on December 22, 1943, to Camp Shanks, New York, the Port of Embarkation, arriving on December 27, 1943.

One can imagine the feelings aboard that train as it passed through all the villages, towns and cities on its way across the U.S., especially on Christmas Eve and Christmas. I wonder, how many men passed within a few miles of their homes and their loved ones did not know it. I wonder if Alex Dunlap, of Miles City, Montana, helped navigate the train across Montana. As we know, his son, Bob, was killed while serving with the Group's 729th Squadron 11 months later.

The group boarded the **Queen Elizabeth** and left on the 2nd of January, 1944, for England. The ship arrived in Scotland on the 8th and they debarked on the 9th and 10th.

Soon, they all arrived by train at Station 142, Deopham Green, England. On February 5th, 1944, they flew their 1st mission to Romilly, France. On May 12, 1944, they flew their 48th mission to Brux, Czechoslovakia. The Group suffered its worst loss on this mission, a total of 14 aircraft and 13 crews. On this mission, 1st Lt. Richard F. Noble's aircraft, the '**Lucky Lady**,' Sn: 42-39941, was lost. From my home town, of New Concord, Ohio, I watched Lt. Noble as he said goodbye to his aunt's family the day he left for Europe. Lt. Noble evaded capture and spent almost three months with the French resistance when he left them to try for the Allied Lines. His grave was later found with the date of death, 4 August, 1944.

On 'D-Day,' June 6, 1944, the Group flew 3 missions, their 68th, 69th and 70th.

On June 21, 1944, the 82nd mission, the Group participated in one of the famous missions of the war, a shuttle mission over Germany to Russia, one target being the Ruhland, German oil refinery. The bomber flew on through Germany and landed at Poltava. The Germans had followed the Group to see where they landed and that night the German Air Force bombed the landing field. Of 73 American B-17 bombers on the field, 43 were destroyed, 19 damaged and with only 7 undamaged. Of the destroyed, 24 belonged to the 452nd Group.

In July, the Group flew its 100th mission to Northern France. The 150th mission was to Cologne on October 15, the second mission to Cologne in two days. On the 162nd mission to Saarbrucken, Germany on November 9, 1944, '**The Lady Jeannette**' was lost.

The November 30, 1944, Daily Consolidated Strength Report showed the following numbers of personnel were assigned to the 452nd Bomb Group:

	Officers	Enlisted Men
87th Sta Com Sq.	17	112
18th Wea Sqdn.	2	8
1284 MP Det.	2	70
214 Fin Det.	1	6
466 Sub-Depot	6	229
1797 Ord S&M Co.	4	73
1230 QM Co.	3	41
872 Oml Co.	2	66
2112 FF Pln.	1	21
275 Med Disp.	2	13
Hq. 452 Bm Gp.	37	89
728 Bm Sq.	116	454
729 Bm Sq.	124	398
730 Bm Sq.	115	452
731 Bm Sq.	116	433
Sub-Total	548	2465
Total		3013

On Christmas Eve, 1944, the Group's mission was to Darmstadt, the day after Christmas to Andernach. A year after the Christmas on the train, the only people left from that train trip would be the ground staff of the group. With 162 missions under its belt, the Group's flying crews would have rotated a bit over four times, on average. Perhaps, some had even come back.

On February 14th, 1945, their Valentine's Day gift was delivered to Tachausonnberg, wherever that is at. One can imagine the Valentines drawn on the bomb loads.

The 225th mission was to Zwickau on March 19, 1945 and the final 250th mission was to Ingolstadt on April 21, 1945. On May 1, 1945 the group participated in the food drops to starving Holland. Several more drops were made on the 3rd, 5th and 6th of May.

V.E. Day, May 7, 1945 was a clear, sunny day with the night made brilliant by the thousands of flares shot off.

To many, the most important mission may have been the Prisoner of War Rescue Missions. Beginning on the 16th of May, the Group flew missions to pick up and return P.O.W.s to airfields in France. Other missions were flown on the 17th, 19th, 20th, and 25th.

The mission on the 30th was extra special as 27 aircraft of the Group flew 521 American P.O.W.s to England. It was also the last operational mission of the Group which then began to prepare to return to the United States. The first of the flying part of the Group began its trip back to the United States on the 24th of June. The ground personnel had to wait until August 6th, when they boarded the **Queen Elizabeth** again for the trip home, arriving at the Cunard White Star Line pier on the 11th of August, 1945.

On the 27th of August, 1945, the 452nd Bombardment Group (H) was deactivated.

World War Two combat action had cost the 452nd Group 437 men, 'Killed In Action' and another four who died in the performance of duty at Deopham Green. Four of those Killed In Action, died at Tincourt-Boucly Boucly on November 9, 1944, in the crash of **'The Lady Jeannette**.' The Pilot, 1st Lt. Donald J. Gott and the Copilot, 2nd Lt. William E. Metzger, Jr. were each awarded the **Congressional Medal Of Honor** for their actions aboard **'The Lady Jeannette**,' that day. Over 1,800 of the men who served in the 452nd have 'transferred' since World War Two ended. In 1997, there were over 1,500 members of the 452nd Bomb Group Association. A growing number of them being associate members, as I am.

You are welcome to join as an associate member to help keep the heritage of this unit alive, well into the 21st Century.

8th United States Army Air Force

452nd Bombardment Group (H)
Aircraft Tail Marking

**728th Bombardment
Squadron (H)**

**729th Bombardment
Squadron (H)**

Labor Ad Futurum
452nd Bombardment Group (H)

**730th Bombardment
Squadron (H)**

**731st Bombardment
Squadron (H)**

Chapter Twelve

Related Crashes and Evaders

As I ended my research into the fate of '*The Lady Jeannette*' and the men aboard the last flight, I found two other events which had traveled with '*The Lady Jeannette*' along the currents of time.

From early 1944 and January, 1945, to the end of my research into the crash of '*The Lady Jeannette*,' they were linked by location and/or the 452nd Bomb Group. One is cross linked to a small boy in Ohio, through a home town and a fondly remembered older friend, Mrs. Noble, the librarian. Neither is a direct part of this book and yet, they are so much, in their own way.

As you might remember from Chapter One, the day that Bernard Leguillier told me about the airman's face he had picked up at the site of the B-17 crash, he also told me about later crawling through the hull of a B-26 that crashed in the Bois de Buirre.

The Bois de Buirre crash site was located about a 3/4 mile from where the B-17 crashed. Bernard had said the B-26 bomber had crashed in February, 1945, during a bad snow storm and that the pilot was killed in the crash. It was interesting, as was the B-17 crash, and sometime I might look into it, but during that summer of 1991, I was looking for a German KRUPP 210 mm shell and World War One places and things of interest. Lots of people were deeply interested in World War Two aviation, I was not one.

During the next six years, as I became more and more interested and involved in the crash of '*The Lady Jeannette* and the grave at Cartigny, I was told by more people of the B-26 crash and what they knew of it.

Later, I often found that the people who remembered seeing one or the other, or both of the crashes tended to mis-remember which was which and get events of the two crashes mixed together.

I remember most vividly a farmer in Tincourt-Boucly who insisted that he had two pieces of '*The Lady Jeannette*.' During the **Remembrance 1994**, we all stopped by his farm yard to see the two relics and as you read, Russell Gustafson had to sign them.

As we stood there in the open yard of the farm compound, he told us, through Bernard Leguillier, of the crash of '*The Lady Jeannette*' as he remembered it.

I immediately knew that he was not describing the crash of '*The Lady Jeannette*,' he had to be describing the crash of the B-26. For as he told it, he was quite young and standing right here in the same farm compound as he listened to the bomber as it circled over Tincourt-Boucly several times. And that the last time it went by, it came from the south. It was quite low, just breaking into sight through the very low clouds as it went overhead, his finger pointing the way the bomber flew off to the north.

He had not heard and seen the '*The Lady Jeannette*,' for she had come from the east and crashed ½ of a mile to the north of the family compound. It had to have been the B-26 that he had seen and heard.

He first showed us a piece of propeller that he had laying in a flower garden by his front door. It was about three feet long and bent in several directions. The outward tip and edges were bent in a U shape and it was broken off in an L shape toward the propeller hub. The second piece was stored on a shelf in his barn. It was the hub end of a propeller blade that had broken off, it looked almost brand new.

As he was asking Russell, through Mr. Leguillier, to sign them, my mind was working on what he had just shown us. Between reading about air crash investigations and watching them on the television, I realized that the propeller tip had to have come from a propeller that was not turning at speed when it hit the ground. Also, since it was evenly bent in a U shape along its length, it meant the propeller had to have hit the ground straight along most of its length. One thing was obvious, the propeller hub end was in too good of condition to have come from any engine on *'The Lady Jeannette'* which hit the earth going straight down.

By that time, Bernard had shown me two pictures he had found in the private collection of a Péronne photographer, who had died since the war, of the B-26 crash and its propeller hub ends were not damaged in the crash. To me, it looked like the farmer had an unbolted hub end of one of the propellers from the B-26.

I do believe, that the propeller tip is the largest remaining relic of *'The Lady Jeannette'* that I have seen. I am certain, that the propeller tip came from the number one engine of the B-17. That was the engine that was stopped and not feathered after the flak hit the bomber over Saarbrucken.

When the bomber dove into the earth going straight down, the propeller would have hit the earth straight on. The dirt formed around the propeller forcing it to bend into the U shape. As the propeller was pushed further into the earth, the outward tip bent backward, breaking it off toward the hub. All this happened very quickly and as it broke off and became loose, the bombs exploded and blew the broken propeller tip out of the crater where it was found and kept by the farmer's father.

Just over two months later, the B-26 crashed in the Bois de Buirre and became a part of this book as a related crash. It was there for sometime before being salvaged and I suspect many items were gone when it was finally salvaged, including one propeller hub end.

As I have written, when Carol and I placed the two new informational marble plaques at the crash site and grave on Memorial Day 1997, it disturbed some of the people of the villages and we were asked to attend a meeting of the Mayors and Councilors of the villages of Tincourt-Boucly, Cartigny and the larger commune, Roisel.

At this meeting another discussion was held about what the various people had seen and heard, and again, I found that people tended to mix up the crash of the B-17 and the B-26. One of the results of the meeting, was that I agreed to begin to research the B-26, which they all agreed crashed in February, 1945, and see if I could find out the American side of the story.

When I got back and started looking into the B-26, I could find nothing in any of the books referring to the Army Air Force February missions that would account for the crashed B-26. I knew from a newspaper article that Claude Leguillier had shown me in 1995, that the 397th Bombardment Squadron (B-26) had been located at the Péronne, A-72 Air Base. The article discussed some of them returning to visit the base a few years earlier. Consulting my American Legion magazine, I called the reunion location number and found out who was the contact of the 397th Group. When I contacted him, he gave me several other numbers to call.

After many telephone calls and many hours on the Internet, I found that the 397th Group just did not have an aircraft that was lost in a time frame that made sense. They had lost a few bombers, but could account for all of them.

Several months passed and as I began to complete this book, I called Bernard and asked him if he would send me a good copy of the B-26 bomber crash photographs. Using a magnifying glass on the copy machine copy he had given me some time before, I could almost make out all of a partial serial number located on the tail. Bernard, good guy that he is, sent me the originals to look at.

When I got them, I looked at them with a magnifying glass and scanned them into my computer and blew them up until they got worse instead of better. There was no doubt in my mind now, the last three serial numbers were 201. Just how many B-26 bombers could have had those three numbers on the tail?

I faxed the Air Force history research people at Maxwell A.F.B., asking them to see if they had any mission missing aircraft with those last three numbers during February, 1945, and I got back in contact with the 397th Bomb Group Association. They came back with the fact that they had no bomber assigned with those last three numbers on its tail. Air

B-26G-1-MA, Sn: 43-34201 '*Where's It At?*'
Photo: Bernard Leguillier

Bois de Buirre, January 22, 1945, Tincourt-Boucly.
Photo: Bernard Leguillier

Force History also called me to say that they had no record of a B-26 bomber lost in action with that possible serial number sequence, during the February time frame. They had even gone a couple of weeks on either side of February just to be certain. Still, the French were certain in their belief that the bomber was on its way back from a mission to Germany when it crashed in February, 1945.

As I have written, one of the directors, Will Henderson, of our small museum is a veteran of the most unsung group of American military personnel during World War One and onward. Graves Registration of old is now named Mortuary Affairs, with its headquarters at Fort Lee, Virginia.

During my research into the B-17 bomber crash at Tincourt-Boucly and the grave at Cartigny, I had been in contact with several people at the Mortuary Affairs. The most recent Director, Thomas Rexrode and mostly with Doug Howard, the Assistant Director.

Somewhere along the line, when it became time to plan for the first combined Graves Registration-Mortuary Affairs reunion of those who have served with both units from World War Two onwards, someone added my name to the list of people to be invited.

I quickly discussed the reunion with Carol, found I had enough Frequent Flyer miles with United Airlines to get a ticket and sent in my fee and made plans to travel to the Washington D.C. area and onward to Fort Lee for the reunion in mid-September, 1997.

As you know, I had been at the National Archives several times before, the latest with Russell Gustafson in June, 1997. Each time, wanting to review the still photographs of the Army Air Force in World War Two. I have been looking for pictures that I might use in this book and I thought, those photographic records might have a lot I would be interested in. Each time before I visited, I called and was told they were at one College Park Archive and when I got there I was told the release of the photographs had been delayed again. The June trip was no different. Upon arrival at College Park, we were told the National Air and Space Museum downtown still had the photographs and that they required an appointment made a month or two in advance of a visit to be able to review the photographs.

I got on the telephone with my old high school friends, Gail and Charles Kettlewell, and asked if I could I spend a few days sleeping on their couch so I could visit the archives? As they did in 1994, they gracefully said, come on in.

I arrived at the home of Gail and Charles, ready to go do the research and locate several items of interest. Something on '*The Lady Jeannette,*' a complete moving picture series from World War One of a KRUPP 210 mm cannon being transported, loaded and fired, and information on the B-26.

A few days later, when I left for the Graves Registration reunion, I had met two of those goals, in some sense of the word. I had found three moving pictures series of the cannon firing. Now, I have to go back sometime and get them copied. I had also found that I had better pictures concerning the events that I was researching than the Army Air Force Files now held. What started out as almost two million photographs has been reduced to far less than half. Most of the photographs I had, were not duplicated in the now official files. In fact, I found none that I considered worth paying the usage fee for.

However, I did accomplish something on the B-26. While talking to one of the National Air and Space Museum archivists, he mentioned a book they had that listed all the serial numbers of the B-26s manufactured.

As I was going through the book, I found there were five possible serial numbers for B-26's and two A-26's, all with the last three numbers being 201. The only problem is, at that time, I didn't know enough to tell if the pictures I had of the crash were of a B-26 or an A-26.

I had sent copies of the two B-26 crash scene pictures to several people and none of them could tell me the difference. That is, until I was given the name of Marvin J. Rosvold, Chairman of Board, Director, of the Ninth Air Force Association, Inc.

Marvin is still working as an architect in Norfolk, Nebraska, and when I called him at his business, he told me to send him a copy of the pictures and he also gave me several names of people who had flown B-26s to contact to ask about the crash.

Off went the pictures and the contacts were made. Not much came of them, but when I next talked to Marvin, he quickly told me, there was no longer any doubt. It was a B-26. "Just look at the air inlets on the nacelles and the Martin Electric Propellers," he said. He followed with, "The tail is rounded and not angled as the A-26's tail was." Good enough for me. Of course, he got me to immediately sign up as an associate member of the Ninth Air Force Association.

The people at the archives and the Air Force Historical Research Center at Maxwell are always way behind with requests such as mine. Funding for that type of work keeps getting cut and one can't even start to blame them.

I had talked to a Dr. Jim Kitchens, back in 1994, when he helped me break the first leads in the B-17 crash and I still had his number. When I called it, it was disconnected or not working, I don't remember which. But, over the years, I have found that if one dials a number one or two on either side, one tends to get someone in the same organization and they are usually happy to give one the correct number.

Well, the fellow I reached was very nice and told me that Dr. Jim Kitchens was no longer with them, but he did give me the number of Capt. William Butler who could help. He also told me their fax number, so I could fax in a request. Before I hung up, I found his name to be Dr. Fred Shaw. The man who had taken Dr. Kitchens place. Nice fellow on the telephone to such a stranger calling in, of course he was the new director.

I immediately sent several faxes with information requests about the B-17 and the B-26. Not much came back quickly, but I had names of some people there now, didn't I? After a few days, I called back and was given the name of a fellow who really got interested and found the records I needed. Mickey Russell, an ex-Marine, took the serial numbers and within a day, called me back and said that he just could not find anything that matched, but he did send me a fax of what he had found.

Of the five B-26 bombers with the last three serial numbers of 201, three were not possible at all and the other two were questionable. Another call to Mickey and he sent me the aircraft records for those two. One had crashed in December, 1944, so it was out, leaving only one. And as everything else it didn't make sense right away. That bomber's record stated it had been written off to the Salvage Board, on December 3, 1945.

A call back to Mickey with the request to please check mission crashes from mid-January to the end of February, 1945, brought no results. During that telephone call, it hit both of us, it had to be the last one because there were no dots, dashes or slashes between the date numbers, it could be January 23, 1945. As it could not have been a mission loss, it had to be something else. Mickey promised to look at the one last chance he had just thought of, the Accident Reports around January 23, 1945.

The call from Mickey, early the next morning, was an exciting one. The B-26, Sn: 43-34201 had crashed in an aircraft accident six miles north of the Péronne Air Base on January 22, 1945. He had found it and said he'd send me all the information at once. Good work, Mickey!

Shortly, I had the Accident Report, along with the crew list and what had happened to them. The French though close, were off. The bomber had crashed on Monday, January 22, 1945, not in February, as they all thought. Second, the pilot was not killed, however, the navigator and flight engineer were.

Time to hit the Internet and seek out people. The pilot spelled his name differently than any other person of that name I could find, he capitalized the third letter, DuBois. Sure enough, I found a person with almost the same name with an e-mail Internet address. I sent an e-mail to him and went back to the net and the next name, the bombardier. After several hours, I had not found anyone who checked out, though I found lots of people with that last name. All I could do was begin to call every tenth person with that name and see if I was lucky enough to find him. After about 20 telephone calls, I had not found anyone who had ever heard of someone with that name in their family. Time to move on to another name, the radio operator/gunner, and it was hard to read, so it was time to call Mickey again and ask him to review the microfilm to see if he could make the name out.

Meanwhile, I scanned the page into the computer and started blowing it up. Soon, I thought I might have the correct spelling and sure enough, I found that last name in the same state the man was said to have enlisted from.

A telephone call to the listed number resulted in a woman answering the phone. As with the first crew man I had located from the B17 crew, the Radio/Gunner of the B-26, Sgt. Samuel M. Assey, had died. I was talking to his widow, Arlene.

Sam and Arlene Assey (pronounced Ace-cey) were married on the 2nd of May, 1966 and she told me, that Sam had died on November 2nd, 1995. However, Arlene was very interested in my research and during several conversations she has told me about Sam's life after the service and that he had several retail stores selling end lots, appliances and such. The more I found out about Sam Assey, the more he sounded like a man I would have greatly enjoyed knowing.

Sam had kept in contact with several crew members over the years and as I later learned, he had traveled to Deale, Maryland, to visit with Lt. Robbins' parents, Calvin Lee Robbins and Ellen M. Wood Robbins to discuss Hugh's death with them.

When I contacted Ethel Nutwell, Lt. Robbins cousin, she verified that Sam had kept in contact with Hugh's parents through the mail and visited them whenever he could until their death. Obviously, a man who believed in Remembrance!

Arlene was so very gracious and she quickly agree to send me a picture of the crew taken before they left the United States for Europe. And, she gave me the address and telephone numbers of the crew members that her husband had kept in contact after the war. She knew he had visited the Robbins family, but since Hugh' parents had died, she did not have their address.

At first I had no luck reaching the Co-

1st Lt. Joseph M. DuBois   Photo: Joe DuBois
1st Lt. Richard P. Britanik
Sgt. Samuel M. Assey
1st Lt. Raymond H. Boettcher
Sgt. William G. Glass
Sgt. Mike Flores
Taken in the bar at the DeSoto Hotel, Savannah, Georgia, on June 26, 1944, just before the crew flew a new B-26 to England.

pilot, Lt. Britanik, at the number I had written down. However, when I called the second number Arlene gave me, I was again able to surprise the man answering the telephone by asking him if he was on a bomber that crashed into a woods on January 22, 1945?

Load for bear or a mission at Péronne A-72 Air Base. Officers of '*Where's It At?*' before their living quarters.
1st Lt. Raymond H. Boettcher
    1st Lt. Richard P. Britanik
        1st Lt. Joseph M. DuBois
            1st Lt. Hugh W. Robbins, K.I.A.
Photo: R. Britanik

Sure enough it was him, Lt. Raymond Boettcher, and we talked for some time. I had called him Richard when he first answered the telephone and he quickly told me that his name was Raymond H. Boettcher and not Richard and that he goes by Ray. It turned out that they had his recorded his name wrong on the Report Of Aircraft Accident, in 1945.

First, he answered my questions about how the two men had died and I learned that the OBOE Pathfinder equipment, weighing about a ton, had broken loose during the jolts and sudden stop and crushed Lt. Robbins and the Engineer/Gunner, Sgt. William G. Glass.

He was able to tell me the bomber's name, '*Where's It At?*' a play on the fact that they were Pathfinders, the lead bombers on a missions who found the target and marked it for the following bombers. They all had wives and girl friends and agreed that it was best not to name the bomber after just one fellow's flame.

A couple of days later, my e-mail dinged at startup and there was a short reply from my e-mail. Yes, he was that pilot, Joe DuBois. It took a couple of more e-mails until he was sure enough of me to give me his address and telephone number and soon, I was talking to him and finding out his view of the crash. One, I could compare with the statement he had written for the Accident Report so long ago.

Between Ray and Joe, I learned that they were on a mission that afternoon and what happened to them after the crash. I also found out a lot about the two men who were killed.

The original crew of 6 had trained together in the states, however when they got to England and took further training to qualify them for their Pathfinder duties they were assigned a seventh crewman, a Navigator, 1st Lt. Hugh W. Robbins, of Deale, Maryland.

1st Lt. Hugh Wesly Robbins, K.I.A. January 22, 1945
Photo: Ethel Nutwell, cousin.

The Pilot, 1st Lt. Joseph M. DuBois told me that Robbins was an excellent navigator and he always got them on target within a minute of the predicted time.

From Lt. Britanik's Flight Log: Jan. 22, 1945, B-26, 43-34201, mission for 4091 Group. Crash landed on return. From A-72 to 7 km N. of Péronne to Zimmerman rail road bridge, Germany. 1 hour instrument and 3 day = 4 hour, 32nd mission.

Though they were assigned to the 1st Pathfinder Squadron (Prov), for combat, they were attached to the 397th Bomb Group at the A-72 Airbase at Péronne. They could be called to lead the 397th and they often acted as Pathfinders for other groups.

Joe DuBois told me, the left engine had begun to cut out on the way in to the target and continued to do so until it died just before the crash. As we will see, that is backed up by the Copilot, 1st Lt. Britanik in his written statement about the crash. Joe said, "that he and Britanik always felt the engine was damaged by flak on the way in."

They dropped their marker bombs right on target, the Euskirchen Bridge and the bridge continued to be bombed by the following Group, the 409th Bomb Group. Their mission, that day, was a total success, trapping 1,500 retreating German vehicles as the Battle of the Bulge continued to wind down. Over half of the German vehicles were later destroyed by fighters of the IX and XIX TAC (Tactical Air Command), along with long range artillery with aircraft spotting.

On the way back to A-72, the left engine continued to momentarily cut out and it appeared to be getting worse. As they approached the base, they found the base weather to be quite bad, with a low ceiling and snow flurries. Lt. DuBois contacted the base air control, Drunkard Control, and continued flying under instrument control.

They arrived back in the area of the base about 14:40 and thus began the last minutes of flight before the crash. This is an excellent place to insert the Individual Aircraft Record Card and the accident report filled out after the crash. The written statements by the men concerning the crash provides an excellent insight into the events leading up the and including the crash.
(Target names differed in Britanik's log and official history, Author.)

(Abbreviated: Author) INDIVIDUAL AIRCRAFT RECORD CARD
Model: B-26G-1   A.A.F. Serial Number: 43-34201 Manuf & Loc. Martin, Baltimore
Contract Number: AC-31733   Final Destination In U.S.: Dow Fld.
Priority Number: A A F Pri I -I   Project: 92665-R
Location Organization   Recipient Next. Dist. Crate/Fly Condition Date Action Remarks
Baltimore Martin   Accepted 5-29
          GLUE Replace C/nia Hunter Fld, GA Avail. 6-19 6-1572 CEI RONP
                2nd Ferry Group F Delivered 6-20
            ATC   "   "   Departed 6-20
Hunter Fld   "   "   "   Arrived   6-20 SAWOrd A F Stop
   "   "   "   "   73 "   " DPR
   "   "   "   "   Departed 6.25 SAW
Dow Fd   "   "   "   Arrived   6-28 DPR
   "   No Atlantic Way DOW   "   Dep US   6-28 C&2
GLUE   9 AF   G B26G   8 43-34201 7-8-44
GLUE   9 AF   A B26G   08 43-34301 6-28-44   7   144
GLUE   9 AF CON SALNBD   R B26G   43-34201   12345   3   645
GLUE   9 AF CON SALNBD   R B26   M 43 34201   12345 3 645

The important entry is the 9 AF CON SALNBD. It stands for Consigned to Salvage Board. The confusing entry was the 12345 as it could also have been December 3,1945.

War Department	WAR DEPARTMENT	Accident-1-22-538
A.A.F. Form No. 14	AAF Station A-27	
(Revised May 14,1942)	U.S. ARMY AIR FORCES	

(1) Place: Péronne   (2) Date: 22 January, 1945   (3) Time: 1500
Aircraft (4) Type & Model B-26GI   (5) A.F. No: 43-34201   (6) Station: A-72
Organization: 9th B.D. Ninth AF   (8) 0-------   (9) 1st Pathfinder Hq
       Command Air Force   Group   (Squadron)

Duty	Name (Last name first)	Rat int	Serial No.	Rank	Per. Class	Br. Or	Air Force Command	Result to Per.	Use of Chute
(10)	(11)	(12)	(13)	(14)	(15)	(16)	(17)	(18)	(19)
P	DuBois, Joseph M.	P	O-677682	1st Lt.	01	AC	Ninth AF	None	No
CP	Britanik, Richard R.	P	O-822630	1st Lt.	01	AC	Ninth AF	Minor	NO
N	Robbins, Hugh W.	N	O-749933	1st Lt.	01	AC	Ninth AF	Fatal	NO
B	Boettcher, Richard H	B	O-766186	1st Lt.	01	AC	Ninth AF	Minor	NO
EG	Glass, William G.	EG	33117765	Sgt.	01	AC	Ninth AF	Fatal	NO
RG	Assey, Samuel M.	RG	20304253	Sgt.	01	AC	Ninth AF	Major	NO
TG	Flores, Mike	TG	39571005	Sgt.	01	AC	Ninth AF	Major	NO

(20) DuBois, Joseph M.   (21) O-677682   (22) 1st Lt.   (23) 01   (24) AC
(Last) (First)(Init)   (Serial)   (Rank)   (Per Class)   (Branch)
Assigned: (25) 9th B.D. Ninth AF   (26) 387   (27) ----   (28) A-71
       (Command & Air Force)   (Group)   (Squadron)   (Station)
Attached for flying (29) 9th B.D. (30) Ninth AF   (31) 1 Pathfinder (32) A-72
       (Command & Air Force)   (Sqdn)   (Station)
Org. Rat. (33) Pilot   (34) 4/22/43   Pres. rat. (35) Pilot   Inst. rat (37) 4/26/44
(Rating)   (Date)   (Rating)   (Date)
First Pilot Hours (at time of accident)   Pres. rat. date (36) 4/22/44
(38) This type.........................1002:05   (42) Inst. time last 6 mo...........33:15
(39) This mode.........................1110:00   (43) Inst. time last 30 days.......08:00
(40) Last 90 days...................... 124:30   (44) Night time last..... 6 mo...06:30
(41) Total..............................11387:30   (45) Night time last 30 days....01:00

AIRCRAFT DAMAGE F-OR-1-onw4-24

	Damage		(49) Lst of damaged parts
(46) Aircraft	M		Complete Wreck
(47) Engine	M		
(48) Propeller(s)			

(50) Weather at time of accident   700 feet ceiling, 200-500 yards visibility
(51) Was the pilot flying on instruments at time of accident   Yes
(52) Cleared from   A-72   (53) Fld. A-72   (54) Kind of Clearance "J" Form
(55) Pilots mission   Combat Mission
(56) Nature of accident Crashed attempting to land
(57) Cause of accident Both engines cut out just prior to landing at A-72
(58) Has Form 54 been submitted? No

Description of accident: At about 1445 on 22 January 1945 aircraft 43-34201 passed over A-72 and asked for landing instructions. Flying control attempted to divert the aircraft but the pilot elected to land due to the fact that one engine was cutting out. At about 1,000 feet the left engine cut out completely and a few seconds later the right engine began to cut out. The pilot was on instruments in a snow storm. The pilot could not hold altitude so he cut the mixtures and switches and bellied the aircraft in approximately six miles from A-72. The plane was a completely wrecked and burnt. The cause of the accident was due 100% to engine failure. There are no recommendations.

Photo: Britanik His friend Bill, they see each other still. Capt. Shirley was his pilot and wrote report about crash.

HEADQUARTERS
1st Pathfinder Squadron Prov.
APO140, U. S. Army   23 January
CERTIFICATE

    On 22 January 1945 at approximately 1445, A/C No. 201, piloted by myself approached A-72 with the left engine cutting out. Drunkard Control attempted to divert the A/C to A-74. I elected to try to land because of the condition of the aircraft. I thought it dangerous to attempt the diversion. After leaving A-72 en route to A-74 the left engine was delivering partial power at approximately 22 hg. And 2300 rpm. The right engine had 45" hg. And 2400 rpm. At this time I experimented more with the carburetor heat control but got no results. The carburetor air temperature gauge was giving satisfactory reading on both engines. It was impossible to climb the A/C above 800-1000 feet altitude. At approximately 1500, the left engine failed completely and approximately 30 seconds later the right engine failed at 800-1000 feet altitude. The mixture controls were cut and the ship was landed straight ahead in a flat attitude with the wheels up.
    The A/C was stalled in from 10-15 feet above the ground at an airspeed of 90-100 mph. And hit about 500-600 yards from a wooded area and continued into the woods approximately 150 feet, hitting a large tree which sheared off the right wing and started A/C burning.
    Actual cause of engine failure unknown. All engine instruments were indicating proper reading. Each main gas tank was indicating over 100 gallons at 1445 (approximately. The weather at the time of the accident was estimated to be 700-800 foot ceiling and 200-500 yards visibility. I was on instruments at the time of engine failure.
    Signed
    Joseph M. DUBOIS
    1st Lt., Air Corps
    Pilot

    Joe suffered no injuries in the crash and he told me of the first thing he saw as the bomber broke out of the low clouds with the engines dead. The field where they had to hit had a big concrete telephone pole right in the middle it. Luck was with them, as they hit the earth hard and the bomber bounced into the air and over the telephone pole. They hit in the field one more time before entering the woods, cutting the light trees as they went. However, right in front of them was a tall, thicker tree and it hit the right side of the plane, shearing off the right wing and starting a fire.

    Joe was called back into the service, in 1950 for the Korean War. He was stationed at the Wright Patterson Air Force Base, at Dayton, Ohio. There he worked on jet engine development. He stayed in the service and retired as a colonel.

Leaving for a mission.   Photo: Britanik

Who left this junk here?   Photo: Britanik

Dragon lady IV with 31 missions under her skirts.
Photo: Britanik

HEADQUARTERS
1st. Pathfinder Squadron Prov.
APO 140, U. S. Army   24 January 1945
CERTIFICATE

On the 22nd. of January 1945, while returning from a mission over Germany, our left engine was cutting momentarily and periodically. I had noticed it had cut like this once before reaching bombline going in, as well as on the bomb run and turn off target. At each time I checked the carburetor heat even though the gauges read satisfactorily all through the flight and were at all times well in the green. Upon reaching the field, at A-72, they tried to divert us to A74 due to weather which I would estimate at 100 feet ceiling and V2mile visibility. The engine sputtered several times and the first pilot thought it advisable to get in while we had a field near. We made three passes and saw the flares on the approach but never could line up due to weather which at the time of the third pass seemed to be zero-zero due to snow flurry. The field tower gave us a heading and we took it up and began to climb. We reached 1200 feet indicated and the left engine cut and the first pilot proceeded to begin single engine operation. Then it cut out again and then out, and were losing altitude fast. Then the right engine cut and we broke through the undercast and immediately saw the trees and telephone pole in front of us. We missed the pole and hit in brushy area. I remember definitely three hard jolts.

In conclusion let me add that at all times during the flight the engine instruments were within normal operating limits, the pilot heat was on for the descent and when the engine cut the rpm would drop about a hundred or so. Each tank had approximately 100 plus gallons in it. I noticed the airspeed was about 110 above the trees and dropping fast. I estimate we hit going about 85-100 mph. The plane was burning upon contact with the ground.

Signed
RICHARD P. BRITANIK
I st Lt., Air Corps
Copilot

When Ray Boettcher and I talked about the crash, he told me that he was standing in the hatchway between the pilots as they were trying to make the landings and when they diverted. He said, the first thing he saw out the front was that telephone pole and it got bigger fast.

He also said, "...that Lt. Robbins was standing behind me with his hand on my shoulder. We had been getting ready to parachute if necessary. However, the bomber never got enough altitude for us to do so and we had to ride it out. Sgt. Glass was standing behind Robbins."

The bomber hit hard each time causing Robbins to bump into Boettcher so hard that Boettcher hit his head opening several large scalp wounds. As the bomber jolted the second and third time, the Pathfinder equipment broke loose and hit Robbins, pinning him and Glass under it, crushing them to death. The equipment and Robbins also hit Boettcher so hard that his back was temporarily paralyzed and he could not move, blocking Lt. Britanik's escape route.

The flames from the burning gasoline leaking from the sheared-off wing, quickly began to set anything burnable afire and the fire was spreading fast, with two men trapped.

Flores and Assey got out through the broken hull. Britanik had to lift and carry Boettcher out of the bomber, an act for which he was later awarded the Soldier's Medal. He told me, he had to, as Boettcher was blocking his way out.

DuBois was able to get out, the only man not hurt. The men then worked on getting Glass and Robbins out. They were dead, but they might be saved from burning. Ray told me that they were able to get

Glass out, but he is not sure of Robbins. Perhaps, that is why the French thought only one man was killed. Glass's remains could have been put in an ambulance or truck before any of the Frenchmen I have talked to, arrived. They must have seen the dead officer being taken to the truck from near the bomber and decided he was the pilot. The crew had to hurry away from the bomber, as the gasoline fed fire was causing the 50 cal. machine gun ammunition to cook off. Once they had moved away from the bomber, Lt. DuBois told them to wait and he would walk down the hill to the village they had seen just before the crash and call the base to report the crash and to request help.

As they waited, Ray remembers Sgt. Mike Flores complaining about burning his ears and arms badly while attempting to get the dead men out. Sgt. Assey had also suffered severe hand and arm burns. Ray just sat there, blood flowing down from his scalp wounds, covering him with blood.

As he described it to me, "You know how bad even a slight head wound bleeds, it doesn't take long to look real bad."

Indeed, l did! When I was three, my father and mother were repairing the roof of a barn for the Paine family a few miles south of New Concord, Ohio. Back then my mom, Luella Claire (King) Cole worked with my dad, Willis S. Cole, Sr., on the roofs, which was a rare thing for a woman in those days.

My sister, Rea, and brother, Dick, and the Paine's son, Tom (I think), along with a couple of other kids all four or more years older than me, decided to feed the hogs in the hog lot to watch them root in the mud for the ears of corn they took from the old fashioned corn crib. The corn crib was a building of sorts, consisting of two long and narrow corn cribs on each side with a roof over both of them to create a wagon shed.

The Paines had put a gate at the far end of the shed to separate the hog lot from the shed and farm yard. They had secured the gate by tying it with wire, a foot or so, down from the top on either side.

The big kids threw the corn ears into the hog lot and watched the hogs come-a-running. The hogs began to root in the mud and the bigger kids climbed up on the gate so they could see better. Being little, I couldn't climb the gate, but I could stick my head through the narrow opening between two of the gate's cross pieces. Boy, could I see those hogs pushing their way to the corn, just to be pushed away by another. Being a towny and not a farm boy, such sights were very interesting to me.

As I stood there with my head through the gate, one more kid started to climb to the top of the gate. Suddenly it pivoted on the two pieces of wire holding it, swinging the bottom up and away and the top down.

That little pumpkin head stuck through the gate received a real good swipe as the little boy was ejected into the hog lot and the bigger kids back toward the farm yard. It took just a second and boy, did I start to cry, loud.

The kids picked themselves up and started screaming that my head was almost ripped off. Everyone came running as fast as they could and I can still see my mother and father scrambling off the roof and down the ladder through a wall of tears, quickly turning reddish.

Mrs. Paine heard the commotion and came running from the farm house. When my Mom got to me, she took one look at me and picked me up on the move, heading toward the house with Mrs. Paine, while Mr. Paine and Dad got the car ready to head for Doctor Bain's office in town.

At the house, they cleaned me up a bit and Mrs. Paine gave Mom a large, very white, Turkish towel which mom wrapped around my head. Then they loaded me up in the car, sitting on Mom's lap. Dad started putting up a dust cloud with that old Plymouth sedan as we made hurried toward town.

Mrs. Paine had called ahead to the Doctor's office and I still remember, pulling up in front of the house that he used as an office and seeing him coming down the steps to the street to meet us.

On the way into and past the waiting area, several patients saw all the blood and I understand, starting, asking if I was going to live? I guess I looked a lot worse than it actually was.

However, I think Mom was finally getting scared too, because the towel had turned red and by the time Doctor Bain got us into his office and took the towel off, it was starting to get quite damp with my blood.

Doctor Bain looked at my head and said it looked like someone had tried to scalp me and had not quite finished the circle. The wood slat of the gate had wrapped up a section of my scalp into a roll.

He asked me to be a strong boy and started to clean my head. I don't remember him giving me anything for pain and he told my mother that the top of the head didn't have a lot of nerve endings in that area.

He unrolled the flap, sprinkled some powder onto my head and began sewing the scalp back into place. I've been lucky to date, my old age has not led to complete balding, I'm just getting a wider and wider forehead. For up there someplace, I have a reminder of that day, that I feel once in a while. A scar around six inches long. Yes Ray, I know how much scalp wounds bleed.

When Lt. DuBois got to the village, Buirre, he stopped at a farmhouse and asked to use the telephone. He called the base, reported the crash and asked for help. However, he did not go back to the woods, as the emergency crew arrived quickly and went up to the woods, while he was taken by one of the American vehicles to the hospital to be checked out.

Up at the crash site, the other men moved to the edge of the woods and waited as the bomber burned behind them.

In 1994, we were taken to a farm house in Buirre, where some of the people insisted someone from the crash of **'The Lady Jeannette'** had walked up and asked to use the telephone to call for help. At the time, to me, it was totally the wrong direction for it to have been a survivor from **'The lady Jeannette'** crash. Talking to Joe DuBois had settled that question, for the French people had again gotten their crashes mixed up.

After DuBois had made his call to the base, the farm people called the Nuttens family in nearby Tincourt-Boucly, as they had the only operating vehicle at that time. They told them about the crash and the men needing help.

Lt. DuBois did go to the crash site a couple of weeks later to see the plane and offer the French compensation, they refused.

During our summer vacation in 1997, Carol and I visited Mrs. Nuttens' son's farm and talked to him about the crash. He called his mother and got her answers to our questions over the telephone.

She and her husband, who has since passed away, had driven up the road to Driencourt to the edge of the woods and then drove along the field next to the woods until they came to the men. They loaded several men, to use her remembered number, into the truck. One of them (we now know that was Flores) had very bad burns on his hands, arms and face. Another had badly burnt hands and arms (Assey) and one looked real bad and very bloody (Boettcher). She didn't give us any information that would answer the question as to whether or not Lt. Britanik was with them.

Once they had loaded the men into their vehicle, they took them to a hospital at Péronne. Apparently a military hospital. Ray Boettcher told me of his most vivid memory of the whole affair, he was in the operating room, literally covered with blood and Lt. DuBois was in the room with him to offer moral support. A young doctor came walking into the room and as he approached Ray, he told Ray excitedly, "You are going to die!" Just then, the doctor's eyes glazed and rolled up and he passed out and fell to the floor. It was obvious that this young Doctor had not been exposed to the bloody wounds of war.

From Lt. Boettcher's statement we know that he had returned to the base by the 24th and a couple of weeks later, when he was about to leave on a mission, an air officer came up to him on the flight line and told him he had something for him, his Purple Heart.

My original plan for this book was to end with the Group's reunion dinner dance in mid-October, 1997, and our special group's **'The Lady Jeannette Remembrance 97.'**

However, completing the research on

'Where's It At?' ran into mid-November and another research project surfaced the night Carol and I prepared to leave for the Group's reunion.

First, however, let me give you the information on the two men who were killed in the crash of the B-26, Lt. Robbins and Sgt. Glass.

1st Lt. Hugh Westly Robbins, Copilot, Sri: O-74993, was the only child of Calvin Lee Robbins and Ellen (Woods) Robbins, of Deale, Maryland. His remains were returned to the United States in late 1948. He is buried in the Cedar-Bluff section of the St. Ann's Episcopal Cemetery, Lot #293, Grave #3, Annapolis, Maryland.

Sgt. William G. Glass, was the oldest crew member and he was called 'pops' by the crew. He was interred at the Epinal, France, American World War Two Military Cemetery, Plot B, Row 42, Grave 36, after the war. To date, I have not been able to locate any next of kin. He listed Altoona, Pennsylvania, as his home of record in 1945.

Sgt. Mike Flores, listed Los Angeles as his home of record. There are many Mike Flores in Southern California and I have not located him. It will take much too long, for this book, to pass a request through the Veterans's Administration to see if he is still alive and if so, locate him.

It does not end here, however. For at the end of September, 1998, during the 80th Anniversary of the end of World War One Memorial Services in France, we plan to unveil a memorial at the same memorial crossroads as the one for *'The Lady Jeannette.'* These seven men and their B-26 bomber will be remembered for many years to come, as people pass, pause and read their memorial.

Two more American's who died near Tincourt-Boucly, Buirre and Cartigny for the Liberty of France, and the men who served with them.

EVADERS

The evening before we were going to leave for Savannah, I was preparing my display about *'The Lady Jeannette'* and *'Where's It At?'*. I was planning to add a list of all the men of the Group who were killed in Europe and who are still buried there. My list would have shown pictures of the cemetery where they are buried and their name.

To accomplish this, I had requested a list of the men from the Washington Office of the American Battle Monuments Commission The Group's yearly roster contains a list of all the men and I had seen a display prepared by Ed Hinrichs for a reunion a few years earlier. Ed's excellent wall of Remembrance told where they were buried and in his two books about the Group and its missing planes, he listed the dead's home of record.

When I had reviewed the list in the past, I recognized none of the men except those from *'The Lady Jeannette.'* However, when I reviewed the list that I received from the American Battle Monuments Commission, a name and home state of record jumped out at me.

1st Lt. Richard F. Noble. 0-453171, 728th Bomb Squadron, 452nd Bomb Group; Buried Ardennes American Military Cemetery: Plot D, Row 4, Grave 19; Died: 4 August 1944, Ohio.

Suddenly, I could see a tall man dressed in an army uniform, with pinkish pants and a darker top. Under his left arm was a large round hat and just above its bill was a large shiny eagle.

From his date of death, if this was who I suddenly thought it was, that memory goes back to when I was about 4 ½ years old. If it was, I saw the man on the list the day he left for Europe. I also remembered that I had heard he had died and that I thought his name was Rex Noble. Rex must have been a nickname.

My sister Rea was friends with the girl, Kay Noble, who lived in the house where I had seen the man. Her mother was the village librarian, so I called Rea. The first thing she told me, after I told her of my suspicions, was that Rex Noble was alive, it was his cousin, Dick Noble who had been killed.

Rea also said that the Nobles had

heard that Dick was shot down and later, that he had been with the French Partisans and that he had been reported missing and presumed dead. Much later, they heard that his grave had been found.

Rea went on to say that Rex Noble had retired from the army and lived in Zanesville, Ohio, where she also lives. And, she and Kay Noble Ballentine still talk once in a while. Kay had married Buck Ballentine, and you know what, I remembered that too.

Rea had a book that listed all the men who had served in World War Two from Muskingum Country Ohio, so she got it out and sure enough.

NOBLE, Richard Francis, 1st Lt enl Army' AF Feb 3, 41; BPS Central Europe; TR EAME; Purple Heart, shot down over Brux, Slovakia, May 12, 44 while piloting B-17 Flying Fortress; presumed dead Nov. 7, 45.
(Bold type represents the dead)

Of course, I knew his actual date of death was the 4th of August, 1944, leaving a very interesting gap in time. Especially since the Zanesville book had been published in 1947. By that time, why didn't the family know about his real date of death and have it corrected in the book?

There was no doubt now, and soon I was talking to his cousin Rex Noble. Rex, Rea had told me, had been awarded the Silver Star during his service in Europe.

NOBLE', Gerald Rex, T Sgt Army Inf Mar 20, 43 Jan 27,46; B.S. Rhineland, Ardennes, Central Europe; TR Am, EAME w/3 BrS, Silver Star, Croix de Guerre avec Etoile de Bronze

---

Rex and I discussed Richard and he told me that the family really did not know what had happened. He told me that Richard had an older brother, Vernon, and that Richard had been married and had a son who lived in Texas now. Well, that helped explain the original listed home address in Alabama, where his wife was probably living while he was in the service.

In 1947, Richard's wife would have had to have made the decision to have his permanent grave in an American cemetery in Europe.

On the 14th of October, I called Mickey Russell and told him about the man I had seen leave for the service and gave him the information I had. A few minutes later, Carol and I left for the Group Reunion.

While at the reunion, I learned more about the mission they were on to Brux, Czechoslovakia. That was the mission on which the group lost the most bombers (14) and crews (13). It was the first major attack on the German oil industry and the Army Air Force lost a lot of planes that day.

Mickey had promised to send me anything he found and soon after I got back, I had the MACR 4819, or Missing Aircraft Report 4819. This 27-page report, along with what I had found in Ed Hinrichs's books and the Group history gave me a solid foundation on what happened to Lt. Noble.

The bomber had been hit by flak directly over Brux damaging two engines, however, they had returned as far as Belgium before the entire crew of their bomber, *'Lucky Lady'* had to bail out. Several were captured that day, but most managed to evade capture for some time before being captured. Others managed to evade until the allied lines came to them. Lt. Noble and his Co-pilot, 2nd Lt. Daniel Viafore, managed to get to Northern France where they spent the next three months with a French resistance group. They and other evaders were kept in a hidden camp.

Viafore has since told me, that Lt. Noble left the Resistance Group that was sheltering them one morning with some French Canadians. They figured that the excellent use of the French language by the French Canadians would enable them to bluff their way to the allied lines in western France.

We don't know what happened to Richard after he left the camp, we just know he died on the 4th of August, 1944, and that his remains were later found by Graves

Lucky Lady, B-17G, Sn: 42-39941

Registration.

During the 452nd Bomb Group's business meeting at the reunion, they asked all the Evaders to stand up. As I am finding, there were many. There were also a lot of the Group who were not able to evade and became P.O.W.

I am depending on 1st Lt. Noble's Individual Deceased Personnel File to tell us where his remains were found and how he died. If his file does not provide further information, other than where his first grave was found, the French **COMMEMO-RANGERS** friends who helped me solve the

secret of the grave at Cartigny will be called into action again.

The memorial crossroads at Tincourt-Boucly will be an excellent place to memorialize Lt. Noble and his crew in 1998. With luck, we will be able to locate the French Resistance group he was with and this memorial will be a very special one, listing both. Only time will tell. *'The Lady Jeannette'* took over a year and a half before I could determine what happened to all four men killed in the crash and almost three years more before I located the last crewman.

'Where's It At?' progressed to all but one man being located in four months. The basic information I have on the *'Lucky Lady' took* less than a month. When this book is finished, I will be free to concentrate on completing my research on the **Related Crash And Evaders**, obtaining final permission for their memorials in France and seeking the donations necessary to complete and install the memorials to those two bombers and their crews.

While talking to the 452nd Bomb Group Association's President, William Roche, he told me about his crash in France, aboard the *'Lucky Lady III.'* As he said, "That must show something about how lucky that name really was." He also told me, that Boeing told him that his *bomber 'Lucky lady III'* had been salvaged by a Frenchman and it is still flying, under a different name, in France.

The **COMMEMO-RANGERS** sold pieces of *'The Lady Jeannette'* encased in a shadow box, with a picture of the only B-17 still flying in France, to raise funds for the memorial at Tincourt-Boucly. It must be Bill Roche's *'Lucky Lady III.'*

I know the target is out there, but the question is?
'Where's It At?'   Photo: Britanik

This is the place alright, see the craters near the bridge from our last trip, let's get it done this time.
Photo: DuBois

Lt. Robbins finds cutting wood for the stove warms twice.
Photo: Ethel Nutwell

Received January 3, 1998

From: Mickey Russell, Department Of The Air Force, Air Force Historical Research Agency
Maxwell Air Force Base, Alabama

It is hard to complete the small work in finishing this book, when each day's mail may bring more information such as this.

Two other related crashes, reference Chapter Eight, page 135, T/Sgt. Robert A. Dunlap's $5 Short Snorter Bill and the serial number of the bomber they flew overseas aboard, Sn: 43-38184.

For the first time, I have a Missing Crew Report with all the correct information recorded, along with the Individual Aircraft Record Card.

The bomber was built by Boeing at its Seattle plant. It was accepted on July 8, 1944 and taken via Great Falls, Montana, to Cheyenne, Wyoming, for a Cheyenne tail gun modification. On July 15th it was delivered to Kearney, Nebraska, and became available for overseas shipment. On July 19th it was flown to Rapid City, South Dakota, where the Gott crew boarded it on the 20th and flew it to Grenier Field, New Hampshire. The bomber and crew departed for England on the 21st, via Newfoundland and Iceland. It was moved onto 8th Air Force inventory records on July 31st, 1944.

On September 1, 1944, the bomber was lead bomber for the 849th Bomb. Sq., 490th Bomb. Group on a mission to Gustavsburg.

As the group crossed the French coast going to the target, at about 11:59 English War Time, the Deputy Lead ship, A/C#941 was seen part way in front of the Lead Ship, A/C.#184. Suddenly, the D.L. ship, A/C#941 rose rapidly and its tail cut off the right wing of the Lead A/C.

Both aircraft began to breakup and fall. Crashing north of Caen, France, east of the village of Deauville. All 10 men aboard the #941 ship were killed and 7 above the #184 ship. B-17G, Sn: 43-38184   K.I.A. = Killed In Action   W.I.A. = Wounded In Action
R.T.D. = Returned to Duty

Lead Commander:	Maj.	Lamond D. Haas	O-427735	K.I.A.
Pilot:	1st Lt.	John M. Kirklin	O-666307	W.I.A., R.T.D
Co-Pilot:	2nd Lt.	Robert E. Russell	O-705995	K.I.A.
Navigator:	2nd Lt.	George J. Kurtz III	O-805173	K.I.A.
Bombardier:	2nd Lt.	Charles D. Crofts	O-542109	K.I.A.
Rad-Opr-Gun:	T/Sgt.	Joe. W. Ripple	18048310	K.I.A.
Engin-Gunr:	T/Sgt.	Oren W. Simpson	85118181	W.I.A., R.T.D.
Ball-Tur-Gun:	S/Sgt.	Lloyd M. Hudson	37537656	K.I.A.
Waist Gunr:	S/Sgt.	Richard V. Weber	12216620	K.I.A.
Tail Gnr:	S/Sgt.	William J. Shiffer	33498522	W.I.A., R.T.D.

B-17, Sn: 43-37941

Deputy Commander:	Maj.	Francis H. Dresser	O-416285	K.I.A.
Pilot:	1st Lt.	Charles S. Frey	O-761918	K.I.A.
Co-Pilot:	2nd Lt.	George W. Hixson	O-768099	K.I.A.
Navigator:	2nd Lt.	Donald J. Hoeffler	O-766267	K.I.A.
Bombardier:	F/O	Lowell Shuman	T-124531	K.I.A.
Rad-Opr-Gun:	S/Sgt.	Thomas H. Gossett	34644630	K.I.A.
Engin-Gunr:	S/Sgt.	Floyd G. Hall	33564703	K.I.A.
Ball-Tur-Gun:	Sgt.	Calvin C. Pulver	38538654	K.I.A.
Waist Gunr:	Sgt.	Donald L. Russell	35226101	K.I.A.
Tail Gnr:	Sgt.	Edward C. Schanhaar	37574644	K.I.A.

Someday, I must visit Deauville and find some villagers who observed the crashes.

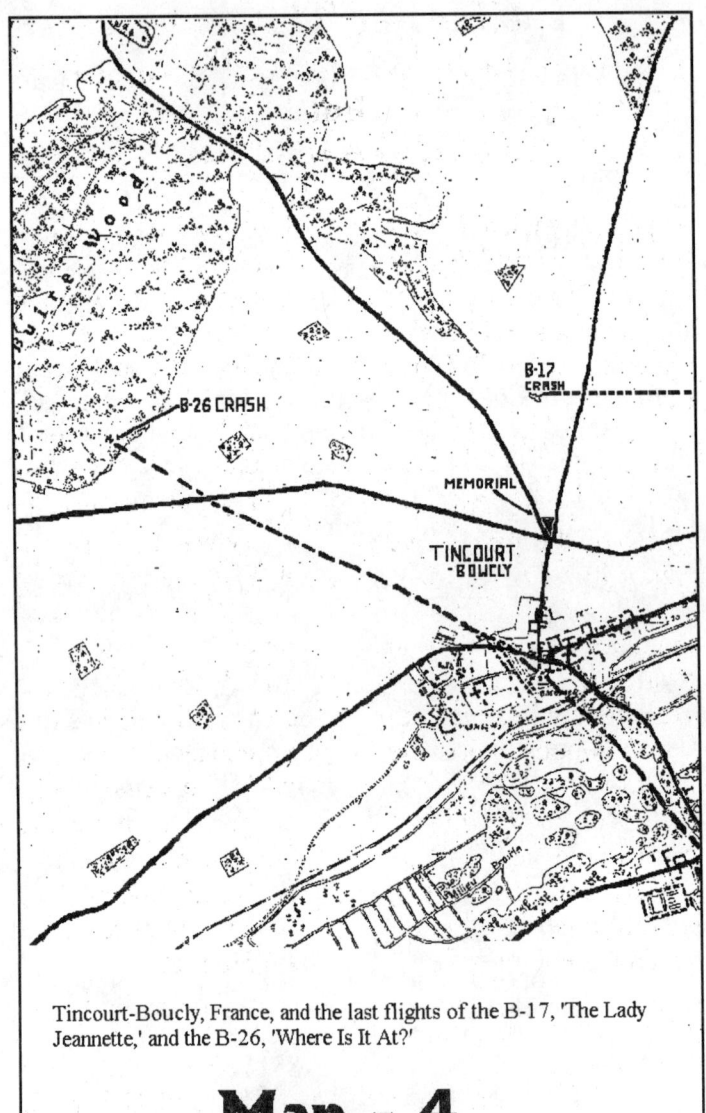

Tincourt-Boucly, France, and the last flights of the B-17, 'The Lady Jeannette,' and the B-26, 'Where Is It At?'

Map - 4

Chapter Thirteen
So You Always Wanted To Go To France
But
You Needed A Good Reason!

But, you can't speak French and your mate isn't interested in military stuff, or you would really love to go to France, but your roomy hates visiting art museums. Of course, you could be single and just haven't had a good reason to visit France.

Wait a second, isn't this a history book? What is this all about? Well, to me history is much more than a dry willowy **Remembrance-Souvenir** of the past. I've been accused of treating it like a dog loves a bone. France is full of such bones, the Somme region has a bone for everyone. You can drive down roads that Roman soldiers laid and stand beside woods where Attila the Hun encamped. Those same woods were the center of terrible battles during World War One and overhead swirled the combat planes of two wars. And somewhere between the dawn of time and the day you stand there, along came tribes, religions, wars too numerous to mention and the growth of a nation.

The purpose of this chapter is to help you decide that a trip to France can be fun, or educational, as you may wish. Either as a couple, or by yourself - woman or man. Carol and I started out as one pulling the other **'over there'** and now both wish we could win a lottery so we could spend more time visiting France.

While planning your trip, you might write the Comite Departemental De Tourisme De La Somme, 21, rue Ernest Cauvin - 8000 Amiens FRANCE and ask for information, in English, on visiting the Somme. Ask for information on visiting the World War One lines and the many other tourist interests in the department. Between the two, any traveling companions will find something they will enjoy. You can take turns visiting what is interesting to everyone!

Surprising, perhaps to most of you, we would spend few weekends in the cities and lots more time in the countryside. We love Paris, for Paris can be lovely in spring or fall, and even in-between. But, our favorite people are out in the countryside, working and toiling just like you and me. Of course, if New York is your bag, then Paris can be your glove. Paris is a place of open and hidden beauty, but personally we have found most of the people in Paris to be just like people in big cities everywhere. Very, very busy and very, very little time for a tourist trying to feel at home.

Well, by now I trust, you have read this book about my experiences searching for the identity of the grave at Cartigny, France and it's time for that promised good reason. How many places are there in the world, where you can stand and envision the exact event, at the exact location of a World War Two air war action that led to the awarding of two of the highest military medals the United States can award, the **Congressional Medal Of Honor**?

I know of two such events in the 8th Army Air Force[65], one was in England, aboard a bomber called *'Ten Horsepower'* of the 351st Bomb Group. The Flight Engineer, Sgt. Archie Mathies and the Navigator, Lt. Walter Truemper were each awarded the **Congressional Medal Of Honor**, posthumously, for attempting to land the B-17 to save the wounded pilot's life. On 20 February, 1944, while on a mission to Leipzig a cannon shell exploded in the cockpit killing the copilot and wounding the pilot. Mathies and Truemper managed to fly the bomber back to their base at Polebrook, England. They lost control on their third attempt to land at the field and crashed. The two men were killed in the crash, the wounded pilot lived through the crash, but later died.

The second dual award of the **Congressional Medal Of Honor** played out in the skies over Germany and France, ending just north of the small village of Tincourt-

Boucly, France. And, as you have read, it continues to play out, even as I complete this book.

We, Carol and I, and our many French friends of the Somme region of France, and the families and survivors of the crew wish to invite you to visit the crash site of **The Lady Jeannette,** the bomber upon which occurred the events for which the medals were awarded, and the Isolated Fifth War Grave of four of its crew.

1st Lt. Donald J. Gott, Pilot
 Congressional Medal Of Honor
2nd Lt. William E. Metzger, Jr., Copilot
 Congressional Medal Of Honor
T/Sgt. Robert A. Dunlap, Radio Operator
S/Sgt. Herman B. Krimminger, Tail Gunner

For our visits to France, we usually leave on a Thursday, meaning we arrive in France early Friday morning and we leave two weeks, and a few days, later on Monday. Coming back is nice, as you are traveling with the sun and you leave France early Monday morning and arrive in Seattle, about seven Monday evening.

We have visited the Somme region without a car, but we have found driving in France to be quite easy and since we spend so little time in the large cities we usually make our car arrangements when we purchase our plane tickets.

It's actually very easy to get to France, all you have to do in enter a magic tube in the United States and before you know it, you are walking out of it into a new country, France. Of course, we ride the cheap seats as much as we can and we have found the last weeks of May and the first weeks of June to be our favorite time. The mustard and canola crops are in bloom and great fields of yellow spread across the land. Along the roadsides and wherever the dirt has been recently disturbed are the bright red blooms of the poppy. Occasionally one will see a whole field of poppies, brilliant in the sun.

To begin this visit to France and the Somme, let's pretend we have just flown into the Charles De Gaulle Airport, arriving at the International Terminal, for just over a week's stay. We arrived about 8:00 a.m. on Friday and we are leaving on the noon flight on the second Monday.

Our plan is to visit the sites of '**The Lady Jeannette,**' and enjoy the World War One areas around the Somme and then to go spend three evenings and two days in Paris before leaving for home. We are going to drive ourselves around for six days, arriving back at the terminal and having the car checked in before the time we checked it out upon arrival, or if you made arrangements you can often drop the car off in Paris at no extra charge. Remember, they will charge for another full day if you are just a few minutes late. You really don't need a car in Paris and unless you are staying for two weeks it's best to check the car in and take a taxi or airport bus to Paris and do the same the day you leave. If you are planning on staying longer, remember, you can park a car on a Paris street late Friday afternoon and not have to move it until Monday morning, just check with your hotel staff to insure you are OK.

After clearing customs and finding our way to the car rental agency and car, we are heading out of the terminal feeling our way through the always crowded traffic. The Charles De Gaulle International Terminal is built in a circle so you drive in circles trying to get out of it. If you miss the exit on your first circle, just go around again and work your way over to the outside of the circle. You will emerge from the overtop parking ramp on the inside of the circle and the exit soon follows, so try to get over as soon as you can. You may have to force it, just ease over. The power of the bluff is another scene of driving in France. Of course, they mean it and give room somewhat grudgingly.

When leaving the terminal, you will find yourself on a double highway just like home and you will quickly come to an interchange with signs that state Paris is to your left. Well, just turn right and head north, you have about 70 miles to go and a new experience if you haven't driven in France before.

The freeway turns into a pay way very

soon and you will have to stop to grab a ticket at a toll booth. When you get off you will turn in the ticket and you will need French Francs. It will cost about 40 Francs or roughly $7.00 to $8.00 depending on the exchange. Knowing the country, we often take the old main north road where there is no fee, however that is when we are not in a hurry and feel like we have time to poke along on the narrow roads.

Another good thing to remember about French roads, is that only the super roads are wide. Most country driving will be done on two lane highways with people darting in and out. It can be scary for a while, until you get used to it. However, by the time you pull off the pay way near Péronne you will begin to feel at ease. Out in the deep country you worry more about tractors on the highway going slow and being hard to get around. The farm tractor is allowed on the roads and they do not give up the right-of-way or necessarily allow you to pass easily.

At the DeGaulle Airport interchange when you turn north, you are turning onto the E15-E19 super road, soon a pay way.

As you pull onto the main road you will quickly notice they are traveling very fast and so are the many semi-trucks. Get used to tailgaters and light flashers for that is life on French roads. Slow traffic to the right and when passing be prepared for a sudden appearance of a dot quickly growing until it is right on your tail with lights flashing. As you get out of the way, you will think, that fool is going 100 miles per hour. Well, he probably is, though 70 to 80 miles per hour is more normal. The speedometer will be in kilometers per hour and the easy way to figure out your speed is to divide the meter reading by 8 and multiply by 5. It's easy, 80 km is 50 miles per hour and 120 km is 75 m.p.h. The same works when figuring out map distances.

Along the road you will find service centers and we recommend that you stop at the first or second one and take a break. There are usually snacks and food available and after a long flight and the first few miles in this traffic, you deserve a break. It gives you a chance to think about the traffic and become more at ease.

When you pass down over a hill and over the river, Aisne, (pronounced somewhat like en) the highway begins to travel mostly along the trench lines of World War One. Off on the left side you will see the new high speed Chunnel train tracks. They still have lots of problems with undiscovered dugouts from World War One collapsing under the new track's embankments. They have had to restrict the speed of the trains due to the track problems. When a dugout is found, they pump it full of concrete and you may see such a project during your trip along the tracks. The trains appear and disappear at surprising speeds and you may see one or two.

After the Aisne river valley, you will start across the Santerre country, meaning good earth. The Santerre region of the Somme is the best farm ground in France.

When you pass exit (12) at Roye, for Amiens and Ham, begin to think of getting off at the next exit (13), or one soon thereafter. Exits here are not marked at its mile or kilometer location. They are numbered from the start of the road. It can be some distance between exits.

As you are approaching exit (13), you are tired and you have been in the air and on the road long enough to want to head for the place you plan to stay first and second, start looking around. Depending upon the type of hotel and the size of the town you want to stay in, there are several options.

Our favorite place to stay is at a Bed and Breakfast located at the north end of the 1916 Battle Zone. However, there are many different B&B's and lots of other places to stay. If you are uncomfortable at one, move around until you find the place you feel fits.

On our first few visits, Carol and I stayed in Péronne because one can walk around the square and town streets, shop, and visit the Historical de la Grande Guerre; Château de Péronne; B.P. 63; 80201, Péronne, FRANCE, just in case you want to write and request information in English. It is the Museum of the Great War located in the old Château at Péronne.

In the recent years, more and more

modern motel/hotel places are opening around France, if you wish more modern facilities.

The St. Claude Hotel, in downtown Péronne, is a typical older French hotel. The old Ramparts Hotel has class and a higher cost, we have only stayed there once and found it quite nice.

In 1995, on a visit to France by herself, Carol stayed for ten days at the Le Provençal Hotel. It is located on the main street at the east end of Péronne. When you come into the square from the west go through the square on past the Mairie and past the next light. Follow the road past the old Britain entrance through the preserved original ramparts. The hotel is located, on the left, a couple of blocks beyond the school you will pass.

It is over the restaurant of the same name. The owner's main business is the multi-star restaurant and the only time you can rent rooms is when the restaurant is open. During the mid-day and in the evening from 7:00 to 10:00 p.m. Once you have made your arrangements they give you a key and you come and go on your own. They are only open during the week, meaning you can stay the weekend, but you have to have checked in by Saturday evening. Carol enjoyed her stay there and insisted I put this hotel in. You will enjoy window boxes at your room window and the shower in the room, however you share a toilet located in the hallway.

There is a nice hotel in Bapaume, but the town does not offer much to see during an evening walk around town. A sister hotel is located at Rancourt, close to the large French cemetery, midway between Péronne and Bapaume, on N17. It is in the countryside and when we stay there, we use it as place to stop and sleep and spend little time in the hotel.

Lots of British people make Albert their base while visiting the English Lines of 1916. Amiens, Cambrai and St. Quentin are all larger cities and offer large city lodging. Amiens Cathedral is one of the trade offs for those who do not care for the military sights.

The Battle of the Somme, the English part, covers an area less than 20 miles wide and it is full of places of interest and monuments to the units and men who fought there. To plan your trip, you should purchase a Michelin Map, Number 53, of France. Number 52 is the same map, however 52 also lists all the British Military Cemeteries. You can always get one at Delville Woods when you visit. They cover the Arras, Charleville-Mézières, St. Quentin areas. Plus, you should read a couple of books, such as the **First Day On The Somme**[66], **The Somme Battlefields**[67] and **Somme**.[68]

Though most British and lots of the French in the Somme area will swear no Americans were present around the Somme, we were there in 1917 and 1918. Not so many at first, but growing in number quickly. Carol and I set a record at our favorite B&B, during our late spring visit in 1997, for length of stay. We day tripped all the way to the Argonne Forest region, near Verdun, and visited Vincent Bentz for lunch followed by a walking tour Cornay and a view of where Sgt. York earned his **Congressional Medal Of Honor**.

During some past visits, we have headquartered at the B&B and left for two or three day side trips. That way, we only had to carry part of our stuff with us all the time. Our load increases very quickly as we visit old friends and get loaded up with the debris, to them and relics to us, of the Great War.

Avril Williams who runs the Tea Room, Bed and Breakfast, at Auchonvillers, north of Pozières, is a very British lady who decided her life was a B&B in the Somme. She has only been open for a few years and each year the place has been improved. The people you meet over her dining table at the evening meal will add so much to your visit.

There you will meet people from Australia and England and other people, such as that damn Sam from the States. Well, it is said in fun, as I do enjoy the interplay and we have been asked to tone it down so the others could sleep as a battle, a general or a Mills Bomb is discussed well into the night.

The best part of being at Avril's place, is that you feel like you are visiting their home as a treasured house guest, not just a person to help pay for the scheme of things.

On nice nights, it takes just a little hint

to get Avril out for a walk along the battle line of 1916. If it is a real nice night and everyone is real interested, you might not get back until after midnight. But, you will never forget Avril's walk and her running commentary on such places as Jacob's Ladder, from where the photographer filmed the famous mushrooming explosion at Hawthorne Redoubt at 7:20 a.m. on the 1st of July, 1916, the first day of the Battle of the Somme.

Don't forget to ask to see her famous basement. The house above was destroyed during the war and rebuilt later, the basement survived and it was used as a dressing station when the front line was in the vicinity and there are several interesting carvings on the wall.

Avril has a personal wealth of W.W.I information which she is happy to share. Nor does she set hours that you have to be gone during the day, as most B&B's there do. If you want to take a day off and just laze, she has a small private bar for her guests and there are always war books to read, relics to see and almost always interesting people to talk to.

Avril's B&B is a working home. Her rooms are well cleaned and her prices are fair.

She sets an excellent dinner table at very fair rates and the large breakfast is included in the room cost and does not come as a surprise when you get ready to leave.

Such establishments tend to come and go, but I have a feeling that when I return for the 100th Anniversary of the 1916 Somme battle, old Sam will be staying at Avril's. Though she might be a bit squeaky by that time, so shall I.

The area we are going to visit is about 30 miles in diameter. Depending on how interested you find yourself becoming, you may find yourself day tripping out 50 miles or more and wishing you had more time to stay.

Not far to the north of Avril's is the Canadian Vimy Ridge Memorial. The walk around and underground tour can take up most of a day if you do it right. A visit there and a stop on the way back at Arras will take a full day.

Figuring this is going to be your first visit to France, or this area of France, we will spend our first night in Péronne at one of the several hotels, as you have come in late May and you will be able to find a room at one of them. We will spend the rest of today and evening, finding our hotel, resting a bit and visiting the World War One museum and walking the streets and square of Péronne.

First thing in the morning, we will begin a tour that will include the sites of **'The Lady Jeannette,'** the Hindenburg Battle Line attack of 1918, the American World War One Cemetery at Bony, and begin to tour the British battle areas of 1916-1918. For the companion who wants to see something else, we will also visit St. Quentin. It will be a full day and, I think, one you will enjoy.

The next day, we will visit the 1916 Battle area and Avril's Tea Room and B&B. You might want to see if you can get a room there for your third and final night, so you can go for a walk. If you want to stay at a fancier hotel, or larger city, such as Amiens, just study your map and join in the circle of the visit and switch your visiting schedule to fit.

As you approach Exit (13) remember that Alan Seeger was killed nearby and a visit to his place of death will be our first stop after paying our toll.

It is always possible that you flew in to England or up north somewhere and are driving down from the north. In that case you might want to get off at the northern Péronne Exit (13I), in that case follow the signs and you will find yourself in the middle of Péronne. Just skip down to the where I write about entering the square. Of course, to make our recommended visit to the place of Alan Seeger's death, just follow the route below backward. It is a nice evening drive.

At the Exit (13), There is a fancy pay way type motel/hotel available at this exit, however, it is at the edge of the pay way and there isn't much to do except sleep. Just follow the signs, if you wish.

After paying the toll, and coming to the regular French-type road, remember this is the main road between Amiens and St. Quentin, watch out for fast approaching cars and trucks, before turning onto it.

Turn left toward St. Quentin and

Péronne, but take the first turn to the left, a very close distance away. Drive down the narrow road toward Belloy-en-Santerre, or Belloy of the good earth. A quarter mile or so before you reach the village, you will find yourself driving along one of the famous sunken roads of France, albeit a shallow one. Off to your left, you will see the hotel across a sloping field with a line of concrete power poles marching across it.

Pull off to the side and get out of the car and look across the field toward the hotel in the distance. On July 1st, 1916, The French Foreign Legion left their line located where the pay way is today. They advanced across the field toward the village. In the sunken road where you are standing, the German machine guns were hidden. The Legion was walking through the old style French wheat which was about chest high to the short French of the time.

Between 5:30 and 6:00 p.m. that afternoon, the Legion charged as they got close to the village. The German machine guns located in the sunken road where you are standing opened fire along the flank of the Legion. Alan Seeger was right out there, just about where the closest concrete pole is located when his life ended, along with several hundred more Legionnaires that day.

Continue on down the road to the village and turn left to find the town square. There you will find the village War Memorial with his name upon it, spelled the French way Alain. Just across the street is the gray colored Mairie, or village hall. By its door you will find a plaque honoring Alan Seeger.

You can go across country to Péronne, but until you are used to it, it is best to go back the way you came, turn left and follow the road to the cross roads at Villers-Carbonnel. You might want to take a few minutes and visit the French Military Cemetery just before you get to the village. It is just one of hundreds of miliary cemeteries you will see, and perhaps visit, in the next few days.

Turn left toward Péronne and before long, you will come to an almost new motel on your left. Depending upon your requirements, you might wish to try for a room here. It is just a short distance into Péronne. I prefer the St. Claude which is just off the square, an old hotel in downtown. You can come and go as you wish, though its best to ask if you will need a key if you will be real late. They also have a restaurant and bar. Carol likes the Ramparts best, which is built into the old city ramparts now mostly torn down. It is well decorated and a nice hotel. They do have a restaurant, but they lock the door and if you don't have a key you can't get back in. I tend to start long talks with people and so do not like such restrictions. Where ever you stay, check on their door locking times. Some never do, others give you a key and others will lock you out.

Drive through the town until you reach the town square. You can't miss it, the Mairie is at the far end as you enter the square. The square is full of parking spaces and you have to pay. There are boxes along the sides of the parking area where you put in some Franc coins and get a ticket to put on your dash.

The St. Claude is on a small side street leading off the square to the Historical of the Great War museum. The street is at the end opposite the Mairie. Make your arrangements at the desk and they will tell you where to park your car for the night.

Make yourself at home and get out of the room and into the town. Walk, shop, visit the Historial, and enjoy the sidewalk tables at the bars. You will find beer is the cheapest thing to drink.

The old moated town citadel has been developed into a Historial of the Great War. It is almost an art museum in its displays and is well worth a visit.

Carol and I, always stop at the super markets and purchase Pepsi Max (diet Pepsi), and some treats to keep the costs down. If you want to do the same, drive past the square and the Mairie and turn left at the first light and follow the road away from the center of town. Bear right until you come to a traffic circle. The large building just beyond on the northeast corner is a large market.

On the southwest corner of the main street where you turned left at the light, you will see a travel trailer kind of thing with a folding front. This is a Frite Wagon, when it is open you can buy the best French fries, ham sandwiches and hamburgers and such. You will spot these all over the country, some never move like this one, others are open along roadsides and you will see a sign saying Frites - 300 meters for instance. They offer quick, decent, well priced meals.

Follow the circle on around 3/4 of the way and go to the front of the super market. Across from the market you will see one of the best places to buy gas. Enter the market, past the fresh fish bar odor, and enjoy your first shopping experience in France. Of course, there is lots of wine, mostly Coke products and some Pepsi, along with various hard products if that is your wish. We often stop at a market first thing in the morning and purchase bread, ham and butter. The first time, we also buy paper towels, mustard and such. That way, we eat one very economical meal a day alongside the road. If we are traveling very lightly, we may not purchase anything other than hot Frites for two or three days.

When you leave this small mall area, you might want to go back a different way, just to experience the town and to become familiar with finding your way around. If you find yourself in an area of fields, you have gone too far, just turn around and feel your way back to the hotel.

Depending on how you slept on the airplane, you might want to take it easy, nap, have dinner and get to bed early, but if you feel up to it, with the late sunny evenings here, this is a good chance to drive around the town and see some of the countryside. In the morning we start our tour.

If you are traveling alone, or your partner doesn't read maps, I have found sitting down and making a list of where I want to go works real well. I have driven hundreds of kilometers across France and not missed a route by more than a few minutes while I am looking for where my road went to.

The French roads use an alpha-numerical identification that can change rapidly. Remember, these roads date back to periods when some people never got more than a ½ day's walk from home. You will pass small stone road markers and now some are inset into the ground along the road.

I start with where I am and write down the road number I am starting out on, as the numbers change and the map shows an obvious interchange I go to the next number. I make certain I write down the larger towns along the route so I can look for that sign too. However, lots of times in France you will see the sign after you have passed the turn. You will also see lots of roads entering at odd angles. That's the way the cows used to walk or the villagers cut cross country to the next village.

You are going to be driving on lots of narrow roads and be prepared to drive onto the shoulder to allow the car that's coming at you to get by, especially one that doesn't want to give any space on their side. Just don't drive onto the shoulder without looking, it might be a ditch. Just pull quickly over as far as you feel safe and they will move over, even though sometimes you think they will not.

When it gets down to the basics, I think I worry more about driving here in the Seattle area than I do there. For there, I expect it. Here, they are supposed to know better.

Here is the route we will follow tomorrow, Péronne, D917, edge of town, D6, Roisel, Tincourt-Boucly crossroads, D184, (memorial). Go to center T-B, D88, Cartigny, turn right Grande Ave (Main street), past church, next left, cemetery up one block on left. (Grave). (*The No. 53 map shows cemeteries as a small box with a cross in it. If it is a military cemetery it will have Brit., Fr., U.S.A., or All. (German) next to it.*) Back on D88 to T/B turn right D6 to Roisel, D6 to Templeux-le-Guerad, D406 to Hargicourt, D331 to Bellicourt. Left on N44 to American Monument, on to D442 to Bony American Cemetery (well signed). After visit, back to N44 head back south to St. Quentin, visit downtown, shop, cathedral (still showing war damage), leave on N29-E44 Amiens road (old Roman road) follow D44 to Péronne after visiting airport on south of road at intersection. Péronne A-72 air base.

In the morning, we will first follow our route to the Tincourt-Boucly cross roads. You can see it a long way off, and there is the memorial you came all this way to see.

As you stand at the crash site memorial at the cross roads of Tincourt-Boucly and look around you, you will see the rolling hills of the eastern part of the Somme Department (80). Just 1,000 feet north of where you stand, the last flight of '*The Lady Jeannette*' came to an end in a large crater that is now a working field.

Take the time to remember what you have read and use your memory to recreate the events that lead to the death of the four men who were heroes there in the sky above you, so long ago. Think about them, read their names out loud, for through you they live.

If the field is not in crop you can drive up the right side road and see the crash site. It will be out in the field on your left, and as you drive up the road, you will see the old fence line bank that starts behind the memorial and goes out into the field. The crash site is about 300 feet from the roadside and it is directly out in the field, about 100 feet, from where that old fence line bank ends. You can make out a low area of ground in the field, if the conditions are right.

In the field to your right as you drive up the road, T/Sgt. Gustafson came to earth and was picked up by the ambulance which took him and Lt. Harland to the hospital. You are also on the same road as the ambulance, containing the men's remains, when it left the crash site to return to base.

If you do not go up to see the crash site, the road, just to your right as you face the memorial, is where the ambulance came to the intersection on its way back to base and, in a sense, it went on to a cross roads in the lives of the living men in it. For they were soon to hide, in an unmarked grave, most of the remains of the War Dead they had just recovered from place of death of '*The Lady Jeannette*' and four of her crew. A burden, much worse than my 'burden of wonderment' to carry for the rest of their lives.

'*Where's It At?*,' the B-26 crashed in the woods on the ridge to your left, on 22 January, 1945. The memorial to that crash will be installed on the left of '*The Lady Jeannette*' memorial facing the woods, the Bois de Buirre.

Those same woods, the Bois De Buirre, held the American Headquarters of the 27th and 30th Divisions from the 22nd of September to the 12th of October, 1918. We are planning another memorial for those divisions at the cross roads memorial garden, to be installed during the 80th Anniversary of the end of World War One.

Further to the left on the low ridge in the distance you will see a brick enclosure with trees around and in it. That is the Tincourt New British World War One Military Cemetery. It held the remains of 136 Americans who died in the hospitals located in the area, until they were moved to the Somme American Cemetery in the mid-1920s. It now contains 2,189 graves. It is worth a visit.

As you drive into the village and come to the village square, you will see the Mairie at the opposite end of the square. You might see if it is open and if someone is there tell them you are Americans and want to see the men's pictures. Up the stairs in the meeting hall, you will find pictures of the six men who were killed in the two crashes. So you don't speak French, point at your self and say "American," point at your camera and say "photographs" and point up the stairs. You will get there.

D88 turns off at an angle to your left as you reach the intersection at the square. You will go past the railroad yard, the tracks have been taken out now and the station is the village Fête hall used for holiday and social functions. Stop and look at the concrete sentry box and think of American bombers dropping bombs on a German train where you are standing. It happened.

Continue on to Cartigny and when you reach the stop sign turn right and drive along the main street. Stop at the center of the village and visit the Cartigny War Memorial. You will find one in every village, town and city and they tend to make you think.

Go on past the church, on your left, and take the next left. A short way up the side street you will find the village cemetery. Park and enter through the gate. Just past the storage area bushes on your left, you will find the Isolated **Congressional Medals Of Honor** Fifth War Grave of World War Two. Yes, it does exist. The families of the men wish to thank you for visiting this grave, unknown for so long.

Take the time to walk among the many other graves in this village cemetery. You will learn how these villages that have been here so long, have a cemetery that does not change in size. As you entered the cemetery you probably noticed that immediately to your right there were some new graves in what looked like an open area. That area contained very old graves. Graves that no longer have living relatives to maintain them or pay rental fees.

In most French cemeteries, one leases a grave plot for, I believe, 99 years. If after that time, no one renews your lease your grave can be removed. Any bones found are placed in the village ossuary and the plot is leased again. You can find examples of all the steps in this cemetery. New graves, old graves, graves disappearing, graves noted to be reclaimed if no one has just cause and graves available for reburial.

Don't forget to find the grave of Emile Berger to think of the care he gave the grave that used to be unknown. It is up the row across from the grave of the men, the one you have come so far to visit. After finding Emile's tomb, follow that row up the end and turn left. Down a few rows, on the corner, you will find the tomb of the village priest who insured the men were given a true grave, CURÉ Étienne Serpette.

Straight down the walk past the grave you will find a small plot with three French World War One graves on your right. Upon these crosses, as you will find upon the men's markers and at the crash site memorial you will see the roundel of the **Le Souvenir Français**. A good place to remember these men of World War One and the organization of volunteers that have and will continue to maintain the sites marked by those roundels.

Once you have completed your visit, drive back to the crossroads at Tincourt-Boucly and continue on down D6 toward Roisel. You might wish to stop there at one of the small café bars for refreshments.

Follow D6 out of Roisel, you will turn left off the main street, and follow the D6 to Templeux-le-Guérard and turn left onto D406 to Hargicourt and take D331 onto Bellicourt. Along this stretch you are crossing from the British/American line in 1918 to the German Hindenburg Line.

Turn left onto N44, going north toward Cambrai. On your left, not far down the road, you will see a large American Monument. It will be well signed. After a visit here, get back on the road and go a bit further north to the turn on to the road to Bony and the American Bony Cemetery.

Follow the signs and you will soon see the cemetery. Be sure you stop by the headquarters building and sign in. The American Supervisor will probably greet you, if not, ask the person there if he is in. Take some time to talk to the Supervisor. They are always full of information you might find helpful. Take your time and do not hurry your visit here. It is a little bit of America. If you had a relative killed in the Wars, ask their help and they can tell you where they are buried, if their remains were left 'over there.' You might find a relative's grave. Carol greatly appreciates the restrooms in the American Cemeteries, about the only equal is at the Delville Wood South African Memorial.

When you leave, turn back the way you came and head toward St. Quentin. Along the way, you will pass the south end of the St. Quentin Canal Tunnel. The Americans fought here, as well as the Australians on to the south. If you are like us, we have been stopping at all the memorials you have seen and along here you will find some more American ones.

Find your way into downtown St. Quentin and enjoy a walk-about. There are nice restaurants, bars, shops and much more to see.

When you are ready to leave, find the

N29-E22 road to Amiens and head west. About ten miles down the road you will come to the Péronne airport at the D44 crossroads. Visit the airport and image a great northeast-southeast runway, now removed, crossing the existing east-west runway. That is the one the two bombers were trying to land on. Ask around and you will find a memorial to the 397th Bomb Group and the Americans that were stationed there during World War Two.

Head back to Péronne by crossing the main road getting on D44 heading north. Just a few kilometers down the road you will see a sign to Cartigny. You are almost back to where you started, keep on to Péronne. If you still feel like seeing some more, stay on D44, which will shift to N17 at the interchange and proceed past the Péronne interchange and go up the hill. That hill is Mont-St.-Quentin, a scene of hard fighting between the Australians and the Germans in 1918. On your left, as you top the hill, you will find the Australian War 2nd Division Memorial to visit.

By now, I expect you are tired and if you go back down N17 and turn right at the first road, you will soon find yourself at the traffic circle by the Super Marché. A good opportunity to pull in and fill your tank and refill your goody bag.

It is probably late Saturday afternoon by the time you get back to the hotel. Take a break and enjoy the small town atmosphere.

By now, you will know if this type of visit interests you as much as you thought it might. If it does, I recommend you call Avril Williams and see if she has a room for tomorrow, Sunday, night. From the U.S., her direct dial number is: 011 33.3.22.76.23.66. Don't forget, it is a six hour time difference from the east coast and nine here on the west coast. In France, it is, 03.22.76.23.66. Feel free to ask someone in the hotel to help you use the telephone. They use a phone card system, where you can purchase a prepaid card at many places. You stick it in the outdoor phones and it subtracts value as you use it. It stopped a large crime problem when remote pay phones were being broken into. Some places, you might still find a coin phone, but often you have to have a card.

As Avril's' business consists of lots of day and three day British trippers, she often has rooms for the first few days of the week, if you didn't make arrangements before you left the states.

Rest up and tomorrow, your last pre-planned day, we will visit the 1916 Battle Lines.

I don't know about you, but our early starts always seem to be about 9:00 am or so. The morning rush is off the roads and the driving does seem much easier.

Head back out to the intersection of N17 north and D44 south and go north on N17 toward Bapaume. If you haven't visited the Australian Memorial, now is the time to do so.

Continue north and you will pass over the Canal du Nord, it was under construction, and dry, when the Australians attacked up and over the hill in early September, 1918.

Before long, you will come to Bouchavesnes-Bergen and on your left is a memorial to the French Marshal Foch to visit. Often there is a Frite wagon there.

Continue up the hill and just beyond the top there is a large Memorial French military cemetery on your right. This was part of the French attack area in 1916. Remember, the French also participated during the Battle of the Somme. Remember Alan Seeger.

Just across the road is a small British cemetery and in the distance to the west you will see a German cemetery. One of the few places where you will find all three right together, British, French and German. After visiting the two closest cemeteries, backtrack a bit and take the road to the German cemetery. Take the time, at each cemetery you visit, to look for and sign the visitor's logs. Your compliments on the condition of the cemeteries are appreciated by the caretakers. We will also be able to see your name, the next time we stop by.

After visiting the German cemetery, get back on N17, continuing toward Bapaume. When you come to le Transloy look for the D19 sign for a road going to your left. There is also a sign pointing to a French memorial. Turn left on D19 and continue until you see a road leaving on your left to the village cemetery located on a slight hill. Pull off and up the road and park.

Inside the cemetery, on your left, you will see a group of monuments. These are to the men of a French Regiment that had many men killed nearby, in 1914. Their sacrifice helped turn the German flank to the east, which in the end, allowed the French to attack the German flank north of Paris during the First Battle of the Marne, saving Paris and France.

Where ever you drive in the Somme region you will see military cemeteries. This one is about 100 yards off the road and in a low travel area. However, I stop there quite often to remember.

From here on, you will be passing many British military cemeteries. It all depends on you if you want to stop. Carol and I, tend to stop at almost every one, even if we have stopped before. The gardening changes over time and it is a rare visit that we don't find another interesting grave. The men's families often submitted short inscriptions which are engraved on the tombstone, these statements can be quite touching.

Along your path yesterday, you might have seen a shell alongside the road, perhaps several, at a marker or propped against a tree. During today's drive, you will see such collections. Do feel free to pull way off the road and look at them and take a picture. However, do not handle them. Almost all will do you no harm, as long as you treat them with respect. But, with your luck you will find the one Stokes mortar shell, German 77 mm shell, or Mills Bomb that will explode. It's just not worth the risk to handle them. You will have an opportunity to purchase such items that have been made safe.

Look all you want, but don't play.

If the weight does not bother you, you can take the safe ones home. Just make certain that they are apart and nothing screwed together. When you pack your bag, make a map of what you pack and list everything you have. Tell the person at the airline receiving line what you have and that it has been demilitarized. Be prepared to open the bag for their inspection.

When you leave the cemetery, continue on down D19 to Lesbœufs. Continue straight on through toward Ginchy. Along the way you will pass an interesting British Guards cemetery. ***The Somme Battlefields***, Martin and Mary Middlebrook's book, it is a great book to carry with you during these visits, as they discuss every British cemetery in the Somme Department.

They also mention many of the individual monuments that might be seen along the road. Each is worth a quick stop and a few minutes of your time.

Feel your way through Ginchy, it is kind of straight ahead, to the South African Memorial at Delville Wood. You have read earlier about Tom and Janet Fairgrieve who are the caretakers. The coffee/tea bar is usually staffed by Janet and she always has an excellent collection of relics for sale. This is a good place to pick up those demilitarized souvenirs.

There is a museum to visit showcasing South Africa's men's service in both World Wars. That countries troops suffered greatly in this woods, which is open for you to walk around. The museum features great bronze panels depicting South African men in their battles. It is a must see!

Delville Wood South African Memorial

Janet also has maps and books for sale that will better inform you of the many places of interest to visit. All the ones that you will not have time to visit during this one short stay. It's enough to bring you back.

As you leave, continue on through Longueval and take D20 on your left to Contalmaison and la Boisselle. Contalmaison had a large chateau at the start of World War One, but it was destroyed and not replaced.

As you leave Contalmaison on D20 you will travel across a shallow valley. There was a battery of German 77 mm cannons captured by the British at the edge of the small woods on your left. If you slow down, you can see the old gun positions at the edge of the road.

Stop and look back at the slope leading to Contalmaison, on the south side of the road, up near the fence, you can see the white spoil of a German trench when the field is plowed and not in crop. A German soldier, of the 106th Saxony (Liepzig), 183rd Infantry Division, by the name Reinhold W. Jülich was captured by the British while sitting in that trench on July 10, 1916. He later moved to the U.S. and raised a family here. His son, Jack C. Julich, is a director of our museum.

Continue on into and through le Boisselle to the far end where you will take a road to your left, marked with a sign pointing to Lochnagar Crater, the result of very large mines blown under the German lines on the 1st of July, 1916. Just past the intersection to your left you can see another crater in the small field. Look on both sides coming and going to Lochnagar, the houses are built along what was several craters in a row.

After visiting Lochnager Crater, come back into le Boisselle and go left or right to the main road crossing on the north side of the village. Watch it, this is a major highway and the vehicles are coming at you very fast on this two lane, narrow road. Turn right and drive on D929 up the hill to the large Pozières British Cemetery. A visit here is a must. There are over 30,000 names of men with unknown graves listed on the walls.

Please visit the grave of John Middleton Brodin, Pvt, 1713, of the 5th Australian Battalion, killed on 25 July, 1916. His grave is located at Row-4P35, toward the far north end, on the right. He was a great-great-cousin of Carol. John's father, Eric Anton Brodin, was shipwrecked on his way to the United States in the South Seas, he was the only survivor and the ship that picked him up went to Melbourne. He ended up living in Australia and starting a family. A lost root of Carol's family tree until just a few years ago. On a hill, in the distance, behind the cemetery you will see the British Monument at Theipval. Don't forget to put your name in the register and show you visited John's grave, that way the next time we look through the register, we will know you were there.

In Pozières, on your right, you will find the old Madame Brihier's café, now owned by Dominic and called 'Tommy's Café.' He is a well known local collector and a stop here is also a must. At a prior establishment he had created a trench line out back and I expect to find one here soon.

We will leave here to visit the Pozières windmill site and the monument to the first tank battle. Drive on through the village and just past the eastern end you will find the Australian Pozières Memorial Site on your left. More Australians died around Pozières than anywhere else during World War One.

Just out there past the mound, all that is left of the windmill, over there by the small road, is where Jacka,[69] V.C., Australian, fought and should have be granted a bar to his Victoria Cross.

Across the road, by the radio relay station, you will find the Tank Memorial to the first battle the tanks were in, on September 15th, 1916. Watch the traffic as you cross.

Look to the west and south, behind the radio station and to the south of Pozières, and you will see a wide slowly sloping field. Out in that field, the Australian 5th Battalion[70] fought the world's worst hand grenade (bomb to them) battle. Cousin John M. Brodin, was killed right out there, within your view.

Tank Memorial - These tanks are about 1 foot long.

About a mile on, by Courcelette, is the Canadian monument to their actions on 15 September, 1916, they were escorted by some of the first tanks. Canadians will want to run up there, depending on your interest and what time it is, that's up to you.

From here we will visit the Monument at Theipval. Drive back into Pozières and turn right, north, onto D73 to Theipval, it is also signed. A little ways out, you will pass a large farm on your right, this is the famous "Mucky Farm," Moquet Farm, and the Australians have recently completed a memorial near the road in memory of the Australian attempts to capture the farm in 1916.

The Theipval Memorial is to the tens of thousands of British and Dominion troops that have no known grave from the Battle in 1916. It is quite impressive. Behind it, is a combined French and British cemetery to show both were involved.

When you leave, you want to turn north, or left on D73, out of the village and head down over the hill to visit Helen's Tower, the 36th Ulster Division Memorial. There is a small coffee bar and museum to visit. At times, the tower is open to climb to the top to get a nice overview of the area.

Leave the tower continuing down the hill and crossing the railroad tracks. Turn left to Hamel and take the next right in Hamel to go up the hill to the Newfoundland Memorial Park. This is a large area and can take a couple of hours to walk around. It is one of the areas where you can walk from what was the British front line to the German front line through no-man's land and back again. It was a particularly bad place on July 1, 1916 and I do recommend you read[71] a bit about it before

The stair way to the Canadian memorial at the Canadian Vimy Ridge Memorial Park.

Restored trenches at the Canadian Vimy Ridge Memorial Park.

275

your visit. You will be impressed with how well it is preserved and how well you can fit what you have read with what you see, a good site specific research place.

As you have visited a lot of places already today, we will pass the memorial for now and go on into Auchonvillers just ahead, to Avril's B&B. When you reach the village, turn right and the B&B is signed and located on your left, next to the water tower.

If you didn't get a room in advance, have a cup of tea and meet Avril. A perfect place to temporarily end your preplanned visit. You can visit the Newfoundland Park on your way back to Péronne, for you have driven in France enough to now guide yourself.

Avril will help you plan your return so you can visit interesting places we have missed. If you have made arrangements to stay, make yourself at home. Don't forget to say hi, for Carol and me, and enjoy the Somme.

Depending on how you have enjoyed your visit to date, you still have four days before you have to return the car.

Talk to Avril about what you have enjoyed seeing, or might want to see. You can easily spend another two days in this area and not get bored.

It isn't far to the French coast where you might spend a night and there are quite a number of famous places not far away. You can easily make it to Reims, in the Champagne grape region to visit the wineries and take a test sip or two.

Don't forget Fort Duhdux and Didier Boniface at Seclin. It is just a short distance past the Canadian Vimy Ridge Memorial.

Perhaps you might make a quick one day visit to Verdun and vicinity, to see the large forts and the American Meuse-Argonne battle area. You can do both and still get back to the airport in time to check in the car. The distances involved are really quite short. You may be tired, but I think you will be happy.

If you have a chance, visit the crossroads and grave again for us, Carol and myself, the French, and the men's families, before you leave.

Avril Williams, breakfast starts at 8:00 a.m., that is unless the bread truck is late.

In **Remembrance-Souvenir**!

Epilogue

As I wrote in the Prologue, the story does not end with the printing of this book. This page is the last page of the book to be written and I completed it on March 3, 1998. There are still several mysteries to be solved and one major step to accomplish. Obtaining an *Act Of Congress* recognizing the **Isolated** *Congressional Medals of Honor* **World War Two 5th War Grave**, at Cartigny. France.

I sent in the request, on behalf of the four men's families, the French and myself at the end of October, 1997. To insure that all United States Senators were aware of the situation, I sent like information packages to every Senator, with the men's home state Senators receiving individual letters and packages.

At the same time, I requested that the families also write personal letters to their home state Senators. To this date, March 3, 1998, I have received letters from the following Senators and Winona Derrick has received return communications from Senator Don Nickles, of Oklahoma. Bonnie Dunlap Owens also has a direct channel of communications with Senator Thrumond.

Senator Paul D. Coverdell, Georgia
Senator Rod Grams, Minnesota
Senator Joseph I. Lieberman, Connecticut
Senator John McCain, Arizona
Senator Arlen Specter, Pennsylvania
Senator Slade Gorton, Washington
Senator Jesse Helms. North Carolina
Senator Trent Lott, Mississippi
Senator Patty Murray,. Washington
Senator Strom Thurmond, South Carolina

The situation is currently the same as the fall of 1994, as the Senators so far have deferred to the United States Department of Army. The D.O.A. stance, is that the **common grave in France** should be disinterred, as well as the four men's officially recognized graves. Any bone fragments found in the five graves would be shipped to the Central Identification Unit in Hawaii. The four men's families will have to submit D.N.A. samples and the D.O.A. will attempt to identify all the bone shards. If they can, they will divide the pile of shards into **four men?** Each man's pile of bone shards will then be interred in their previous official grave. If they cannot identify all the bone shards, the United States Department of Army will **establish a new *common grave*** at a National Cemetery midway between the surviving families. We believe this demand by the D.O.A. to be nonsense and an excessive waste of United States Taxpayer funds.

The families of Lt. Gott, Lt. Metzger, T/Sgt. Dunlap and S/Sgt. Krimminger and I consider such an action to be a desecration of the men's graves and will continue to insist that the United States not disturb any of the existing graves. We will continue with our drive for that Act of Congress doing the honorable thing and recognize the grave for what it is. An **existing *common grave***, which owes its existence to the only **witnessed and documented case of *American Soldiers* recovering and hiding *American War Dead***!

Several mysteries remain to be solved. I want to locate, if possible, any of the surviving men who were in the ambulance and who hid the four men's remains from the B-17 crash on November 9, 1944. The families have long forgiven them and wish that they might know that the remains did not stay hidden next to a deserted road. Also, it would be much harder for the United States to refuse to recognize the ***common grave in France*** with a living participant. A grave containing the remains of four men airmen of World War Two, two of them *Congressional Medals of Honor* awardees.

I have still to locate Sgt. Mike Flores, one of the five survivors from the B-26 crash on January 22, 1945.

And, I have still to receive the file on Lt. Richard Noble so that I might locate where he died and find for his family, just what did happen to him 54 years ago.

Authorities And Sources

1. **A Time For Trumpets, The Untold Story Of The Battle Of The Bulge**, Charles B. MacDonald, Bantam Book, Toronto, New York, London, Sydney, Auckland, December, 1995. ISBN 0-553-34226-6

2. **A Time For Trumpets, The Untold Story Of The Battle Of The Bulge**, Chapter Ten: *Kampfgruppe Peiper*.

3. **The Price Of Glory, Verdun, 1916**, Alistair Horne, MacMillian & Co. Ltd., New York, St. Martin's Press, 1962.

4. **The Canvas Falcons**, Stephen Longstreet, Ballantine Books, 1970. ISBN 345-02500-8-125

5. **The Balloon Buster**, Norman S. Hall, Bantam Books, August 1966.

6. **In Flanders Fields and Other Poems**, Lieut.-Col. John McCrae, M.D., Toronto, William Briggs, 1919.

7. **American Armies And Battlefields In Europe**, Center Of Miliary History, United States Army, Washington, D.C., U.S. Govt. Print., 1938.

8. **WAR - Underground**, Alexander Barrie, A Star Book, W. H. Allen & Co. Ltd., 1961.

9. **Verdun And The Battle For its Possession**, Michelin Illustrated Guides To The Battlefields (1914-1918), Michelin & Cie., Clemond-Ferrand, Michelin Tyre Co. Ltd, 81 Fulham Road, London, SW., Michelin Tire Co., Milltown, N.J., U.S.A.

10. **A German Deserter's War Experience**, Translated by J. Koettgen, B.W. Huebsch, New York, 1917.
    Chapter XXI - IN THE HELL OF VAUQUOIS.

11. **Letters And Diary**, Alan Seeger, Charles Scribner's Sons, New York, 1917.
    Poems, Alan Seeger, Charles Scribner's, New York, 1916.

12. **The Vanguard Of American Volunteers**, Edwin W. Morse, Charles Scribner's Sons, New York, 1922.

13. **A Soldier Of The Legion**, Edward Morale, Houghton Mifflin Company, Boston and New York, 1916.
    Kelly Of The Foreign Legion, Letters of the Légionnaire, Russell A. Kelly, Mitchell Kennerley, New York, 1917.
    The French Foreign Legion, John Robert Young, Thames and Hudson, 1984. ISBN 0-500-27382-0
    American Fighters In The Foreign Legion, Paul Ayers Rockwell, Houghton Mifflin Company, Boston and New York, The Riverside Press, Cambridge, 1930.

14. **La Grande Guerre, vécue-Racontée-Illustrée Par Les Combattants**, Asistide Quillet, Editeur, Librairie Aristide Quillet, Paris, 1922.
    Der Krieg 1914-19 in Wortlund Bild, Emeiter Band, Deutfches Ferlagshaus Bong & Co., Berlin, Leipzig, Lbien, Stuttgart.

15. **The French Foreign Legion**, A Complete History Of The Legendary Fighting Force, Douglas Porch, Harper Collins Publishers, 1991. ISBN 0-06 016652-5

16. **The Illustrated Encyclopedia Of Artillery**, Ian V. Hogg, Chartwell Books, Inc. New Jersey, 1987. ISBN 1-55521-310-3
    A Military Atlas of the First World War, Arthur Banks, Leo Cooper, London 1989. ISBN 0-85052-1459

17. **Final Disposition Of World War II Dead 1945-51**, Edward Steere and Thayer M. Boardman, QMC Historical Studies, Series II, No. 4, Historical Branch, Office Of The Quartermaster General, Washington D.C. 1957.
    QMC Historical Studies, The Graves Registration Service In World War II, Number 21, Historical Section Office Of The Quartermaster General, April, 1951.

18. **Before Endeavors Fade, A Guide To The Battlefields Of The First World War**, Revised Edition, Rose E. B. Coombs, MBE, An 'After The Battle' Publication, Plaistow Press Limited, London 1990. ISBN 0-900913 61-4

19. **The Tanks At Flers**, Trevor Pidgeon, Fairmile Books, Cobham, Surrey, England, 1995, 2 Volume Set..
    ISBN 0-9525175-2-3

20. **American Armies And Battlefields In Europe**, American Battle Monuments Commission, United States Government Printing Office, 1938, Page 381.

21. **Order Of Battle Of The United States Land Forces In The World War**, American Expeditionary Forces, Divisions, United States Government Printing Office, 1931.

22. **American Memorials And Overseas Military Cemeteries**, The American Battle Monuments Commission, MCMXCIV

23. **American Armies And Battlefields In Europe**, United States Printing Office, 1938.

24. **Order Of Battle Of The United States Land Forces In The World War**, Divisions, United States Printing Office, 1931.

25. **The Army Air Forces In World War II - Combat Chronology - 1941-1945**, Compiled by Carter, Robert Mueller, Albert R. Simpson Historical Research Center, Air University and Office of Air Force History, Headquarters USAF, 1973.

26. **The Mighty Eighth**, Roger A. Freeman, Motorbooks International, Publishers & Wholesalers. Arms and Armor Press, 1991. ISBN 0-87938-639-X

27. **D-Day, Operation Overload**, SMITHMARK Publishers Inc., New York, N.Y., 1993. ISBN: 0-8317-2188-X

28. Bill Fannon, Letter - March 16, 1995 and telephone interview August 26, 1997.

29. S/Sgt. William R. Robbins' personal notebook, listing all the missions he flew.

30. Interviews, personal and telephone: August, 1994 - June, 1997, with Russell W. Gustafson..

31. Letter from Pilot's Mother to Navigator's Mother, 29 November, 1944.

32. Interview with Jerry Collins, June 18, 1997. "Memories of his crew members."

33. 452nd Bomb Group History Microfilm, Page 0674, Mission 162, Flight Path Over Europe, showing E.L.F. (See Pg. 216.)

34. **Over Here**, Steve Snelling, Eastern Daily Press, The Breedon Books Publishing Company, Derby, England.(1996) ISBN 1-85983-066-8

35. HQ USAAF Station 142, Office of the Intelligence Officer, Unit History Report for the Saarbrucken Mission, 9 November, 1944. 1 December, 1944. Major Harold P. Thoreson.

36. Interviews with 452nd Bomb Group Association members, during the reunions, 1994, 1995, 1996 and 1997.

37. Lead Navigator's narrative (report) for Mission of 9 November, 1944, "A" (729th) Squadron.

38. **Mighty Eighth War Manual**, Roger A. Freeman, Motorbooks International, Publishers & Wholesalers, 1993. ISBN 0-87938-508-1

39. Even though most of France had been Liberated by this time, it was still referred to as the Enemy Coast.

40. Operations Officer's Report of Mission, 9 November, 1944, "B" Squadron.

41. Operations Officer's Report of Mission, 9 November, 1944, "A" Squadron.

42. Interview with William R. Robbins, May, 1996.

43. SO #224, HQ USAAF STA 142, 17 Aug '44

44. SO #227, HQ USAAF STA 142, 20 Aug '44

45. Telephone Interview with Irving Hirsch, 23 June, 1997.

46. Missing Crew Report, A/C: 904, Squadron: 729, Group: 452, Date: 9 November, 1944.

47. Battle Casualty Report, 452nd Bombardment Group (H), 10 November, 1944.

48. Interview with William W. Fannon, October, 1994.

49. Interviews with family of John A. Harland, July, 1994 and 21 June, 1997. Verified by Joseph F. Harms, 19 June, 1997.

50. High School Paper, "**A Little Philosophy,**" Wilhelm Metzger (Wilhelm, a play on the German Language, he was studying.).

51. Interview with Harold E. Burrell, 2nd Lt. Metzger's original crew, October, 1994.

52. Individual Deceased Personnel Files - Report Of Burial, Graves Registration Form No.1.

53. Individual Deceased Personnel File - Disinterment Directive, Krimminger, H. B. - 22 Apr 48

54. Individual Deceased Personnel File - Disinterment Directive, Dunlap, R.A. - 22 Apr 48

55. Individual Deceased Personnel File - Disinterment Directive, Gott, D.J. - 22 Apr 48

56. Individual Deceased Personnel File - Disinterment Directive, Metzger, R.A. - 22 Apr 48

57. Included in the History of the 452nd Bombardment Group (H), November, 1944. Available on the microfilm copy of the Army Air Force Official History of the Group.

58. Lead Navigator's Narrative for Mission of 9 November, 1944, Stephen H. Rhea, 1st Lt., Air Corps, Lead Navigator.

59. **Missing Planes of the 452nd Bomb Group**, 2nd Edition-1995, Compiled by Edward Hinrichs, 7582 North Shore Circle, Forest Lake, MN 55026, (622)464-5121.

60. Personal Records - provided by James O. Fross's widow, Mary Fross, McAllen, Texas

61. 452nd Bomb Group Microfilm History, Missing In Action Report, Robbins report, as amended, 26 Nov 44.

62. **Over Here**, The Americans In Norfolk during World War Two, Steve Snelling, Eastern Daily Press, The Breedon Books Publishing Company Limited, Breedon House 44, Friar Gate, Derby, DE1 1DA., 1996. ISBN 1-85983-066-8

63. **Sergeant York And His People**, Sam K. Cowan, Grosset & Dunlap Publishers, Funk & Wagnalls Company, 1922.

64. **A Story Waiting To Be Told**, Lowell W. (Pete) Black, Oklahoma.

65. **The Mighty Eighth, A History of the Units, Men and Machines of the US 8th Air Force,** Roger A. Freeman, Motorbooks International Publishers & Wholesalers, Osceola, WI, 54020, USA 1993. ISBN 0-87938-638-X

66. **The First Day On the Somme**, 1 July, 1916, Martin Middlebrook, W.W. Norton & Company, Inc., New York, New York, 1983. ISBN 393-05442-X

67. **The Somme Battlefields**, A comprehensive Guide from Crécy to the Two World War Wars, Martin & Mary Middlebrook, Penguin Books, 1991. ISBN 0-14-01.2847-6

68. **Somme**, Lyn Macdonald, Michael Joseph, London, 1983. ISBN 0 7181-2254-2

69. **Jacka, VC**, Australia's Finest Fighting Soldier, Ian Grant, Sun Books, The MACMILLIAN Company of Australia. ISBN 0 7251-0620-4

70. **"Over There" With The Australians,"** Capt. R. Hugh Knyvett, Charles Scribner' Sons, New York, April 1918.

71. **Beaumont Hamel, Somme**, Battle Ground Europe Series, Nigel Cave, Publisher Leo Cooper Printer.: Redwood Books, Trowbridge, Wilts, 1994. ISBN 0-85052-3982

Recommended movies:

Apartment For Peggy, 1948, life on the G.I. Bill, married college student's problems.

Since You Went Away, Selznick International Picture, the problems of a family with the father in the service during World War Two.

The Best Years Of Our Lives, 1946, the trials of three veterans returning home.

Index

101st Airborne Division 51
104th Infantry, 26th Division 240
11th Engineers 60
13th Airborne Glider Division 237
13th Combat Wing 72
19th Tactical Air Command 70, 186, 251
1st Division 52, 61, 63
    Big Red One Division 58
1st Lt. Charles S. Frey 261
1st Lt. Donald J. Gott, M.H. 64-66, 71, 73, 78-80, 82, 84, 85,
        92-95, 98, 102, 103, 115, 117, 123, 134-139,
        141, 142, 144, 147, 151, 154, 155, 157, 158,
        160, 163, 164, 167, 168, 176, 177, 186, 191,
        195, 207, 212, 219, 220, 224-226, 228-230,
        232, 234, 239, 241, 243, 261, 264
    A. A. Tuck 226
    Alice Fincham Gott 226
    August Peil 225
    Bert Allard, Jr. 226
    Billy Wayne Calhoun 226
    Bonnie Pauline New Compton 226
    Brent Compton 226
    Calvin Eugene Derrick 226
    Chad Ryan Compton 226
    Cheri Denise Compton 226
    Clarence Hokweiler 226
    Clarence John Gott 225
    David William Gott 226
    Donald Max Compton 145, 166, 195, 226
    Donald Max Compton, Jr. 226
    Earl Lee Hartley 226
    Earline Mann (Barton) 227
    Gary Joseph Compton 145, 226
    Hazel Cathryn Gott Peil 143, 146, 225
    Ione Donoghe Gott 226
    Jared Monte Compton 226
    Jimmie Lee Gann 176, 177, 226
    Joan Brooks Compton 226
    John Allen 226
    Joseph Eugene Gott, Father 115, 134, 142
    Kenneth Chalmers 226
    Kenneth Cleo Compton 226
    Kenneth James Gott 226
    Kenneth Sherrill 227
    Kevin Eugene Allard 176, 177, 226
    Krista Dawn Gann 226
    Leroy Zigler 226
    Loren Schneider 227
    Lorrie Ann Compton 226
    Lucille Magdalyn Gott Compton 143, 225
    Lucille Schneider 226
    Mary Lucy Hanlon Gott, Mother 115, 142
    Monte Ray Compton 226
    Otto James Gott 142, 143, 146, 226
    Patricia Ann Ryan Compton 226
    Patricia Corinne Compton Gann . . 145, 176, 177, 226
    Peter James Gott 226
    Ralph Persons 226
    Raymond Compton 145, 225
    Raymond File 226
    Raymond Schneider 226
    Sammie Rude Compton 226
    Starla Kay Compton 226
    Terrie Lynn Compton 226
    Theron Eugene Compton 145, 226
    Troy Theron Compton 226
    W. B. Catlin 226
    Winona Colleen Compton Allard Derrick . . 123, 145,
        161, 162, 166-169, 176-178, 195, 207, 225, 226
1st Lt. Gerald W. Collins 69, 70, 74-76, 94-96, 98,
        102, 123, 205, 219, 220, 239
    Angie Collins 220
    Ashley Collins 220
    Beverly Collins 220
    Beverly Grace Bergstrum Collins 219
    Bryant Collins 220
    Don Curtis Collins 219
    Donald Collins 220
    Harold Collins, Father 219
    Harold Collins, Jr. 219
    Hazel A. Builderback Collins, Mother 219
    Lauri Collins 220
    Pamila Collins 220
    Pres. of the Nat. Defense Transport Assoc. 220
    Ronald Collins 220
    Scott Collins 220
1st Lt. Hugh W. Robbins 249, 250, 252, 254
    Calvin Lee Robbins, Father 257
    Ellen Woods Robbins, Mother 257
    Ethel Nutwell 250, 260
1st Lt. John M. Kirklin 261
1st Lt. Joseph M. DuBois 249, 250, 252, 253, 256
1st Lt. Kenneth F. Bickford 95
1st Lt. Marshall R. Duncan 154
1st Lt. Ralph P. Goldsticker 99
1st Lt. Raymond H. Boettcher 249, 250, 252, 254-256
1st Lt. Richard F. Noble 242, 257-259
    Kay Noble Ballentine 257
    Rex Noble 257, 258
1st Lt. Richard P. Britanik 249, 251-254, 256
1st Lt. Robert S. Marquis 95
1st Lt. Stephen H. Rhea 71
1st Lt. Walter R. Green 138, 139, 149, 238
1st Pathfinder Squadron (Prov) 251, 254
27th Division 270
285th Field Artillery Observation Battalion, Battery B 2
295th Military Police Company 2
29th Division 55
2nd Lt. Donald E. Roberts 238
2nd Lt. Elmer E. Gerard 238
2nd John J. Reilly, Jr. 95
2nd Lt. Daniel G. Viafore 259
2nd Lt. Bruce Clago 259
2nd Lt. C. J. McCollum 231
2nd Lt. Charles D. Crofts 261
2nd Lt. Donald J. Hoeffler 261
2nd Lt. Earl L. Penick 70, 94, 126, 130, 135,
        146, 207, 239, 240
    Carlton Penick 207, 239
    Lavona 240
    Michael Lee Penick 240
2nd Lt. Frances W. Myers 95
2nd Lt. Fred Prado 95
2nd Lt. Frederick W. Hardin 231
2nd Lt. George J. Kurtz III 261
2nd Lt. George W. Hixson 261
2nd Lt. John A. Harland . . . 71, 73, 78-81, 84, 88, 89, 93, 94, 96,
        98, 102, 113, 117, 124, 133, 135, 138, 140,
        157, 158, 160, 194, 196, 205-207, 210, 229,
        230, 232, 239, 270
    Debby Harland 206, 230
    Dianne Harland Kowar 230
    Elizabeth (Liz) Harland 230
    Ida M. Miller 133, 229
    Judy Harland Galloway 230
    Kathy Harland Greinier 206, 230
    Scott Harland 157, 159, 206, 230
2nd Lt. Joseph F. Harms . . . 71, 73, 80, 83, 84, 88, 93, 94, 96, 97,
        99, 101, 102, 133, 158, 160, 191, 194, 200,
        205, 210, 230, 231
    Brooke Wood 231
    Christine Woods Ianello 231

Elsie Gray Harms, Wife 231
Ernest Edward Harms, Father 230
Gerard Vincent Harms 230
Jean Lynne Harms Witte 231
Karen Jean Harms Wood 231
Mark Ianello 231
Mary Justina Rigney Harms, Mother 230
Mrs. Elsie Harms 133
Regina Delores Harms 230
Richard Witte 231
Richard Witte, Jr. 231
William Witte 231
2nd Lt. P. L. Koob 140
2nd Lt. Phineas Indritz 130-132, 151
    Ida Chemda Indritz Krimminger 149
2nd Lt. R. Laule 259
2nd Lt. Robert E. Russell 261
2nd Lt. Robert L. Hester 95
2nd Lt. Steven A. Mem 231
2nd Lt. William E. Metzger, Jr., M.H. . 65, 66, 71, 73, 75, 77, 78,
        80, 81, 84, 85, 87, 92, 93, 96, 98, 102, 116,
        117, 136, 138, 141, 144, 149, 154, 155, 163,
        164, 166, 167, 169, 170, 176, 177, 187, 191,
        195, 207, 212, 229, 231, 235, 237, 238, 243, 264
    A LITTLE PHILOSOPHY 238
    Alexander Wm. Rubiera 237
    Betsy Ann Fredericks Intellini 237
    Cecil Carr Fredericks 148
    Cecilia Marie Rubiera 237
    Christina 237
    Deborah Lou Fredericks Coate 237
    Dian Sue Fredericks Rubiera 237
    Ethel Badeau Metzger, Mother 130, 134, 143,
        144, 151, 235
    Frances Louise Metzger Fredericks 116, 144,
        209, 237
    Frank Prado 237
    George W. Scholfield 148, 236, 237
    Ginger Segal Scholfield 237
    Identification Bracelet 141, 146
    Jeanne Elizabeth Metzger Scholfield .. 116, 141, 144
    Krista Prado 237
    Kristen Intellini 237
    Laura Jane Fredericks Creer 237
    Lauren A. Intellini 237
    Lauren Alexandra Creer 237
    Lisa Mc. Coate 237
    Lynely Intellini 237
    Magan Prado 237
    Phyllis Lynn Scholfield Prado 237
    Rebecca Morgan Creer 237
    Rosco Bradford Creer 237
    Samuel Schofield 237
    Stephanie 237
    Stephen Wayne Scholfield 237
    Tess Scholfield 237
    Thomas Eugene Scholfield 237
    Wendel B. Coate "Bud" 237
    William E. Metzger, Sr., Father .. 116, 137, 141, 143,
        144, 147, 151, 235
    William J. Rubiera 237
    Woodlawn Cemetery 163
2nd Lt. William W. Fannon 95, 122
2nd of the 317th Infantry of the 80th American Division 60
30th Division 270
351st Bomb Group 263
388th Bombardment Group (H) 69
397th Bombardment Group 70, 246, 272
3rd Air Division 70, 72
3rd Sidney 2, 64, 233
3rd Army 270
409th Bomb Group 251
4114 Hospital Plant 93
452nd Bomb Group Association. ... 98, 204, 207, 208, 210, 260

452nd Bombardment Group (H) 64, 65, 69, 76, 93-99, 101, 102,
    118, 121-123, 125, 129-132, 137, 140, 147.
    153, 158, 159, 166, 169, 171, 172, 220, 222,
    225, 227-231, 233, 235, 240, 242-245, 257, 259
    1230 QM Co. 242
    1284 MP Det 242
    1797 Ord S&M Co. 242
    18th Wea Sqdn. 242
    2112 FF Pln. 242
    214 Fin Det. 242
    275 Med Disp 242
    466 Sub-Depot 242
    728 Bm Sq. 242
    730 Bm Sq. 242
    731 Bm Sq. 242
    872 Oml Co. 242
    87th Sta Com Sq. 242
    Hq. 452 Bm Gp. 242
    The Queen Elizabeth 241, 242
45th Combat Wing 69, 72
4th Combat Wing 72
5th Calvary, American 58
606th Graves Registration Company 17, 90, 172
609th QM Graves Registration Company 92
693rd Airborne Anti-Aircraft Battalion 236
6th Division 2, 6, 237
    The Sightseeing Sixth 2
70th Repl Dep 231
728th Bombardment Squadron (H) 69, 257
729th Bombardment Squadron (H) 65, 69-71, 73, 76, 88, 93, 96,
    97, 99, 130, 147, 158, 172, 220, 222, 225,
    228-231, 233, 235, 240-242, 244
730th Bombardment Squadron (H) 69, 241, 244
731st Bombardment Squadron (H) 69, 99, 241, 242
7th Calvary 168
7th Corps 67
80th Jubilee W.W.I 205
82nd Airborne Division 48-51
87th Station Complement Squadron 99
8th Air Force 64, 69, 70, 132, 136, 139, 160, 261, 263
92nd Combat Wing 72
93rd Combat Wing 72
96th Bombardment Group (H) 69
98th General Hospital 93
Air Force Historical Research Center 67, 162
    Capt. William Butler 248
    Dr. Fred Shaw 248
    Dr. Jim Kitchens 248
    Mickey Russell 248, 258, 261
Alain Leguillier 55
Alan Seeger 7-9, 11, 24, 56-58, 62, 63, 156, 267, 268, 272
    I HAVE A RENDEZVOUS WITH DEATH 8
    Maktoob 63
American Avion INCONNU 107, 108
American Battle Monuments Commission 18, 156, 257
American Hidden Grave 105
American Isolated War Grave 18
American Legion Post 161, Redmond, Washington 196
American St. Mihiel W.W.I Cemetery 92
ANZACs 60
Army Air Force Photographic Collection 205
Attila the Hun 263
Australia
    Australian Air Force Museum 196
    Canberra 195
    Canberra War Museum 195
    Childers 196
    Mullumbimby 196
    New Castle 195
    Sidney 196
    Williamstown 195
Australian 5th Battalion 275
Aviator AMERICAN UNKNOWN 18, 31

Entry	Pages
Unknown American Aviator	31
Avril Williams	182, 190, 201, 266, 267, 276
Kathy	181, 190
Marc	181
Sebastian	181, 182, 190
Tea Room, Bed and Breakfast	181, 190, 201, 265, 272
B-17 'Snake Eyes'	125, 132
B-17, Sn: 42-102931	95
B-17, Sn: 43-37833	95
B-17, Sn: 43-38184	261
B-17, Ten Horsepower	263
B-17G, Sn: 42-39941, 'Lucky Lady'	259
B-17G-35VE, Sn: 42-97904, 'The Lady Jeannette'	69, 162
B-26G-1-MA, Sn: 43-34201 Where's It At?	247, 249, 257
Barbara White	11
Barry Brodin	195
Battery Corporal Willis S. Cole Military Museum	163, 166, 176
Battle Of The Somme	7, 27, 42, 60, 195, 266, 267, 272
Belgium	2, 46
Bastogne	3
Baugnez	2
Brussels	46
Malmédy	17
Port of Antwerp	152
Belmont High School	219
Bernard Delsert	20, 21
Bernard Leguillier	1, 12, 14, 17, 19, 23, 27, 33, 34, 39, 53, 61, 157, 174, 176, 178, 189, 197, 202, 204, 208, 245-247
Régine Leguillier	12
Valerie Leguillier	12
Blue Trenbeath	196
Bob Bautcelmess	162
Bomb Disposal, North France	21, 91, 183, 184
Brigadier General McAuliffe	3
Brigitte Coquel	49
Bud Wortman	11
Buncher Beacon	71
California Public Utilities Commission	219
Capt. Carl Eminger	158
Capt. Jack R. Ginter	145
Capt. James T. Passman	92, 123
Capt. John E. Jordan	142
Capt. Shirley	252
Capt. Stiles	139
Carl Phillips	154
Carol Lorraine Cole	1, 2, 6, 12, 34, 86, 170, 195, 236
George E. Smith	225
Cat-Cat (4x4)	15, 28, 29
Caterpillar Club	
S/Sgt. James O. Fross	223
S/Sgt. William R. Robbins	125
Cathy Osmont	48
Center for Air Force History	67
Central High School	138
Chaplin Frank L. Whitney	118
Charles King	233
Christian Kowal	12, 21, 29, 183, 184
Claude Coquel	41, 43, 46, 53
Claude Leguillier	12, 15, 19, 34
Claude Obert	202, 212
Coghlins, Inc.	126, 241
Col. B. L. Wilson	144
Col. Butte	123
Col. James N. Soligan	167
Col. John E. Bodle	144
Comite Departemental De Tourisme De La Somme	263
COMMEMO-RANGERS	41, 42, 46-53, 55, 66, 67, 157, 161, 164, 173, 174, 177-179, 182, 183, 185, 190, 201, 208, 212, 259, 260
Company D, 108th Infantry of the 27th Division	46
Congressional Medal of Honor	136, 138, 140, 141, 143, 144, 147, 155, 159, 209, 210, 243, 263
1st Lt. Donald J. Gott	191
2nd Lt. William E. Metzger, Jr.	117
Lt. Frank Luke	4
Lt. Walter Truemper	263
Sgt. Alvin York	172, 203, 266
Sgt. Archie Mathies	263
Coors Beer	
Peter Coors	51
Cordell Taylor	167
Cpl. Edward L. Polick	231
Cpl. Edward T. Gorman	238
Cpl. John Steele	48
Cpl. Marley R. Conger	231
Cpl. Oscar B. Lane	231
Cpl. Paul F. Tickerhoof	149, 238
Cpl. Robert J. Falsey	149, 238
Cpl. Walter Jankowski	149, 238
CURÉ Étienne Serpette	53, 106
Czechoslovakia	
Brux	241
Daily Oklahoman	141
Cullen Johnson	141
Débarquement en Normandie	41, 46
D-Day 50th Anniversary	34, 41, 46, 48, 50, 52, 56, 67, 69, 157, 163, 165, 230, 233, 236, 242
Deopham Green, Station 142	71, 94
DeSoto Hilton Hotel	210, 249
Dick Huff	11
Didier Boniface	197, 203, 204, 276
Doctor Bain	255
Dominic Zenardi	27, 274
Don Williams, State Senator	167
Dr. Jene Miller	167
Drunkard Control	251
Dwight Pugh	167
E. Elirn Gerard	149
E.L.F. (Emergency Landing Field)	70, 80, 81
Earl Mitchell	167
Eastern Daily Press	
Above and Beyond	195
Steve Snelling	195
Ed Hinrichs	258
Emile Berger	iv, 108-110, 165, 179, 203
Marc Berger	202
England	
Deopham Green, Station 142	70-72, 88, 94, 101, 149, 241, 243
Lowestoft	96
Mildenhall	72
Norfolk	94, 195
Eric Brodin	
Nance Brodin	196
Eugene and Gisele Lelouey	48
Catherine	48
Evelyn Lombardo	19
Everett C. Olson	188
Face of an American aviator	12
Fairleigh Dickinson College	229
Family - Nuttens	107, 256
Fargo High School	142
First Battle of the Marne	273
Flight Officer Lowell Shuman	261
Floyd Dew	154
Foie de Gras	19
France	196, 274, 275
A-72 Air Station, Péronne	70, 81
Aisne River	265
Albert	22, 27, 201, 202, 266

American Ardennes W.W.II Military Cemetery . 257
American Epinal W.W.II Military Cemetery ... 257
American Limey Temp. Military Cemetery .. 92, 133,
141, 145, 152, 187, 188
American Lorraine W.W.II Military Cemetery .. 156
American Meuse-Argonne Memorial 6
American Meuse-Argonne W.W.I Cemetery 4
American Monument at Cantigny 56
American Normandy W.W.II Military Cemetery .. 52
American Oise-Aisne W.W.I Military Cemetery .. 38
American Somme W.W.I Military Cemetery . 33, 55,
61, 106, 267, 270, 271
Amiens 38, 52, 61, 182, 263, 265-267, 269, 272
Arc de Triomphe 182
Argonne Forest 203
Arras 267
Asseviliers 11, 182
Auchonvillers 181, 190, 266, 276
Australian War 2nd Division Memorial 272
Avocourt 6, 36
Bancourt 28, 66, 185, 207
Bapaume 23, 41, 43, 53, 61, 266, 272
Basilica "Notre-Dame de Brebieres 22
Battle of the Somme 7, 13, 173, 181, 196, 272
Bellicourt 269, 271
Belloy-en-Santerre 8, 11, 56, 62, 268
Bernes 16
Bois de Buirre 46, 107, 177, 205, 245, 270
Bois de Compiégne 56
Bony 33
Bouchavesnes-Bergen 272
British Monument at Theipval 274, 275
Butte de Vauquois 6, 7, 36
Caen 52, 261
Cambrai 189, 266, 271
Canadian Vimy Ridge Memorial Park 267, 275
Canal du Nord 24, 272
Cantigny 61-63, 183
Cartigny 17-19, 21, 31, 33-35, 38, 41, 52-54, 56,
61, 66, 67, 90, 104-106, 108, 109, 163, 164,
166, 168, 171, 173, 174, 177, 178, 185, 188,
190, 191, 200, 201, 204, 206, 208, 210, 217,
220, 225, 233, 235, 245, 246, 257, 260, 263,
269, 270, 272
Champagne 58
Charles De Gaulle Airport 15, 200, 264, 265
Charleville 266
Château Bellinglise 9, 56
Château Craonnelle 57
Château de Péronne 265
Château le Blanc-Sablon 57
Chemin des Dames 57
Cherbourg 67
Cologne River 104
Combles 22
Contalmaison 274
Cornay 203
Cote 304 37
Courcelette 275
Craonnelle 57
Deauville 261
Delville Wood South African Memorial 21, 59,
61, 273
Driencourt 12, 15, 16, 39, 41, 44-46,
104, 107, 171, 256
Estrée-en-Chaussee 13
Ferme de LELOUEY 47
Ferme de LERCHER 21
Flamicourt 1
Flers 42
Foreign Legion 63
Fort de la Malmaison 57
Fort de la Pompelle 58
Fort Duhdux 203, 276

Fort Tavannes 3
Fort Vaux 4, 172
French National Ossuary 4
Gare de Nord 52
Ginchy 21, 273
Gouzeacourt 60
Grave at Cartigny 21
Ham 265
Hamel 275
Hargicourt 269, 271
Hattonville 188, 189
Hawthorne Crater 190
Hindenburg Battle Line 60, 267
Historical de la Grande Guerre 265
Jacob's Ladder 191, 267
La Boisselle 60, 274
Laon 57, 81
le Transloy 272
Lesbœufs 23, 273
Lille 72, 203
Lochnager Crater 60, 274
Loire River Valley 53
Longueval 27, 274
Martin-de-Varreville, Le Vallee 47
Mesnil 22
Metz 64
Metz-Thionville 233
Meuse-Argonne 2, 44, 172, 233, 276
Mont-St.-Quentin 272
Montauban-de-Picardie 61
Montfaucon 6
Mourmelon 56-58
Newfoundland Memorial Park 181, 275
Normandy 43, 46, 47, 49-53, 55, 56, 67, 157, 174
Nurlu 64, 189
Omaha Beach 48, 52, 55
Paris 1, 53, 163, 170, 182, 205, 263
Péronne ... 1, 7, 11, 17, 19, 34, 35, 41, 42, 46, 53, 56,
70, 79, 106, 107, 171, 173, 182, 189, 200,
212, 246, 249-251, 256, 265-270, 272, 276
Pozières 27, 38, 42, 60, 173, 266, 274
Pozières British Cemetery 195
Province of Picardy 211
Punchy 19
Rancourt 266
Reims 31, 36, 56-58, 276
Roisel 182, 183, 269, 271
Roisel British Military Communal Cemetery 183
Romagne-s/s-Montfaucon 4
Romilly 241
Roye 265
Santerre 265
Seclin 203, 276
Somme Department (80) 270, 273
Somme River 1
St. Avold 156, 171
St. Mihiel 4
St. Quentin 81, 182, 266, 267, 269
St. Quentin Canal 60
St. Quentin Canal Tunnel 271
Ste. Laurent-sur-Mer 52
Ste-Mere du Mont 47
Ste-Mere-Eglise 17, 48, 50-52, 55, 56
Sword Beach 52
Tank Memorial, Pozières 274
Templeux-le-Guérard 271
Theipval 274
Theipval Memorial 60
Thionville 64
Tincourt New British W.W.I Military Cemetery . 270
Tincourt-Boucly .. 12, 16, 41, 66, 82, 84, 93, 98, 103-
108, 162, 171, 173, 174, 176, 177, 188, 190,
201, 202, 204, 220, 224, 233, 235, 243, 245-
247, 256, 257, 260, 263, 269, 270

284

Tours	53
Trench of the Bayonets	172
Utah Beach	47, 48, 52
Vauquois	203
Verdun	2-4, 7, 36, 37, 44, 56, 78, 80, 158, 171, 172, 193, 266, 276
White City	191
"Mucky Farm," Moquet Farm	275
Frank D. Lucas, U. S. Congress	167
Frêdêric Loyer "Freddo"	60, 201, 202
French 75 mm cannons	22
French Marshal Foch	272
Frite Wagon	269
Gail and Charles Kettlewell	39, 207, 208, 247
General Custer	168
General Hap H. Arnold	142
Gerald King	233
Gérard Leguillier	19, 21
Baptiste Leguillier	21
Catherine Leguillier-Lercher	19
German 77 mm cannon	15, 22, 274
German 77 mm shell	273
German Potato Masher	3
Germany	2
Andernach	242
Berlin	126, 223
Bielefeld	126, 223
Bremen	126, 223
Cologne	126, 223
Darmstadt	242
Dusseldorf	2, 4, 126, 223
Frankfort	126, 223
Gustavsburg	261
Hamburg	126, 223
Hanover	126, 223
Heligoland	223
Ingolstadt	242
Kassel	126, 223
Leipzig	263
Ludwigshafen	126, 132, 223, 224
Mainz	223
Merseburg	126, 132, 223
Minster	223
Neunkirchen	126, 224
Nürnberg	126, 223
Regensburg	125
Ruhland	242
Saarbrucken	58, 64, 65, 70-72, 82, 91, 93-96, 98, 125, 126, 136-139, 143, 148, 150, 153, 158, 163, 164, 188, 220, 222, 224, 225, 228-230, 233, 235, 240, 242, 246
Tachausonnberg	242
Weisbaden	126, 223
Gibson Girl Portable Emergency Radio	100
Glen Dorr	167
Glenn T. Fuller	135
Graves Registration	55, 188, 247
Graves Registration - Mortuary Affairs Association	206, 208, 247
Greenland	99
Hank North	160
Harold Snyder	154
Harry Otstott	154
Hitler	57
Hotel Residence Marceau	182
How the Howitzer	10
Iceland	99, 100, 205
Ida Chemda Indritz Krimminger Hoff	234
Fulton Street Playgrounds	235
Ida Hoff Fieldhouse	235
Irwin S. Hoff	234
Jonathan Hoff	234
Judy Hoff	234
Ken Hoff	234
INCONNU (Unknown)	33, 34
Unknown American Airman	35
Irving Math	98, 102
Isolated Congressional Medals Of Honor Fifth War Grave of World War Two	271
Jacques Notebaert	48, 52, 53, 176-178, 183
James Ryan Arthur	67
Jamestown High School	228
Janet Fairgrieve	38, 59, 60, 273
Jean-Jacques Gorlet	205
Jean-Pierre Cilliez	40-42
Nicolas Cilliez	40
William Cilliez	40
Jess Erickson	169
Jocya Charlet	50, 51, 164-169
Joel Felz	61
John D. Miller	167
John Manning	186
John Middleton Brodin	38, 41, 173, 195, 196, 274
John Witte	159
Jules Roy-Schenkers International Freight Forwarders	200
Jupiler Beer	11
Keith Johnson	169
Kelly Farnsworth	196
Kim Sasaki	190
Korea	34
KRUPP 210mm Lange Mörser	11, 29, 38-40, 46, 195, 204, 208
KRUPP 210 mm shell	13, 14, 21, 29, 245, 247
Lawrence E. Rice	206
Le Courier Picard	202
Le Provençal Hotel	266
Le Souvenir Français	iv, 17, 18, 108-110, 174, 186, 191, 212, 217, 271
Le Stromboli	61
Legends' of the Grave	31
Les Amis De Vauquois et de sa région	36, 37
Lima Electric Motor Co.	138, 237
Little Big Horn	
Greasy Grass, Battlefield	168
Longhorn Bar	167
Louis Wolfe	154
Lowell (Pete) Black	167
Lowell Thomas	150
Lt. Col. Burnham L. Batson	97, 122, 132, 138
Lt. Col. Charles S. McCormick Jr.	93
Lt. Col. John McCrae	5
Lt. Col. Mayo A. Darling	133, 141
Lt. Col. Van Der Wolk	145
Lt. General Joseph Lawton Collins	67
Margarit Rubino	67
Lt. J. J. O'Hara	145
Lt. William M. Silbert	144
Lt. Wyatt F. Hundley	138
Lucky Lady III	260
Luella Claire King Cole Rice	206, 255
Luftwaffe	70
Madame Josiane Brihier	27
Mr. Brihier	27
Maj. Francis H. Dresser	261
Maj. Lamond D. Haas	261
Major General Frederick L. Anderson	143, 144
Major General H Feldman	156
Major General J. A. Ulio	113, 132, 135
Major General Robert B. Williams	142
Major Harold P. Thoreson	95
Marc Berger	202, 203
Marcel Gauthier	7, 9, 11, 14
Margaret Siegfried Schinz	
World War One Nurse	196
Marge and Jim Dawson	196
Market Street Presbyterian Church	163
Martin and Mary Middlebrook	273
Mayor David Berger	165, 166, 170, 206
Mayor George T. Kurkowski	162, 164, 168

Mayor Jean-Claude Jonville	204
Mayor Joseph Lefever	63
Mayor Madame Yvonne Gronnier	175, 176, 204
Mayor Michel Boulogne	176, 204
Mayor William O'Dwyer	153
Messerschmitt	125
Metal Detecting	15, 22, 23, 35, 41, 42, 45, 46, 91, 108
Michael Vieillard	43, 50, 164, 165, 169, 209, 212
Michel Lelouey	48
Michelin Map	266
Mills Bomb	13-15, 22, 24, 27, 28, 41, 58, 60, 165, 201, 266, 273
Monty Wedd	195
Morocco	19
King of Morocco	20
Meknes	19
Port Lyautey	236
Mortuary Affairs	
Asst. Director, Doug Howard	247
Director, Thomas Rexrode	247
Mr. Cassel	103
Mr. Chaulieu	103
Mr. E. M. Soward	153
Nancy Carol Gibson Cole	236
Napoleon	189
National Air and Space Museum	207, 208, 247, 248
National Archives	39
Netherlands	
Arnheim	126, 223
Groesbeek	46
Nijmegen	46, 52
Oorlosgmuseum	46
Overloon	46
Waal River	46
New Zealand	60
Norman F. Maclean	188
Oklahoma Aviation Hall of Fame	
1st Lt. Gott's Medal Of Honor	195
Olivier Coquel	50
Ossuary	3, 4, 33, 34, 106, 172, 271
Paula and Bob Lorenzi	209
Pepsi Max (Diet Pepsi)	20, 268
PFC Jack E. McBride	154
Eleanor McBride Protsman	154
James McBride	154
Mr. and Mrs. Levi McBride	154
Pvt. Paul Allen McBride	154
PFC Robert Leach	172
PFC. Robert B. Wallace	153
Charles Wallace	153
Dewey Wallace	153
Mrs Charles Greenland	153
Mrs Irene Hirn	153
Pierre Linéatte, Councillor General du canton de Péronne	210, 212
Pierre Segers	15, 41, 46-48, 52, 53, 61, 66, 67, 157, 165, 171, 176, 185, 201, 207, 209, 212
Bernard	15
Portugal	48
President Clinton	52
President Roosevelt	131
President Truman	143
Pvt. John T. Bodwell	156
Quiring Monuments, Inc.	197
David Quiring	197, 200
Ramparts Hotel	266
Ray Glover	169
Ray Sallgren	169
Rea Mae Cole Huff	255, 257
Rebecca Lynn Cole Willsey	iv
Red Cross	122
Reinhold W. Jülich	274
Jack C. Julich	274
Remembrance-Souvenir	15, 63, 157, 173, 212, 276
Rev. E. J. Penhorwood	153, 154
Rev. Paul Graser	154
Richard Boniface	12, 14, 22, 33, 61, 201, 203
Michelle Boniface	61
Peter Boniface	61, 201
Romain Boniface	61, 201
Richard Hulliner	154
Richard K. Cole, "Dick"	11, 255
Richard K. Cole, Jr. "Rick"	10
Robin Cole	10
Robert Lefevre	16
Robert Patton	154
Roland Ringenbach	186, 212, 217
Roman Lala	169
Russia	
Poltava	242
Ryan Arthur	157
S/Sgt. Albert R. Richards	95
S/Sgt. Aldo Valenzano	95
S/Sgt. Donald E. Turman	95
S/Sgt. Floyd G. Hall	261
S/Sgt. George B. Bush	259
S/Sgt. Herman B. Krimminger	71, 74, 78, 81, 82, 84, 85, 90-94, 96, 98, 99, 102, 115, 118, 124, 130-133, 135, 140, 141, 148, 152, 155, 158, 160, 166, 177, 185-187, 191-194, 205, 209, 212, 227, 232, 233, 264
Bessie Autrey Krimminger, Mother	115, 233
Betty Jo Rowell Krimminger	233
Darren Neil Krimminger	210, 233
Ginger Louise Martin Krimminger	233
Haley Nicole Krimminger	233
Hugh Clifford Krimminger, Father	233
Hugh Carson Krimminger	115, 233
Ida Chemda Indritz Krimminger	115, 124, 131, 148, 151-153, 192, 229, 232, 234, 241
Mary Elizabeth Riggins	233
Michael Hugh Krimminger	233
Otis Riggins	233
S/Sgt. Jackson C. Britt	95
S/Sgt. James O. Fross	71, 73, 75, 78, 82, 84, 88, 93, 96, 97, 102, 113, 116, 124, 134, 139, 158, 160, 191-196, 210, 212, 222
Cecille Ling Fross, Mother	134
Jacquelin Fross	102
Kimberly Fross	210
Mary June Alderman Fross	210
Michael Fross	210
S/Sgt. Leon H. Navies	259
S/Sgt. Lloyd M. Hudson	261
S/Sgt. R. Munn	259
S/Sgt. Richard V. Weber	261
S/Sgt. Richard Weemes	231
S/Sgt. Robert G. Williams, Jr.	95
S/Sgt. Robert M. Long	95
S/Sgt. Thomas H. Gossett	261
S/Sgt. William J. Shiffer	261
S/Sgt. William R. Robbins	71-75, 78, 80, 82, 84, 87, 91, 94, 96-98, 102, 112, 124-126, 129, 135, 137, 148, 150, 153, 158, 160, 191-195, 207, 212, 229, 240
Charles Russell Robbins, Father	240
Derek Joshua Blodget	241
Derek Matthew Lambert	241
Helen Josephine Robbins, Mother	240
Howard Frederick Robbins	240
Kevin Dumphy	241
Lisa Marie Lambert Blodget	241
Scott Blodget	241
Shirley B. Robbins	118, 134, 240
Tami Marie Robbins Dumphy	241
Todd Andrew Robbins	241
Tracey Ann Robbins	241
Wendy E. Robbins Bosse	241
William R. Robbins, Jr.	241

Sally McDonald, of 'The Seattle Times'	55, 56, 58, 64
Sandwich Jambon	171
Scott Love	210
Secretary of War Henry L. Stimson	131
Senate Committee on Armed Services	91
Senator Arlen Specter, Pennsylvania	277
Senator John McCain, Arizona	277
Senator Joseph I. Lieberman, Connecticut	277
Senator Patty Murray, Washington	277
Senator Paul D. Coverdell, Georgia	277
Senator Rod Grams, Minnesota	277
Senator Slade Gorton, Washington	208, 277
Senator Strom Thurmond, South Carolina	277
Senator Trent Lott, Mississippi	277
Sgt. Albert E. Wyant	117, 149, 238
Sgt. Calvin C. Pulver	261
Sgt. Donald L. Russell	261
Sgt. Edward C. Schanhaar	261, 263
Sgt. Edward McCarty	46
Company D, 108th Infantry of the 27th Division	46
Sgt. Edward T. Gorman	149
Sgt. Irving David Hirsch	135, 209, 210, 212, 232
Bryan Wolf Hogeorges	232
Chad Hirsch	232
Charolette Winkler Hirsch, Mother	232
Cybil Adel Hirsch Miller	232
Edward Hirsch	232
Jill Schmidt Hirsch	232
Joseph Hirsch, Father	232
Lee Hogeorges	232
Robert Allen Hirsch	232
Ruth Schwartz Hirsch	232
Ryan Miller	232
Sharon Allison Hogeorges	232
Tracy Miller	232
Sgt. Mike Flores	249, 252, 255, 256
Sgt. Philip Caldwell	95
Sgt. Samuel M. Assey	249, 250, 252, 255, 256
Arlene Assey	249
Sgt. Vernon L. Moody	259
Sgt. William G. Glass	249, 252, 254, 257
Short Snorter Bill, 'Lucky Piece'	93, 149, 187, 261
Shot At Dawn	182
Snake Eyes	132
South High School	240
St. Ann's Episcopal Cedar-Bluff Cemetery	257
St. Claude Hotel	266, 268
Stalag Luft III	95
Beleria Compound	95
Stecher Mortuary	
Franklin Stecher	154
Stokes mortar shell	273
Sylvan Boniface	25, 30
T/Sgt. Charles J. Turner	95
T/Sgt. Eugene E. Van Loozenord	95
T/Sgt. Harold DeYoung	95
T/Sgt. Harold E. Burrell "Tex"	117, 149, 170, 195, 237, 238
Florine Burrell	195
T/Sgt. Joe. W. Ripple	261
T/Sgt. Lloyd A. Martin	259
T/Sgt. Max N. Srodawa	95
T/Sgt. Oren W. Simpson	261
T/Sgt. R. Atkins	259
T/Sgt. Robert A. Dunlap	71, 73, 75, 78, 79, 81, 84, 85, 88, 90, 92-94, 96, 118, 121, 131, 132, 135, 136, 146, 153, 155, 156, 158, 159, 162, 164, 165, 168, 169, 172, 176, 177, 187, 191, 192, 212, 222, 239, 261, 264
Alexander Dunlap, Father	121, 134, 162, 239, 241
Angela Owens Whitesell	176, 177, 182
Bonnie Dunlap Owens	115, 118, 135, 140, 152, 162, 164, 165, 169, 176-178, 181, 182, 187, 212, 221
Diana Herndon	169
Don Herndon	165
Don R. Herndon	169
Leigh Herndon	165
Mark Cyr Herndon	165
Marsha Io Dunlap Hendron	162
Martha Schmitt Dunlap, Mother	115, 162
T/Sgt. Russell W. Gustafson	71, 73-79, 81, 82, 84, 85, 88, 89, 93, 94, 96-98, 101, 102, 112, 117, 125, 131, 132, 134, 135, 138-140, 150, 151, 158, 159, 167, 168, 171, 175-177, 188, 193-195, 205, 207, 212, 219, 220, 227-229, 245, 247, 270
Amy Elizabeth Gustafson	229
Edith Gustafson, Mother	228
Erick William Gustafson	229
Kerry Ann Gustafson	229
Lee Marie Gustafson	229
Michael Gustafson	229
Phyllis Williams Gustafson	229
Robin Ann Gustafson	229
William Axel Gustafson, Father	228
T/Sgt. Wilmer E. Henderson "Will"	2, 17, 52, 55, 56, 67, 90, 247
Texas Buttermilk	210
The 452nd Bombardment Group (H)	
Opal Barnes	241
S/Sgt. Marvin E. Barnes	241
The American Legion	56, 64, 168
The Lady Janet	66
The Lady Jeannette	67, 69, 71-76, 80-85, 87, 88, 93, 95, 97-99, 101, 102, 108, 109, 122, 123, 125, 130, 132, 136, 155-157, 159, 163, 164, 166, 169, 171, 173, 176, 177, 183, 184, 186, 188, 194, 196, 197, 201, 205-210, 212, 217, 219, 220, 222, 225, 228-230, 233, 235, 240, 242, 243, 245, 246, 256, 257, 260, 264, 267, 270
The Lima News	137, 163
Mike Lackey	163
The Miles City Daily Star	131, 162, 164
Bonnie Dunlap Owens	136
The Rev. Peter Weaver	154
Tilton General Hospital	151
Tincourt-Boucly	12
Tom Fairgrieve	38, 59-61, 273
Tom Paine	255
Tom Starbuck	167
Tommy's Café	27, 38, 274
Total Army Personnel Center	185, 192
Tulely High	232
U. S. Soldier Unknown	53
U.S. Army Casualty and Memorial Affairs Department	190
Union Nationale Des Combattants En Afrique De Nord	183
United Airlines	64, 67, 170, 193, 195, 197, 200, 247
Sue Zorn	197
United States	
Alexandria, Louisiana	130
Allentown Cemetery, Ohio	154
Altoona, Pennsylvania	257
Amarillo, Texas	228
Annapolis, Maryland	257
Arlington National Cemetery, Virginia	152, 166
Arnett, Oklahoma	64, 123, 134, 136, 137, 143, 145, 160, 161, 163-165, 167, 169, 179, 225, 226
Augusta, Georgia	162, 164
Bakersfield, California	114, 164
Bethesda, Maryland	220
Boston, Massachusetts	194
Bridgeport, Connecticut	227
Brooklyn, New York	112, 133, 192
Camp Perry, Ohio	237
Camp Shanks, New York	241
Camp Young, California	138, 237
Cheyenne, Wyoming	261
Chicago, Illinois	134, 207, 229, 232
Cimmeron Field, Oklahoma	240

Colorado Springs, Colorado	144
Dayton, Ohio	253
Delphos, Ohio	154
Denver, Colorado	165
Detroit, Michigan	130
Douglas, Arizona	237
Dulles International Airport, Virginia	157, 205
Ellis County, Oklahoma	152, 161
Enid, Oklahoma	227
Fairmont Cemetery, Harmon, Oklahoma	225
Fargo, Oklahoma	141
Fort Benjamin Harrison, Indiana	231
Fort Bliss, Texas	236
Fort Dix, New Jersey	160, 240
Fort Lee, Virginia	206
Gardner Field, California	227
Geiger Field, Washington	241
Great Falls, Montana	261
Greensboro, North Carolina	231
Grenier Field, New Hampshire	261
Harmon, Oklahoma	115, 152, 224, 225
Jamestown, New York	112, 160, 228
John Hopkins Hospital, Baltimore, MD.	152
Kansas City, Missouri	113
Kearney, Nebraska	146, 261
Keesler Field, Mississippi	154
Kirkland, Washington	163, 169
Lancaster, California	237
Laredo, Texas	148
Lawton, Oklahoma	130, 146, 207, 239
Lima, Ohio	116, 134, 136, 137, 160, 178, 235
Los Angeles, California	219
Manassas, Virginia	39
Manchester, Connecticut	138
Marfa, Texas	220
Marshville, North Carolina	187, 233
Maxwell A.F.B., Alabama	67, 162, 246
McAllen, Texas	113, 193, 194
Midway Airport, Illinois	206
Miles City, Montana	131, 134, 136, 155, 162, 165, 168, 239, 241
Monroe, North Carolina	210, 233
Muskingum Country Ohio	258
New Concord, Ohio	1, 10, 206, 242, 255
New Milford, New Jersey	200
Newark, Ohio	39
Oklahoma City, Oklahoma	229
Oxnard, California	220
Palm Springs, California	169, 170
Rapid City, South Dakota	237, 241, 261
Redmond, Washington	196
San Antonio, Texas	223, 240
Santa Ana, California	138, 227, 237
Savannah, Georgia	208, 249
Scott Field, Illinois	241
Seabring, Florida	138
Seattle, Washington	165, 189, 264
Shattuck, Oklahoma	167
Shawnee Township, Lima, Allen County, Ohio	152
Sioux Falls Army Air Field	115
Sioux Falls, South Dakota	115
Spencerville, Ohio	154
Springfield, Colorado	166
Tinker Field, Oklahoma	144
Toledo, Ohio	237
Tucson, Arizona	195
Twenty-Nine Palms, California	237
Washington, D.C.	135
Wichita Falls, Texas	241
Will Rogers Field, Oklahoma	142
Woodlawn Cemetery, Lima, Ohio	152, 235
Woodward Air Field, Oklahoma	145
Worcester, Massachusetts	112, 125, 126, 148, 192, 240
Zanesville, Ohio	10
United States Air Force	19
Unites States Army Air Force	33, 34
V.J. Day	150
Veteran's of Foreign Wars	168
Victoria Cross	
Jacka, V.C., Australian	274
Vincent Bentz	36, 203, 266
Warren White	11
Western Union	113, 115, 117, 122, 230
William Roche	210, 260
William Spencer	154
Willis S. Cole	1, 6, 237, 255
Willis S. Cole III	iv, 1, 2, 6
Willis Samuel Cole, Jr. "Sam"	1, 9, 156, 164, 166, 167, 176, 177, 266

Battery Corporal Willis S. Cole Military Museum

A NONPROFIT CORPORATION
13444 124th Ave. NE, Kirkland, Washington, 98034-5403   U.S.A.
E-mail: ww1@ww1.org -- http://www.ww1.org